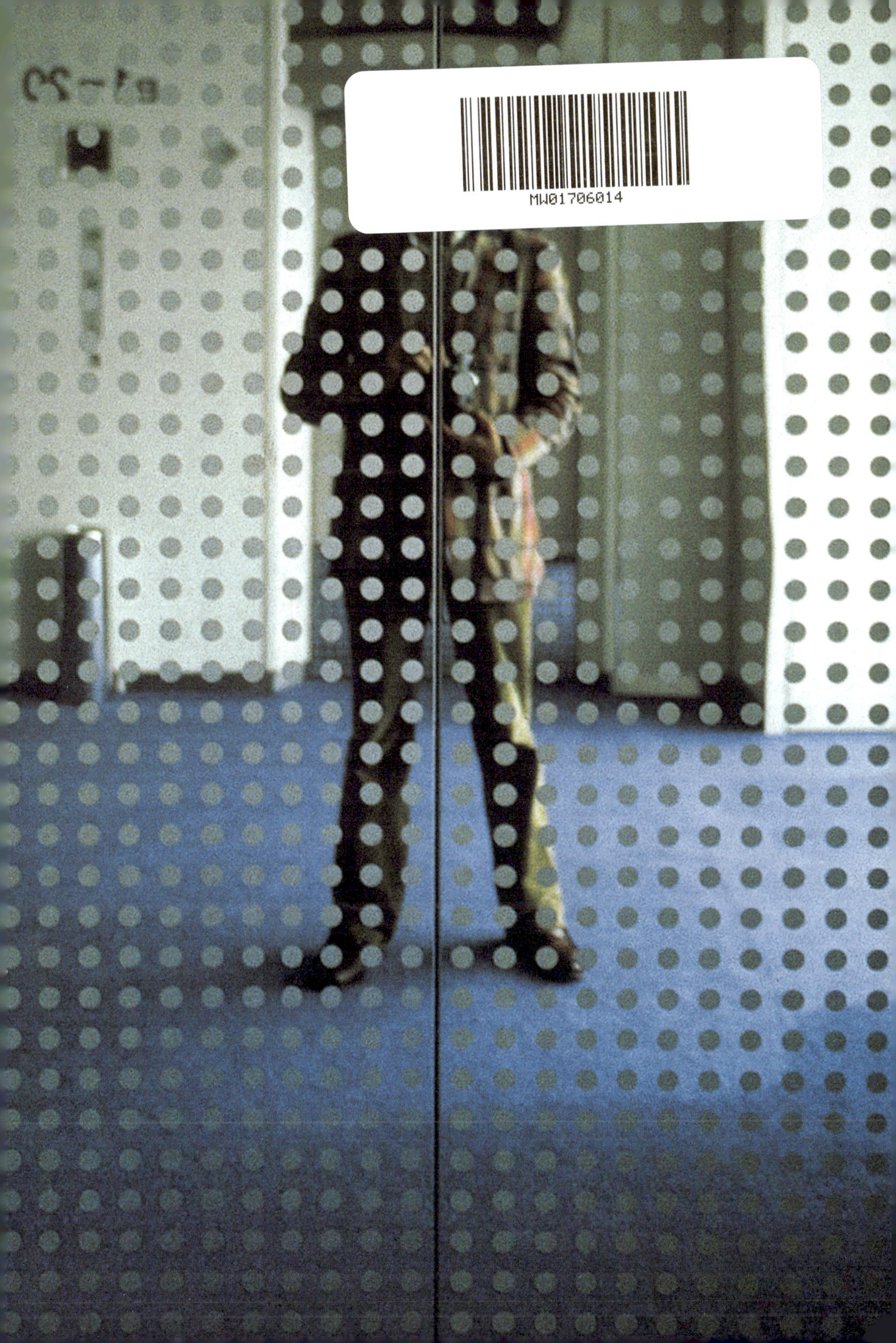

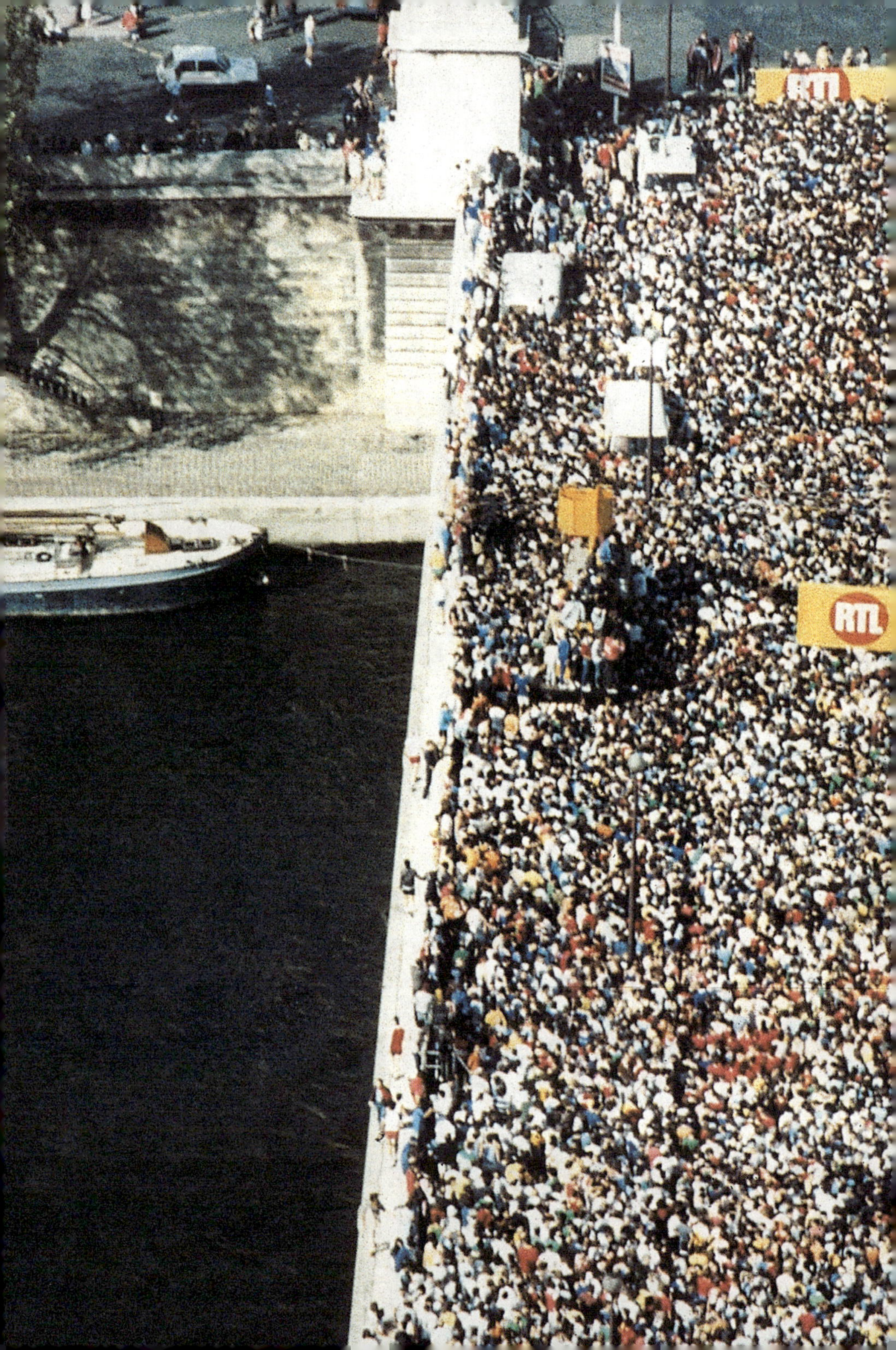
RTL
RTL

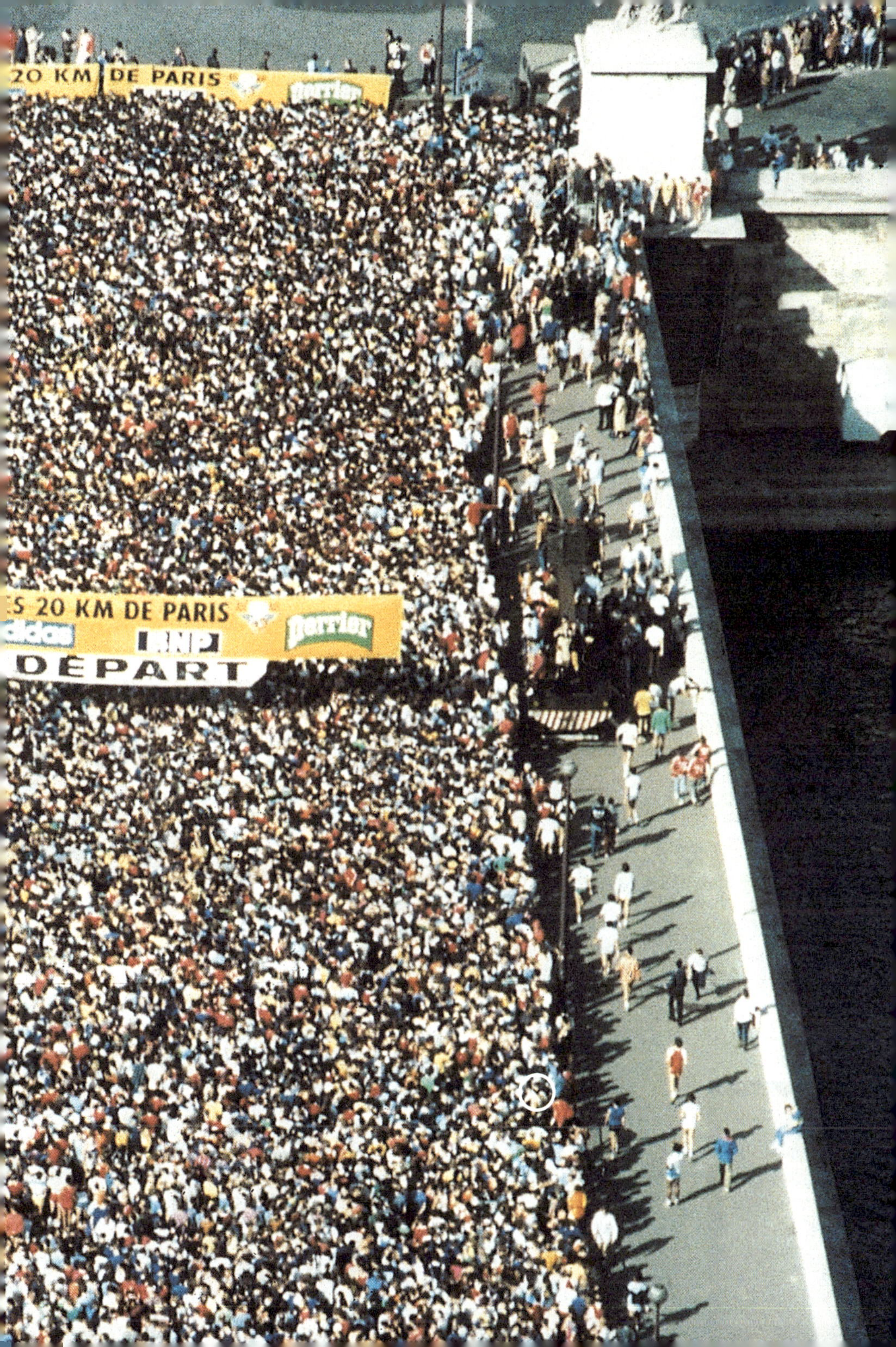
20 KM DE PARIS
Perrier
S 20 KM DE PARIS
adidas
BNP
Perrier
DÉPART

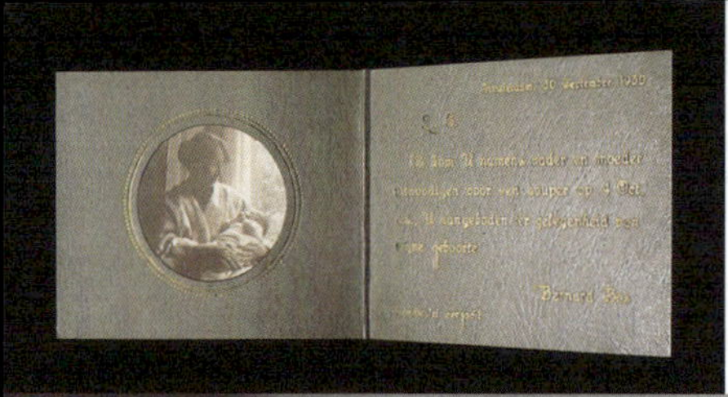

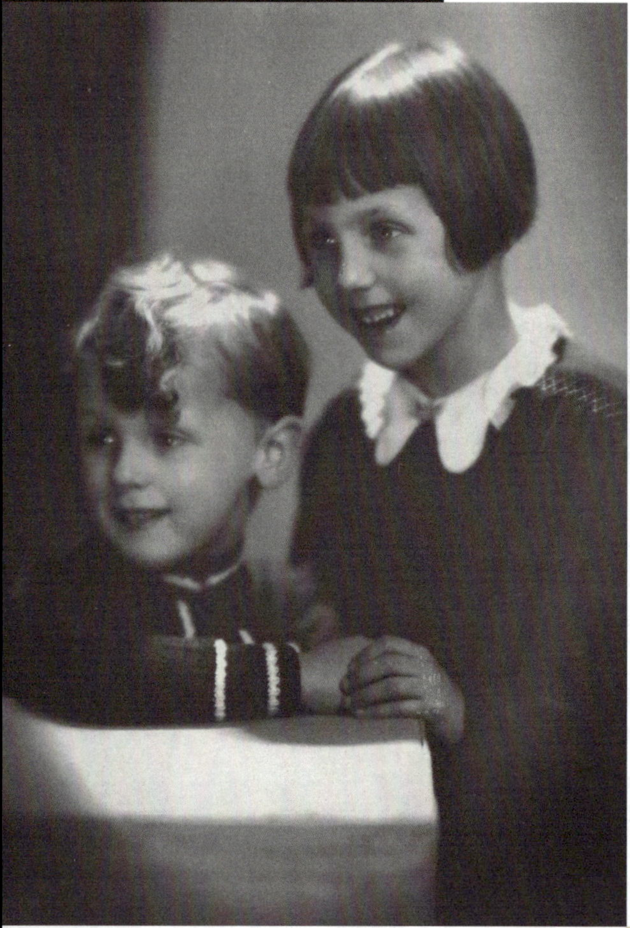

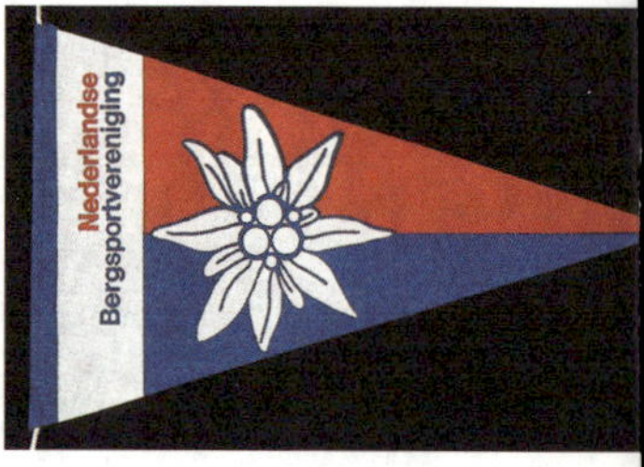
Nederlandse
Bergsportvereniging

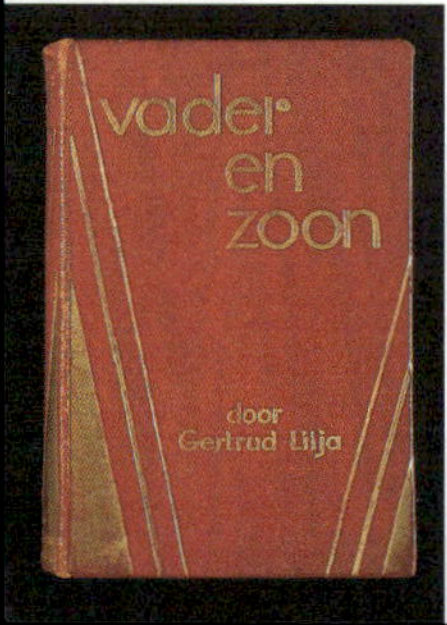
vader en zoon
door
Gertrud Lilja

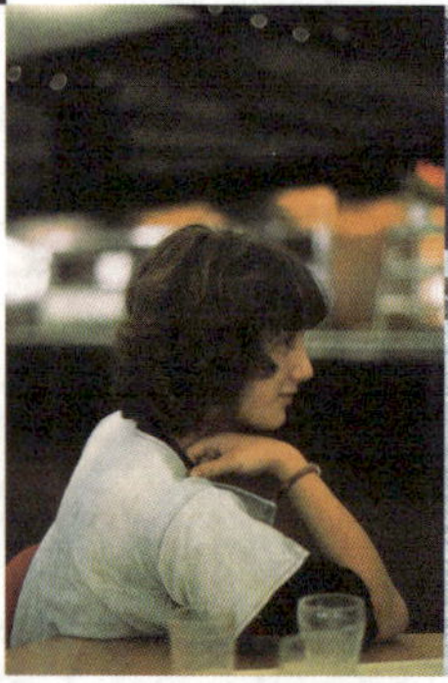

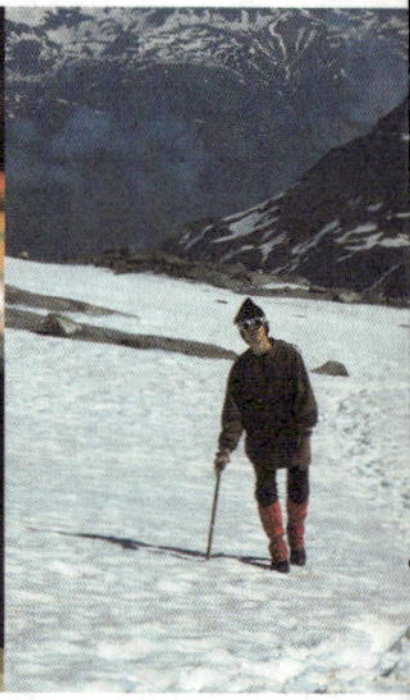

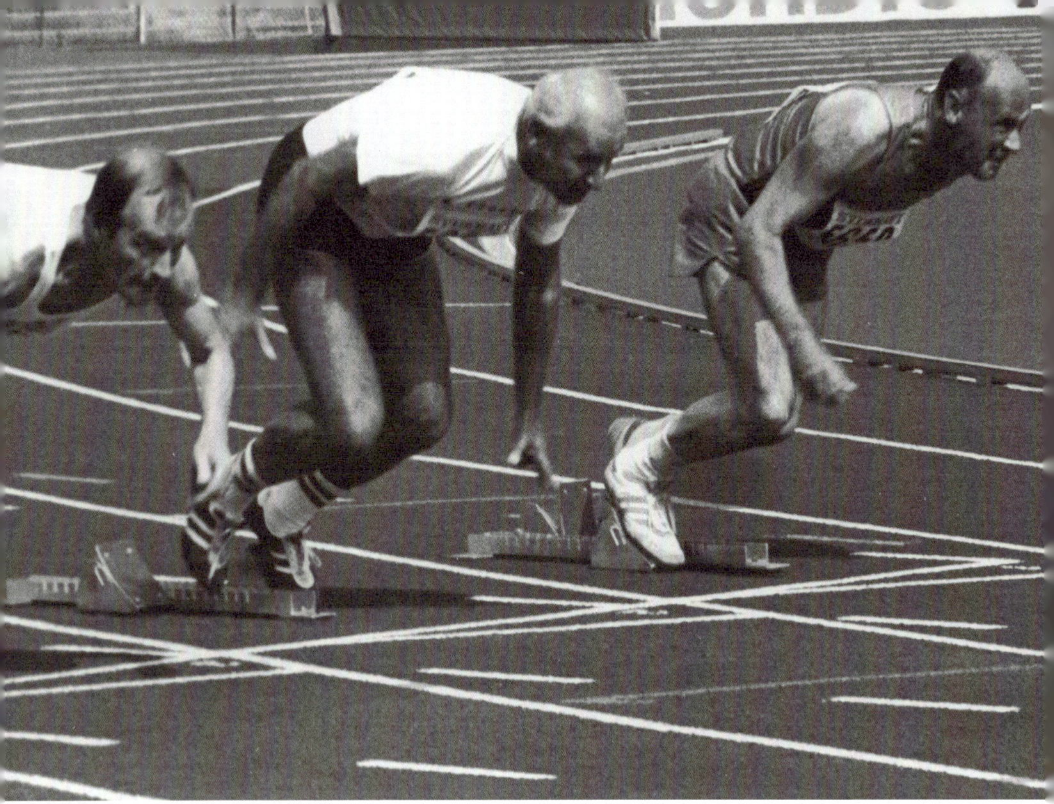

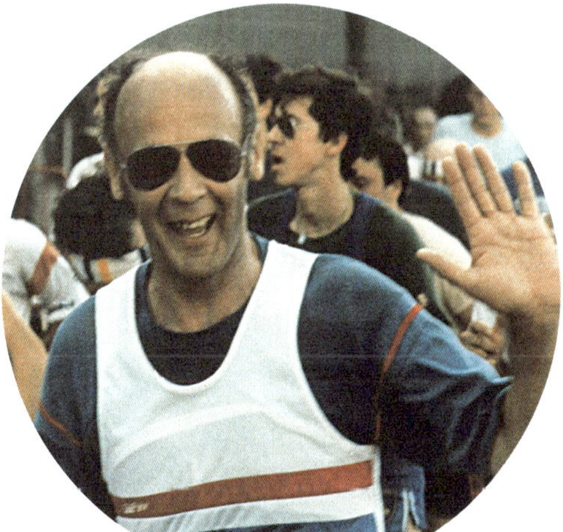
adidas

For Jantien,

whose idea it all was
and who got it under way.
Thank you, my dearest dear.

Ben

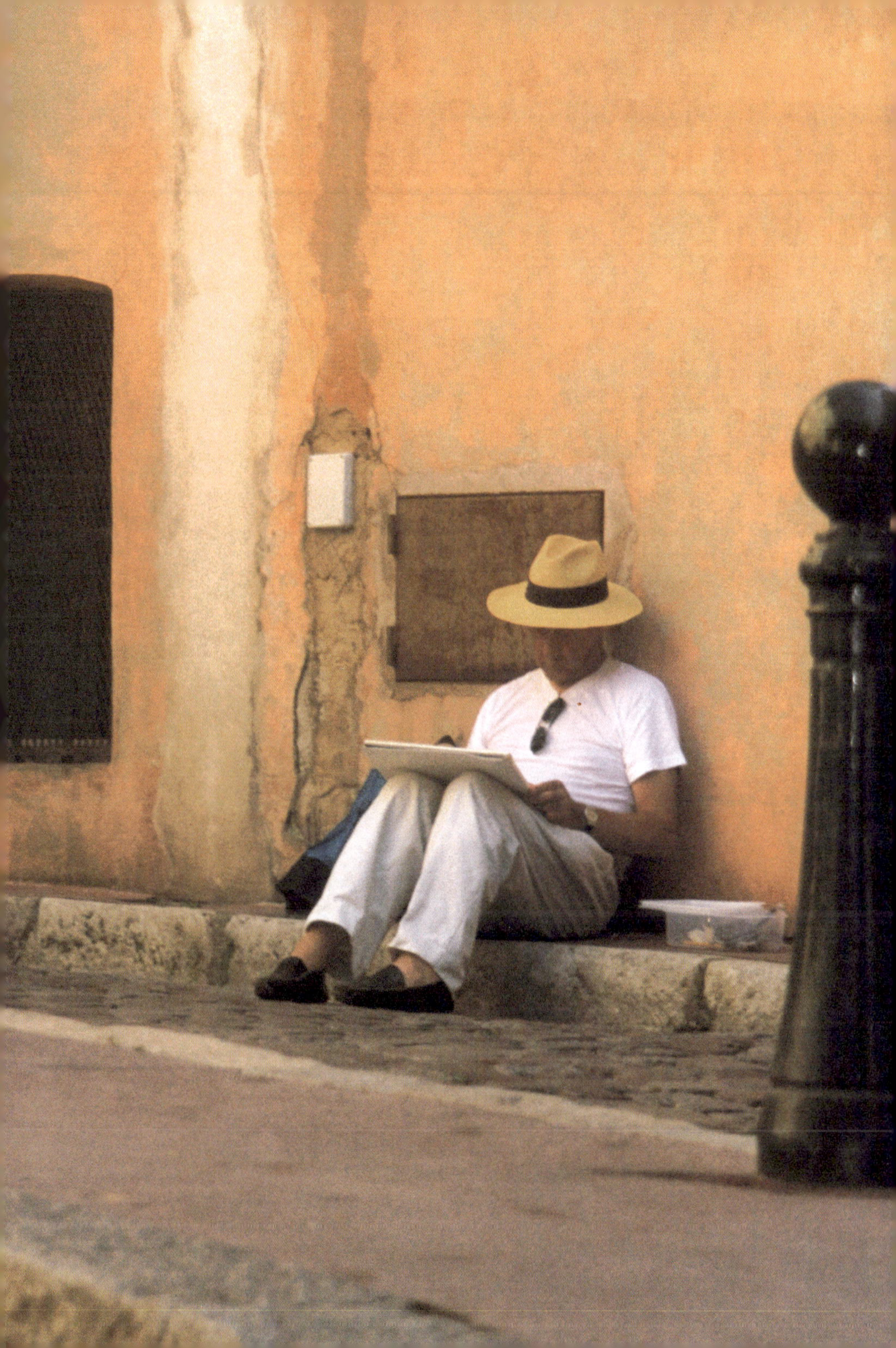

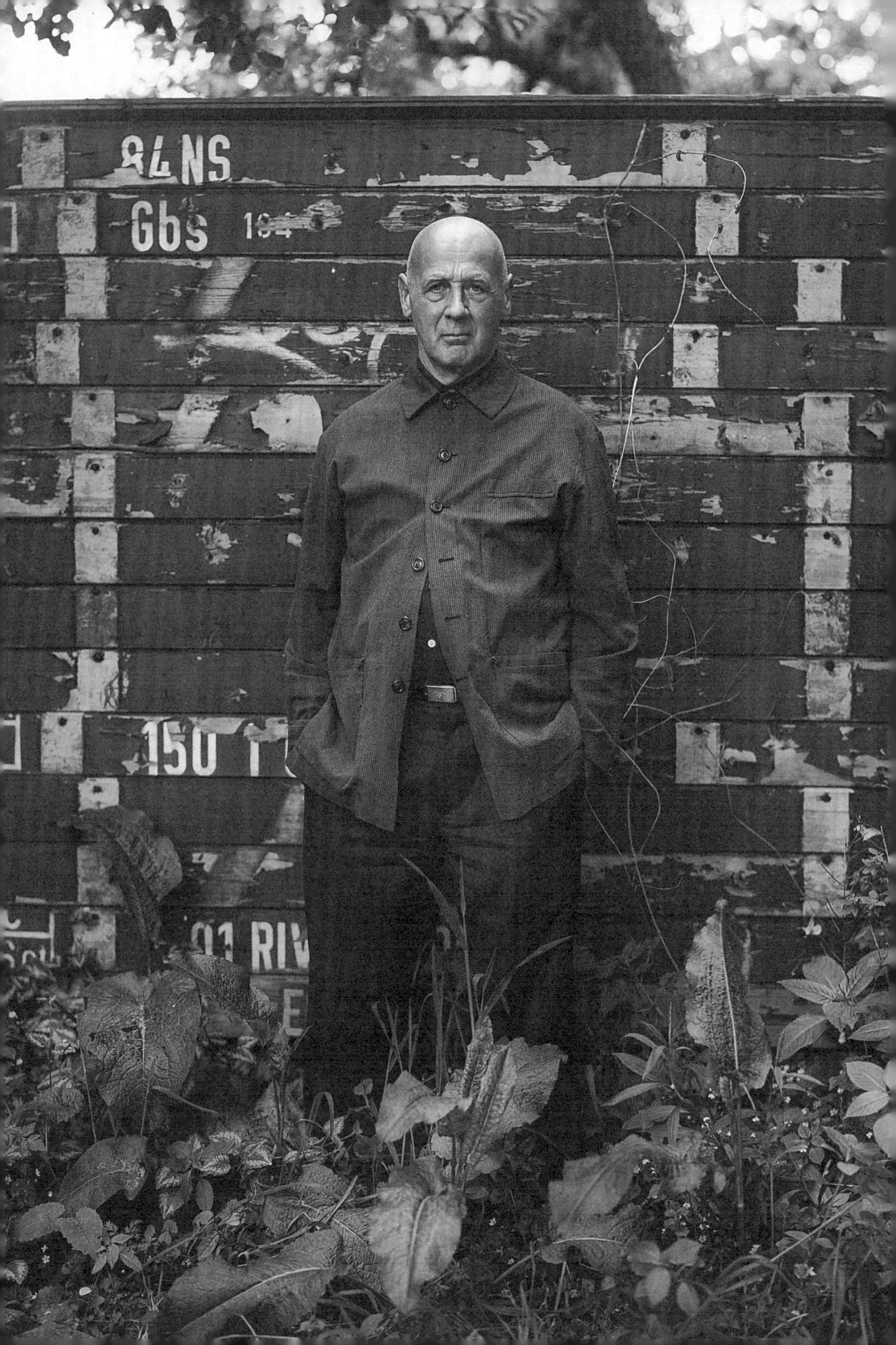
84NS
Gbs
150
01 RIV

Design of a Lifetime

Ben Bos

Dirk van Ginkel and Paul Hefting

BIS Publishers Amsterdam

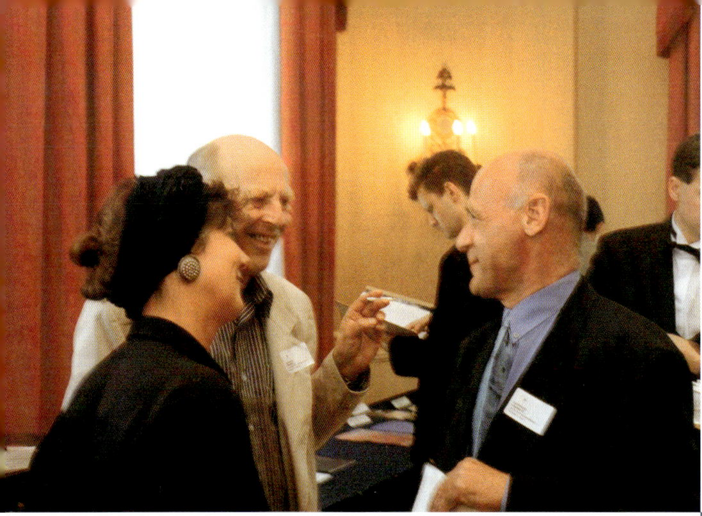

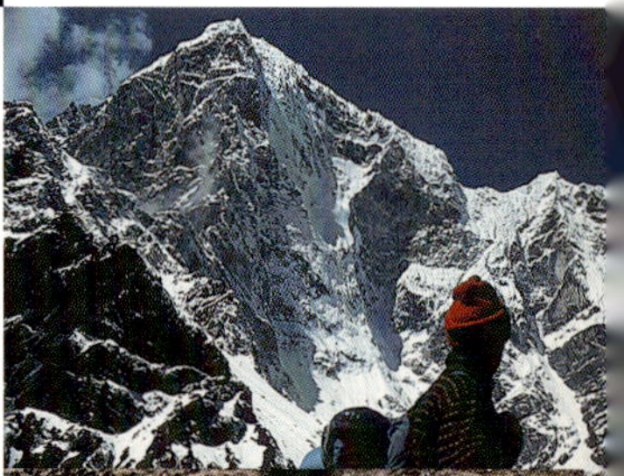

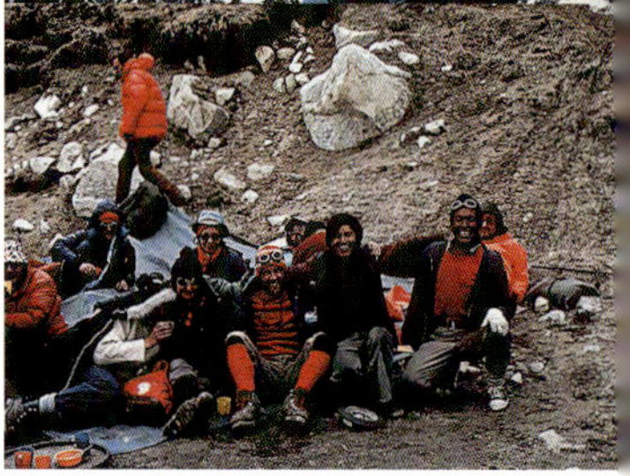

He leans on the table, puts his hand under his chin, looks at you wide-eyed, allows his gaze to wander and return to you, puts his glasses on his forehead and speaks. True words. Ben Bos at Plantagekade, within hearing distance of Artis zoo. For many years he worked for TD, Total Design, which earned him a reputation as a 'Matterhorn in head and heart.'
In English: 'a cold fish'.

No way.

OK, he did find himself in a severe climate and was an austere designer. But someone with an eye for detail will perceive the respects in which he differs from his then colleagues. Ben gave thought to the identity of his clients, each and every one, explored the limits of the grid and transcended them. OK, he was a teacher, he could be pedantic, give reprimands and was occasionally nicknamed 'parson Bos'. However, he was driven to this behaviour not by the rules, by unwritten laws or by any doctrine, but by enthusiasm and affection. OK, he was a stickler for precision who almost maniacally accounted for his working hours and minutes. However, this was not motivated by mathematical precision, but by honesty and loyalty: towards the design studio, towards the people of whom it was composed and towards the clients.

Much may go hidden under a surface.

In Ben's early years the Netherlands woke up. Crumbling sectarianism, Sandberg's expressiveness, Dekkers' reductionism, provo's naivete, flower power's optimism. These left their imprint on Ben. He understood his age, but was no uncritical follower. He remained true to himself, steered clear of fashions and trends, but did employ social photography – even pictures of strikes in a staff magazine. Now, many years later, nothing has changed: Ben observes, reflects, selects the essential and integrates it through his vision. In an animated way, not mechanically. Coherently, consistently, never on autopilot. Adverse to compromise and mediocrity, with a penchant for beauty and purity, a passion for detail and an urge towards proximity.

Ben and I live in the same era and work in related professions. We share ideals and memories, heroines and heroes. Initially these things remained unspoken of. We knew each other, knew each other's work, saw parallels. I listened to his well-crafted sentences and read his transparent texts. Jantien shattered the silence, the unnecessary distance, perhaps the shyness. She levelled the shells into which we retreated, brought warmth and joy to the surface, to the heart.
I have never considered Ben to be an exponent of the Swiss school and the chilly polder landscape. No way. Yet there is thin ice between a hunch and a certainty. Ben piloted me across. He moved me to tears in a sea of flowers, white and blue, he moved me when he was seventy, he makes me feel comfortable talking, laughing and smiling over a cup of cappuccino or over an excellent glass of wine.

Will you write the preface? **Jantien asks on a balmy evening.** Short and sweet, **Ben admonishes on a clear morning.**

With pleasure.

Paul Mertz

Contents

Introduction

In 1978 Ben Bos was invited to join the Alliance Graphique Internationale, an association whose membership is composed of the crème de la crème of the international design world. It was a glorious moment for Bos. It constituted nothing less than a recognition that he belonged to the happy few who were 'bigshots in the profession'.
In the past he had had a similar experience, albeit on the national level. In 1961, during his studies at the Instituut voor Kunstnijverheidsonderwijs, he designed a poster for printing company Steendrukkerij De Jong & Co which to his mind approached the attitude and standard of the work of Wim Crouwel, his great example. The knowledge that he was capable of producing a 'little Crouwel' was just as liberating as the membership of the AGI was to be in later years.
When in 1963 Ben Bos was invited to join Total Design – the first multidisciplinary design studio in the Netherlands – his life as a designer began for real. He would be employed by the studio for thirty years.

In one of her contributions to Mode en module, a monograph on Wim Crouwel, Frederike Huygen describes Ben Bos's position in Total Design as that of the 'outsider-insider'. Although Bos worked longer at Total Design than anyone else and was the stablest factor of all staff members in the tumultuous history of the studio, he did play 'a suspended role'. As a senior designer and member of the management he enjoyed the same rights as partners Wim Crouwel, Benno Wissing, Friso Kramer and the Schwarz brothers. However, he was not a co-owner. Bos's position also differed in other respects. As Huygen writes: He guaranteed the continuity of the studio. On a business level his team was always stable in the sense that it always – and sometimes as one of the few – guaranteed ample profits. However, he was much less interested in innovative design than the other partners. To some extent Bos's manner of operation was that of an outsider-insider as a result of this suspended role. His position in relation to the partners was now equal, now unequal.
But there are other reasons why Ben Bos's position is hard to define. Although he may have been a less gifted theorist than the TD partners, his interests ranged much wider than theirs. Bos is a prime example of the Renaissance man. He was not only a designer, but also a competent journalist and copywriter. True, in his youth he didn't make it as a professional freelance writer, but he did write dozens of publications, including a number of books. And, as Huygen states: His background as a copywriter facilitated his writing of publications and brochures on Total Design. In 1968 he even produced a film on grids with Dick Schwarz that was intended to familiarize clients with the use of the grid.
Add to that the fact that all of his working life Bos integrated his hobby of photography into many of his designs and you get an impression of a versatile, disciplined and loyal person. Someone who has meant a lot to the profession in various ways: as a designer, studio manager, administrator of the professional association, teacher, guest lecturer, initiator and chairman of the Nederlands Archief Grafisch Ontwerpers and of course as an author on design.

Bos's life appears to be dominated by long-term relations. The Big Adventure, as he called his stay at Total Design, lasted from 1963 to 1991. His work for Ahrend began in 1953 when he was hired as advertising assistant. But even in the new century he still monitors the production of promotional publications for this client. His activities for Randstad also continued for a long time: some thirty years. While the names of other designers are associated with certain movements or a recognizable 'handwriting', Bos's name appears to be essentially linked to those of his clients. Furness and the city of Capelle aan de IJssel deserve to be mentioned, but Ahrend en Randstad are the main ones. That is why this book contains two articles that consider the importance of Bos to these clients in greater depth.

However, we start out with Bos discussing his own place in Dutch design against the background of the development of graphic design during his lifetime. If he did not emphatically set himself up as a representative of some movement, if he did not become famous for a clear personal signature, what does the designer Bos stand for? That is a question which this book attempts to address by telling about the role that Ben Bos played in a personal and anecdotal fashion.

Paul Hefting and Dirk van Ginkel

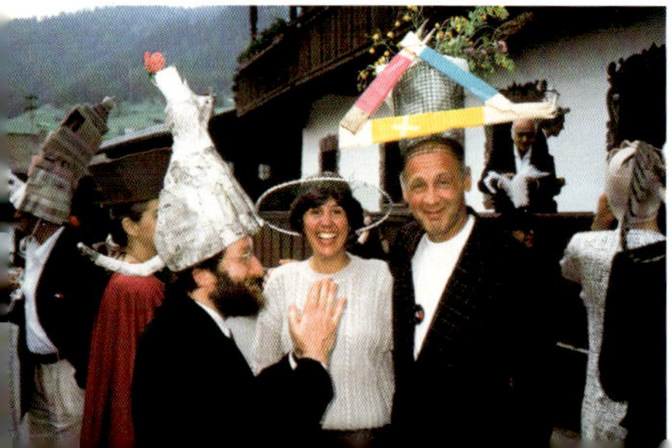

Paul Hefting

The time and the backgrounds

The history of cultural reception is the story of our emotional and rational response to the changing situation in society.

Raymond Williams

Its a lovely holiday cottage. We like it immensely. The collection of abominable stuff, bad taste and monstrosities is huge and is headed by the stacking white plastic one-piece garden chairs. **This is a quote from Ben Bos's 1991 book** Design, de ontworpen meerwaarde **[Design, the designed added value].**
At the time of writing, Ben and Jantien stayed at beautiful Isle sur la Sorgue in the Vaucluse. I know the region quite well and I remember Pierre Pessemesse's auberge, hidden away in a beautiful valley of the Luberon. The rocky road towards it gave you the feeling you had taken a wrong turn, until a small sign with a sloppily written caption Auberge sans étoiles **gave some reassurance. I hope it still hangs there and hasn't been replaced by a more sensibly designed signpost.**
These surroundings with their gorgeous ruggedness appear to resist design. It is a different, almost innocent world, untouched by designers and production processes. It is a world that is opposed to ours, where, as Bos writes, product design is an inescapable process. It effectively started with the shaping of the prehistoric stone celt. Human beings produced **[functional, non-aesthetic, PH]** tools. And now, in this postindustrial era, it is inevitable for each non-handmade mass product to be conceived and planned and drawn and specified.
He is right and things should be allowed to stay the way they are, on condition however that the above and many other oppositions – good and poor design, variation and originality – continue to exist. The consumer must be able to compare and choose for himself.

Ideals **In the second half of the nineteenth century designing an 'aesthetically and functionally sound' object was viewed as a moral obligation to society. After all, the 'beautiful form' from one's own time – i.e. not an imitation of the past, as the World Exhibition of 1851 in London demonstrated – has an educational value, as the dominant opinion was at the time. These 'aesthetics' were thought to ultimately improve society, make it more humane and more critical. Morris and Crane initiated this movement in England, although their response to the far-reaching industrialisation was an attempt to rehabilitate the arts and crafts. This proved a romantic dream, an echo of the ideas of the eighteenth-century French philosopher Jean Jacques Rousseau. He believed that man is essentially good and should aim to recover simplicity, the source of life, nature. Socialist and paternalist ideas also were at play in the background and in fact have always been present in the innovative arts and crafts movements: in the Wiener Werkstätte, in the Deutsche Werkbund and in the Nederlandsche Vereeniging voor Ambachts- en Nijverheidskunst.**
However, the aesthetics of industrial products was also an important concern – Henry van de Velde even speaks of the 'aristocracy of the product', manufactured by der neuen machinellen und industriellen Herstellungsart.
If the common man could not afford the products from the Wiener Werkstätte, the large quantities in which the sound industry product was

manufactured could change that. What was more: everyone should be brought in touch with the 'beautiful form' in all spheres of life.
Jean François van Royen, administrator of the Nederlandse Staatsbedrijf der Post Telefonie and Telegrafie [Dutch mail, telegraph and telephone company], believed that the government also had a certain responsibility. Van Royen propagated the good form at the PTT. In his opinion it improved both the working climate and the standard of public services. It wasn't just a question of amusement or passing the time – there was more at stake. The ultimate goal was the creation of a better world: not an unattainable ideal, but a necessary link between layman and professional, between layman and artist, necessary but also possible, if the yearning awakens towards a wholly animated human life, not restricted by the particularism of specialist knowledge, but combining a skill in one's own profession with open-mindedness and receptivity, sharp wit and responsiveness to all spiritual expressions, as these originate from the heart of life that is common to all.
In 1922 Van Royen stood for parliament as a candidate for the Onafhankelijke Partij, through which prominent artists, academics (including the historian J. Huizinga), architects and musicians hoped to bring culture to society.
As material considerations have now become inordinately dominant, the correct balance between material and spiritual values must be restored. Ultimately this is the spiritual elevation that is the be-all and end-all of all politics, **as the party manifesto reads. In the end the party did not get enough votes for a seat in the Second Chamber of the Dutch parliament.**

Purism **In those years the efforts to create a different, new world intensified. In the De Stijl group this took the form of a desire for an 'international unity in Life, Art and Culture' (Van Doesburg). The new, purified image and the new spatial conception were expressed in art, architecture and typography. New media and techniques (photography) changed the appearance of printed matter, not only as a 'constructive unity of content and form,' but also in a 'dadaist' sense (Mécano/Van Doesburg). Although at the time De Stijl was a small movement, it was internationally well-connected and exerted a great influence, even long after 1946. The movement aimed for a kind of purism, an expurgation of superfluities, the search for the quintessence – an effort that has been undertaken in all ages. In industrial art and architecture the matter-of-factness, the expurgation of subjectivity, was emphasized. Piet Zwart wrote:** I hope I will sometime have the opportunity to sit under a linotype for a week and listen to the rhythm of the linotype in order to root out my baroque tendencies, because that is the modern plague: our enforcement of changes and reforms of old categories as expressions of modern life. **Like Van Royen, he felt he had an obligation to society.** Design is not a matter of taste, but an expression of our attitude to life, dictated by the meta-cosmos. Design and the use of materials are not matters of personal taste, but responsible factors in society.
These words, which have often been quoted, reflect the seriousness and working methods of these 'maniacs', while curiously enough the 'meta-cosmos' (whatever Zwart meant by this) was supposed to justify this attitude to life.
Gerrit Rietveld wrote: The main value of an interior resides in quietness and clarity – i.e. a degree of simplicity or a lack of ambiguity, yet it is a result of many interacting factors. We will successively consider the interior **[through the eyes of the occupant and maker, PH]** in the light of the function of the house in relation to the inhabitant's attitude. Openness versus closure, material versus empty space, the visibility of the construction versus spatial image. Everyday maintenance, economy

1959 At home in Slotervaart, Amsterdam
Photography by Arjé Plas

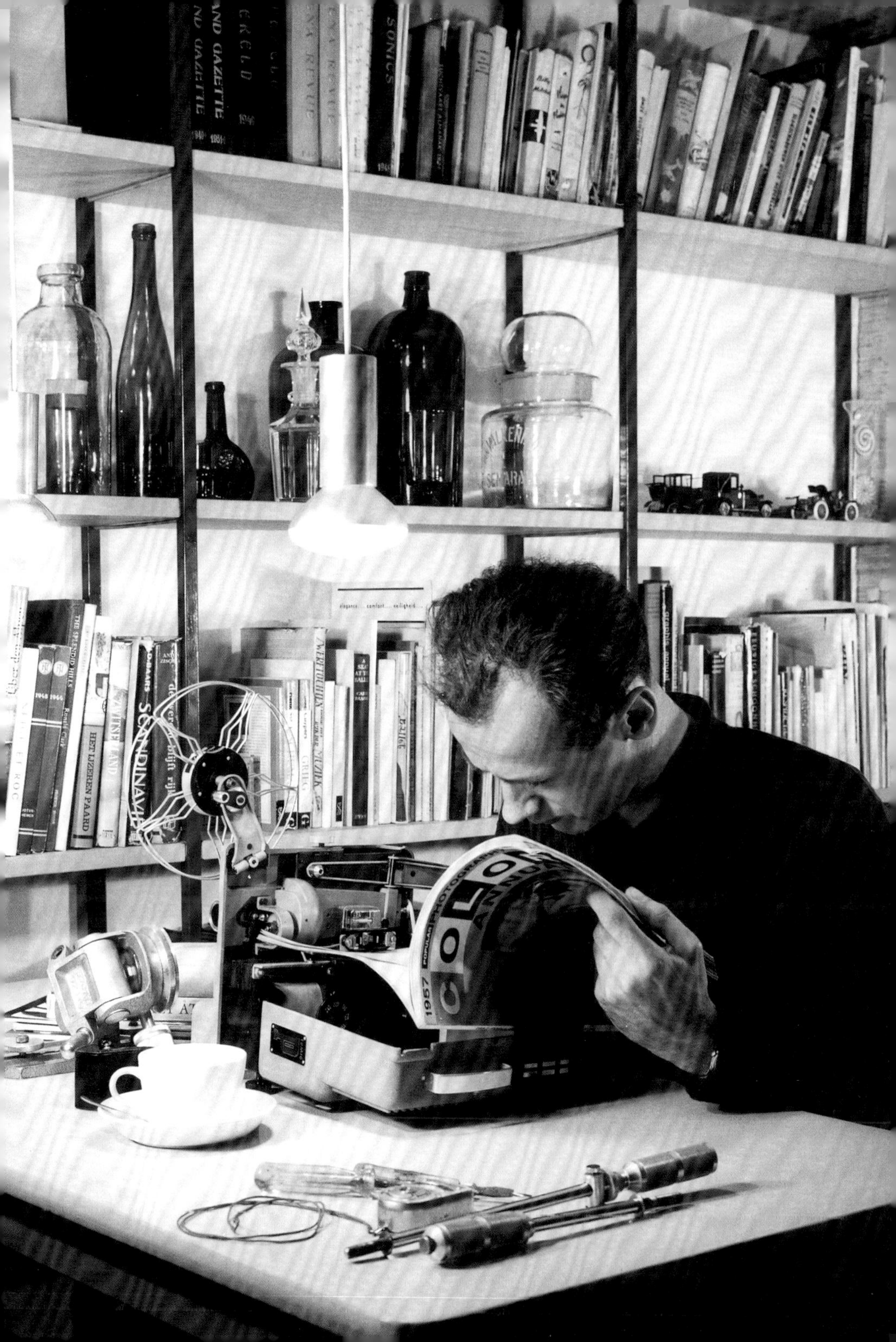
AND GAZETTE
SONICS
THE SPLENDID HILLS
HET IJZEREN PAARD
elegance.... comfort.... veiligheid....
1957

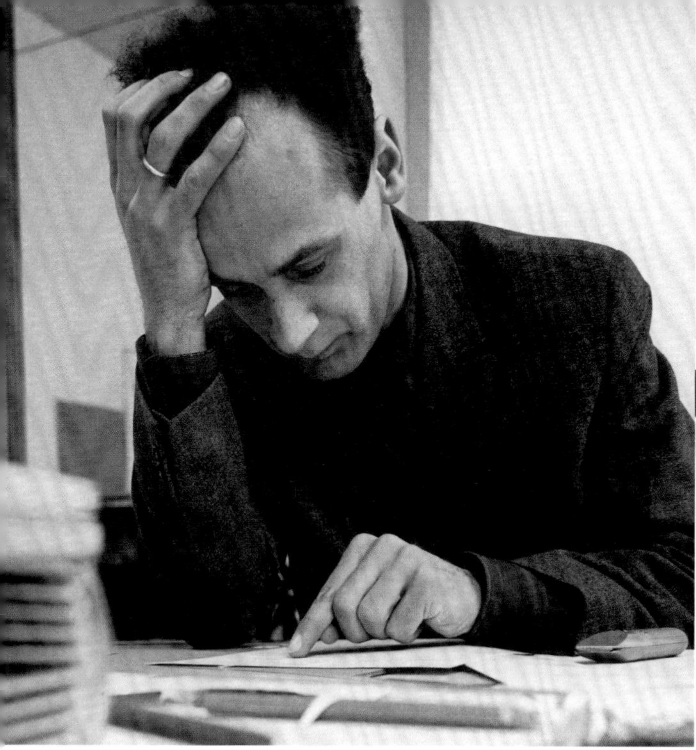

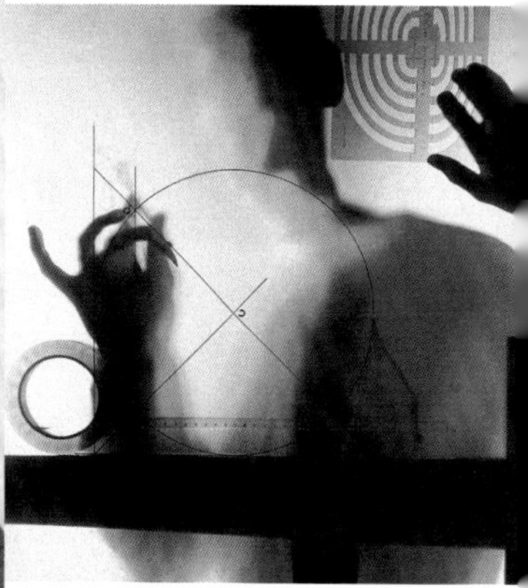

Early sixties Starting out at Total Design

1959 Illustration for drawing materials brochure Ahrend, Model Ben Bos Photography by Jan Versnel

and construction costs. The practical versus the beautiful. Colour and plasticity of the interior. The manufacture – manual or by machine. The personal and the serial product. The industrial form. No compromise between the many requirements and oppositions. An interior is only good if it testifies to an outspoken opinion on these possibilities, without the residents being continually confronted with these problems.
Didn't Rietveld's crate furniture from 1934 exemplify the 'cheap beauty' that everyone could construct during the Depression?

Decency and resistance **World War II with its fear and terror wiped all that out. The ideal of freedom continued to be cherished underground, where people dreamed about the future, the reconstruction after the war was over. The paternalism that underlies all idealism of the early twentieth century re-emerges in 1945. On the first New Years' Eve after the liberation Prime Minister W. Schermerhorn addresses the Dutch people:** Thought still reaches higher than matter. If our people can muster the strength to direct its thoughts to the one common goal, matter will also bend before its will.
After all, youth was being morally corrupted by the cinema and the unrestrained reading, dancing, bathing and camping in scanty clothing. And those are just a few of the subversive types of entertainment.
The Nationaal Instituut that was founded after the war, and that existed for only one year, was intended to change all that. Its objective was to enliven and raise our national awareness. **The objective of this institute was to ensure** that our people knows and sings its own songs; that it resumes making music and playing games, learns to enjoy art, the theatre and folk dancing; that it devotes its attention to Dutch literature; in short, that it regains

awareness of its quintessential values. **Folk dancing, which evolved out of Dutch traditions, is held in high esteem:** Dancing can sublimate the relations between boys and girls, which are currently subject to flirt and piquancy. **The aim was to restore these home-grown traditions.**

This atmosphere of respectability and decency and the resistance to it is portrayed in Gerard van 't Reve's novel De Avonden. **A search is also undertaken to find the indigenous in the arts, the Dutch quality of visual art. G. Knuttel Wzn. described this in his book** Tot het hart der mensheid – Het Nederlandse in de Beeldende Kunst: **'Just a matter of honour, or is it a real "value"?,' he wondered. In fact he hoped for a return to seventeenth-century fame. However, the Dutch people were busy with other values, with rebuilding the country. The Netherlands pulled itself out of a slump and faced the – economic – future with optimism. 1951's stamps to benefit children – featuring photographs by Cas Oorthuys – show children with happy faces standing before houses under construction, smoking chimneys and apartment buildings: a Dutch Social Realism facing the future.**

Black plane **There is a bolt from the blue in the visual arts. As an alternative to the well-behaved painting and the carving of war memorials, Sandberg presented some uninhibited painters in the Stedelijk Museum. The COBRA exhibition of 1949 caused a shock. We had lost our colonies, communism was wreaking havoc, and then there was the first Russian nuclear bomb, the Cold War, Korea, Cuba, China and Vietnam... All of these constituted major threats and now art was degenerating, too. True, innovations were also being made in the applied graphic arts, but these were not quite as shocking to the untrained eye. The experiments of the thirties had already familiarized the public with these. Otto Treumann, Dick Elffers (whose painterly posters were great favourites with the public), Willem Sandberg, Jan Bons, Jurriaan Schrofer and Wim Crouwel: these were the innovators of the public 'message' in typography and image, which was partly based on the clarity of earlier German design (Bauhaus) and the work by Swiss typographers that they saw after the war. Their responsibility also differed from that of artists. They had to communicate the message of their clients: museums, exhibition organizers, theatres or companies.**

Society grows more complex. Prosperity gradually increases and the Dutch people is informed in all sorts of ways about the best design for living. There was an abundance of patronizing – including that of a positive kind. The NVSH (Dutch association for sexual reform) showed how to improve your sex life, Goed Wonen **showed how to improve your interior. At the same time building contractors were in a position to realize the ideal of the prewar city planners: broad streets, sun and light, but at an extremely low price and producing very poor quality. There was a great housing shortage.**

Companies raised their profile. They had to improve their familiarity and attract customers. America was the main example in nearly all fields of life: political, economical and social. Although the general public was unfamiliar with the Dutch word ontwerp **– let alone 'design' – the growing number of visual advertisements appearing in the streets gradually became more lucid. The designers received a growing number of commissions. This was the start of an incredible and rapidly increasing prosperity (in Western countries), of the never-ending communication flow that we now know and tolerate. Quantities increased, speeds rose, content became more diffuse, frequently meaningless, pressure increased. And now, in our age, we must try and find our way through this jungle of images, among the bombardment of useful and useless visual attention seekers, and develop some way to select this information. The**

graphic design profession has changed into 'design and communication'. The lines of the communication network (company/client/consultancy) are so short that they create a black plane on which words like quality, excellence, functionality, information and communication have lost all meaning. Everything revolves around consumption, the economy, turnover and profit, while advertising slogans patronize the public and the service industry increasingly leaves the public to fend for itself. However, there are also positive aspects: more options to choose from, easier ways to reach people, a higher employment rate, more study programmes and, for those who are desirous and capable of it, a better and more critical approach to society.

Faded ideals In these years of rapidly increasing prosperity, design techniques also underwent profound and rapid changes. Scissors, pencil and glue were integrated in the computer. The ever-evolving graphic industry employed the latest typesetting and printing techniques. The number of clients continued to rise. Awareness of the importance of design grows not only in the corporate sector – having a corporate identity becomes imperative – but government organizations and private institutions also call in the aid of designers.
In 1984 Total Design introduced the revolutionary Aesthedes: a huge machine fitted with three monitors, a complicated operation panel and an enormous printer. Nowadays, every designer can do about anything he needs using a much smaller computer, a printer and a scanner. The time has come when the designer is both typesetter, lay-out artist and lithographer. All data can be transported via telephone lines or on CDs to the printing firm or even directly to the printing press, which finishes the job. In the graphic design departments of academies pencils are conspicuous by their absence. The number of designers has greatly increased – when Ben Bos joined the GKf it had 110 members, while today the bNO has thousands of members – and graphic design features all the movements that are familiar from the visual arts and architecture: conceptualists, minimalists, classicists, functionalists, new fauves and others. All this led to a great quantity of printed matter, which often raises the question what is the essential content of the profession.
In this river of social change and technical development flowing ever more rapidly, Ben Bos worked at Total Design from 1963 to 1991 as designer, team leader, creative manager, teacher, writer and editor. Initially the ideals of the twenties (creating a better world) were still at play at this design studio, but they gradually made way for the aim to enhance the image of enterprises or cultural institutions by means of contemporary forms that were lucid, businesslike and above all functional.

This is a rough outline of the times which shaped the life and work of Ben Bos, and which he largely witnessed himself. His biography must be viewed against this background. Ben Bos has a great love for the profession and, as Wim Crouwel said about the Total Design years: In that period we developed our own, intractable view on design which we actively advocated. We infected each other and had an unshakeable faith in our credos. I often was under the impression that Ben was probably the best guarantee for loyal continuity among all those egos.

Lucid, practical and efficient The war had made a deep impression on Bos. It was a cruel chaos which fed his desire for lucidity, order and comprehensibility in a better world. As a son of a hard-working bookbinder he did not have a very cultured background, apart from the fact that his parent's house was furnished with sober and immoveable furniture of the Amsterdam School. There were many moral do's and don'ts, which led to his whole-

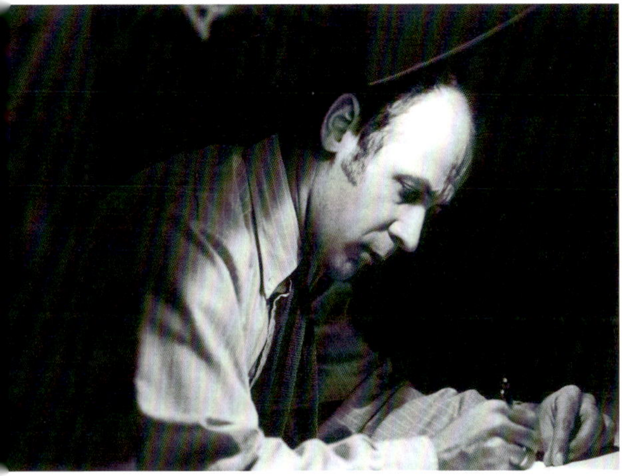

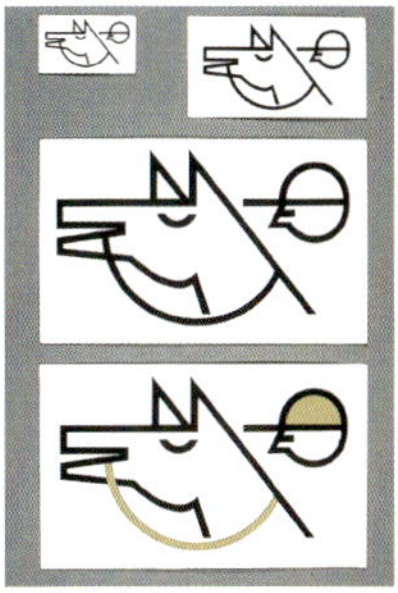

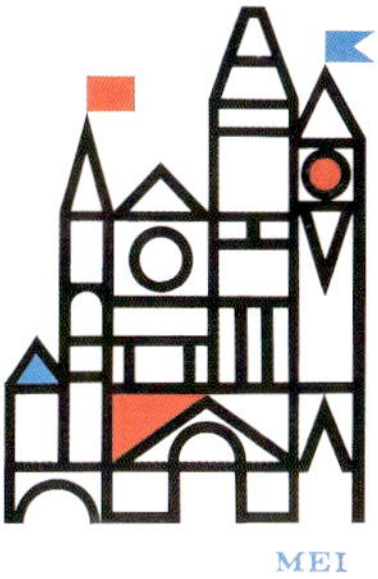

1960-61 Academy assignments

hearted rejection of the nineteenth-century mentality. Things needed become more tolerant, but above all more practical and efficient. The social-democratic atmosphere in the family of a girlfriend exposed him to an alternative to petty bourgeois life. A new world opened up for him. Bos wanted to be loyal, conscientious and 'lucid' and accordingly fulfilled his military service at a time of new threats (Russia, China) in which a better army would be able to resist the enemy. Deep down he was a humanist and social democrat, but unlike many people in the arts aznd design world he did not have any communist sympathies. Ben Bos was a journalist, draughtsman and photographer, joined the Ahrend firm, and at the ripe age of 26 registered at the Instituut voor Kunstnijverheidsonderwijs, where his teachers included Wim Crouwel, Charles Jongejans and Tom de Heus.

Ben Bos joined Total Design in 1963, the year in which the studio was founded. This first multidisciplinary design studio in the Netherlands aimed to create a conceptual unity among all public expressions of a client such as letter paper, trademark, packaging, product, advertising and PR, exhibition stands, but also the spatial design of the factory itself. Bos became a colleague of Wim Crouwel, Benno Wissing and Friso Kramer, people whom he regarded with admiration.

Total Design (the English name, unusual for the period, reflected the multidisciplinary and international orientation of the studio) set high standards and in a sense imitated enterprises outside the Netherlands with an outspoken design culture like Olivetti, Braun and IBM as well as English studios such as Design Research Unit and Fletcher, Forbes, Gill (later called Pentagram), which had been founded in 1962.
In those years the idealistic aim to

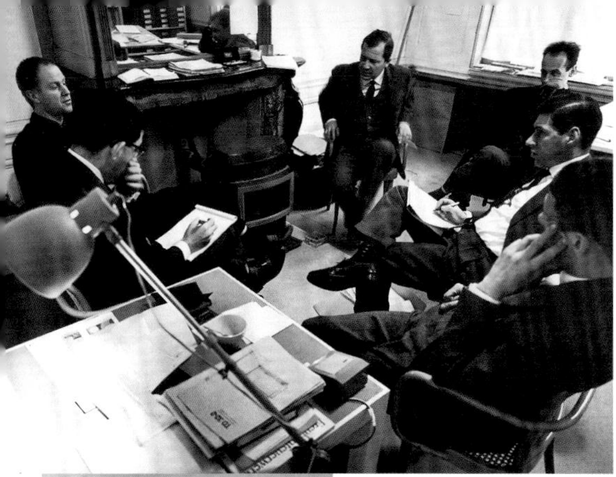

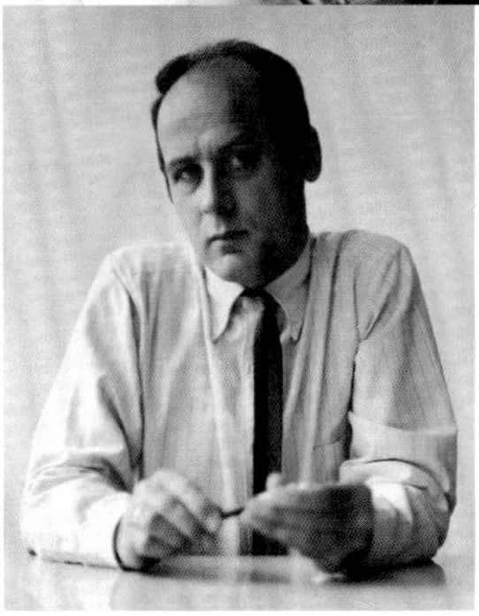

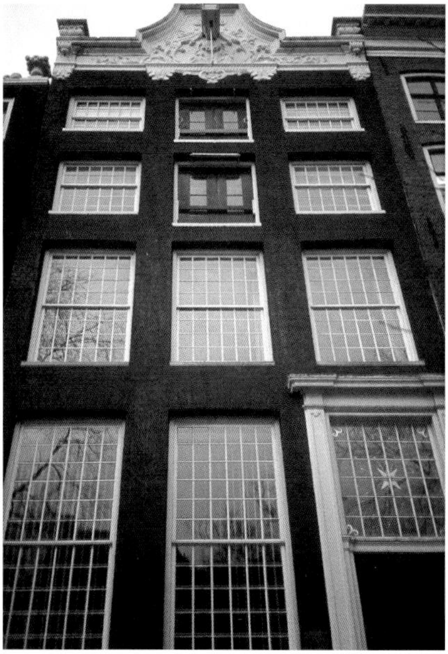

1963 Management and staff meeting at Total Design
Dick Schwarz, Friso Kramer, Benno Wissing,
Ben Bos, Paul Schwarz, Wim Crouwel

Herengracht 567, Amsterdam
This is where Total Design started in 1963. It would remain here until 1987

contribute to a better, more livable world, an ideal to which Ben Bos also subscribed, still counted. In the context of that idealism the sound, practical form was viewed as a kind of service. An interview with Friso Kramer in Goed Wonen **magazine of 1964 contains a statement that has a similar import as Rietveld's words:** One of the ground rules is that a product must be designed in such a way that is does not bother people with the idiosyncrasies of the designer and manufacturer. All his life, the designer must learn to omit the inessential during the design process. Likewise he has a duty towards society to be aware of the latest results of scientific research and to apply these in order to render them useful, understandable and livable for users. The results of academic studies (in science and philosophy) will be decisive factors in the long run.
A photograph of the partners of those years – Crouwel, Wissing, Kramer, the Schwarz brothers and Ben Bos as 'junior designer' (a title that he himself chose in the belief that he still needed to prove himself) – shows the seriousness and ambition of this studio.

The history of Total Design has already been described in detail by Frederike Huygen in the monograph on Crouwel, in which the ups and downs, the turnover of staff, the projects and the importance of the studio are all discussed. She also provides a partial analysis of Ben Bos's role at Total Design: Bos was a stable factor at the studio. He was steady as a rock and displayed an almost unconditional loyalty to the studio. He guaranteed the enterprise's continuity. On a business level his team was always stable in that it always generated ample profits – sometimes as one of the few. However, he was much less interested in innovative design than the other partners. To some extent Bos's manner of operating was that of

an outsider-insider. His relation with the partners was variable: now equal, now unequal. That wasn't always easy.
Ben Bos's importance for Total Design certainly lay in this loyalty, but also in his versatility and the social skills that he displayed both in and outside the studio. The fact that he still has a working relation with Ahrend – where he started his career – and continued working for Randstad long after he left Total Design is telling. However, unlike other partners he did not deliberately set out to maintain a high profile, although in the end he did become widely known.
Bos is not a theorist but a doer. That was clear from the very start: at home he noticed the inefficient design of his mother's kitchen, he was an avid supporter of Goed Wonen **magazine and a life-long advocate of lucidity, readability and communication transfer without an excess of signals in the graphic industry.**
At the IvKNO Bos learned from Crouwel and from the designers whom Crouwel admired. These belonged to the Bauhaus, the Hochschule für Gestaltung in Ulm and the Swiss Neue Graphik: Max Bill, Müller-Brockmann, Anton Stankowsky, Armin Hofmann and Celestino Piatti. In 1961 Ahrend sent Ben Bos on a study trip to Milan, the Mecca of design, to visit the exhibition of AGI members that would be held in the Stedelijk Museum the following year. The 1962 Christmas issue of Drukkers Weekblad Autolijn **– 'Print around the clock' – was devoted to this exhibition. It provides an excellent impression of an era and offers a good international survey of graphic design in those years. It already was a highly varied and – I would say – unpretentious and friendly impression of information, that has now become much more aggressive and complex. On those occasions he sensed in which direction he would finally move: towards graphic design.**

Opposites **The sixties in Amsterdam were a turbulent period, with Dylaby, the Nieuwe Liga, Fluxus, Vietnam demonstrations, the provos, the royal wedding of Beatrix and Claus, the happenings, the meetings at Spui square, the democratisation movement, the anti-authoritarian and anti-government actions. Society was undergoing a metamorphosis. In graphic design this was reflected in the work of Swip Stolk and Anthon Beeke and ten years later in that of Wild Plakken and Hard Werken,** groups walking like unicorns in the geometric park.
Total Design was their opposite, with its emphasis on the grid and structures that dictated the appearance of its design. Although during the provo period Benno Wissing occasionally changed his clothing from formal to 'youthfully informal', Total Design stuck to its principles and anyway the studio couldn't make a major switch without offending most of its clients. A different mentality prevailed there, which was directed at functionality, and not at the ephemeral, the political comment and social commitment that people like Jan van Toorn propagated in the seventies.

Instrumental creative labour **No matter how much Total Design changed and developed among the ever-growing prosperity, Ben Bos remained loyal to this studio, and it shows in his visual work. His designs for two major clients Ahrend and Randstad display a consistency which is wholly in keeping with Bos's principles and 'lifestyle': lucidity, functionality and instrumentality. The designer remains in the background: his objective is not art for arts's sake, artistic design or personal expression, but the clearest possible communication of the message and the content.**
In his own words: A designer is someone who provides a shape for a piece of information that is usually supplied by others through the use of form, colour, structure, image, typeface, time or space, and who usually assumes

responsibility for its adequate realization and/or reproduction. Design is no free expression, but a kind of instrumental, creative labour that is generally performed by order.

Many people testify to the fact that relations between Ben Bos and his clients were excellent and involved debates full of sound argumentation during which both parties kept an open mind. It should not be forgotten that this was many years ago, when these discussions were still personally conducted by managers and not by marketing managers, as is common practice today. On top of this, the mergers, joint ventures and all other attempts to achieve a higher position on the world market are disastrous for designers, especially for those who have maintained relations with a company over many years. The same applies to corporate identities that are either modified or completely abandoned.

Ben Bos's main activity was designing for various kinds of enterprise. These circles usually were in need of a design consultant. They often considered the status quo as the easiest and cheapest option. Innovations in this field were considered unnecessary and wasteful. But when the neighbour and the competitor make the effort, you cannot afford to stay behind. It is a difficult road. In the case of the PTT, which had a rich design tradition, the introduction of a corporate identity took twelve years. Bos had always strongly advocated that companies adopt an identity and had gradually become a specialist in this field. He has also published a fair amount on the subject. Many of his logos, such as those for Kluwer, Furness, Dronten, Capelle aan den IJssel and Randstad have survived for decades, often to this very day.

Corporate identities are always a question of money, and in some cases a lot of money. The most expensive option is to have no identity. A corporate identity is an investment that requires maintenance. Many corporate identities suffer from malnutrition. **As far as possible, Bos has kept an eye on this maintenance, ensuring that the corporate identity is correctly used in branch offices both at home and abroad, that employees do not take initiatives such as producing new routing systems or suddenly introducing a different typeface. A corporate image or corporate identity requires strict regulation.**

After all, it forms part of a company's existence, its reliability and familiarity.

A corporate identity designer is a Jack-of-all-trades, because the entire company must be pervaded by that image, down to the smallest details.

He also is the person who must impress the importance of clarity and recognizability upon the people in charge.

After all, it is a 'product' that does not have a clear-cut value which can be expressed in figures. In the case of Ben Bos it also was a matter of ethics ('a sense of moral responsibility'):

Once you accept a commission, you undertake to monitor and maintain it until the end of time. He was loyal to the companies for which he worked.

He is one of the many designers of the twentieth century who – following German architect Behrens, who designed AEG's identity – effectively propagated the sound form to lay people. So perhaps there is some kind of educational mission after all, a functional aesthetics to which Ben Bos, as a designer, writer and teacher remained true all his life.

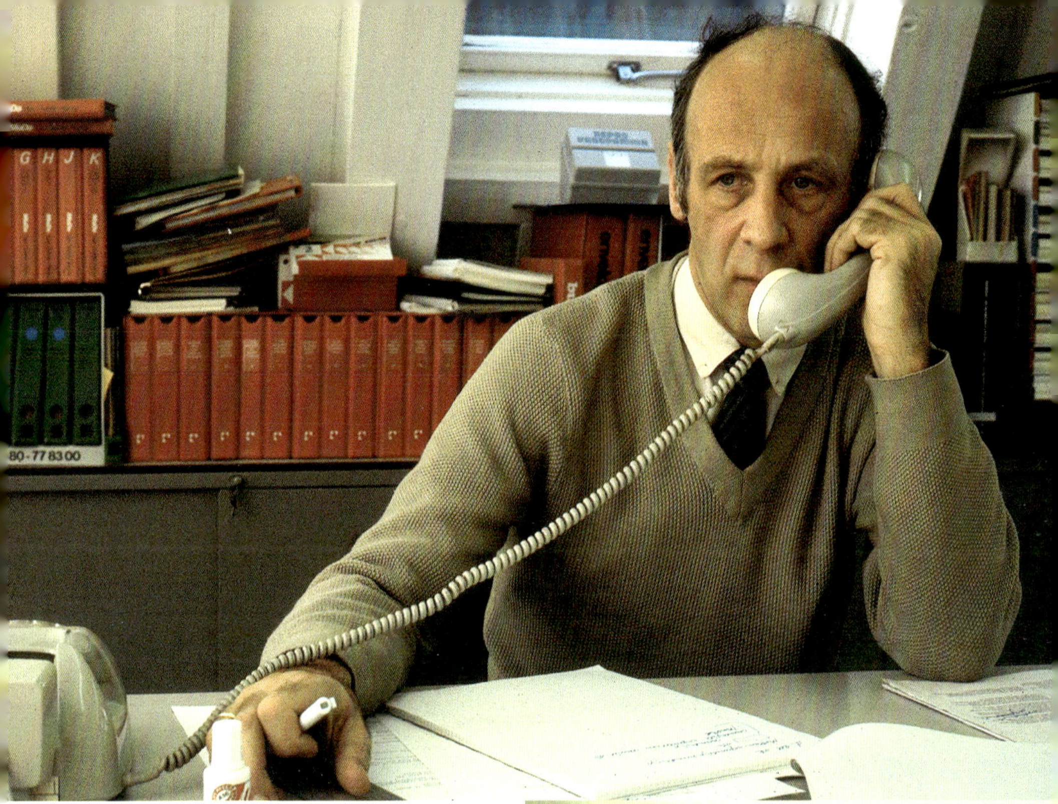

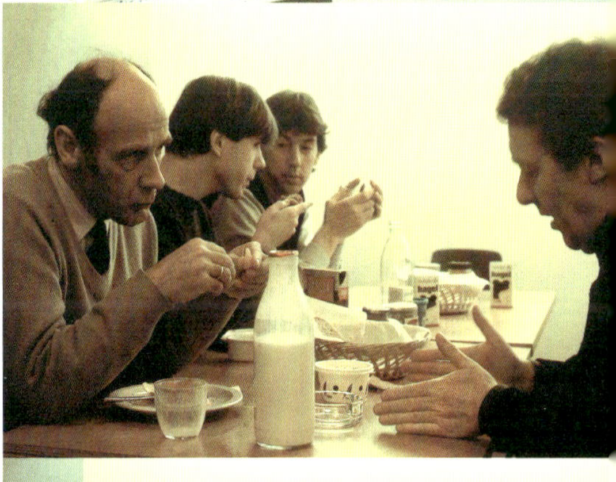

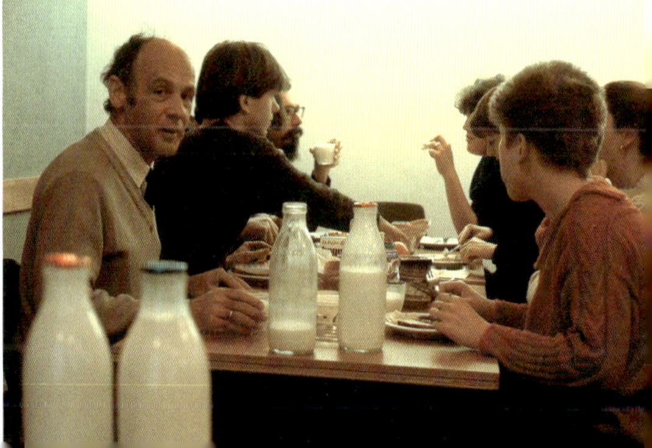

Lunch at Total Design

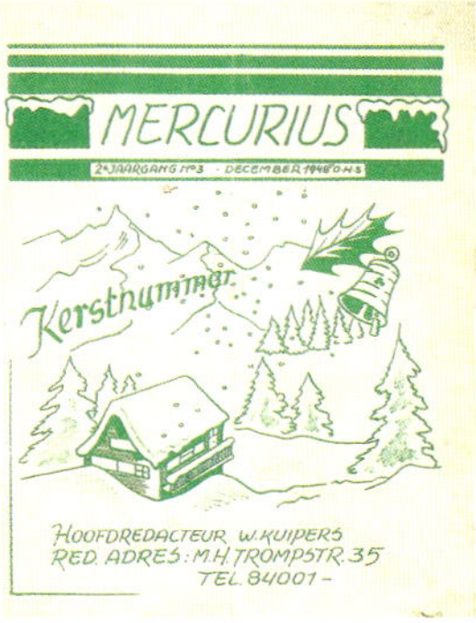

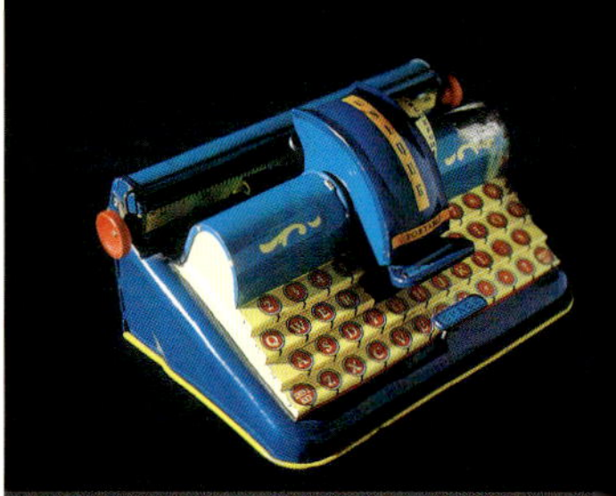

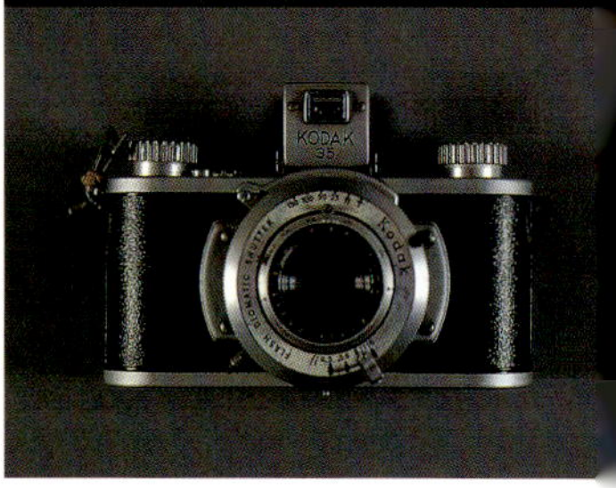

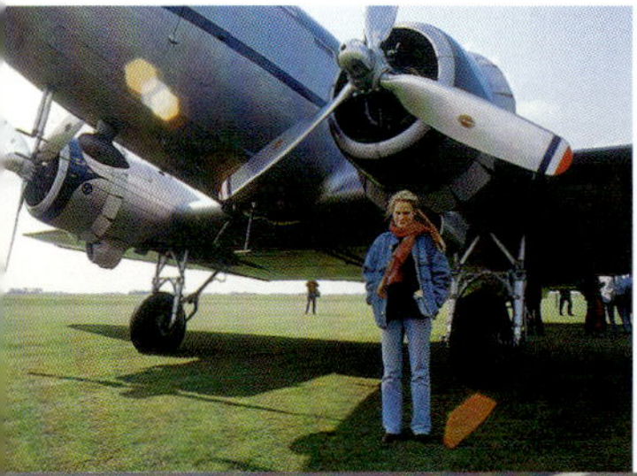

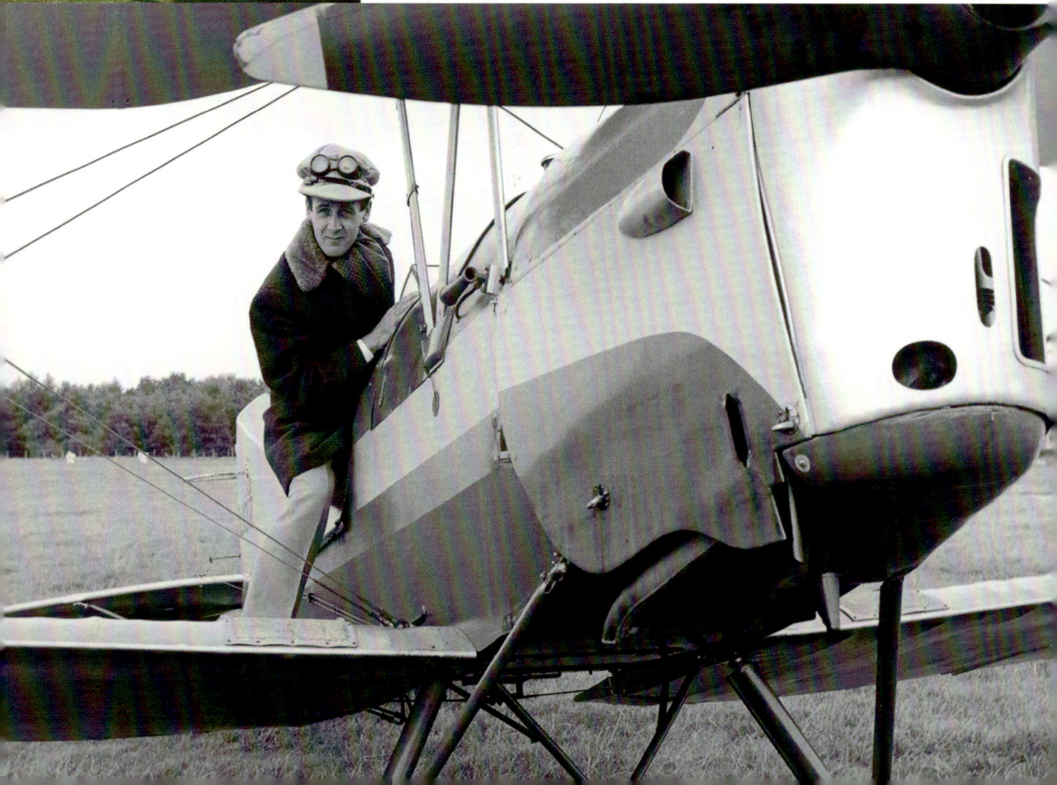

1948 School magazine 1e OHS, Amsterdam

1992 Jantien's daughter Jacobien Peeters flies to Texel in a Dakota

1964 Ben Bos posing with a Tiger Moth
Photography by Arjé Plas

1942 Children's typewriter
1946 Kodak 35

Dirk van Ginkel

Doubly gifted

Impressions of a designer's life

Ben Bos definitively opted for design at the ripe old age of twenty-four, when he was employed as a copywriter by the multi-faceted trade enterprise Ahrend. He decided to attend the one-year night study programme in Lay-out at the Amsterdam Graphic School and subsequently moved on to the five-year night study programme at the IvKNO, which would later become the Rietveld Academie. After graduating with distinction from both study programmes Ben Bos – by then over thirty – could rightfully call himself a designer. However, until his twenty-fourth he had been developing his talents for photography, drawing, written journalism and design without a premeditated plan, and without a clear preference for any one of his talents.

I was quite late in making a definitive choice of profession, **says Bos.** However, you should consider the circumstances under which I grew up. I am a member of the generation that was badly shaken by World War II. Not only was our education much delayed by the closing of the schools, immediately after the war we also developed a deep and manifest fear of the Chinese and the Russians. In response to that I rather protracted my national service. I believe I was not alone in doing so. On top of that I come from a family where we didn't lack any of the essentials, but that was about it. I had to deny myself extracurricular activities that were not obligatory, like music or dancing lessons. So there were many things of which I remained unaware and that I was unable to enjoy. That's why I had to teach myself all sorts of things: drawing, writing, photography...

I was a little lacking in a sense of direction.

However, this 'directionlessness' proved conducive to a high productivity. It led to a series of single-handed publications such as school magazines, the periodical of the athletics club of which he was a member and publications of the airplane spotters club of which he was the secretary. Eventually these activities resulted in a 'real' job for an employer for which he would still be undertaking activities in the autumn of his career: Ahrend.

I knew Toon Bogers through AAC, the athletics club, and he was head of publicity at Ahrend. He had read enough of my stuff to offer me a job in 1953 as advertising assistant and copywriter, **Bos recalls.** Oddly enough, this text-oriented function inspired a real passion for design.

One-man productions **Photography, drawing, writing, athletics, aviation... Ben Bos had many hobbies which he avidly practised. Although this was one of the reasons why he postponed the choice of profession for so long, he was quite sure what he did not want.**

I really didn't consider a career in my father's business as an option. He was a bookbinder, had a company with some seven employees and worked like blazes day and night. And he paid dearly for that in terms of his physical condition. On top of that, it didn't exactly turn him into a happy person. So that was not for me.

Nevertheless he feels he owes a debt to his father's profession.

My father was himself the son of a bookbinder and I believe that it is due to this family history that my interest in everything related to text and illustration came naturally to me. At an early age I was given a little children's typewriter with which I produced small newspapers.

And I was overjoyed when immediately after the liberation a sailor cousin gave me a 35 mm camera that enabled me to produce realistic illustrations. Prior to entering military service in 1950 I had always been able to give full rein to this urge to combine my talents and hobbies in graphic one-man productions.
In 1948 Bos finished secondary school and started working as head of the central booking liaison department at KLM. This was a job that, if only indirectly, tied in with his interest in aviation. This also applied to his time in uniform which lasted until 1953. Bos fulfilled his national service at the Dutch Royal Airforce and for a period worked at the Photography and Film Department and the pilot examination department. In his spare time he wrote as much as he could.
In that period I wrote numerous articles on aviation for soldier weeklies. I had frequent contacts with the aviation industry and airline companies and obtained my information through them. It was not just a way to turn my interest in aviation to practical use, but I also considered it as a foretaste of my future. At the time I thought I would go on to become a freelance journalist. That is why I took a correspondence course in journalism during my national service. But these plans to become a writer never materialized. It proved impossible for me to make a penny on it. I very briefly worked at the Dutch Dairy Promotion Bureau as a PR assistant and then Bogers turned up and asked if I would like to join Ahrend.

Promotional writing **In 1953 Bos was appointed at nv Wed. J. Ahrend & Zoon as advertising assistant and copywriter. At the time Ahrend had its own publicity department. Due in part to the innovative contribution of industrial designer Friso Kramer the company had developed a clear philosophy about furniture quality standards. And over the years it developed ideas along the same lines about the standard of its graphic expressions. The fountainhead of these ideas was Cor Walstra, a full-time designer who worked alongside Bos and who was employed by Ahrend from 1953 to 1993. Bos describes Walstra's graphic output as lucid, simple and maintaining high standards with regard to the typographical rules of the game. In retrospect, Ben Bos takes a slightly more critical view of Walstra.**
His work was not boring, but it was well-behaved. He himself did not have a playful approach. We made some very fun things together, but it became apparent what he lacked when I left in 1963. Nevertheless, Ahrend published a lot of beautiful graphic work from his hand.

Making Crouwels **Quite soon after joining Ahrend, Bos decided to attend a study programme in lay-out at the Amsterdam Graphic School. He witnessed every day how Walstra processed the texts that he had written and concluded that he would also be able to express himself in design work. Perhaps he could even go one better.**
On top of that, design seemed much more fun than writing texts about furniture, drawing materials and instruments. I wanted to be able to do what Walstra did. That was my reason for attending that course and immediately after moving on to the night study programme in design that was taught at the IvKNO. Fortunately I got the opportunity to put into practice what I had learned almost immediately. True, Walstra initially gave me hardly any room in the regular Ahrend publications, but I was given free rein in Ahrend's staff magazine that I was given the chance to reanimate. I could write for it, draw for it, design it. So once again I was making something that I could assemble according to my own views. That was a familiar feeling. Thc first freelance commissions also started arriving in that period.
Disciplined as always, Ben Bos mounted his bike four or five nights a week and cycled to the design classes. He received instruction from, among

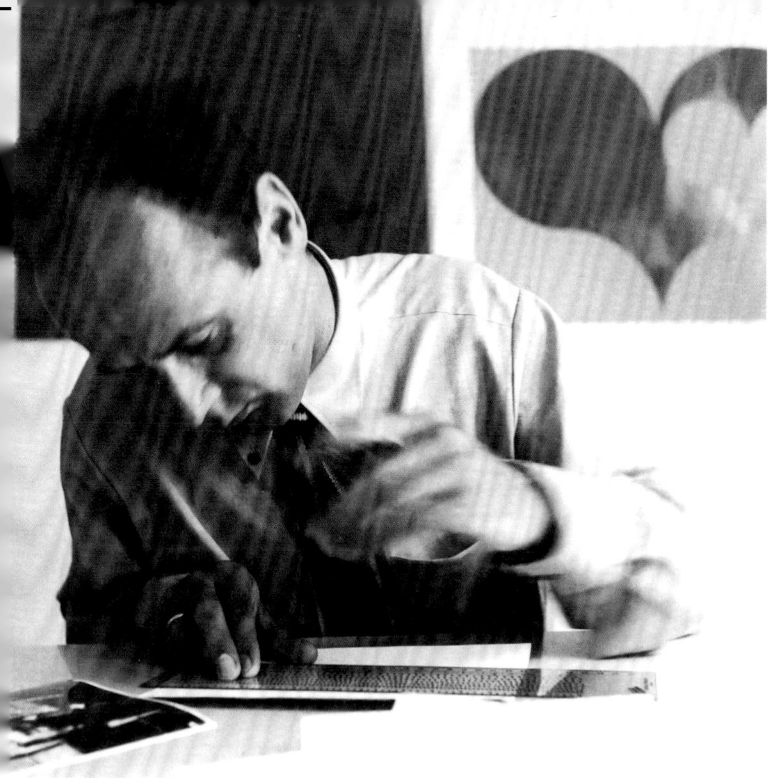

1969 In the background a Bijenkorf poster

others, Jan Elburg, who taught formal theory, draughtsman Piet Klaasse and typographer Charles Jongejans. And Wim Crouwel was there too, the man who Bos regarded as the absolute maestro.
I hero-worshipped Crouwel. I was strongly attracted to the Neue Graphik, a movement of which he was a strong supporter and which advocated clarity, simplicity and clear structures in the organization of the material. I still am a great admirer of the functionalism of masters like Ifert, Scheidegger, Müller-Brockmann, Hofmann and Neuburg. Crouwel also was a functionalist in heart and soul, and dogmatic to the bone to boot. When in the eighties he was given yet another professorship I heard him deliver a lecture on functionalism that in no way differed from what he was saying forty years earlier. But at that time it made a profound impression on me.
On the other hand, as Bos emphasizes, there was not much else around to be impressed by. In a sense, functionalism was the only real movement – Pieter Brattinga, Benno Wissing, Tom de Heus and Charles Jongejans and others had also been converted to it. Other designers worked very individually, on the basis of personal concepts. Otto Treumann and Dick Elffers produced work in which a colouristic, almost painterly approach dominated. And although Bos highly regarded their work, he was looking for a different approach to design. Why did he not try to link up with Piet Zwart and Paul Schuitema, who were also protagonists of the lucid design school and who had many followers?
Schuitema and Zwart worked on the basis of a typographical approach that was very modernist. And they made frequent use of photographs. As the pre-war photographers could not provide them with what they needed, they developed their own photographic vision and used self made photographs in their designs. That was a great

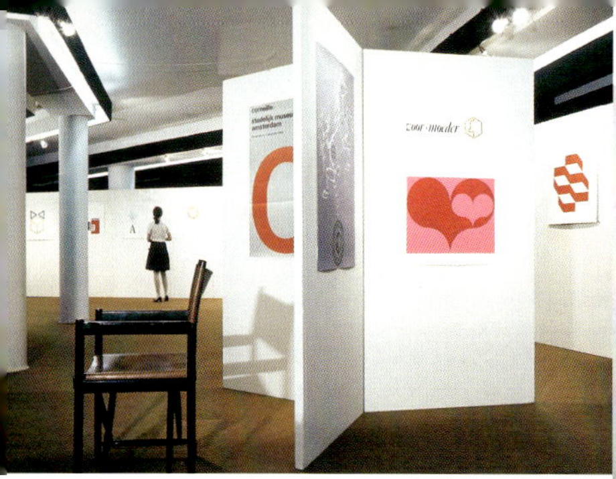

1970 Total Design exhibition at BMW Munich

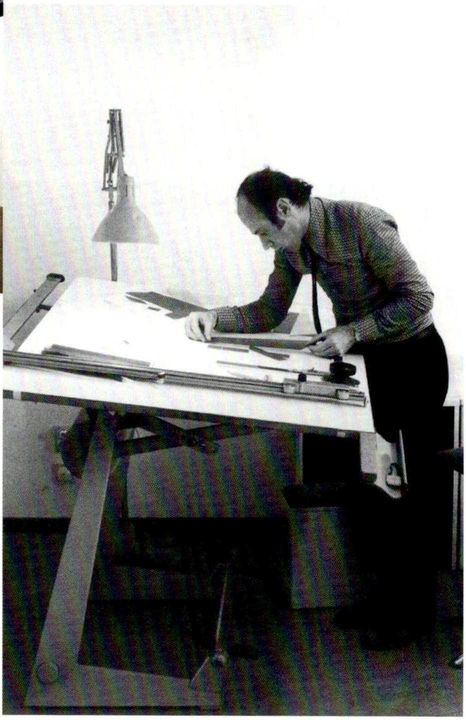

inspiration. For many years I also used photography as my main source of images. It was mainly due to practical considerations that I did not study with them in The Hague or Rotterdam. In those years there existed hardly any mobility, and you didn't have any money either. Moreover, it was physically impossible for me as a young father in Amsterdam with a full-time job to attend evening classes in another city. And then you have to consider the time I spent on freelance projects I worked on in the few hours that remained. At the time Crouwel ran a studio with interior designer Kho Liang Ie and he sometimes farmed out work to me. Of course I couldn't refuse that.

So apart from Functionalism and Modernism there was not much that could help Bos find his bearings. He reminisces that when he joined the GKf in 1964, this professional association had just 110 members, including a fair share of very illustration-minded designers. It was a very small world. That's why Wim Crouwel's conceptual world was so attractive and inspiring. At one stage there was nothing I wanted to do more than producing little 'Crouwels'. Incidentally, I already succeeded in doing so during my studies at the IvKNO. I was once given a school assignment to design a poster for the printing company Steendrukkerij De Jong & Co and when I had finished it I thought: 'That's my first real Crouwel'. I'm not ashamed of my attitude at that time. As far as I'm concerned, it's quite normal that you use a kind of personal beacon when you're trying to find your bearings.

In spite of his full-time job at Ahrend, frequently did projects for Crouwel and when his great example was away on travel he would keep an eye on his studio. I was very much Crouwel's part-time right hand. A few years later we would be cooperating full-time at Total Design.

Humanity **In the book** Wim Crouwel: Mode en module **Frederike Huygen writes:** Bos will remain one of Crouwel's most faithful disciples. **This claim does not only imply that Bos grew up in Crouwel's shadow, but also that he never stepped out of it. Does Bos agree with Huygens' observation?**
During the preparations for my professional practice I made a dedicated effort to develop a style that built on what I knew from Crouwel. I have never tried to hide that. To **Leerling/Meester**, a Tecno publication from 1994, I contributed a story entitled 'The maestro'. In this I state emphatically that Crouwel was my idol and that for some time I wanted to follow in his footsteps. That shows how much affinity I felt with the man and his work. However, it later dawned on me that I also possessed qualities which Crouwel himself lacked. I was better than him at producing work that was emotionally charged and infused with a kind of humanity. In design terms: I was better at editorial design than Crouwel. His oeuvre is largely defined by his work for museums. The really interesting pieces are the posters and the catalogue covers. The internal layout of these catalogues usually is a systematically elaborated system based on the premise that reproductions of works of art should be presented whole, should never be cut, not to speak of adding anything to them. This led to beautiful and reliable printed matter of a distinctly institutional nature, nothing more and nothing less. I have tried, more than Crouwel, to tell a story on the basis of the carefully inventoried wishes of the client. The nature of my commissions demanded that anyway. **With reference to the abstract product of client Randstad Uitzendbureau Bos states that he always aimed to enliven brochures and other corporate publications with what he calls 'committed, social photography'. It is a type of photography that you also see with Ad van Denderen, Dolf Kruger and Cas Oorthuys.**
That kind of pictorial strategy, which you wouldn't expect from an ambitious and commercial company like Randstad, was something I have always deliberately aimed for. I later did the same for Ahrend. Ahrend sometimes received complaints from abroad that their brochures were so 'dry' and aesthetic. I tried to remedy this, for instance by placing used coffee cups on desks that were photographed to show that the furniture was designed for living or working. Or I arranged for a secretary to walk past, out of focus. In Crouwel's work you will look in vain for this humanisation of the setting. In that sense I believe I have liberated myself from his influence and made a personal contribution.
Although Bos calls himself a functionalist, he believes he uses a broader definition of Functionalism than his teacher. That was also borne out by several commissions that he accepted. From 1957 to 1991 he worked for Hulp voor Onbehuisden [Aid for the Homeless]. Bos wrote and designed begging folders and edited the organization's magazine. He also worked for two years in the construction team for the old people's home Nieuw-Vredenburgh, a commission that started with a routing system and led to a far-reaching involvement with the interior drawings by architects Van Gendt & Mühlstaf. Once again the objective was to add warmth, livability and thereby humanity.
Obviously, these are activities that are socially relevant. To my mind, Functionalism has more dimensions than Crouwel attributes to it. It involves more than a clear, direct and uncluttered information transfer. A little more passion can't do any harm. Imposing order is very important and readability is a good thing, but an added emotional charge renders communication more effective and therefore is also functional.

The big adventure **In 1963 Bos embarked on 'The Big Adventure', as he called it in Tecno: his career at Total Design, the first Dutch multidisciplinary design studio. Bos, who had risen to the function of art director at Ahrend, started working there as studio manager. The partners – in addition to investors Paul and Dick Schwarz, these were designers Wim Crouwel, Friso Kramer and Benno Wissing – had contributed their own staff members and Bos was expected to act as their manager. This was a gross miscalculation, since these staff members were used to cooperating directly with the big guys and accordingly did not accept Bos's intermediary position. It didn't take long before Bos concluded that he would be wiser to form his own team inside TD.**

Bos soon traded in his design guru Crouwel for Benno Wissing.

I quickly started rubbing shoulders with Wissing. Not only did he have a great store of theoretical knowledge, but he also was an expert at passing it on. Wissing was the 'party theorist', the mastermind of the grid as the designer's tool. He made it possible for all designers to use various sheets on which column widths and line positions were preprinted. This allowed us to work more efficiently and freed us to devote more time and space to the creative side of projects. On the basis of Wissing's theory Dick Schwarz and I produced a 16mm film entitled **Straminologie** (gridology). This was intended to allay the fears of designers and clients who believed that the use of grids would restrict their creativity and the number of formal variations.

Incidentally, this was the complaint that motivated the 'smear campaign' against Total Design in the late 'seventies. Vrij Nederland **columnist Renate Rubinstein, backed by a small army of others, held Wim Crouwel cum suis accountable for the New Ugliness.**

The nagging of Rubinstein and her supporters mainly concerned the telephone directory that Crouwel had designed. To my mind it was a great improvement on the previous version. From a purely production-technical perspective it was a major step forwards: typesetting was simplified, more text could be fitted onto a page, which reduced the bulk of the whole thing, it was easier to read... In short: easier for the user and cheaper for the client, due to the enormous amount of paper saved. I have to give Wim Crouwel credit for the fact that in the ensuing public debate he accepted full responsibility, although it would have been easy for him to say that all or many of these 'criticisms' should really be directed at the client. I thought it was very chivalrous of him to protect the PTT. The whole tussle was just a load of nonsense.

Other reproaches that were hurled at Total Design – like the claim that 'the power of the grid' had turned it into a design factory that left no room for artistic innovation – are swept from the table by Bos:

Those attacks came from another angle. People were accustomed to the image of graphic designers as a kind of artists who operated as individuals. In the minds of those people TD represented a power block. After all, we could handle commissions that were too big for people who operated individually. It also worked the other way around: the big clients knocked on our door. As the British designer Henrion once said: 'Institutions like to talk to institutions'. That's just the way it works. But people did not like that back then.

Ten years after **In the seventies Total Design had greatly changed compared to the sixties. The Schwarz brothers had left the company, as had Friso Kramer and Benno Wissing. Which changes had been made at the studio where Bos had worked as a creative co-manager since 1966?**

As far as Friso Kramer is concerned, the story is simple: He was more comfortable in the model workshop of a factory than behind a desk at the Herengracht. That is supported by the fact that his

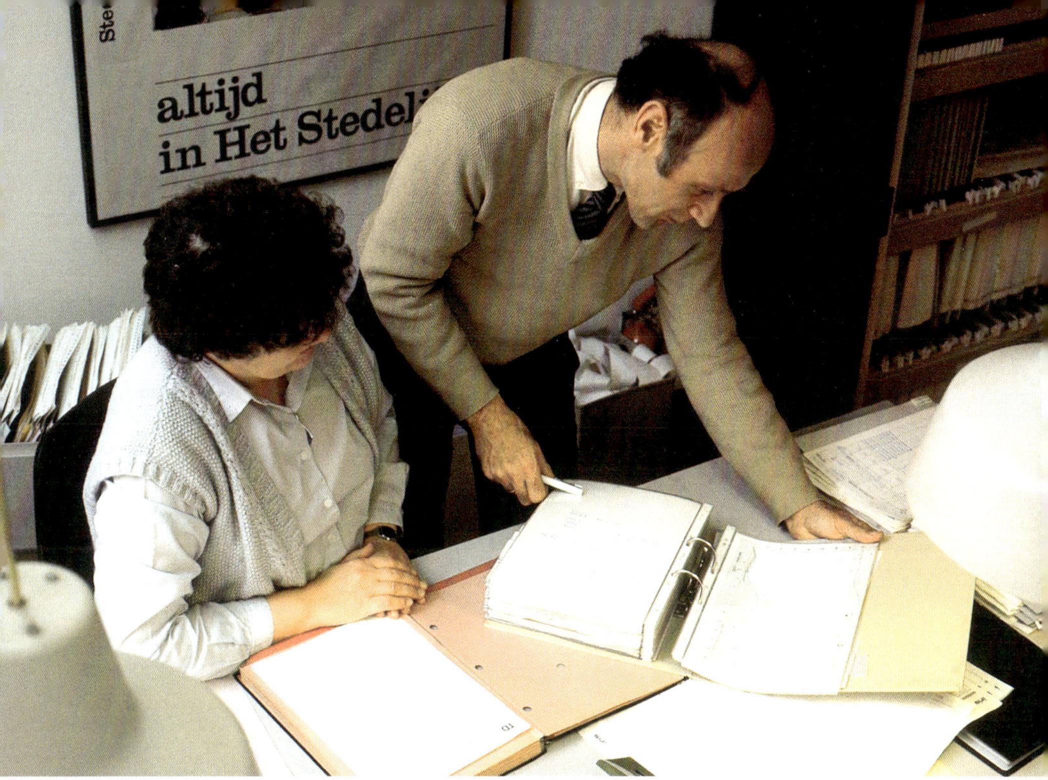

output steeply rose after he left us. His departure also meant that the multi-disciplinary character of TD became a thing of the past. We have never really managed to get the industrial leg of the operation off the ground. The situation with regard to the Schwarz brothers and Wissing was more complicated. Wissing maintained: 'Total Design is a design studio, so designers call the shots.' He believed that the brothers insufficiently understood what mattered in design and maintained that they should essentially restrict themselves to pulling out the chequebook during fallow periods. With Benno and his team, that was occasionally necessary around 1970, when the cost on commissions simply exceeded the returns. That led to heated conflicts with the outcome that both parties left.

Incidentally, Bos has a reputation as the team leader who always managed to work at a profit with his team. In the book on Crouwel Frederike Huygen calls him 'a tower of strength'.

Bos: My team was the cork which kept the agency afloat. One of the reasons was that I managed to attract commissions that were more profitable than the cultural projects. Moreover I think a had a better eye for expenses and profits, probably due to my education at a trade-oriented secondary school and my experiences at Ahrend.

Administrative worries in the seventies

By this time, he financial position of the studio, where business was not always flourishing, had by this time become quite opaque. Who really owned TD, now that nearly all founding partners had gone? Ben Bos certainly didn't. From the very start the arrangements for his financial position in the studio had been a little 'unusual'. His first three-year contract had been based on his last salary at Ahrend. Before the expiry of this contract, Bos reported that his income from freelance activities, undertaken in the evenings

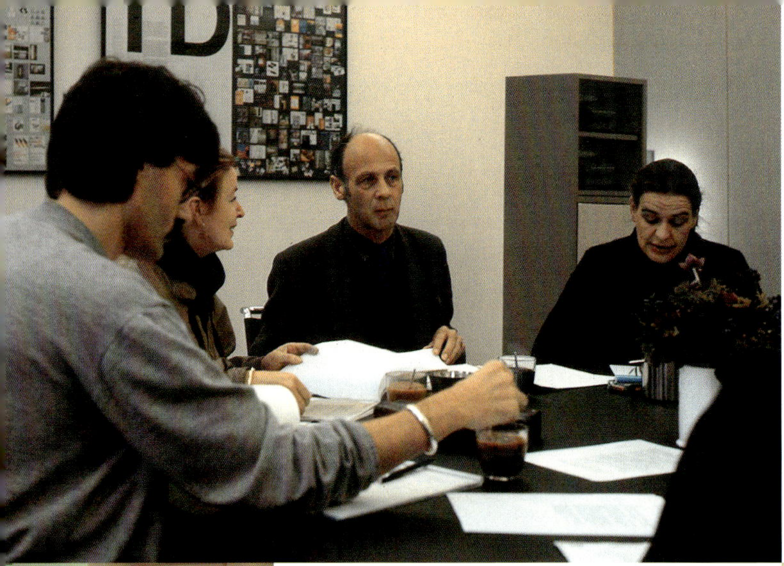

Meeting at Total Design
Jelle van der Toorn Vrijthoff, Daphne Duijvelshoff,
Ben Bos, Jolijn van der Wouw

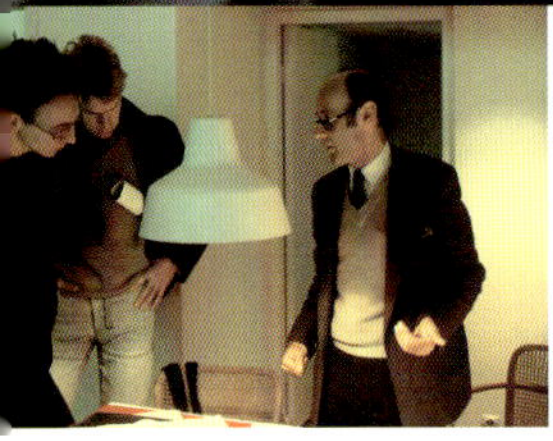

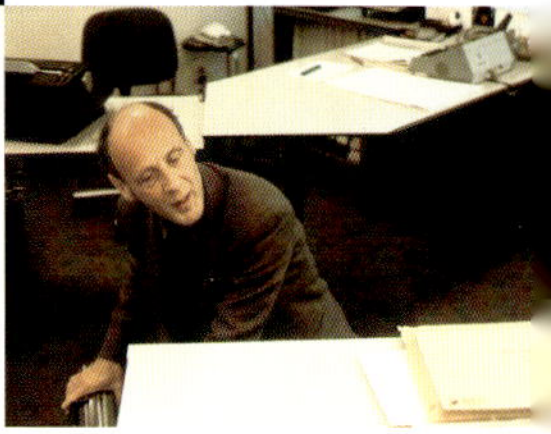

and during weekends, were considerably higher than the salary he was paid by TD. Something had to be done. The chosen solution was that Bos introduced his own clients, headed by De Bijenkorf, in exchange for which he was appointed as manager.

My salary was also raised to management level, **says Bos.** However, my goodwill was not converted into shares, unlike that of the three designer-partners. In those days the word 'shares' was not on the tip of everyone's tongue, at least not the way it is now. Still, you can say that when I was admitted to the management in 1966, I neglected to cash in on the clients I introduced. And the founders didn't bother to point that out to me. A little more assertiveness could have improved my position considerably.

After the departure of Friso Kramer, the Schwarz brothers and Benno Wissing a new management was formed, that was composed of Wim Crouwel, Hans Wierda and Ben Bos. Crouwel's shares were formally the only ones which still conferred 'power'. Those of the Schwarz brothers were in 'the dead hand'. Once again Bos, or Wierda for that matter, was not offered any shares.

Incidentally: in 1972 Bos and his right hand Wim van der Weerd repaid Total Design's debt to the Schwarz brothers in one fell swoop.

Crouwel was not quite happy with his formal 'force majeure'. This was one of the reasons why a few years later the BV was converted into a foundation – as an administrative format. This did not bring about any change in the ownership situation for the company's managers. That only happened in the late eighties, when a renewed Foundation issued share certificates that could be purchased by the managers according to a certain ratio. The value of these certificates rose spectacularly towards 1990 due to the recovery of the company assets to

which this value was linked. However, Bos was unable to profit from this. On leaving Total Design in September 1991 the regulations stipulated that he handed in his portfolio. On final quittance, a hectic year later, its value proved to be hardly any more than the amount he had deposited.

Spirograph riders **Huygen has divided the history of TD into three periods.** During the first period, which lasted until 1972, the partners made up an evenly balanced team, while the work they produced was cutting edge, innovative and intelligent. The general prosperity and the absence of competitors contributed to the reputation that TD acquired. The second phase lasted until 1980. During this phase Crouwel initially was the TD face, but he gradually withdrew into the background. After the 1972 crisis he made a considered choice to continue the studio, which necessitated a compromise between design principles and business considerations. The studio sailed an unsteady course since it lacked a clear sense of purpose. The work made in the TD offices started to show signs of routine, while the organisation became unmanageable. Crouwel's output fell below the artistic standard of the early period. There was increasing competition by other design studios while the economy was in a slump. In the absence of strong creative impulses TD's work bogged down into a treacherous swamp. (...) During the third phase, which started in 1980, these developments culminated in a professional and financial crisis.

Crouwel expected that the appointment in 1982 of Jelle van der Toorn Vrijthoff would benefit the organisation. The management of that time – which included Ben Bos and Loek van der Sande in addition to Van der Toorn Vrijthoff – sanctioned a number of changes: the aim to improve efficiency and – on the instigation of Van der Toorn Vrijthoff – the deployment of a design computer that was then unique and which was expected to put the studio back on the creative cutting edge. The businesslike atmosphere and the investments in the computer almost caused bankruptcy. In spite of this, Huygen writes even as late as 1997: Van der Toorn Vrijthoff's management role cannot be evaluated at this moment.

Two years later, Ben Bos does not find this at all difficult:

Van der Toorn Vrijthoff was responsible for a policy that was wholly based on the Aesthedes: the computer which we owned and that was supposed to help us move forward. He thought: We can do something with this thing that nobody else can do, and we are going to turn that to our advantage. From then on, TD was managed from the computer rooms, so to speak. Human beings no longer counted. According to Van der Toorn Vrijthoff the time of the great talents had passed. Human beings could not match the precision with which this computer worked. As a result, designing at TD appeared to become largely a matter of applying computer tricks. You could see at a glance if, and even when, a design had been made using the Aesthedes. Whoever had mastered the tricks used them. In principle I approved of the presence of the computer, just as I had applauded those forms of Benno Wissing's, because it relieved you of a lot of boring and time-consuming work. However, what actually happened was that a large number of commissions were realized as if they were bank notes. Each design was suddenly given a kind of infinite multi-layeredness. Everything fitted together in a marvellous, but extremely anaemic manner. I remember an annual report for the Suiker Unie with all those crystals and other knickknacks that were knitted together and overlayed. It was awfully clever, but you no longer saw what it was all about. The message was completely obscured. And that was in the order of the day. When my children were given a spirograph by their grandmother, I said: Put the wrappers back around that rubbish. What you make with it is completely uncreative. Those endless concentric circles are totally boring. Those spirograph riders at Total Design went on using the Aesthedes for quite a while. The design process was as it were dehumanized by the specific application of the computer. Wasn't I one of the managers who allowed all that to happen? Don't I bear some responsibility for that? Yes, I do. It wasn't very smart of me to think: The next generation has new ideas. I will only try to critically coach them from the sidelines. I probably should have interfered even more actively than I did. But I am so damned modest.

Return Amsterdam - The Hague **According to Van der Toorn Vrijthoff the era of the major talents had passed. That is why, says Bos, in 1985 he did not try to retain Wim Crouwel for Total Design some wayor other.**

And then it was my turn, **says Bos.** After all, I was the preserver of the past, the guardian of the old standards. Not only those regarding work methods, but also regarding the way you deal with people. And the way they dealt with me went against my sense of decency. I belonged to the management, but I was excluded from the deliberation during which a decision was taken about a collaboration with a Danish studio. I was not even introduced to those people when they visited the opening of Total Design Brussels, which I had set up in 1991. That sort of thing happened too often. So during a management meeting I announced: 'Gentlemen, If you show so little respect for me, I have no choice but to fall back on my self-respect.' Then I left. And they have suffered for it. When I left the studio, it employed 65 persons. Many, and certainly not the least among them, soon followed my lead. Quite a lot of people in and around the profession are of the opinion that TD has never really managed to get back on track since then. I'm sure the TD-ers themselves do not agree. They still get big commissions. Unfortunately I am rarely charmed by the visual results. Other things matter now, and that's a part of this era. The era of the big money.

Then Bos was invited to join the management of 2D3D design studio in The Hague. This studio was reputed to believe that the world ended at the outskirts of The Hague.

Be careful, **says Bos.** In the secretariat they had maps of Leiden, Delft and even Rotterdam lying ready in a drawer. When I saw those, I said: 'You probably know Amsterdam by heart and I'm sure you don't need a map of Holland at all!' They appointed me in order to enlarge the studio's clientele. I was expected to raise its profile by contributing innovation and upgrading. They believed that this would be a challenge. But I was really shocked when I started working there. Not only was the work often rather fiddly or excessively layered, the studio also had a culture of conducting meetings that was lethal. I had no idea people could chatter so long about so little.

Bos would not stay for long, just over two years. He refused to introduce clients such as Randstad, since he believed that the studio lacked the qualities to serve such a major account. However, he did introduce clients like the FNV [Dutch Trade Union Congress] and publisher Misset to 2D3D and also arranged for an important number of commissions by Ahrend and PTT Post. However, when Frits Goldschmeding rang to ask if he would like to participate in Randstad's American adventure Ben Bos did not hesitate to leave. Back in Amsterdam and on his frequent visits to Atlanta he resumed work on two clients for which he had always worked with heart and soul: Randstad and Ahrend. Incidentally, Randstad had ceased to be an exclusive client with Total Design soon after Bos left.

Goldschmeding told me: 'Since you left TD, everything is twice as expensive and in my opinion only half as good.'

1984 Randstad corporate design exhibition
Waterland Museum, Purmerend

1988 Exhibition 'Ben Bos, 25 years Total Designer' De Beyerd, Breda

1996 Presentation of the Oeuvre Award to Benno Wissing
Stedelijk Museum, Amsterdam

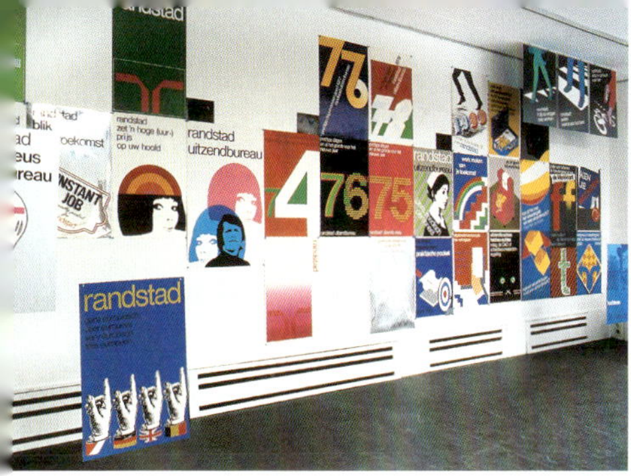

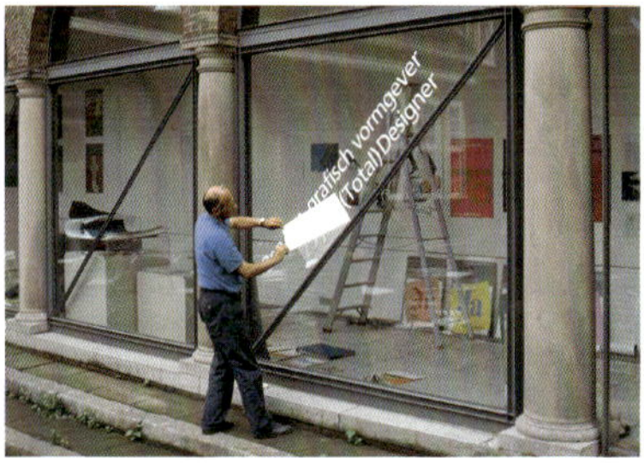

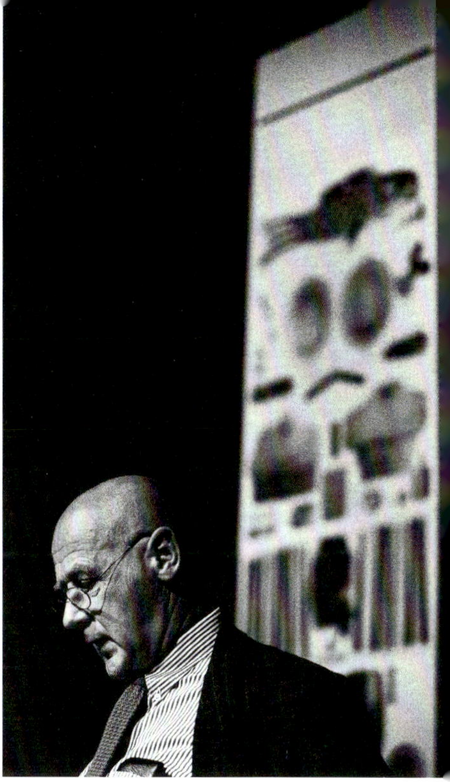

He believed it suffered from a lack of vision, management and consultation.

During his 2D3D period Ben Bos once again started writing in order to improve the studio's image. Although he had always published intermittently, his writings now began to appear more frequently. These publications included *Design, de ontworpen meerwaarde*, a short book on design management, and a publication on Benno Wissing, the subject of an exhibition in the Stedelijk Museum that he had designed. Since leaving TD he also appears in other capacities. He frequently lectures at national and international events, participates in exhibitions and forum discussions, is involved in design management study programmes, is the founder and chairman of the Nederlands Archief Grafisch Ontwerpers and frequently contributes to design periodicals *Art View*, *Design in Business* and later *Identity Matters*, the magazine into which the two aforesaid titles were merged. So he is still tirelessly busy with all things related to design. But then, he already was as a child.

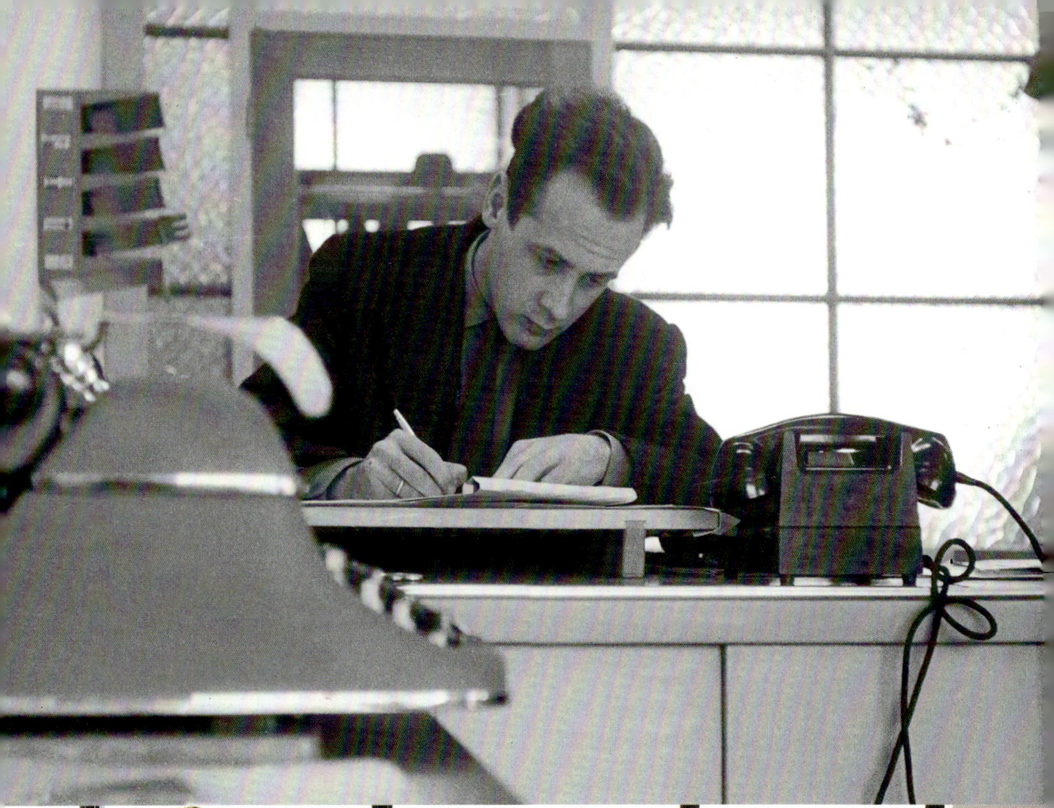

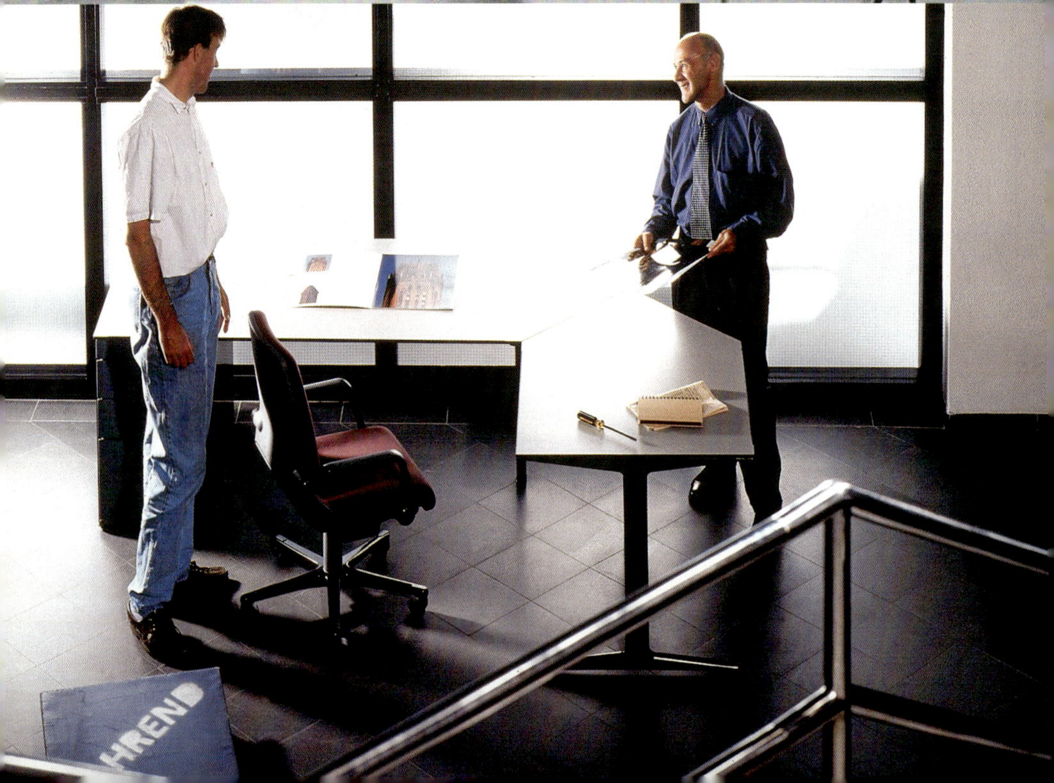
HREND

Ahrend

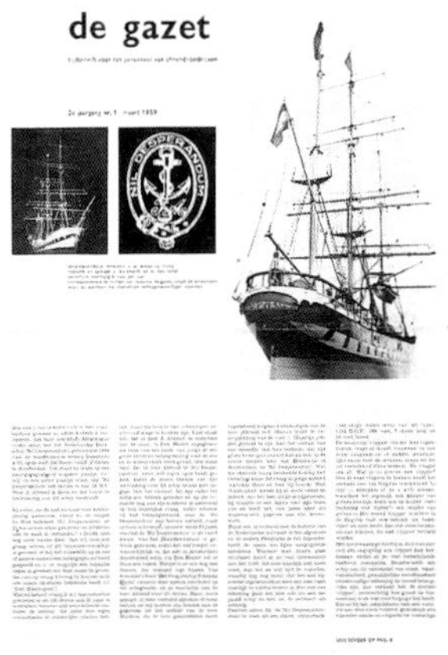
de gazet

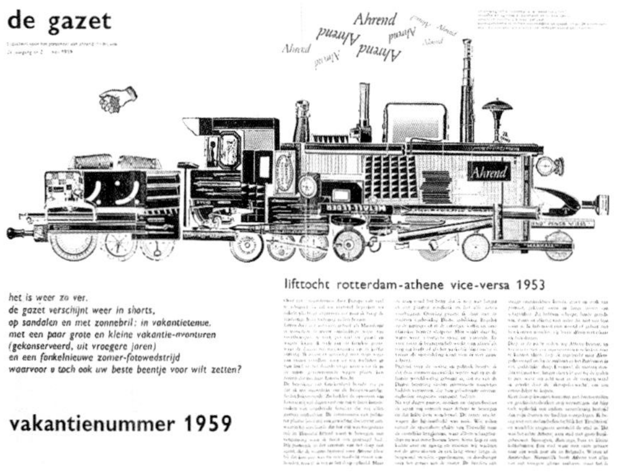
de gazet

het is weer zo ver.
de gazet verschijnt weer in shorts,
op sandalen en met zonnebril: in vakantietenue.
met een paar grote en kleine vakantie-avonturen
(gekonserveerd, uit vroegere jaren)
en een fonkelnieuwe zomer-fotowedstrijd
waarvoor u toch ook uw beste beentje voor wilt zetten?

vakantienummer 1959

lifttocht rotterdam-athene vice-versa 1953

1959
Staff magazine 'de gazet'
Editing, design and illustrations by
Ben Bos

1959
'Facetten'
'Peek-a-Book': visual rhymes
using photographs by Arjé Plas
and Jan Versnel
Concept and art direction by Ben Bos
Design by Cor Walstra

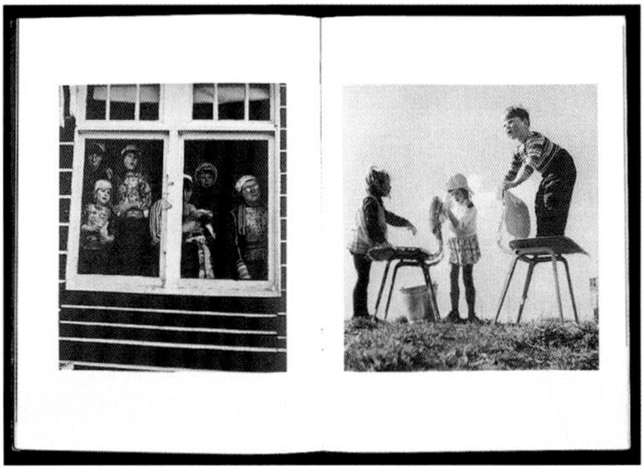

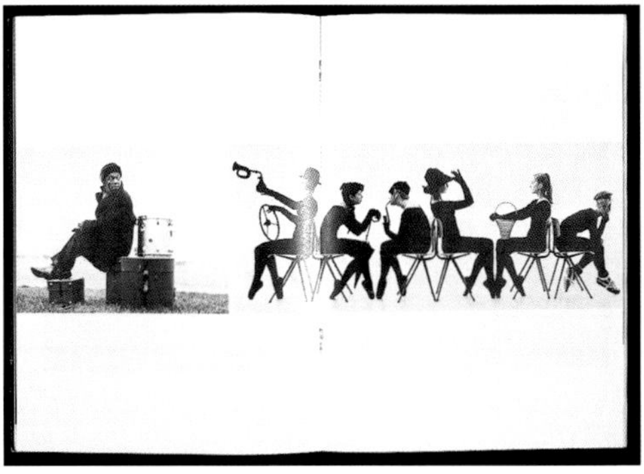

Imaginative, colourful and lyrical

Wim Crouwel met Ben Bos when the latter registered as a student at the Instituut voor Kunstnijverheidsonderwijs, which later became the Gerrit Rietveld Academie. Teacher Crouwel was impressed by his student and a few years later invited him to join Total Design. On several occasions Bos testified that Crouwel was his great example.

Even when he was still a student, Ben distinguished himself through his great dedication. I was quite impressed by his determination to acquire various skills. I also admired him for his versatility: he could draw, photograph and write like the best, not to speak of his feeling for design. He was someone who gave me the feeling that there was nothing left for me to teach him. Ben himself thinks otherwise, but as far as I'm concerned he was already fully formed. I have always taken him completely seriously. That's why I didn't waste any time hiring him as an assistant for several projects of the studio that I ran back then.

Like myself, Ben admired the Swiss typographers. They really understood that less is more. Ben was a great adherent of that approach and I too have always aimed to achieve that. However, if I compare my work to his, mine is much drier and more straightforward. Ben's oeuvre is imaginative, colourful and lyrical. He has a penchant for making things beautiful and arranging them. You also noticed that when you visited him at home. His interior was much more decorative than mine. Later I discovered that in my own work I often chose to consistently stick to certain principles, although sometimes, with works that formed part of a series, I could have achieved more pleasing results if had been less strict. For twenty years I produced the catalogues for the Stedelijk Museum. When I look at them now, I think: 'If you had stuck less rigidly to your grid, you could have improved them.' I'm sure that Ben would never have allowed that sort of thing to happen.

In some respects it was an advantage that he was much less steeped in theory than I was. He thought all that stuff was quite interesting, but due to his great versatity he participated more actively in the outside world than I did. That's why he approached his work more pragmatically. Total Design has greatly profited from this. I did not only think he was a gifted designer, I also thought he was highly independent. Unlike some, he was no copycat. His preference for the design methods that I also favoured was entirely his own. We both had a markedly analytical approach: You should consider a problem from all angles before you start designing and try out several variations, that sort of thing. Most designers start sketching when they have barely heard half a word. I believe that the description in *Mode en module*, the book that was written about me, of Ben as a follower, the eternal follower-up, is mistaken. He is a marvellous designer who has his own identity. His work for Total Design was invaluable, even if only because he guaranteed its continuity and financial security. But his importance is much greater than that.

Since you ask, I do think that Ben himself significantly contributed of his image as the 'eternal follower-up'. For a publication by Tecno Forum about teachers and pupils he wrote an article about me, 'The maestro', in which he names me as his 'great example'. It is a panegyric which made me quite uncomfortable, even though I was flattered. Of course I have my heroes, too, but in my article I chose people who established their name several decades before me. It is a delicate affair if you choose someone from your immediate environment, someone with whom you have collaborated for so many years. I didn't know very well how to react. And I didn't understand it either. Ben himself has so many qualities that he has no need to be so self-effacing. He is big enough as he is.

The only negative thing I have to say about Ben is that he could be such a damned macho. His temper could flare up dangerously. If he was under the impression that you were cutting corners, you had better stay out of his way. With Anthon Beeke who, like Jurriaan Schrofer and Paul Mijksenaar, was invited to join the studio in an attempt to break free of Total Design's 'severity', he went through a phase that was characterized by a certain degree of stand-offishness. Anthon worked at night, had the nerve to produce work that was highly deviant, and was utterly incapable of cooperating with colleagues. On the other hand he did have a very individual sense of duty and loyalty, while his negative traits were compensated by the positive aspects that had been our reasons for inviting him to join us. However, Ben was unable to surmount his objections to these negative traits. He was never very good at putting things in perspective. In that sense he was a difficult man. I also think that as a result of his sensitivity he experienced his departure from Total Design very differently than the other persons involved. That's why he looks back in anger, unfortunately.

DvG

Paul Hefting

Ahrend's man of ideas

One of Ben Bos's most important clients was Ahrend NV. He maintained relations with this company for 46 years, which may be considered exceptional. This is illustrative of the trust that existed on both sides. After all, Bos contributed significantly to the company's 'look' and familiarity. He started working for this family business in 1953.
Ahrend had quickly recovered after the war, because there was a great demand for the company's wares and services among its customers. In the years following 1947 branch offices were opened in Eindhoven, Maastricht, Groningen, Hengelo, Rotterdam, Middelburg and even in Antwerp, while the distribution of Ahrend products was eventually extended to other European countries. In 1953 Ben Bos was appointed as advertising assistant. His job description was later expanded to include copywriter and business journalist and in the period from 1960 to 1963 he worked as designer and art director. In later years he worked for Ahrend with variable degrees of intensity, both at Total Design, at 2D3D and at his own studio FORMatie 2.

Hundreds of publicity expressions **In his book** 60+40 is waarschijnlijk honderd: Ahrend – passers, pennen, potloden en projecten **Dirk de Wit devotes a paragraph to 'Produkt, industriële en grafische vormgeving' (product, industrial and graphic design). Much of the information below is derived from this source.**
The century of company history is in effect the history of – especially – Jacobus Ahrend, who, with considerable inventiveness and entrepreneurship would expand the painting and drawing supplies agency of 1896 into one of the biggest office interior companies under the name NV Wed. J. Ahrend & Zoon. In its first decades the shop's supplies not only included compasses and drawing supplies, chairs, drawing boards and cupboards, but also sextants, nautical and geodetic measuring instruments, heliotype machines, radios, cameras, typewriters, paramedical equipment as well as books on architecture and technology. (Ahrend had an in-house printing press, publishing company and bookshop.)
To promote the sales of its extensive product range Ahrend published hundreds of illustrated folders, price-lists, brochures and catalogues with florid texts and a highly variable design. They looked like advertising brochures from the nineteenth century, such as the publications of big American mail order companies like Sears, Roebuck & Co., but over the years the covers also conformed to the fashion of the day: Jugendstil, Berlage style, Amsterdam School, Art Deco and New Realism. Still, these publications were not designed by well-known designers of the period, but probably by the printing firms themselves. Albert Hahn is the only name we encounter. Another form of advertising was printing the company name on buildings and the company fleet. However, there was no real consistency in these expressions, apart from the intention to improve the company's familiarity in various ways.

Interior office design **In the thirties Ahrend started to specialize increasingly in office furniture. It established relations with the Oda companies in St.-Oedenrode that manufactured steel furniture and with De Cirkel in Amsterdam. This company also produced steel tube chairs, which were designed**

by its owner Jan Schröfer in the Bauhaus style (Marcel Breuer, Mies van der Rohe, Mart Stam) or the Gispen furniture that was becoming more popular with the business world in the thirties. After many conflicts and a tug-of-war for power Ahrend, Oda and De Cirkel merged into the Ahrend holding in 1967. Jan Schröfer was a great advocate of steel furniture that was technically and aesthetically sound, and of the sound industrial product in general. He was also one of the persons who inspired the foundation of the Instituut voor Industriële Vormgeving in 1949.
During the reconstruction period there existed considerable competition between furniture manufacturers. Customers were offered considerable discounts for, as Schröfer called it, incompetence and an utter lack of aesthetic sensibility. At De Cirkel he created a climate where much attention was devoted to design. Until 1966 Friso Kramer, Wim Rietveld, O. Kolthof en Schröfer himself were responsible for this. Friso Kramer contributed significantly to the revival of interest in industrial design with his Revolt, the living room and office chair from 1952/3, which became so well-known in part because it was constructed out of bent sheeted steel instead of bent tubes. Ahrend initially regarded this piece of furniture with scepticism, and in fact it did initially have a lot of growing pains. However, a breakthrough was gradually achieved and the chair became the first in a long series of new designs for chairs, drawing boards and tables.

Ahrend is given a 'look' The reputation that Ahrend had acquired with its 'aesthetic' furniture, was reflected in the graphic design of its catalogues, folders, staff magazine, advertisements and price-lists. From the very start these PR media were of crucial importance to Ahrend, as the company did not sell its products through retail, but supplied directly to customers.
For a long time founder Jacobus Ahrend personally produced the advertising material and as a result of his experience in a publishing firm he also had any affinity with design. Still, Ahrend's publications were not motivated by any 'aesthetic' ideal: they merely served to improve sales.
From the fifties on, Anton Bogers was responsibile for publicity. He was assisted by designer Cor Walstra and Ben Bos, but designers from outside also contributed. These included Charles Jongejans, Jan Bons, Gerard Wernars and the photographers Jan Versnel, Peter Marcuse en Arjé Plas. Even the poet Jan Elburg wrote some texts for Ahrend. An in-house design studio for publicity printing was set up and its design increasingly came to determine the Ahrend look – its corporate identity, in fact. The advertising campaigns started receiving awards. From 1958 on Ahrend published a periodical sales magazine with special issues that were called Facetten. Also much attention was devoted to the design and construction of showrooms.
Whatever ups and downs Ahrend was going through, the company's familiar graphic image persisted. In 1963 Ben Bos joined Total Design and realized his projects for Ahrend in that agency. One of these was the publicity for the complex office furniture system Mehes, that is now famous and was even sold to the Shanghai Banking Corporation in Hong Kong. The English architect Forster, who designed this building, did not only choose this furniture, but also Total Design's routing system.
The Mehes system had developed out of the Facet system and was intended i.a. for the open-plan offices, which were then booming. It continued to be added to over the years and eventually became Ahrend's best-selling system product.
The design climate at Total Design – the 'style' of lucidity and transparency – reflected the mentality that prevailed at the time, certainly in the business world. However, it is still an essential part of Ahrend design, produced under

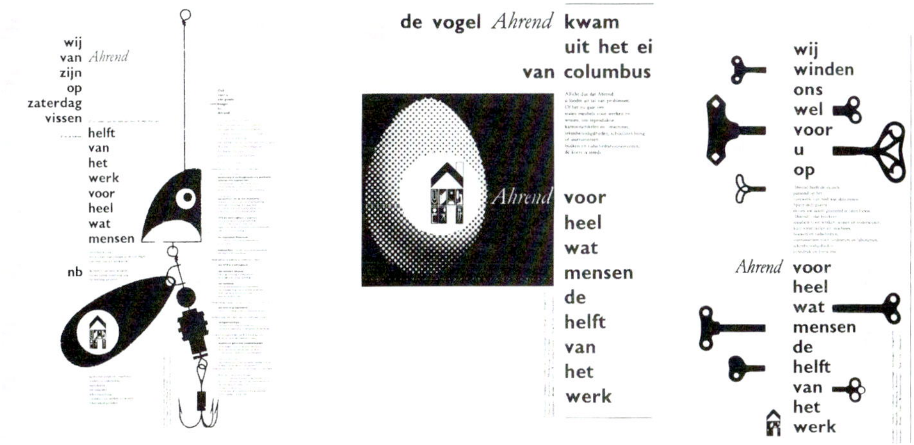

1961
Newspaper advertisements
Concept and texts by Ben Bos
Design by Gerard Wernars

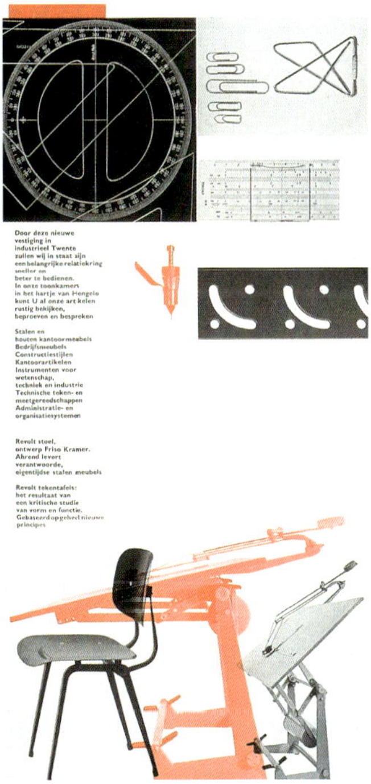

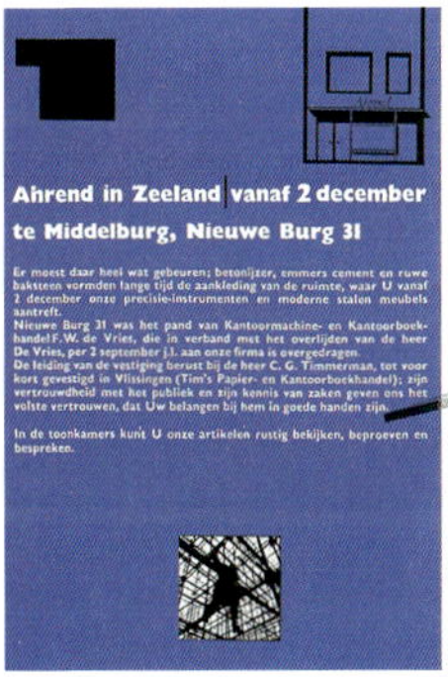

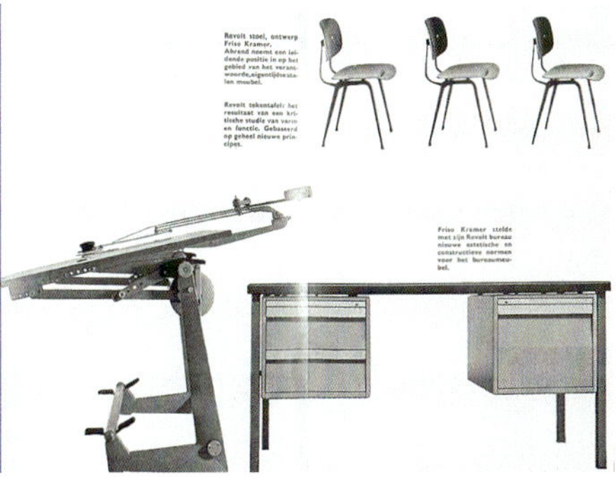

1960
Brochures new Ahrend branches

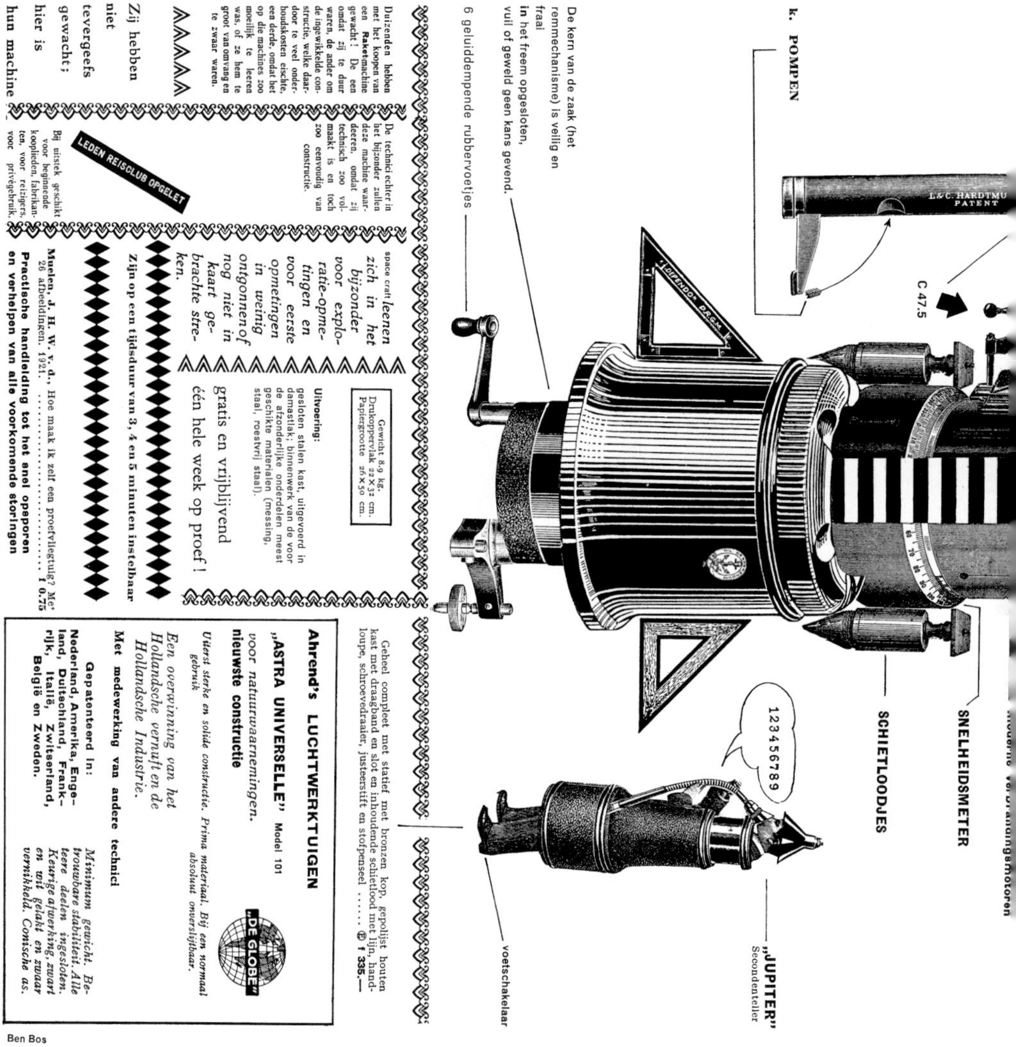

Ben Bos

1962
Illustration for ladies' issue of 'de gazet'

Levering kan niet door tusschenkomst van andere handelaren geschieden.

LUCHTSCHEEPVAART
afd. ruimtevaart
Ahrend-Fijnmechaniek nv

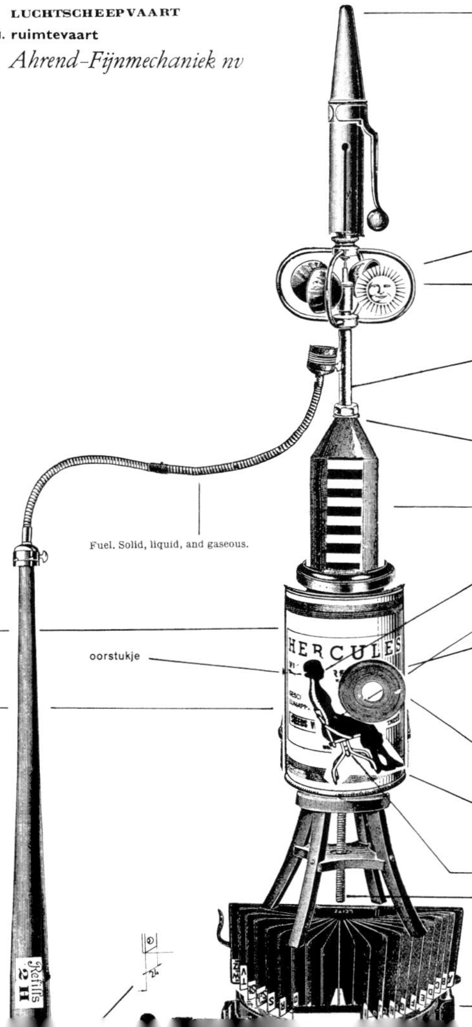

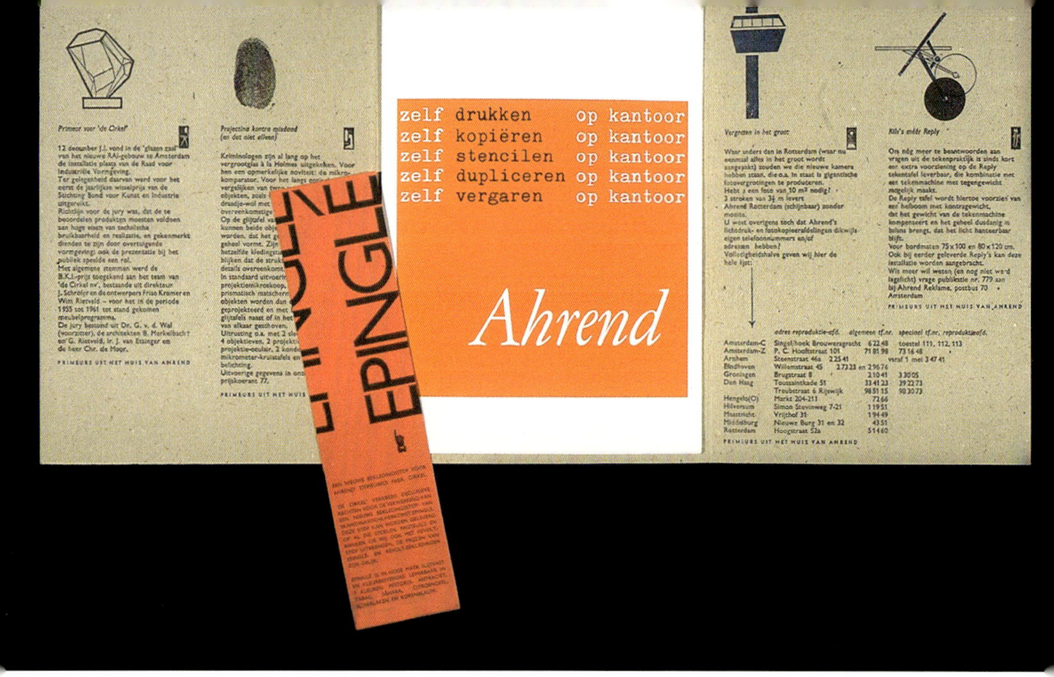

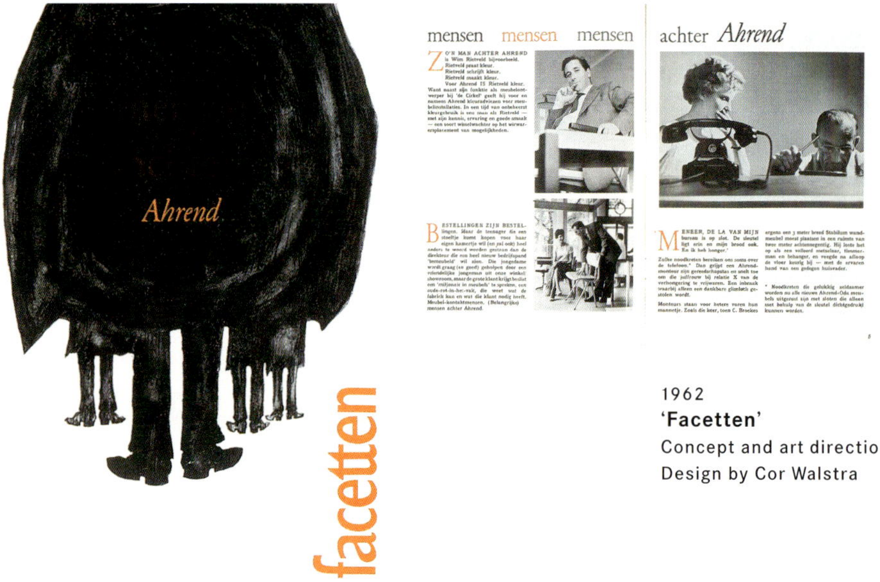

1962
'Facetten'
Concept and art direction Ben Bos
Design by Cor Walstra

direct responsibility of the manager who guards this uniformity. It is vulnerable, since the management must also have affinity with design and be aware of its importance to the company. The present manager J.C. Koenders's previous work experience with the graphic industry make him a committed 'supervisor'. He is assisted by Fred Gerrets, who has headed the Publicity department since the mid-seventies.

Both word and image **Ben Bos has significantly contributed to Ahrend's image. In his early days at this company he familiarized himself with, as he calls it, the 'essentials' of each product. This enabled him to word the product descriptions more precisely, while he also helped make the company's graphic 'product' more lucid and simpler. In his first years he worked in a small department that consisted of a head, a designer, a secretary and an assistant.**

And what did I do? Reduce by half a big pile of catalogues that had been filled over the years with texts that were largely written by Mr Ahrend himself, and upgrading the quality of the contents in the process. It was an excellent exercise: saying the essential with fewer and fewer words, mainly by eliminating unnecessary fustian.

In the long run he proved to be the man of ideas. He edited de gazet **staff magazine, developed topics for** Facetten **sales magazine, was editor, illustrations editor, wrote texts for the advertising campaigns, supervised the photography and got good designers and photographers interested in contributing to Ahrend's public image. How does Bos look back on this period and how does he view his own development at the time?**

Jan Elburg came up with things that were wholly different, brand new, more poetic. That taught me to take greater liberties with language. I became more daring and more skilful. Walstra designed my texts and suddenly I started finding that more interesting than my own job. That led to my attending evening classes in lay-out at the graphic school for two years, shortly after I began working for Ahrend. I subsequently moved on to the evening study programme at the IvKNO, which now is the Gerrit Rietveld Academie.

In the mean time I had been commissioned to reanimate the staff magazine. That was a good platform me. I was allowed to write and draw for it and to design it. Walstra did not allow me full play in the regular Ahrend publications, but the staff magazine was all mine. Of course I was up to the challenge, with all the experience I had gained. At the Rietveld Academie Schelvis, Jan Broer and Piet Klaasse helped me to improve my drawing. And I was a great admirer of Wim Crouwel, in whose footsteps I wanted to follow. He propagated a lucidity and transparency that fascinated me and which I also wanted to introduce in my own work.

In my later years at Ahrend as art director and copywriter I was mainly the man of ideas. I contributed campaign texts such as: 'The Ahrend bird came out of Columbus's egg' and Gerard Wernars would make something wonderful out of that. With a one-haired brush Gerard would draw the shades of the egg in screen dots. That kind of thing was still possible then. Really crazy. We received several awards from the Genootschap voor Reclame for the advertisements and for **Facetten** magazine. During the greatest period of **Facetten**, which continued appearing for some time after I left – however, without its former playfulness – we thought up topics, such as Colour and Peek-a-Boo, and presented them in a highly original fashion.

Later, during my period at 2D3D design studio, but especially after that, in our own little company FORMatie2, I did a lot of work for Ahrend, including package design. In 1996, for Ahrend's centenary, I initiated the exhibition **De vorm van Ahrend** that took place in De Beyerd in Breda. I subsequently succeeded in creating a company museum at Ahrend's head office that provided a survey of Ahrend furniture and featured some of the best publicity material. So the history of the company is at least partly preserved. I selected the exhibition items, designed the structural alterations and described and designed the whole thing.

There have been two periods during which Ben Bos intensively occupied himself with Ahrend: from 1953 until his move to Total Design and the period after 1991. During his long stay at TD Bos worked for Ahrend only intermittently. When he left TD in 1991, his relations with Ahrend intensified and in the last years of the century Ben Bos has continued to work for Ahrend, mainly as a consultant and to a lesser extent as a designer. Ahrend works with several free-lance designers, but nevertheless manages to maintain a certain consistency in its design policy, without producing a rigid corporate design.

1972
Printed matter for the introduction of Ahrend's office furniture system Mehes
Photography by Arjé Plas

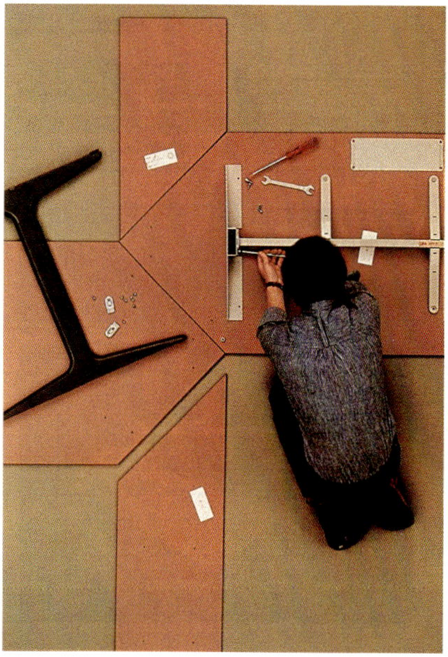

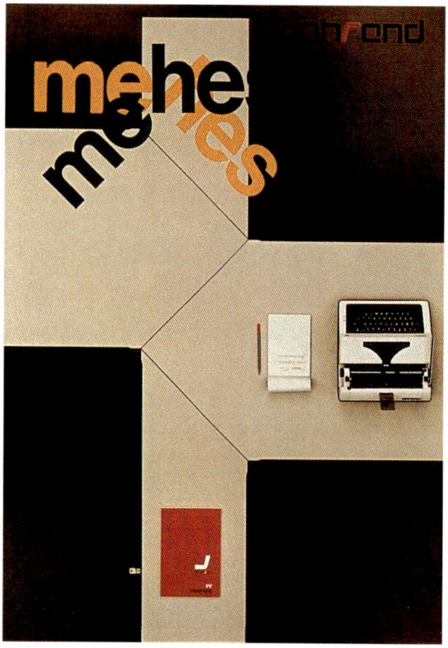

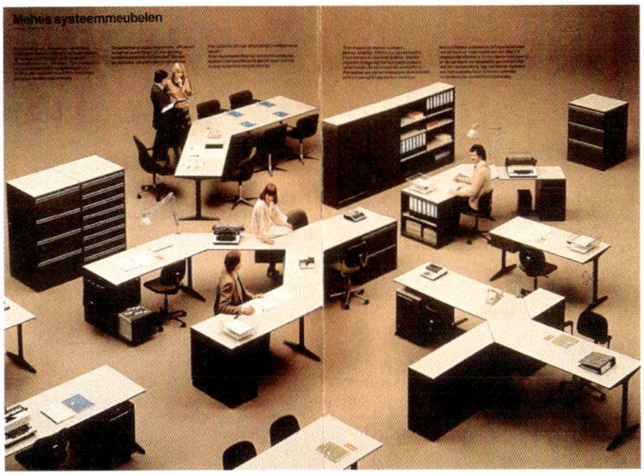

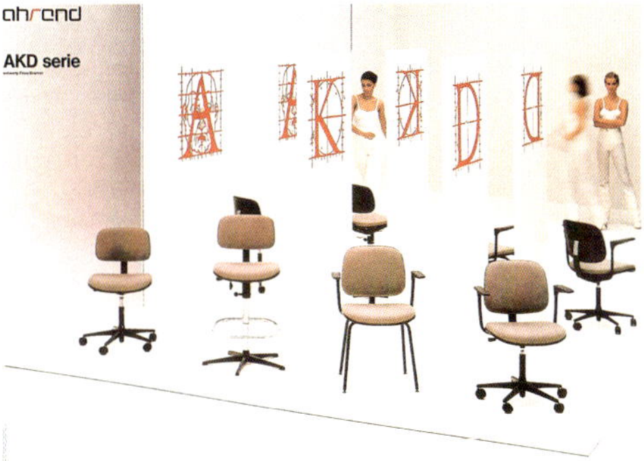

1972
Brochure Mehes furniture system
Photography by Arjé Plas

1972
Folder introducing AKD office chairs
Photography by Arjé Plas

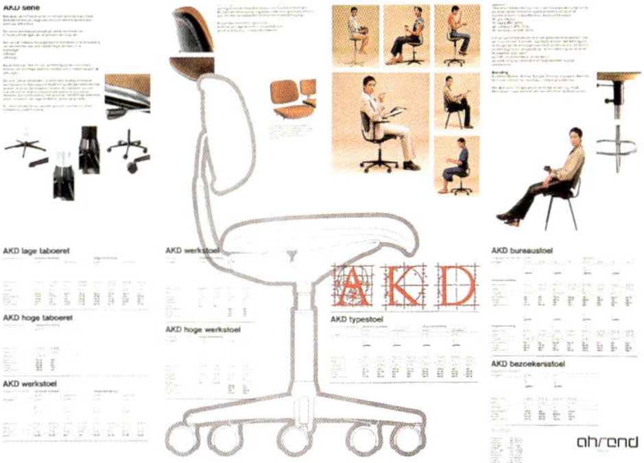

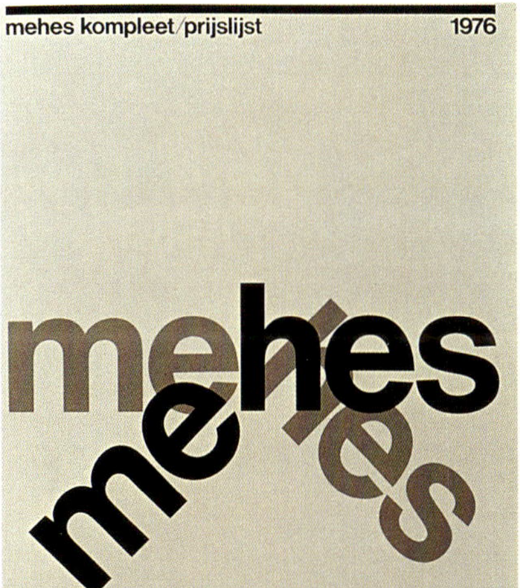

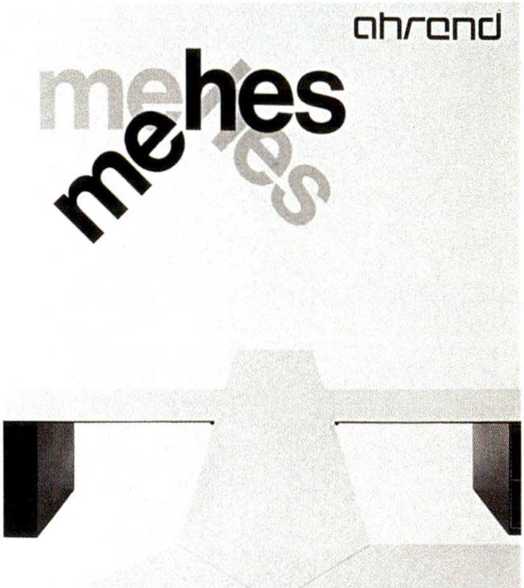

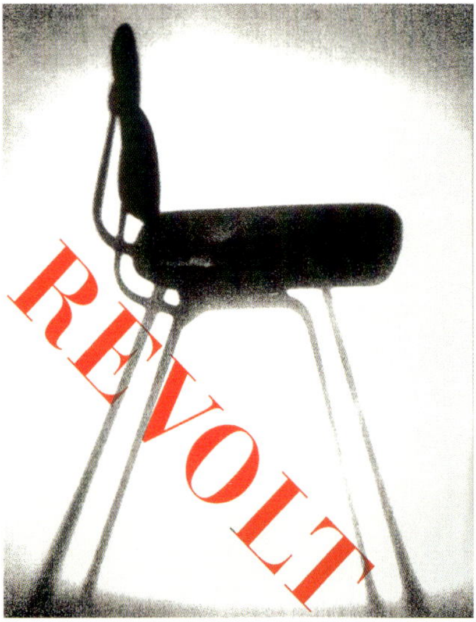

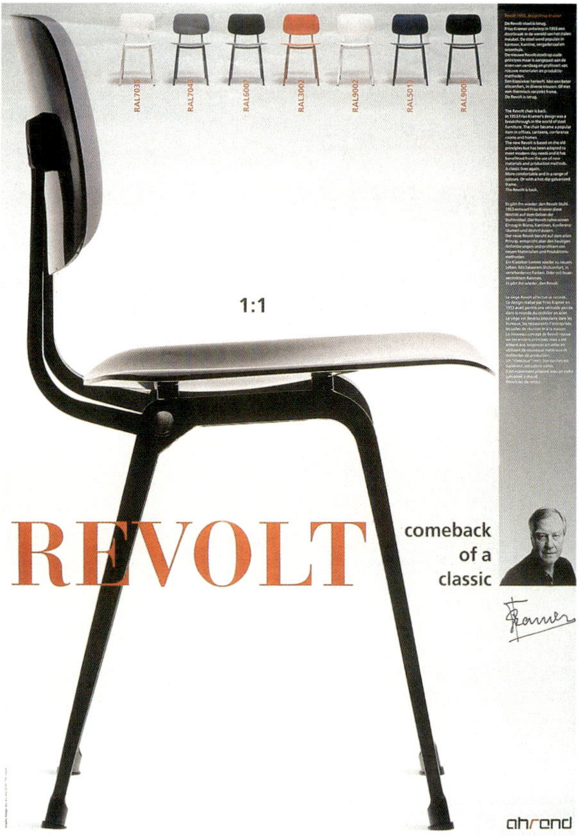

1993
Invitation to the introduction of the remake of the Revolt chair
Photography by Bert Berghuis

1993
Poster introduction of the remake of the Revolt chair
Photography by Bert Berghuis

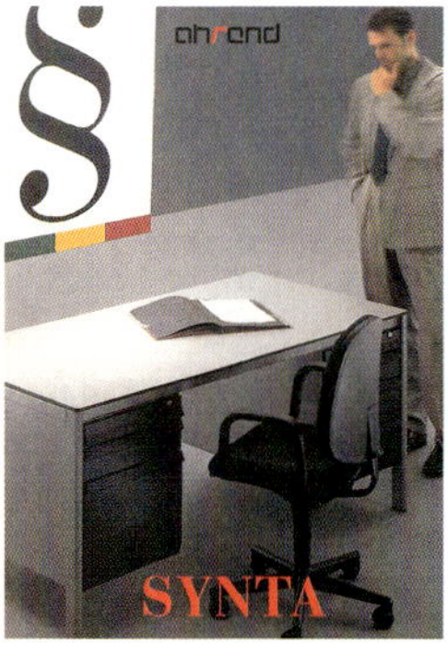

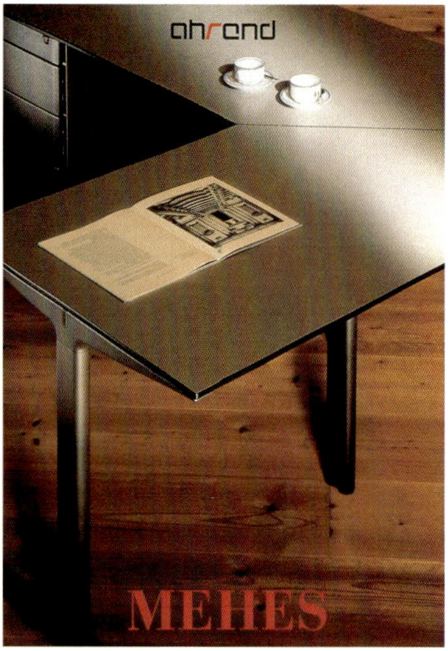

1993
Brochure on Synta office furniture
Photography by Bert Berghuis

1993/94
Brochures on Mehes and Athos furniture systems
Photography by Bert Berghuis

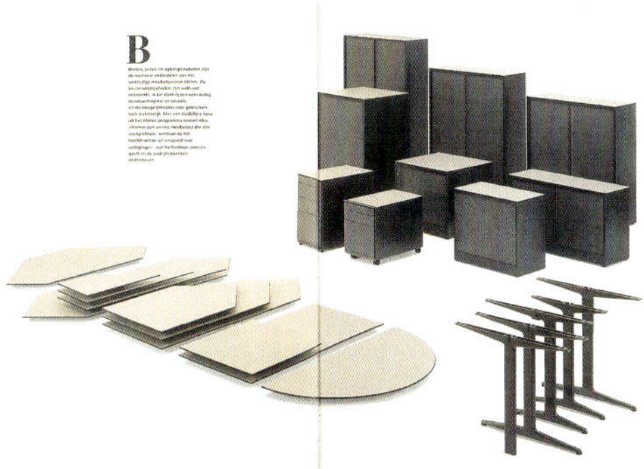

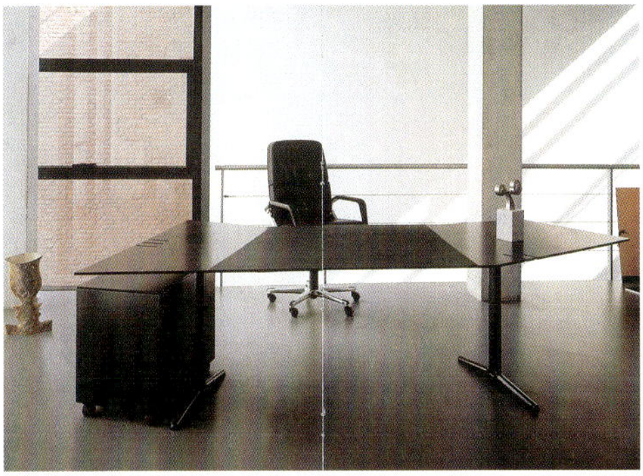

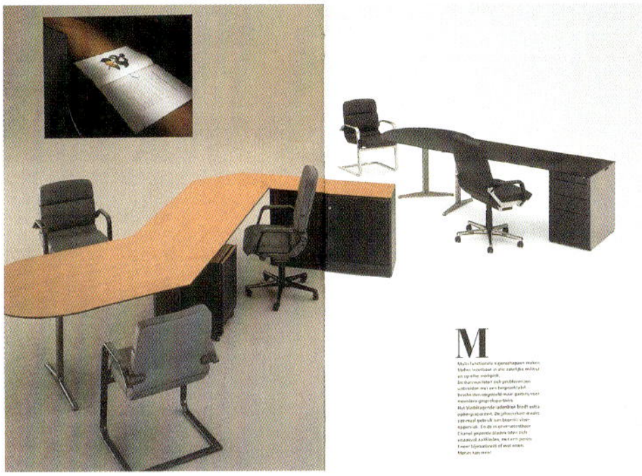

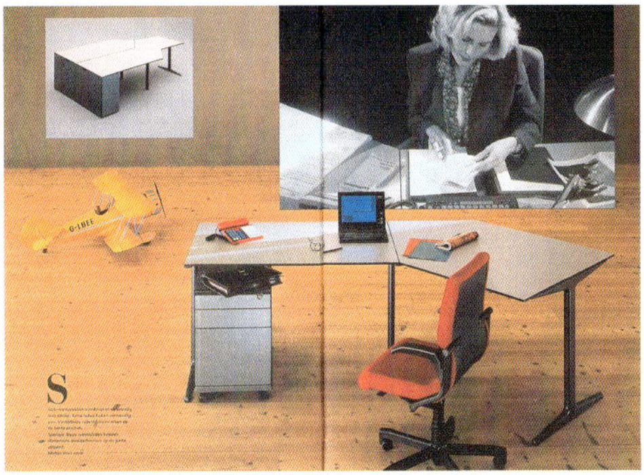

1993/94
Brochures meubelsystemen
Mehes en Athos
Fotografie Bert Berghuis

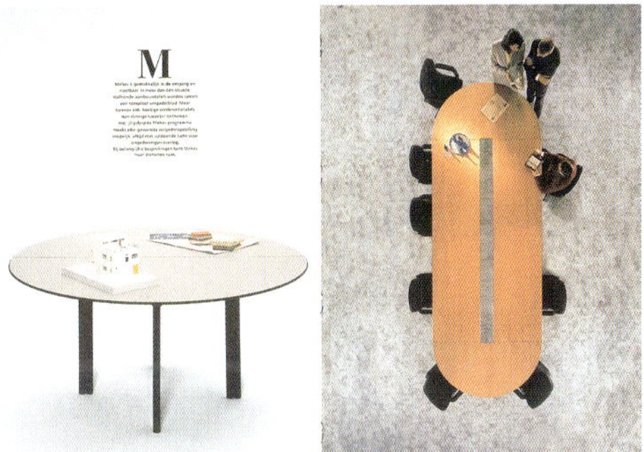

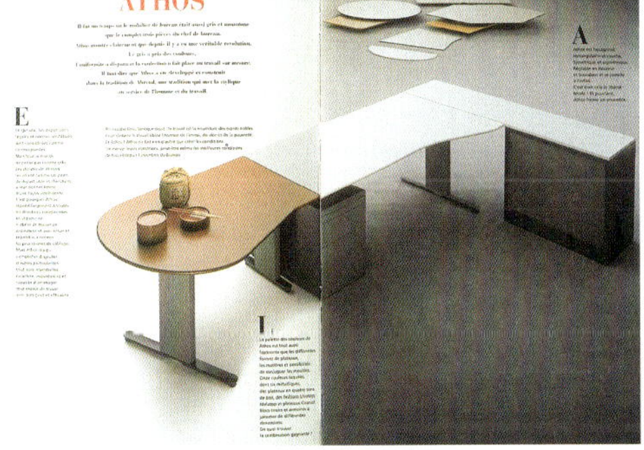

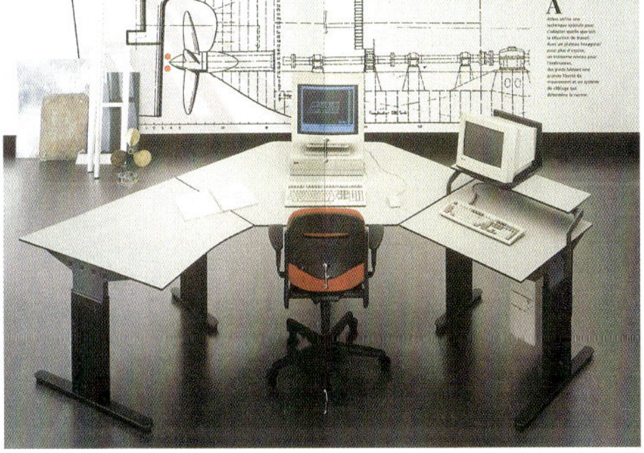

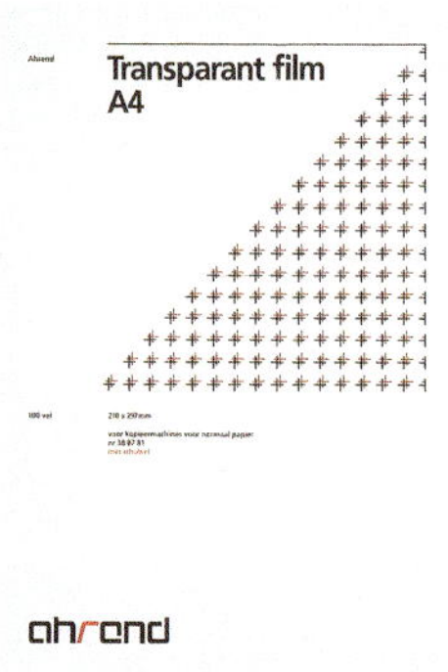

1994
Packaging/printing office supplies

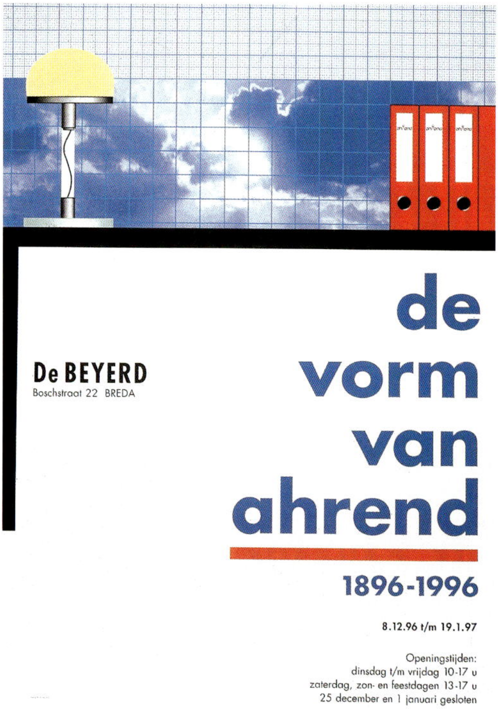

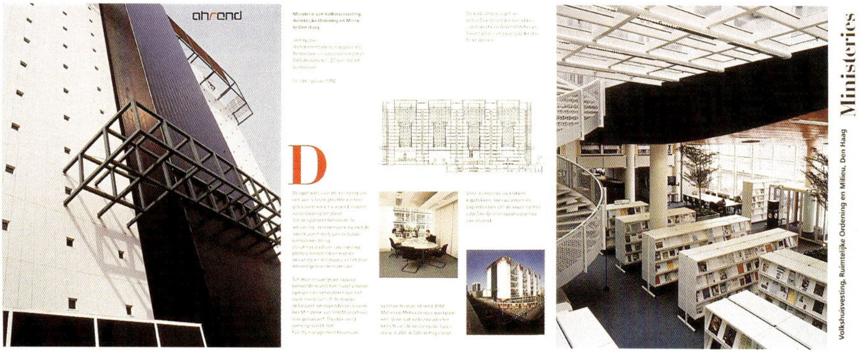

1996
Poster for exhibition celebrating Ahrend's centenary
De Beyerd, Breda

1995
Project folders

1996
Logo Koninlijke Ahrend
Centenarian Ahrend NV receives the royal imprint

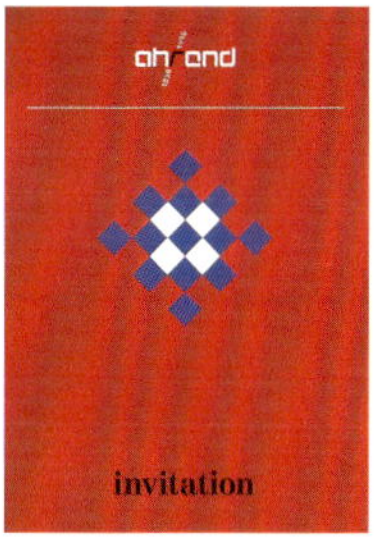

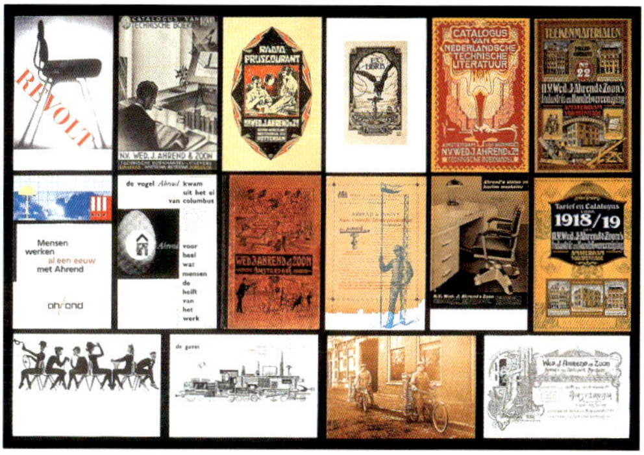

1996
Invitation to jubilee dinner

Series of postcards celebrating the centenary

1997
Design, brochure and logo Ahrend Museum, Amsterdam

1996
Exhibition 'De Vorm van Ahrend'
De Beyerd, Breda
Concept Ben Bos
Design by Meyer/Van Gerwen

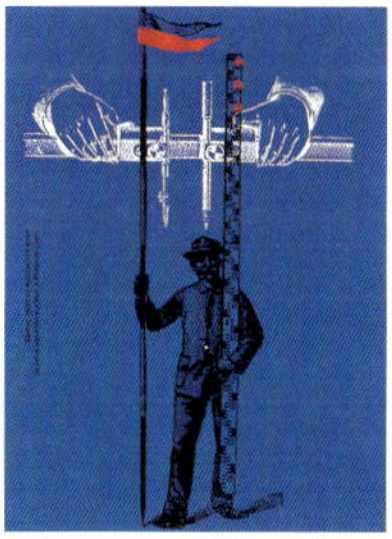

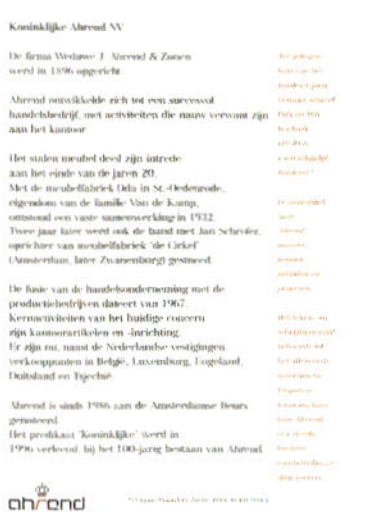

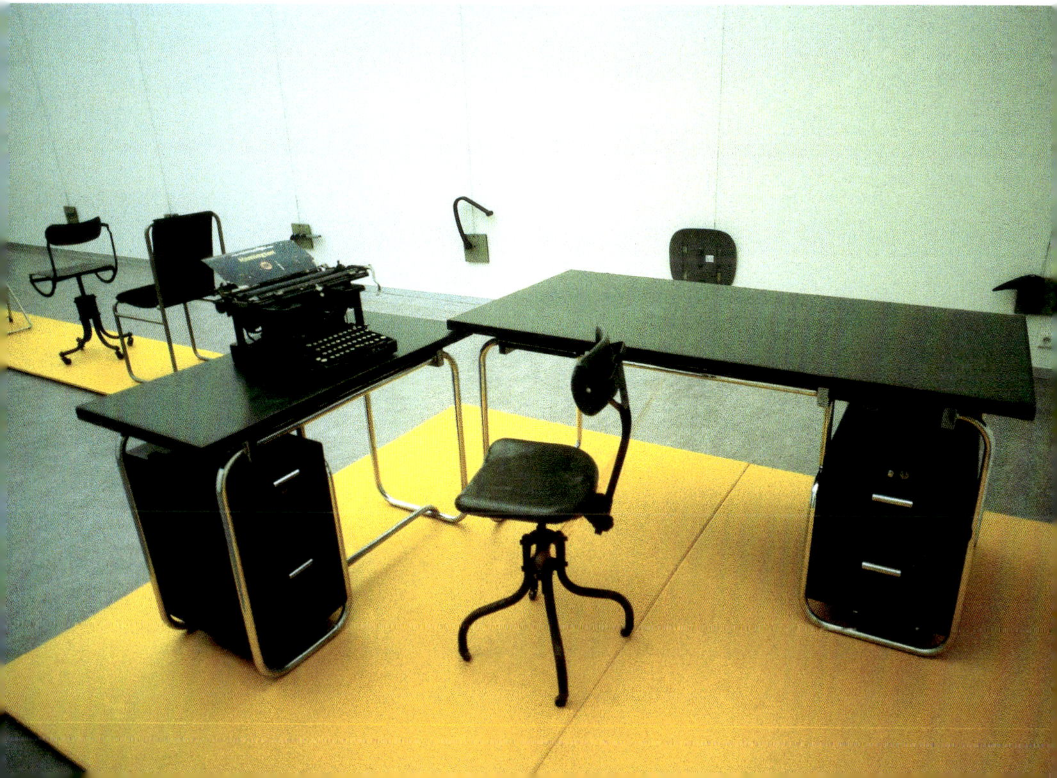

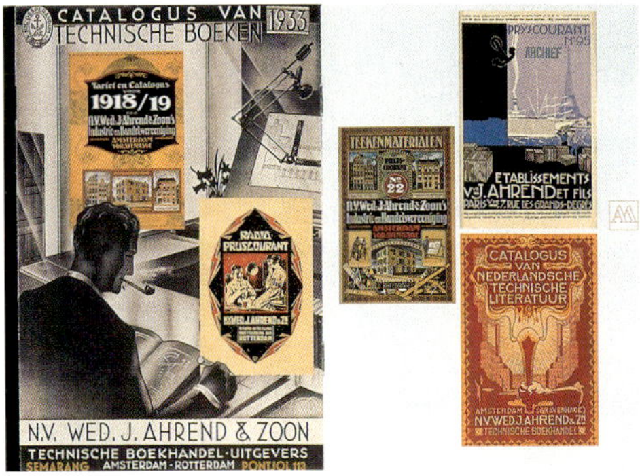

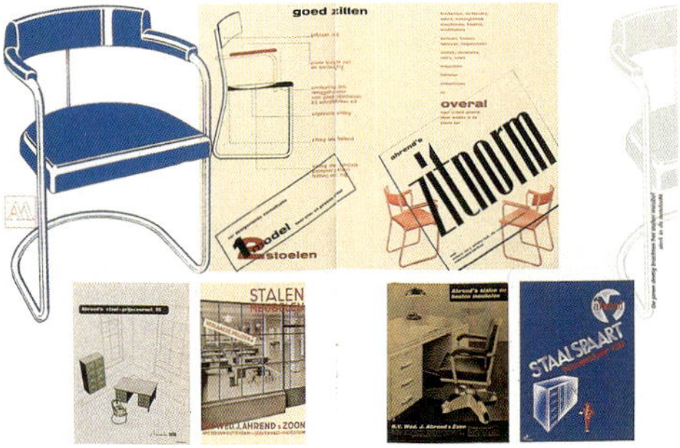

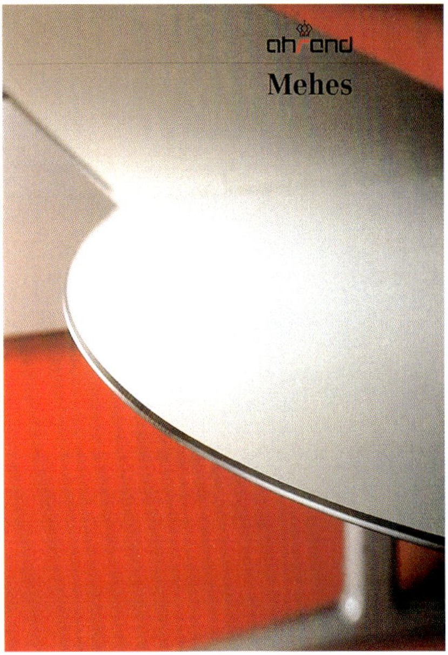

1997
Brochure Ahrend Museum

1998
Brochure Mehes system
Photography by Yves Paternoster

1998
Ahrend playing cards

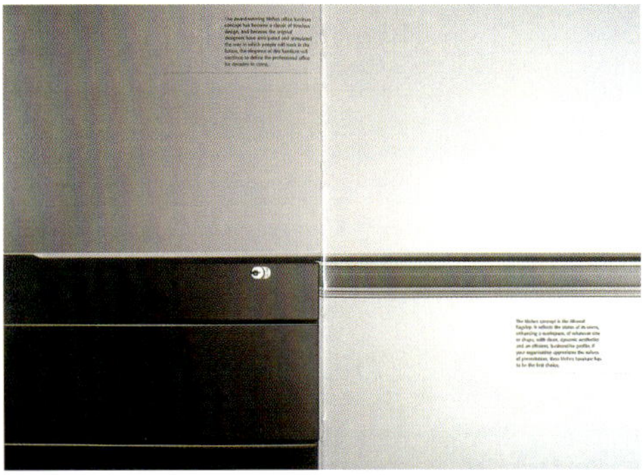

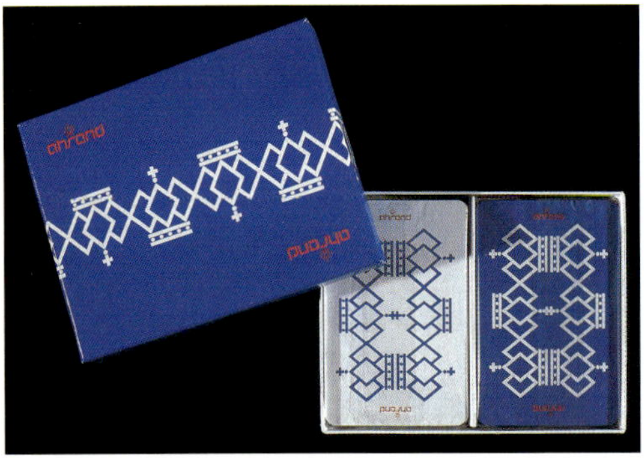

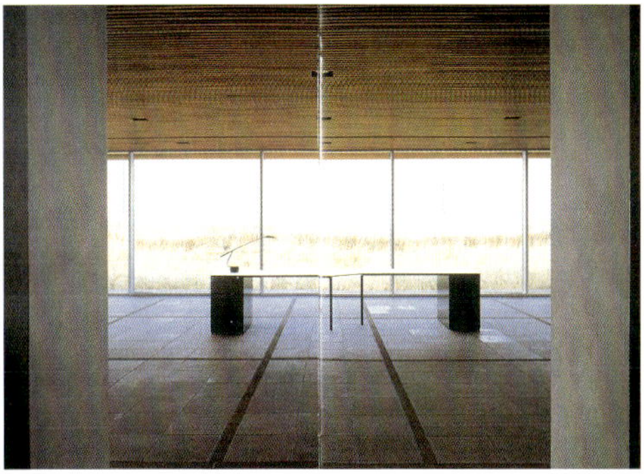

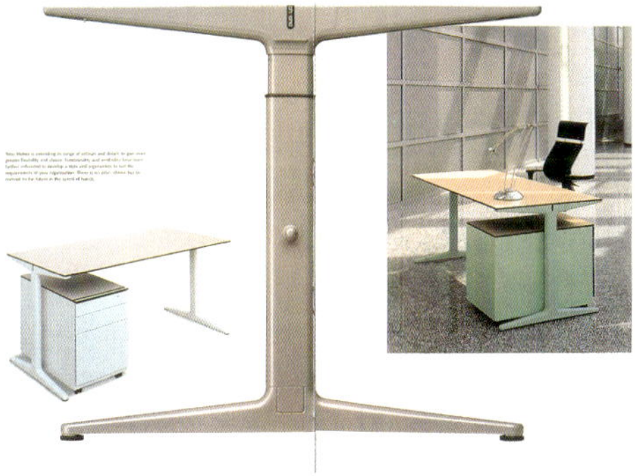

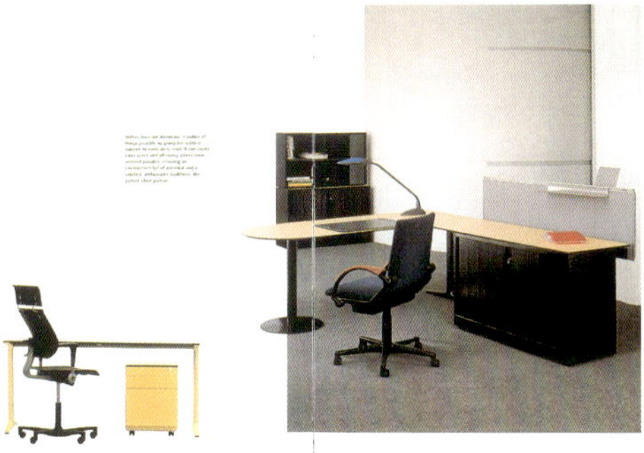

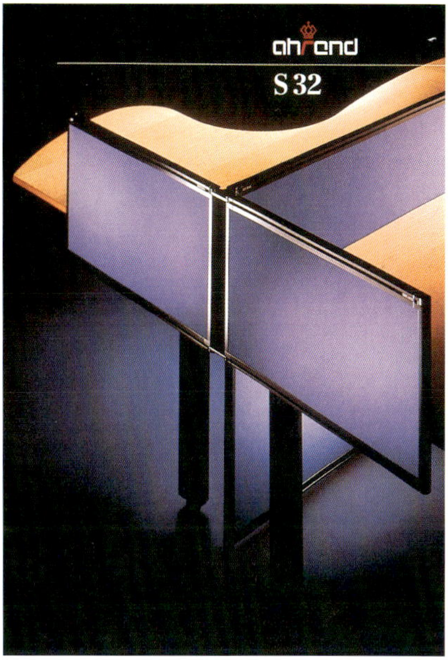

1998
Brochure cover
S70 screens
Photography by Yves Paternoster

1995
Logo and corporate design
Gwinner & Ulrich, Munich
A company taken over by Ahrend

GWINNER & ULRICH

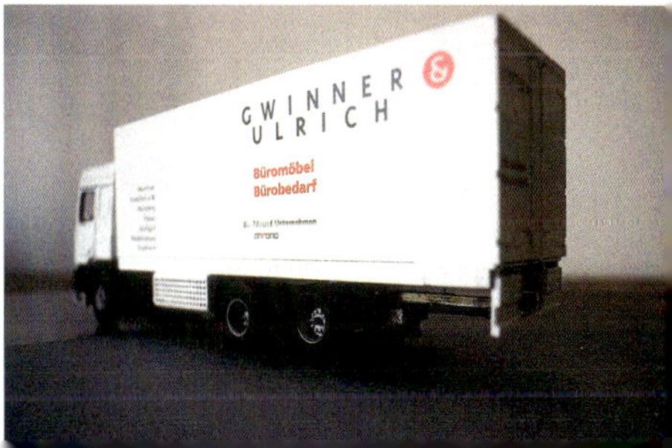

1998
Invitation to presentation
tables designed by architect
Wim Quist

1999
Invitation to exhibition
Manchester

1996
Ahrend trade fair stand
London

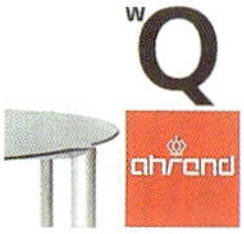

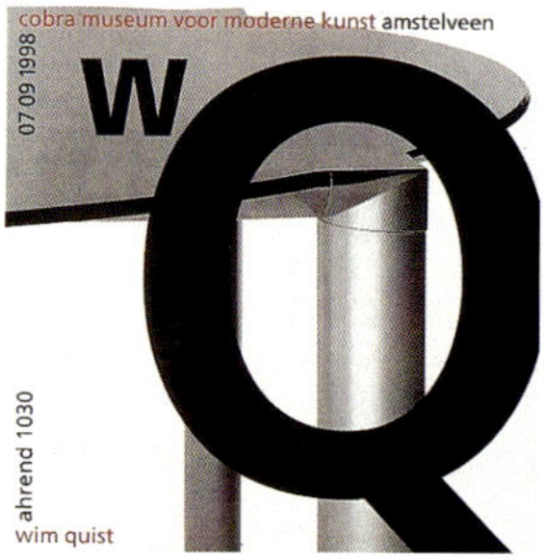

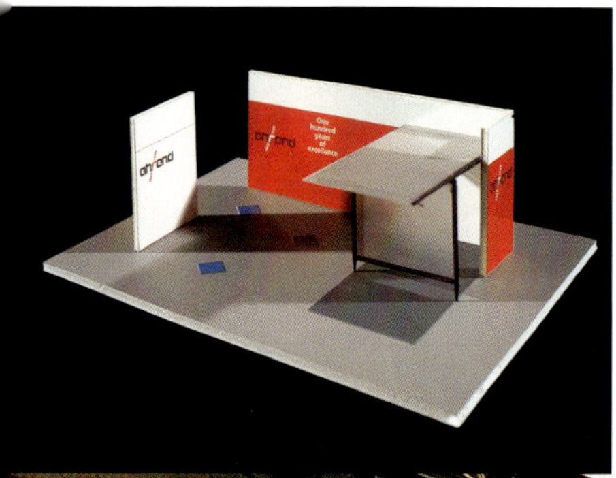

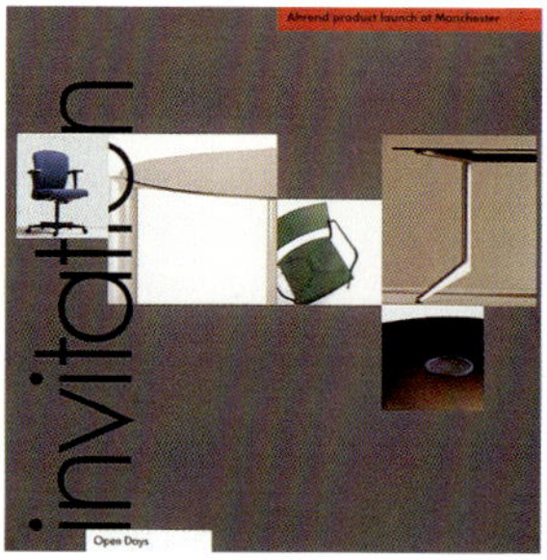

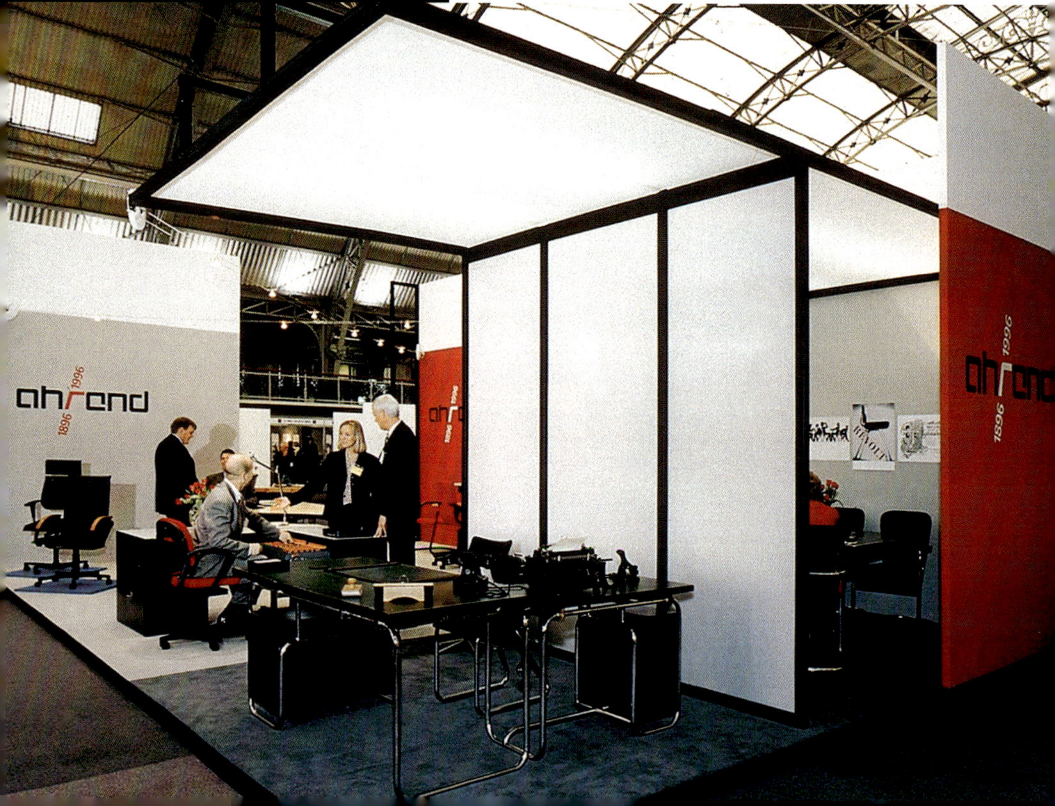

Strict and emotional

Daphne Duijvelshoff joined Ben Bos's team (at Total Design) in 1968. Prior to this she had worked for one year at the smaller DDM studio. Then she joined the design studio that was the ideal of many designers. However, it proved to be a school of hard knocks. Duijvelshoff currently works as a free-lance designer.

Ben was very strict and always looked over your shoulder. He gave instructions, but he could also hurry you quite badly. Nevertheless you could learn a lot from him and his criticisms. There was always too much work for the team of four, which was already quite big.

Ben was temperamental, which could express itself in angry outbursts, but also in an extravert enthusiasm when something had gone unusually well. He invested a lot in his staff members. Ben was a hard worker who made long hours. He was never ill. He highly taxed himself, but then he was under a lot of pressure due to the many projects that had to be finished. After all, Ben did ensure that TD remained in business.

After some time our team relocated to the building next door to Herengracht 567. That was where the De Gruyter room was situated, where Ben worked with people like Wim van der Weerd on commissions for that chain of supermarkets. And then there was De Bijenkorf, for which Ben also turned out a lot of work. We also produced a large number of staff magazines, which was a speciality of Ben's. He has also published on the subject. He had a background in journalism and wrote the best articles.

His designs were very lucid. He was clearly inspired by Pentagram and Alan Fletcher. He was much less doctrinal than Wim Crouwel and used ornamentation, for instance. This rendered his work more humane, so to speak. When he worked, he would collect all sorts of stuff and create a big mess around him, but out of this chaos he would conjure up a beautiful poster in no time. His work is actually rather charming, like his work for De Bijenkorf. He also had a great feeling for colour. Combining the doctrinal with the colourful and the decorative came naturally to him. Ben frequently cooperated with photographers – Cas Oorthuys, Aart Klein, Jan Versnel – and also took a lot photographs himself. Those pictures were always circulating around the studio.

After four years I joined Wim Crouwel's team, where I enjoyed much greater freedom than during my work with Ben.

PH

Randstad

1968
Staff recruitment stand
Home economy trade fair
RAI, Amsterdam

1967/68
Series of folders
Photography by Ben Bos

1968
Branch office Düsseldorf

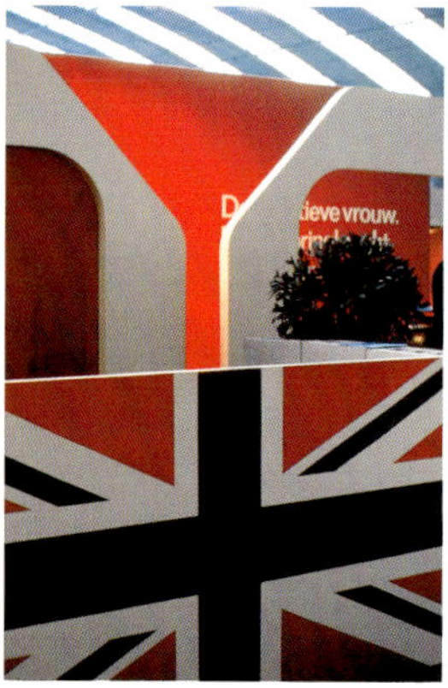

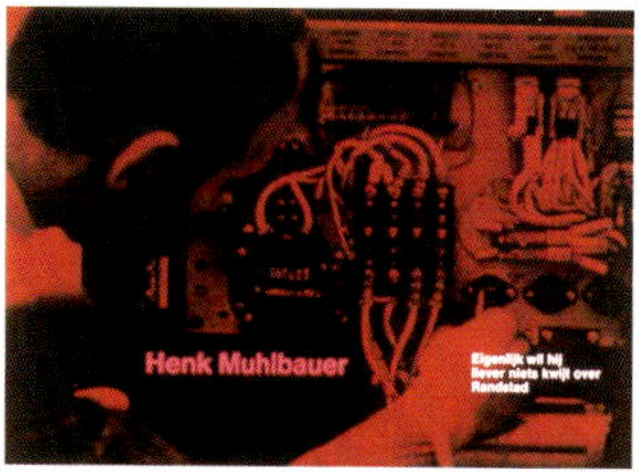

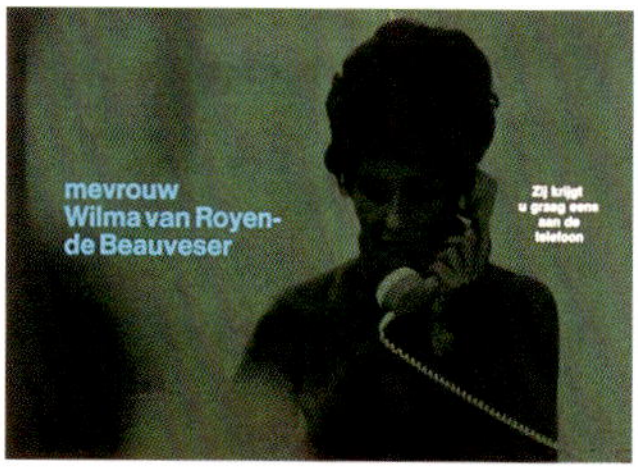

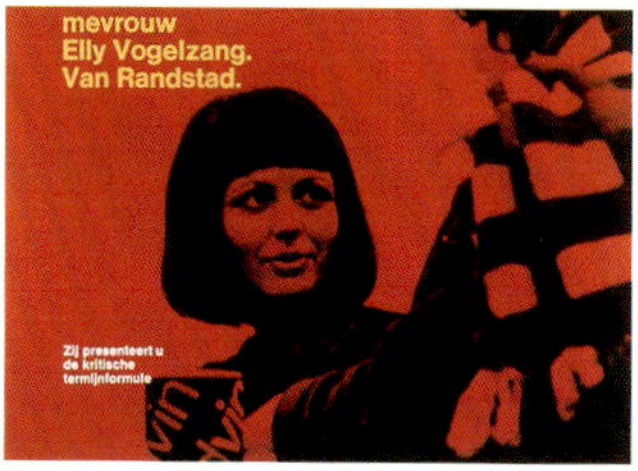

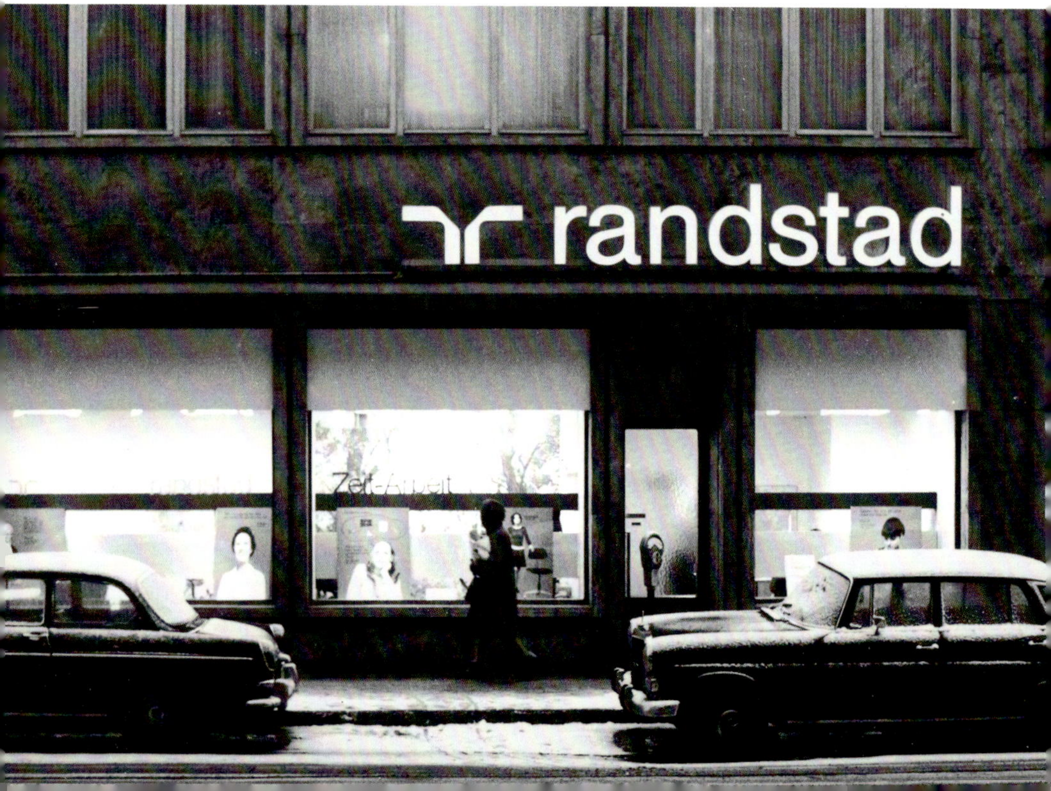

Dirk van Ginkel

Aiming for perfection: Randstad's corporate design in its time

In 1996 the phenomenon of design management seemed about to enter its Golden Age. Westminster University in London and the Ichthus Hogeschool in Rotterdam introduced part-time study programmes catering to the growing demand for talent in this field. The first internationally oriented European Designer fair was held in Maastricht, while the prestigious Design Management Institute from Boston decided to institute a annual conference in Amsterdam. The Dutch publishing house BIS Publishers launched Design in Business **magazine, which was wholly devoted to the subject.**
The sky seemed to be the limit. At last, the faith of the enlightened avant-garde in the value of design for increasing a company's familiarity seemed to be broadly supported. 1996 was the year in which a new job was officially created: design manager. KLM, the Dutch Post Office, Randstad and the Dutch National Railways, the familiar design-driven enterprises that had been setting a good example since the early sixties, would at last be imitated on a grand scale.
In this atmosphere of professional euphoria Ed Bolk, the Strategy Development and Public Relations manager of the Randstad holding, seemed about to vent strong criticisms when, on the invitation of the aforementioned Ichthus Hogeschool, he delivered a lecture under the title 'Design is too important for service organizations to delegate it to a design manager'. Was the importance of design management, which was at last being recognized, coming under attack after all? This fear quickly proved unfounded. Bolk started by establishing that to his mind design was so important that it should be a concern of the enterprise's upper management. Of course design managers were welcome, but design management should primarily remain a management issue. As Bolk stated:
Corporate design is a method for influencing corporate staff. It is a tangible expression of the corporate culture. It renders the invisible service visible, so to speak. It also confirms the ideas (perception) of a company and expresses its identity. Such an essential aspect of a company is too important to farm it out to a design manager. In an organisation such as Randstad it is the management that ultimately decides in these matters.[1]
Randstad itself is an outstanding example of this approach. Throughout its almost forty years' existence the corporate management has proved in word and deed that design can contribute in many ways to the achievement of company objectives. Ben Bos has rendered valuable services to Randstad in this field over a great number of years. Bos advocated design management not only as a designer, but also as a writer and consultant (he helped set up the part-time study programme at Ichthus Hogeschool). At Total Design he developed Randstad's well-known corporate design, supervised its restyling in the mid-eighties and continued to advise the Randstad management after leaving the studio in 1991. Until 1998 he also worked abroad for this company. How did Randstad deal with the design phenomenon over all these years and why did it make the choices it did?

[1] Report of the Symposium 'Design management In Nederland', Ichthus Hogeschool, 1996

Myth and reality **To every success story a myth attaches itself, and Randstad is no exception. Tradition has it that Randstad was a design-driven enterprise from its very inception. It is widely believed that during its long existence the company never lacked the strong corporate design for which it became famous, even outside the Netherlands. Frits Goldschmeding, founder of the present temping giant, had barely developed his temporary employment concept when he started discussions with Total Design, one of the first, and certainly one of the most influential design studios that the Netherlands has ever known. All of this is a lie. Even Randstad employees in high positions contribute to this confusion of fact and fiction. As late as 1997 one of them told** Design in Business **magazine that in 1966 it wasn't easy for Goldschmeding to be accepted as a client by Total Design client:** (...) the temping industry did not have a very good reputation in those days. Total Design had to think twice about wanting to do business with Randstad.[2] **The reality is a little more prosaic, although it doesn't make this history any less impressive.**

The Randstad holding developed out of a graduation thesis on 'temporary employment' written by Free University student Frits Goldschmeding. It was an initiative in a field that was still virgin soil in the Netherlands. Therefore it was important to create sympathy for these new staffing services. How do you do that? As Susanne Piët writes: Even in the pioneering stage Goldschmeding must have realized that a lucid visualisation would be the basis for communicating the service concept, which at that time was still quite hazy.[3] **Randstad started inserting adverts in** Het Parool **newspaper that distinguished it from its competitors, but was soon imitated. The distinctiveness of its presentation was lost in no time. About the expressions in the early days Goldschmeding said:** Of course Ben's stomach would have turned three times if he had seen what we made back then. But the weird thing is that countless people started imitating our advertising style. You saw 12 point letters all over the place. After six months I discovered that as a temping agency we were ahead of our competitors, while our design was really very amateurish. In 1963, when I graduated and felt the need for a professional approach, I went to advertising agency Nijgh and Van Ditmar. They designed folders and a letterhead with a logo composed of a curious-looking R that ended on a tittle typing arm.[4] **However, that also made Ben's stomach turn.** It was a sort of failed typewriter's key, **he says.** The people of that agency produced some very silly stuff. **Goldschmeding and his advisers must have thought the same at some stage. When Randstad financiers Paul and Dick Schwarz introduced him to Total Design, which the two brothers had co-founded, the groundwork was laid for a relationship that would last 25 years and for a corporate design that would survive even longer. So there existed a financial connection between the two companies. As Ben Bos recalls, Total Design's alleged abhorrence of Randstad is a fiction:** Any misgivings I had were caused by the fact that I didn't quite know how to deal with this company, since temporary work was still brand new in 1966. That Total Design's status could be impaired by accepting Randstad as a client simply didn't occur to us. There were some shady figures who operated in that line of business, but Randstad was far from shady.

2 **Dirk van Ginkel, 'Vormgeving is leuk, jongens! De democratisering van design management'. Interview with Diana Krabbendam in** Design in Business, **Vol. 2, no.5**
3 **Susanne Piët, 'Kennen, vertrouwen and dienen. Nieuwe huisstijl na explosieve groei bij Randstad'. In:** Randstad Data **1, special issue on corporate design, 1988**
4 **Id.**

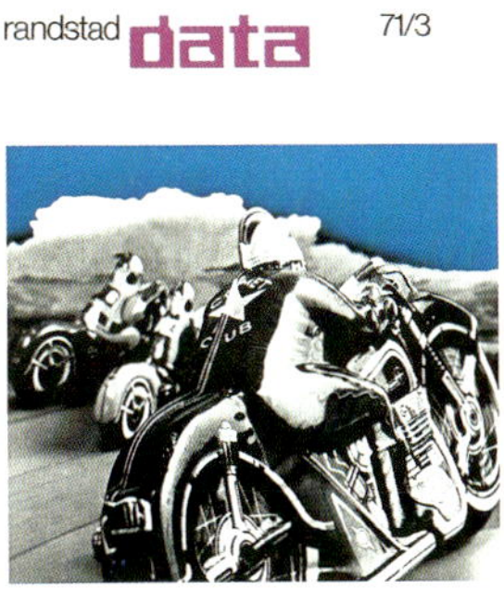

1971
'Randstad Data'
Quarterly magazine
In collaboration with
Daphne Duyvelshoff
Photography by Hans Pelgrom
and Aart Klein

1969
Inflatable pillows
Present for employees

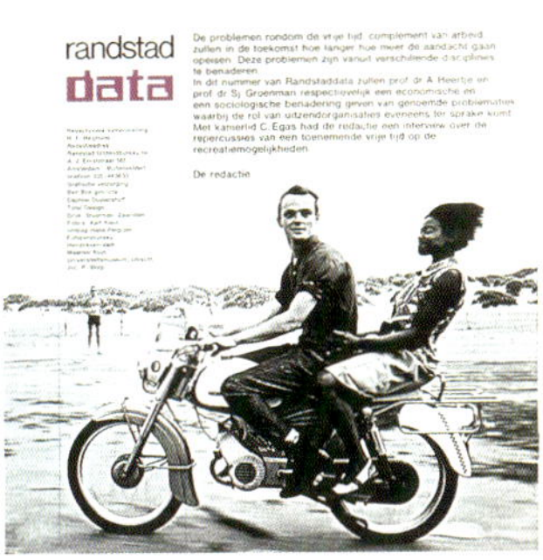

randstad data

De problemen rondom de vrije tijd, complement van arbeid zullen in de toekomst hoe langer hoe meer de aandacht gaan opeisen. Deze problemen zijn vanuit verschillende disciplines te benaderen.
In dit nummer van Randstaddata zullen prof dr A Heertje en prof dr Sj Groenman respectievelijk een economische en een sociologische benadering geven van genoemde problematiek waarbij de rol van uitzendorganisaties eveneens ter sprake komt. Met kamerlid C. Egas had de redactie een interview over de repercussies van een toenemende vrije tijd op de recreatiemogelijkheden.

De redactie

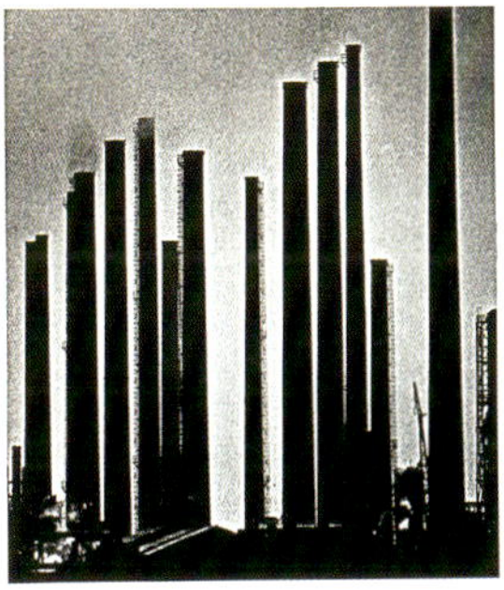

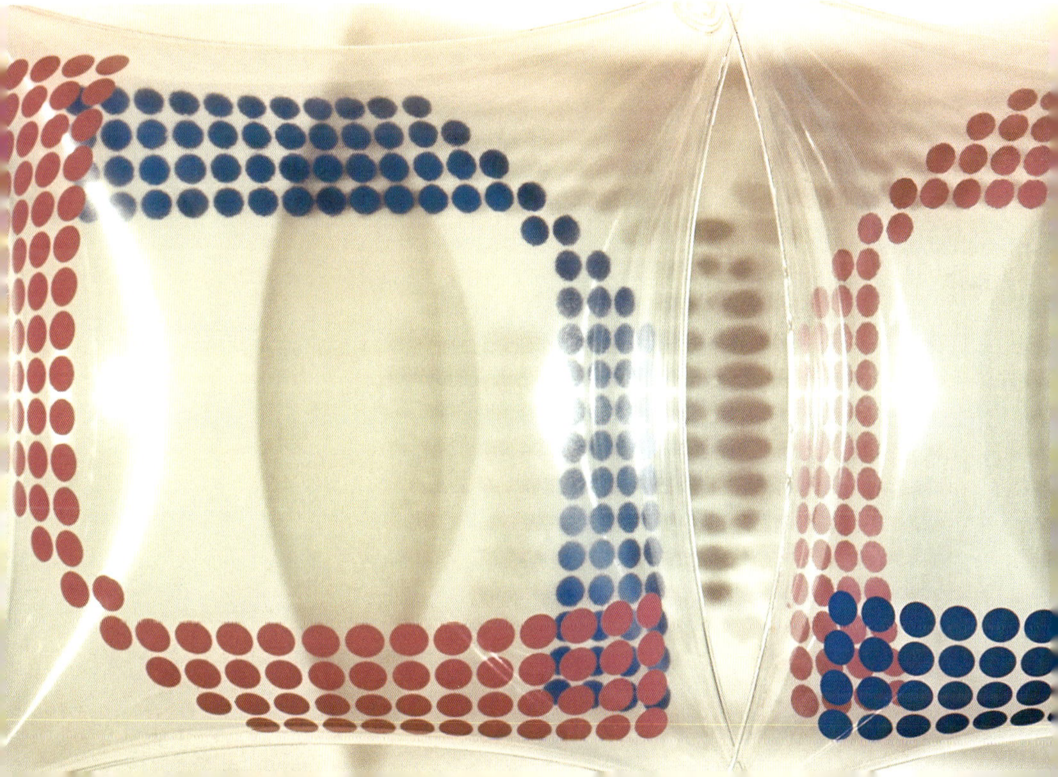

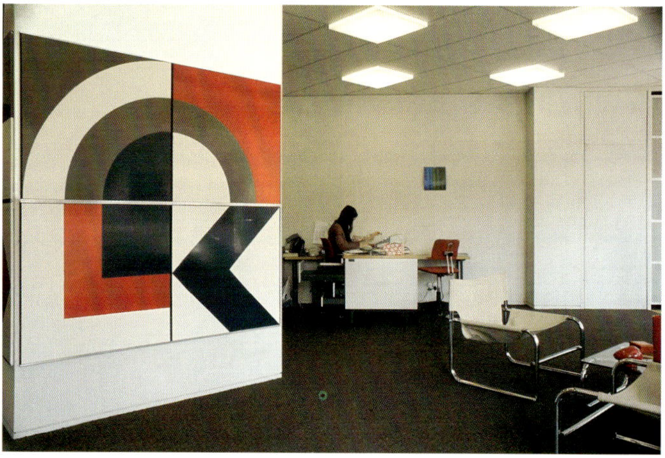

1971

Interior design for a branch office in Amsterdam

Furniture and 'mobile' art object

1971

Separation wall

between office space and restaurant

Amsterdam head office

In collaboration with architect Theo Tempelman

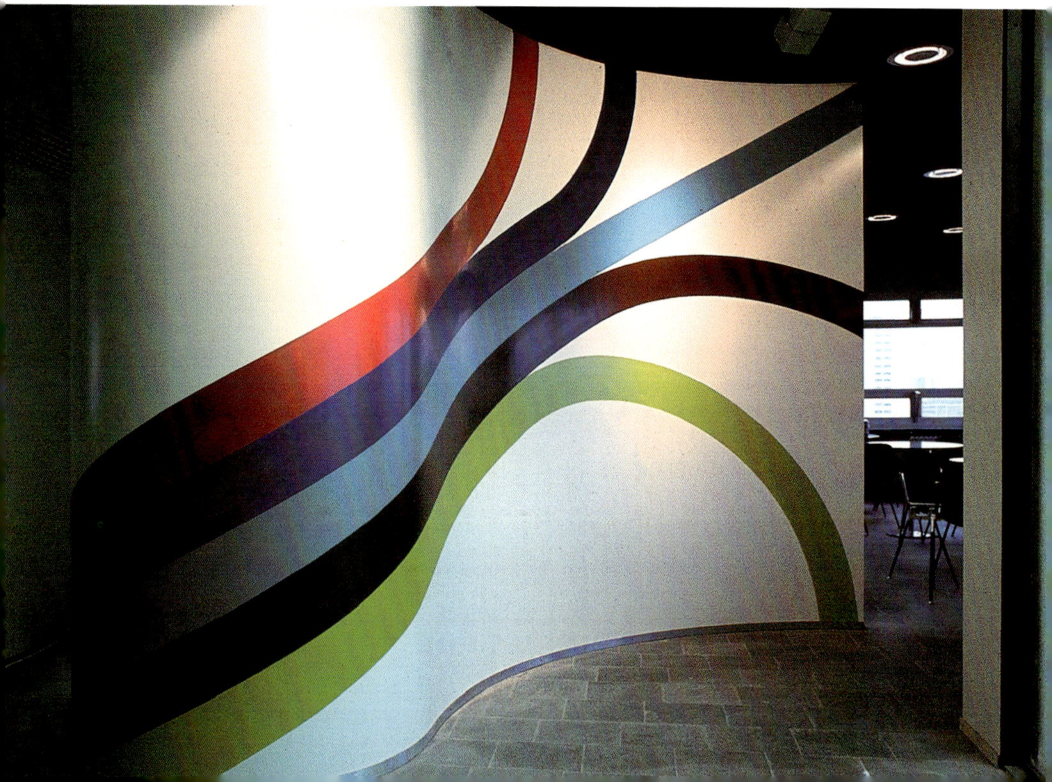

The Randstad brand **Between 1960 and 1968 the temping industry went through a period of rapid expansion. Dozens of temp agencies, all struggling to maintain a high profile, competed for a share of the market which was still relatively new.** People printed and messed around like there was no tomorrow, **Goldschmeding said to Piët.** I collected a lot of that stuff and gave the whole bunch to Ben. I said: 'That's what I do not want. I want to distinguish myself from the others.[5] **Mercedes's star, PAM's stylized drop... Goldschmeding hoped to see something with that kind of strength and simplicity. Ben Bos promised to do his best. The result is widely known. About the Randstad logotype Bos said:** It contains a trace of an alphabet for which TD colleague Wim Crouwel was receiving a lot of attention at the time. His computer alphabet led to a marked simplification of the standard letter shape. And then I thought: I just have to make a very beautiful R. This R became markedly more elegant. I tried to imbue it with both exactitude and refinement to express Randstad's dualistic role. On the one hand we had to appeal to temporary workers, most of whom were women. On the other we wanted to communicate exactness to clients. When the single R proved too shaky we added another one in reverse. That created a balance. But then I am talking about a logo. On the subject of corporate design, we should hasten to add that a corporate design is not a logo, while a logo is not a corporate design. In any case I showed them just this one concept. And I have to say they didn't waste much time accepting it.[6] **Bos subsequently ensured that the logo was also employed in other corporate expressions: calling cards, letterheads, forms, the interior design of branch offices, etcetera.**
Although Randstad did not present itself from the very start in the tailor-made suit that Total Design cut for it, it nevertheless was one of the first companies to take its corporate design seriously. In 1988 Bos recalled: In the Netherlands this has only been a serious concern, a part of deliberate corporate policy, for some 25 years. In 1963 KLM was the first Dutch enterprise to introduce a genuine corporate identity. The National Railways soon followed suit and then the Post Office. So Randstad was an early bird.[7]

The culture **For decades Randstad has honoured the view that design is one of the main tools for communicating, both internally and externally, the enterprises's principles and standards. As Ed Bolk claims, this does not apply to service companies only.** I believe it is equally important to all types of enterprise. However, its value in the service industry is beyond doubt. If you consider that at this moment some 85 per cent of the Dutch labour population works in service jobs, you can imagine how important it is to distinguish yourself through your presentation.
When Bolk joined Randstad in 1976 that was no less important. He recalls that some figures in the temping industry made it necessary for you to count your fingers after you had shaken their hands. **The branch offices of the various temping organizations did not inspire sufficient confidence. According to Ben Bos they looked a lot like dubious coffee houses. The industry did not have a very good reputation, while the political world also regarded these companies with suspicion.** The FNV trade union thought that all temp agencies should be banned, while the Dutch Labour Party included similar plans in its party programme, **says Bolk. Randstad's businesslike, efficient and functional style compared favourably to the dubious orange-and-brown interiors of many competitors. The company**

5 **Susanne Piët, 'Kennen, vertrouwen and dienen. Nieuwe huisstijl na explosieve groei bij Randstad'. In:** Randstad Data **1, special issue on corporate design, 1988**
6 **Id.**
7 **Id.**

presented itself in brightly lit branch offices, generally situated in busy shopping streets, that gave the impression of great openness. The message was: Randstad has nothing to hide.
All of our expressions were, and still are, motivated by this one idea of aiming for perfection, **states Bolk.**
And with the aim to achieve perfection an important aspect of the Randstad culture has been named.

In the booklet De PZ-Pocket: Diensten, cultuur and management[8] **that is issued to all Randstad relations, Ed Bolk discusses the importance of a corporate culture to service organizations. After emphatically stating that the role of the service provider, the person who maintains personal contact with the client on behalf of the service organisation, is crucial to the service process, Bolk writes:** Inspiration, striving to achieve a higher goal, makes it possible for people to keep on providing services in the long run. A higher goal is an inspiration. Therefore the task of the service organization is to direct the service workers' motivation towards the long term. Not merely in order to prevent burn-out, but also to create a positive relation between the standards of individual employees and those of the organisation. Corporate culture plays a major role in this. After all, the culture consists of the traditional working methods that everybody shares and includes the long-term objectives that inspire the employees. Therefore the management of a service organisation has the important duty to define, monitor and communicate the corporate culture. (...) A culture that is shared improves organizational efficiency and reduces the risk of error. After all, the corporate culture tells everyone how things should be done. (...) A strong culture provides identification models and thereby increases the chances that individual needs are satisfied, because it is clear that individual and corporate principles and standards are in accord. It improves performance by stimulating the mental capacity, which increases the production of the enterprise as a whole. This generates pride in the enterprise, based on security and emotional bonding. (...) In a service enterprise especially a strong communal culture is the only effective control instrument.
Bolk goes on to discuss the features that characterize the culture of the Randstad service organisation:
- **functionality**: The first criterium for acting must always be that the costs of an effort must not exceed its return.
- **aiming for perfection**: Within the limits of the economically feasible, perfection should be aimed for.
- **other-orientation:** A service worker should be genuinely interested in the client.
- **anticipation:** Providing services implies that the service provider anticipates possibilities that he perceives, but that may not yet have occurred to the client.
- **unanimity and consensus:** Important decisions must be taken with the approval of all persons concerned.
- **good faith:** Good faith is the awareness that all the service provider's actions are motivated by the interest of the client and therefore indirectly that of one's own organisation.

Aiming for perfection **This set of uniform, unchangeable criteria forms the quintessence of the Randstad culture. In 1976 these features were codified by Goldschmeding and Bolk. The last of these emphasizes that they did not so much serve to introduce regulations as to render explicit a practice that had already existed for a long time.**
The origin of these criteria can be traced back, **says Bolk.** Everything is related to Dutch Calvinism, the Free University in Amsterdam, to the person of the founder, to the people with whom he surrounded himself. The criteria are now observed by all 16,000 Randstad

8 **Ed Bolk,** De PZ-Pocket. Diensten, cultuur and management, **1996**

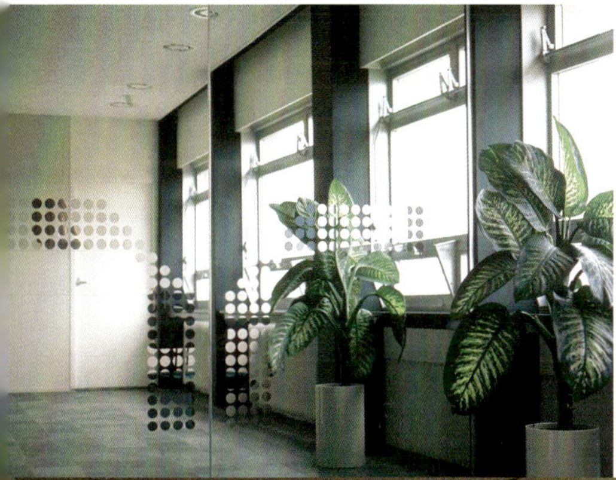

1970
Plastic carrier bag

1971
Mirror wall with transparent logo
Amsterdam head office

1970
'Mobile' magnetic art object
Amsterdam head office
In collaboration with architect
Theo Tempelman

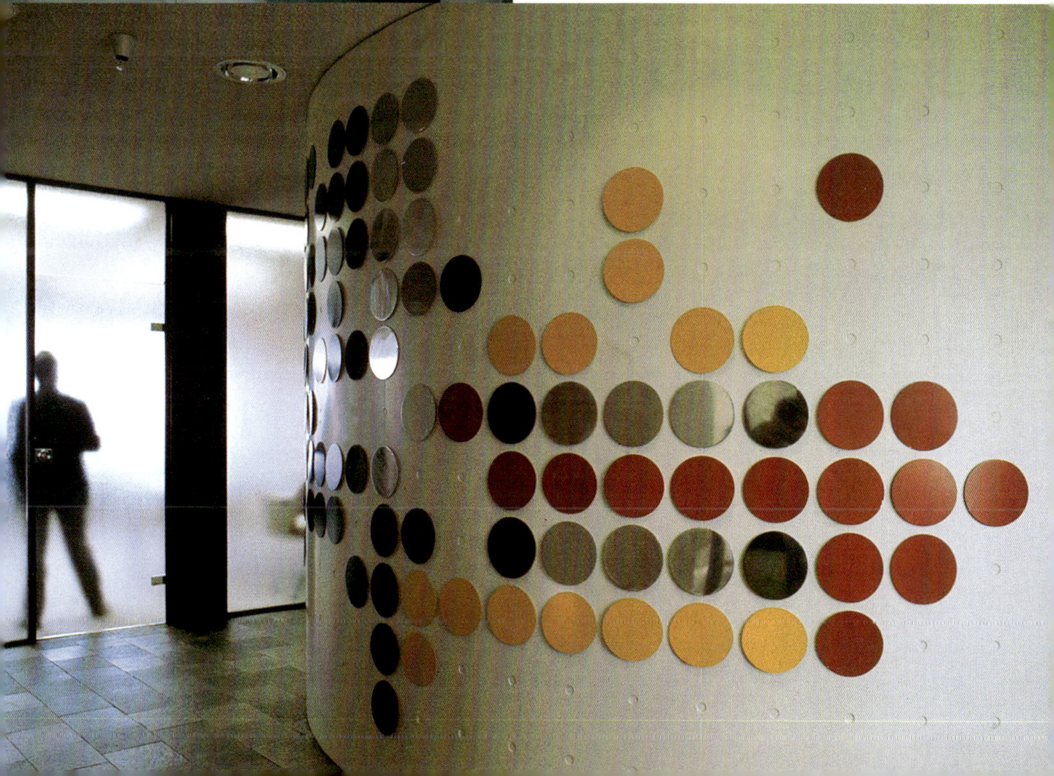

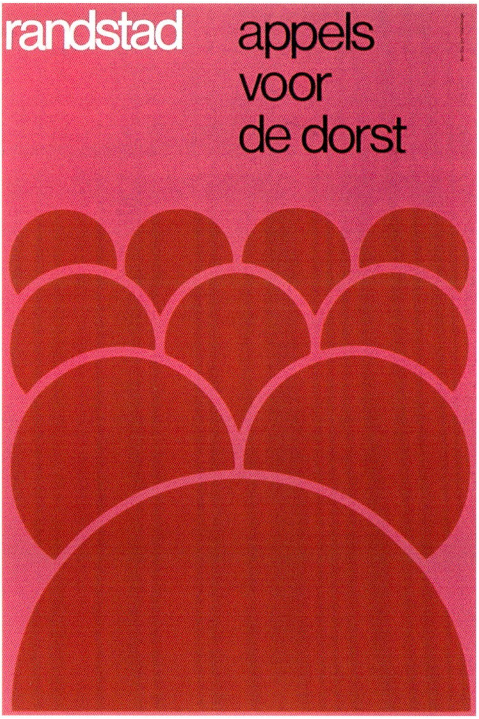

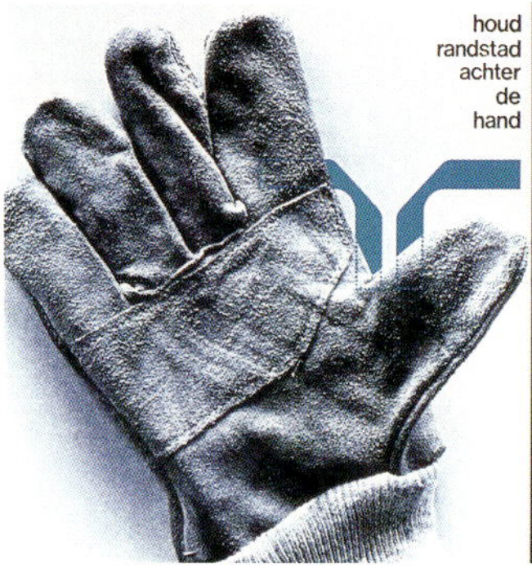

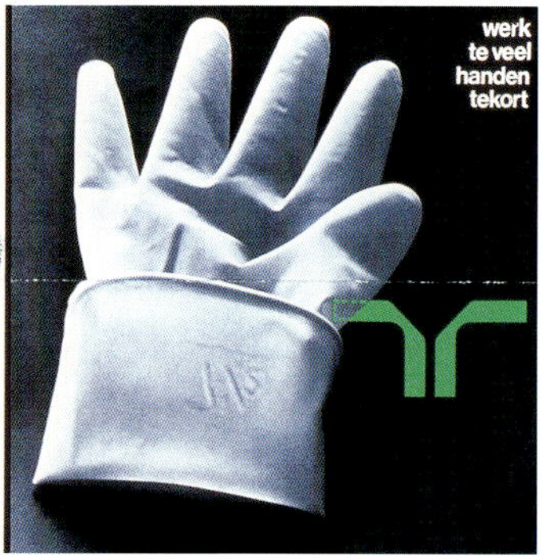

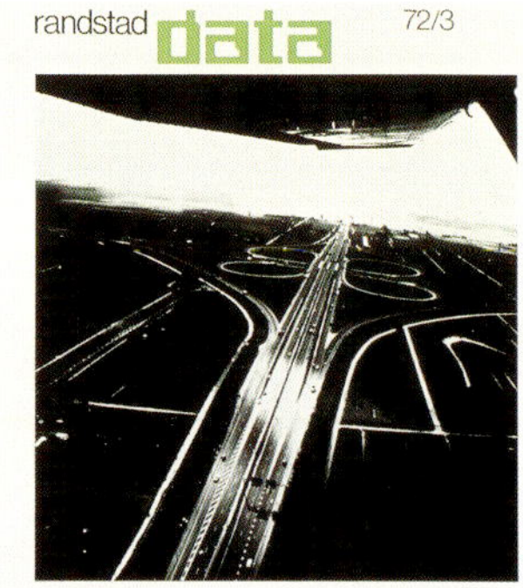

1971
Poster

1972
Folders
Photography by Peter Marcuse

1972
'Randstad Data'
Quarterly magazine
Photography by Cas Oorthuys

employees. **And this is done with a view to what is nowadays called stakeholders value: the protection of the interests of all parties who are directly and indirectly involved – employees, clients, temp workers, suppliers and society. In the minds of Randstad employees, this simultaneous representation of interests has been summarized in three central concepts: knowledge, service and trust.**

What is the relation of the present Randstad culture to the corporate identity that Ben Bos designed in 1967? How do these reinforce one another? And what is the role of corporate design in the 'instilling' of corporate principles in the minds of its many new employees? Ed Bolk claims that the last happens almost automatically: Since 1967 Randstad's activities have been remarkably consistent, not only in its formal corporate design, but also in the style of the house: the behaviour of its staff. As a result of this consistency certain people are attracted to your company while others are not. A clear identity is always functional in terms of attraction and repulsion: it serves as a first selection. This ensures that people working at Randstad have affinity with our corporate culture, and this makes the horizontal transfer of this culture among employees highly effective. The role of the management is to further encourage this transfer by behaving in a way that is guided by the same principles. Design is one of these forms of behaviour. Publications for staff, forms, desk materials, the interior of branch offices: all of these reflect this perfectionism. These corporate design expressions reinforce the culture, the internal transfer and the Randstad feeling.[9]

Total Design could be trusted to translate the Randstad feeling into corporate identity expressions. Total Design was Randstad, **says Bolk. However, the bulk of the communication budget was not spent on design, but on adverts, in which it proved to be more difficult to convey the Randstad feeling. Randstad showed itself to be an extremely critical client – after all, it aimed for perfection – and an advertising agency like Ogilvy & Mather had difficulty coping with that.**
We have always had skirmishes with advertising agencies, **Bolk recalls.** It happened with JWT and to an even greater extent with Ogilvy & Mather. I have repeatedly been forced to ask Ben if he could once again give those advertising folks chapter and verse about our objectives. **Ben Bos also speaks of** enormous tensions. **He tells that O&M went to considerable trouble to trip up Total Design.** Their creative department came up with proposals that were totally unacceptable in view of the entire structure that we had built. For instance, they wanted to use a completely different typography in the campaigns, came up with various counter proposals for staff magazines, you name it. Those were hefty battles. **Ed Bolk kept flying back and forth between the two agencies as a grey dove of peace.**
Still it would be many years before Randstad hired another advertising agency. These was due to the enormous risk of damage that such a switch entails. It always takes around two years to really get to know our company, **says Bolk.** That goes for both our employees and our suppliers. If you trade in one advertising agency for another, you can count on a year and a half's expenditure without any visible results. That's why we hesitated so long to switch.

9 **In his book** Relatie als nieuwe waarde. Relatiediensten organiseren en verkopen **(1999) Ed Bolk extensively discusses the internal and external importance of communication and corporate design for service brands. Especially chapter 5, 'Promotie of relatiediensten', is highly relevant.**

Refreshment and dynamism **For about twenty years Randstad had managed very well with Total Design's corporate design. However, around 1987 it was decided that a complete overhaul was due. The limit had been reached. Or, as Bolk says, the surprise had gone. Although predictability can be an asset for a corporate design, Randstad always wanted just a little bit more, due to its aforementioned perfectionism.** My angle always was, **says Bolk,** that I wanted to see proposals that were completely recognizable on the one hand and surprising on the other. If they were, I approved them. But over the years the surprise wore off, and a certain datedness crept into what we already had, so something needed to be done. In the mid-eighties we were about to open a whole series of new branch offices. That was a good occasion for upgrading our corporate design.

Ben Bos had already noticed that the existing light frames in the branch offices were no longer adequate. Their construction was really unsound. It allowed the light to shine between the sheetings and the frames. He proposed to revise the construction and restyle the lettering at the same time. The Helvetica has many virtues, but it was clear that by now it was too old for our purposes. After some experiments we decided to submit a proposal that was a radical departure from the existing design, while nobody would notice the difference.

Bos started by inviting four young designers working at Total Design to develop new ideas for Randstad's corporate identity, but the results of this exercise did not please him. He then requested colleague and right hand Wim Verboven to make a inventory of the main developments in design over the past twenty years and to introduce replacement components on the basis of an analysis of these. Thus the Helvetica was replaced by the Frutiger, which had many potential advantages. In terms of typesize, leading and readability the Frutiger was a considerable improvement. We had to start changing our style of writing, **says Bolk.** Texts had to become shorter, sentences had to become shorter, more white, wider leading... As by this time even academics were having trouble reading long sentences, the accessibility of our printed matter had been lost.

TD also introduced a second typeface to end the perpetual conflicts with advertising agencies. They always wanted to use other typefaces than the Helvetica, but never came up with anything suitable. So we thought: If we give them two types that they can use, we will have fewer headaches. Finally we also replaced the two basic colours Process Blue and Reflex Blue by a more subtle colour to which we also added a blue gamma, a grey gamma and a collection gamma. These colours have an optical effect that was in balance with the new colour blue.

The result? Refreshment, dynamism and readable texts, **says Bolk.** For non-initiates the differences were small enough to allow for a phased introduction. We did not have to replace all old light frames overnight, for instance. So the solution also proved very economical. In addition we were able to save a lot of money by cutting hundreds of forms. Randstad suddenly looked completely revitalized. And of course it was also very important that there was consistency in spite of the change: in the service industry the clients always wonder whether they have made the right choice. Therefore the worst thing you can do is to take a drastic step in matters like this.

A change in brand policy **Randstad's corporate identity does not merely reflect its corporate culture, but also testifies to the 'kinship' of the various Randstad brands. In addition to the Randstad Uitzendbureau temping agency, subsidiary companies have been created with names such as Randstad Interimkader or Randstad Polytechniek. The corporate identities**

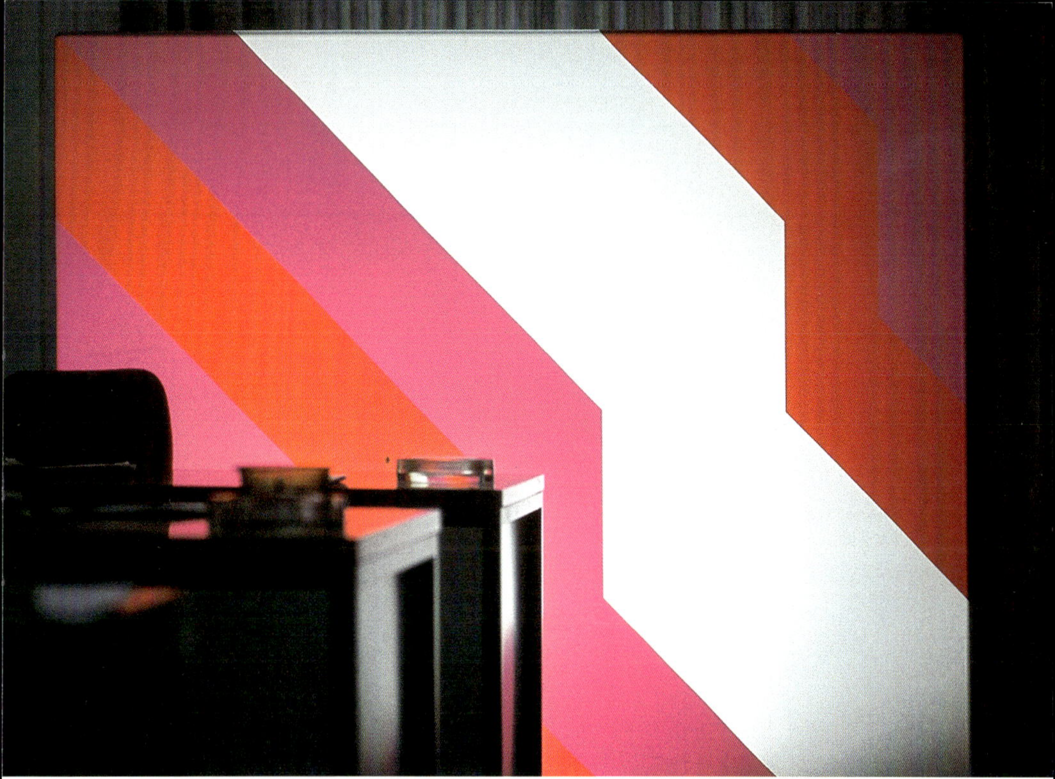

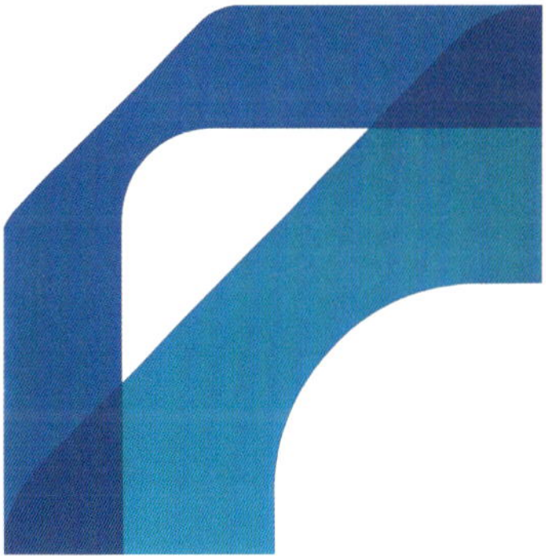

1972
Separation wall
Utrecht branch office

1972
Cover of company brochure

1972
Logo and corporate design for Interlabor
A Belgian Randstad subsidiary

Apart from the overall corporate design, Bos's involvement was incidental, and largely limited to the design of branch office fronts. Randstad holding feared that the corporate identity of the two companies might become too similar.

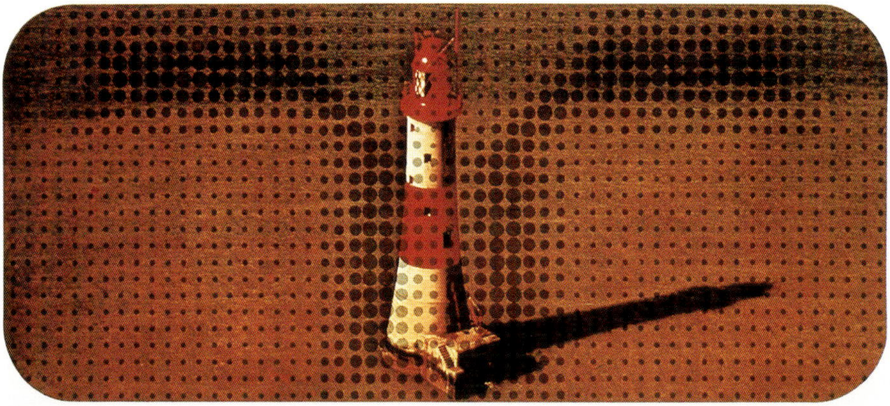

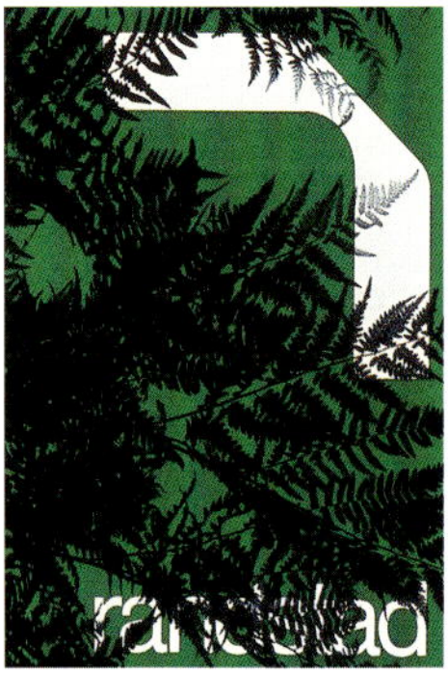

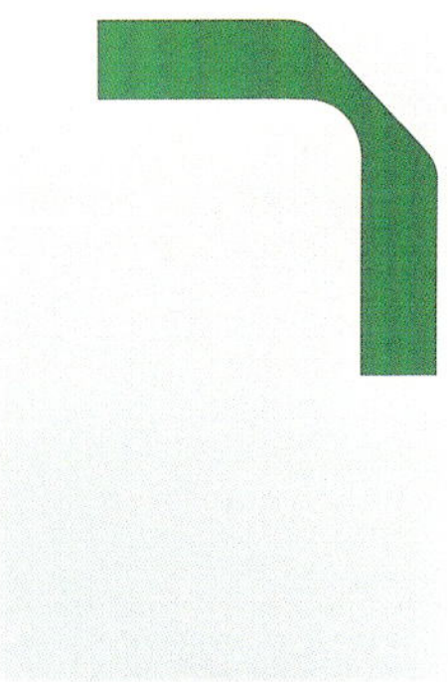

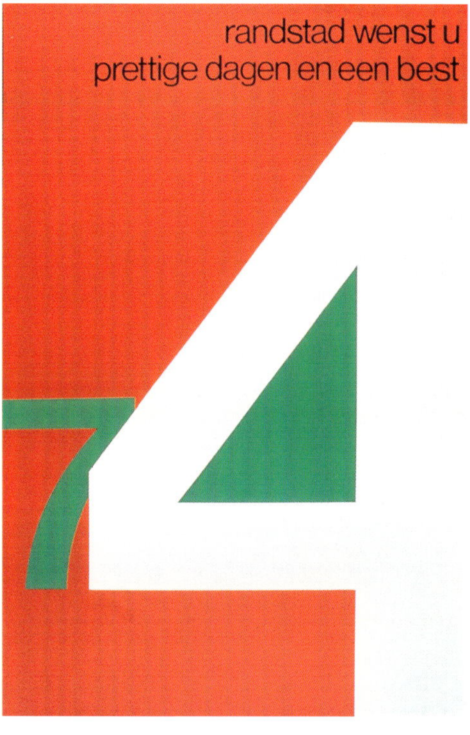

1972
Guide for temp workers
Photography by Carel Blazer
In collaboration with
Daphne Duyvelshoff

1972
Postcard

1973
New Year's poster

of these are based on the same design principles. Incidentally, Randstad's brand policy is considerably more complicated: not every new subsidiary is automatically given the Randstad name.

To use Olins' categories,[10] **says Bolk,** you can say that the Randstad holding conducts both a monolithic, an endorsed and a branded brand policy. Randstad Interimkader may be called monolithic, Capac is endorsed, because Capac always states it is a member of the Randstad group, while Tempo Team is branded, because it has no interest in publicizing it is a Randstad company. At one point we had expanded so much that we were no longer able to reach certain groups with this one name Randstad Uitzendbureau. That's why we started looking for alternatives. It goes without saying that activities that could harm the Randstad brand were given a separate brand name, and accordingly received their own corporate identity.

The Randstad holding has greatly expanded its activities, even outside the Netherlands. It may be interesting to consider the enterprise's American plans, especially in view of the fact that the typically American service industry with its instrumentality is completely at odds with everything that Randstad stands for. The set of uniform, unchangeable criteria that form the basis of the Randstad culture must be applied by Randstad employees in an authentic, personal and pluriform manner. If they fail to do so, they cannot form a relaxed, personal relation with clients. Americans have quite a lot of difficulty with the latter, claims Bolk. Americans in the service industry are anything but relaxed. They use standard expressions like 'How are you today?' But you mustn't try and answer them, for they are not interested in your actual feelings. That is a highly instrumental form of service. That works very well with instrumental purchasers, who want to be efficiently served and nothing else, for they are also discount buyers. But principles-and-standards buyers are another story. They seek partnership. You can describe the relation between Randstad and Total Design as follows: the effectiveness of the partnership was more important than the fee that the agency charged.

Randstad in America **When Randstad started to explore the situation in America in 1992 it already had a strong foothold in European countries such as France, Germany and Britain. The Spanish market was also being studied at that time, as the fastest economic expansion in Europe was expected to occur on the Mediterranean coast. Randstad also intended to gain a strong position in the United States. After all, Europe and the US jointly make up 80 per cent of the world market in temporary work. Incidentally it was in the US that the basis for temporary work was laid. The oldest American employment agency, which Randstad purchased in 1998, was founded in 1890.**

Randstad studied the quality and composition of the economy in the various states and concluded that the South-Eastern states offered the best prospects. The North-East was highly dependent on electronics, the Mid-West on heavy industry, while California with its agriculture, defense and electronics was also too one-sided to serve as a springboard. In addition to their considerable economic diversity, the South-Eastern states had the advantage of being situated in a convenient time zone, that there were two planes flying there daily, that the infrastructure was sound and the legislation favourable. There also was a fair amount of competition. That was good news, a sign that the market had developed. It was also bad news, because the market had already developed. However, Randstad interpreted it as good news and set up

10 **Wolff Olins,** The New Guide to Identity: How to Create and Sustain Change through Managing Identity, **1995**

business in Atlanta. It purchased the small TempForce chain, which owned twelve branch offices in Atlanta. Then they faced the question: What to do about the brand name?
Eric Vonk, who was in charge of the American operation, recalls: We requested the advice of two prohibitively expensive brand name gurus. We told them the whole Randstad story and asked whether or not we should introduce our own brand. The first one associated the Randstad name with a German steel manufacturer and said that this brand name would be **a nail in our coffin**. The other one was reminded of Haagen-Dasz and interpreted it as a sign of quality. Moreover he thought that the logo looked very stylish and encouraged us to use it. So their answers were yes and no. Then we still knew nothing. Until one rainy afternoon we discovered in a hotel room that Randstad was an anagram of **Standard**. That settled it. We decided to use the word Randstad as often as possible in combination with expressions like **standard** and **new standard**. The rest is history. So we immediately renamed TempForce.

Vonk set up an extensive programme to ensure that the Randstad culture and the market positioning would be accepted by the TempForce staff.
We wanted to retain those people, **tells Vonk.** After all, when you purchase a chain you buy goodwill, clients and experience. When you lay off experienced staff, you destroy capital and that's no good. However, many changes needed to be made. And these would form the basis for the **New Standard** that Randstad wished to set.
A major difference with the situation in Europe is that in the American staffing industry the purchase and sales officers operate independently of each other. The salesmen go on the road and attract orders from companies. They then inform the recruiting officers that company A has so many of temporary vacancies and is prepared to pay so much. Then it is up to the recruiting officers to try and find those people at that price. In Randstad the functions of recruitment and sales have always been integrated. After all Randstad believes that to cement relations temporary work should not be organized around a set of job requirements but around an affinity with, and an understanding of, a company and its culture. On the basis of this other-orientation Randstad intermediaries award vacancies to persons who do not only meet the job requirements, but will also fit in with the company in question.
To allow for such matching, TempForce's office window interiors had to go. According to the Randstad principles optimal operations can only be achieved in open office spaces. There is always a chance that a colleague is talking to an applicant who is just right for a vacancy that has been impossible to fill for two days.
A third difference between the American and European working methods is the rewarding of staff in the form of commissions. Randstad works on the basis of fixed salaries with a partly variable reward based on a collective measurement.
A fourth and final difference relates to push versus pull marketing. Even today, many staffing agencies can be described as push marketeers. Salesmen working on a commission basis go to extremes in order to score deal after deal. It will be clear that this does not accord with Randstad's ideas about its brand. That was also something in which the staff needed to be instructed.

While Vonk cum suis were implementing the Randstad culture and procedures, they rang Ben Bos and asked him whether he would be able to adapt the existing corporate identity to the American situation. What did Bos, who had left Total Design two years previously, find in the US?
The appearance of those branch offices was quite shocking, anything but **New Standard**. They were filled with the kind of furniture that in Holland you can

An artisan

Joost Klinkenberg joined Total Design in March of 1980 and stayed on until the end of 1987. During those years he was a member Ben Bos's team. Klinkenberg currently is director of HS Totaal studio.

I quickly became Ben's assistant. By 1987, when I left Total Design, I headed my own team. I cooperated with Ben for six years and never experienced him as a leader, but rather as a colleague. Although he was formally responsible and had considerable 'presence', which was often almost tangible, he was not the kind of leader who rushed you in a manner that was suffocating. He gave you much freedom to do your own thing, perhaps a bit too much – he provided little in the way of support or supervision. We were barely kept in check, although some people needed to be. There were no evaluation meetings, no wage disputes, no discussions about the profession and inside the team you could be your own boss. You had your own clients, with whom you would also confer. For these clients you were the contact.

In 1980 Ben immediately involved me in the annual report for TwijnstraGudde. Ben had laid the groundwork and I elaborated it. I was immediately taken along on visits to the client and subsequently realized the project by myself. That was actually quite rash, because I was just setting out as a designer. I did have some experience, including with annual reports, but still... Ben had confidence in me and anyway, at the time he had a lot on his mind, also in the personal sphere. You could tell. He was a little absent-minded and also you shouldn't forget that by then Ben had been working at Total Design for 17 years. There were also various problems with Loek van der Sande and Anthon Beeke which Ben took rather personally.

I view Ben as a master. I have learnt a lot from him, although he hasn't taught me much. However, I was in a position to see a lot of him, his approach to design, his working methods, the way he did things. It was a professional approach that I admired. He could write, was a good photographer, an expert designer and illustrator. He had a way with concepts and was clearly present in the details. He also made good spatial designs, both on the large and small scale, and in that sense I consider him an all-round designer, on a level with Piet Zwart: a driven and emotional Renaissance man who can turn his hand to anything.

His other side was his short temper, his grumpiness or bluntness. He could not always achieve what he wanted. He was capable of giving people a 'thrashing', but I am not the type to let myself be walked over and would tell him to cut it out. Then we discussed and solved the problems at hand.

He was the moving spirit behind Total Design. He achieved a lot with his team. They worked hard and did a lot of business. It bothered him that other departments of the studio didn't do likewise. That led to a conflict between his modesty and his vanity.

In fact, Ben propagated the ideals that Total Design stood for, especially in the early days. He was loyal. He got on well with clients and due to this loyalty and his strong personality he managed to retain them. That was also due to his persuasive manner of speaking, of teaching almost. He was a master at that, also during public speeches and lectures at academies. On top of that there was something authoritarian about him, which you need for those things.

I also appreciate his work because it is a mixture of advertising (like his work for Ahrend and Randstad) and lucid 'canvassing'. He could pack a lot of clout in his designs. He edited or stage-managed the integration of text, photography, headings, image and colour. He's very good at that. And he was good at managing and motivating people, both clients and printers, lithographers and photographers. He could explain with great precision how he wanted something done. Of course there was the occasional flop, but those were relatively rare.

I did regret that inside the team we rarely discussed each other's work, design in general, professional issues. There was no exchange of ideas and everyone operated individually.

In 1984 the Aesthedes arrived, mainly on the instigation of Jelle van der Toorn. He wanted to look ahead, to the world of the new media. This rather frightened some people, who feared that the handiwork would be lost. Actually Total Design was running behind in the field of automation: people still cut and pasted and typed on IBM typewriters. Those were the early days of the switch to electronics and Jelle thought that Total Design should move with the times, or the studio would miss the boat. There was no in-house expertise on computers whatsoever. Jelle changed all that and I played an active role in this change. In retrospect, the expensive Aesthedes had very few features compared to the Mac. Computer design was still in its infancy. At Total Design people were still unable to think in computer terms. Only in recent years has that really changed. Deep down Ben was opposed to it. He is an artisan, a craftsman. For him the preservation of his handwriting was sacrosanct.

What I learnt from Ben is that a design can have 'clout' and that in order to achieve that you must have a drive, a profound love of the job, commitment as well as emotion.

PH

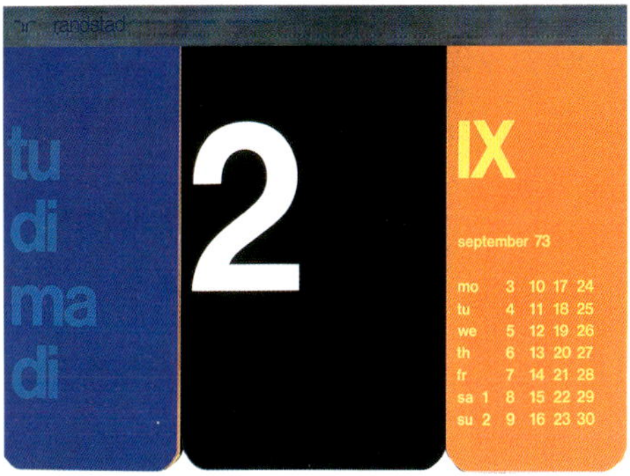

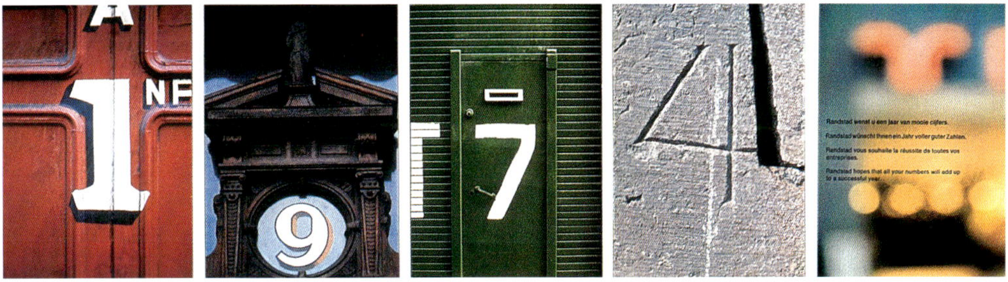

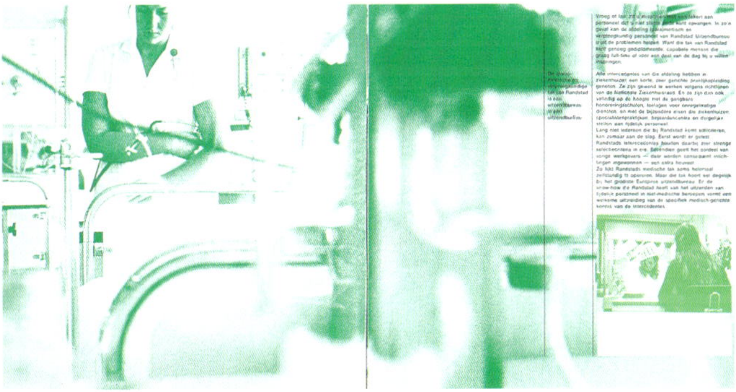

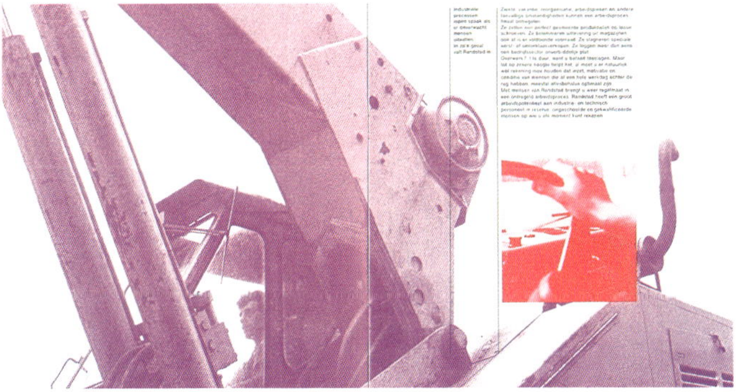

1973
Perpetual wall calendar

1973
Series of New Year's cards
Photography by Ben Bos

1973
Folders for medical and industrial staff
Photography by Peter Marcuse and Arjé Plas

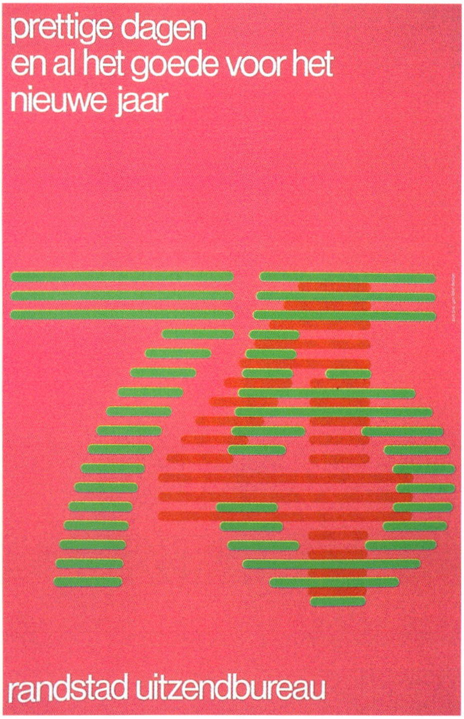

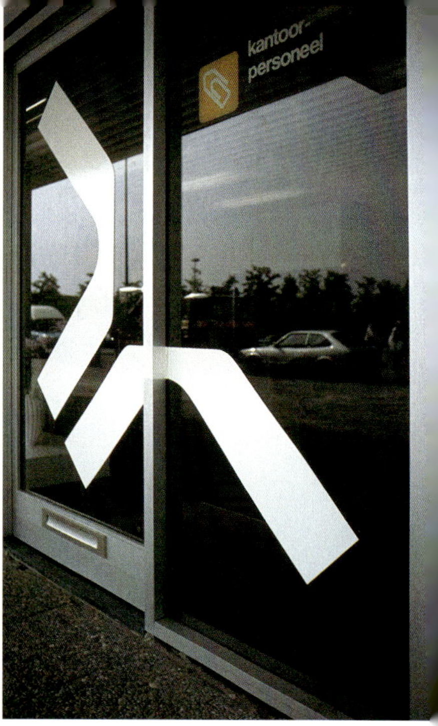

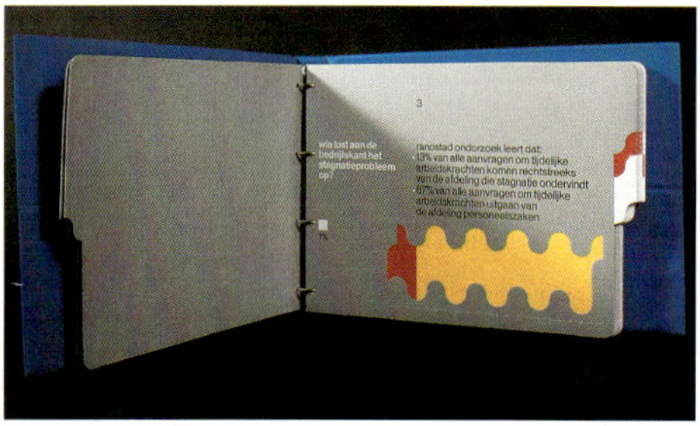

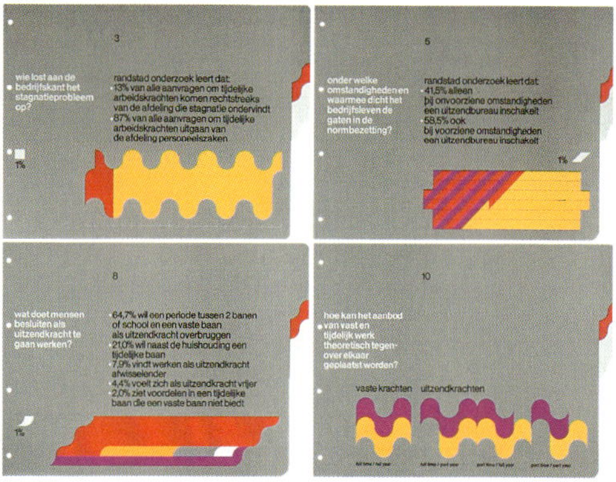

1974
New Year's poster

1974
Lettering for Amsterdam-Noord branch office

1974
Acquisitions book

buy in the city during the Queen's Day jumble sale. The desks were imitation mahogany and the wallpaper had a flower motif. The Christmas decorations were already or still there when I visited. They also used office windows, which gave you the sensation of being inside a police station. Dreadful. But there was a lot to be gained. At least TempForce was special in the sense that it had ground floor branch offices in shopping streets, just like Randstad did in Europe, while its competitors were accommodated in office buildings on the fourteenth floor.

If Bos was none too enthusiastic about the interior design of the branch offices, he did not really warm up to the graphic corporate design either.

I saw a lot of well-meaning personal initiative by branch office staff who created all sorts of stuff using scissors, glue and felt tip pens. For some time we had a **Wall of Shame** on which we collected expressions of this type. That proved highly effective, and these personal initiatives soon belonged to the past. Incidentally the situation with Jane Jones, the second chain that was purchased, was hardly any better.

As the initial expenses of the new enterprise that Randstad envisioned were very high, Bos was unable to change the branch offices and their paperwork overnight. Initially his main concern was to provide the current staff with the necessary tools with which they could most efficiently perform the purchase and sales activities that were now integrated.

Initially I mainly shifted a lot of graphic work, **Bos remembers.** We had to revise an inordinate number of forms, including their contents. Form by form and letter by letter we investigated, reorganized and sanitized everything. It took a couple of years before this process had reached the stage where the American Randstad people worked according to the European Randstad methods using materials that met European standards.

As a part of this project Bos established relations with a local design studio, Copeland & Hirthler, that he subsequently trained in the Randstad mentality. Later on Randstad itself appointed its own communication officers. It goes without saying that Bos could not handle all of this by himself.

A new market positioning **The question begging to be asked is: What was the effect of the New Standard that Randstad set? Did the competitors continue as before or did they adjust?**

I observe a fair amount of imitation, **says Vonk.** I have even seen blatant copies. No doubt the other participants have started to take their own brands much more seriously. The brand expressions and the behaviour of the competitors' staff have become much more professional.

That is hardly surprising if you consider the fact that in six years Randstad has become a formidable player in the US. The National Association of staffing agencies has 8,000 members, including many small players, but also some of the biggest in the world. Randstad occupies a ninth position with 550 branch offices in 36 states. On a normal working day Randstad employs some 75,000 dispatched persons. A number of these operate under the Randstad name, a number of them not yet. In the long term all purchased brands will sport the Randstad name.

In that respect**, says Vonk,** we conduct the same policy in Europe and the US. You could say that we are busy reorganising into three divisions. The largest of these is Randstad, which will lose its name extensions such as **Uitzendbureau** or **Interimkader**. Secondly a division will be created – which has already been introduced in the UK and the Netherlands under the brand name Yacht – that will concentrate on the upper market segment, i.e. well-paid, highly specialized professionals. A third division will concentrate on mass production: dispatching large

numbers of people for relatively simple labour, such as 400 storage workers needed for three days. This division will also be given its own brand name. Randstad itself will, on both sides of the Atlantic, continue to concentrate on the middle segment, with the same market approach and the same corporate design. Incidentally, a brand such as Tempo Team will continue to exist.
The last remark equally applies to Randstad's corporate design. In the long run Vonk expects it to evolve some more, but only in the distant future. That is quite remarkable if you consider that Randstad is also raising its profile in the slipstream of this reorganisation into divisions, which is a result of the enormous increase in temporary work.
In 1990 the Bureau of Labour Statistics reported that 15 per cent of the labour population did not have a traditional labour agreement, **says Vonk.** This means that a large minority temped, worked on secondment or had a contract for a limited period. In 1999 this number is expected to be 55 per cent. Add to this the fact that the largest group in the labour market with a traditional employment contract, the age group between 30 and 45, changes jobs 8.8 times per ten years, and the picture is complete. There is an extraordinary amount of migration. That's why the starting point for our positioning is that we no longer wish to be associated with temping. After all, that only had any value in a rigid labour market. Now that hardly any permanence is left in employer-employee relations you have to look for a different attitude. For us that is: Randstad wants to act as an agent for talent and as a workforce services provider for employers. That has been a major and risky about-turn of strategy: instead of generating demand we are now selling supply. We focus on the labour market and recruit talent, even if we do not have any jobs for them yet. The old situation in which we generated demand and subsequently looked for supply to meet it, belongs to the past. We now possess supply, chart the demand in enterprises by means of productivity and efficiency analyses, and then proceed to advise them.
Such a set-up works only if the industry has great faith in Randstad. Vonk says that it has.
Randstad is one of the best performing companies in the staffing industry. Our goal is not to become the biggest player, but we do aim to achieve a leading position. Including the brand, the image and the promise that it holds...
It proves to be so pliable that the Dutch concept from 1966 can be very successfully used in the US in 2000. That is quite exceptional, and if there was only one message I could give, that would be it.

A number of the initiatives developed in 1996 in the field of design management did not live for very long. The European Designer fair was never repeated after the one event while the magazine Design in Business **was discontinued in the summer of 1998. The Ichthus Hogeschool can still use a few more design management students, while the Design Management Institute finds it more difficult every year to fill the seats at its conference. Never again has the future looked so bright for design enthusiasts as it did that year.**

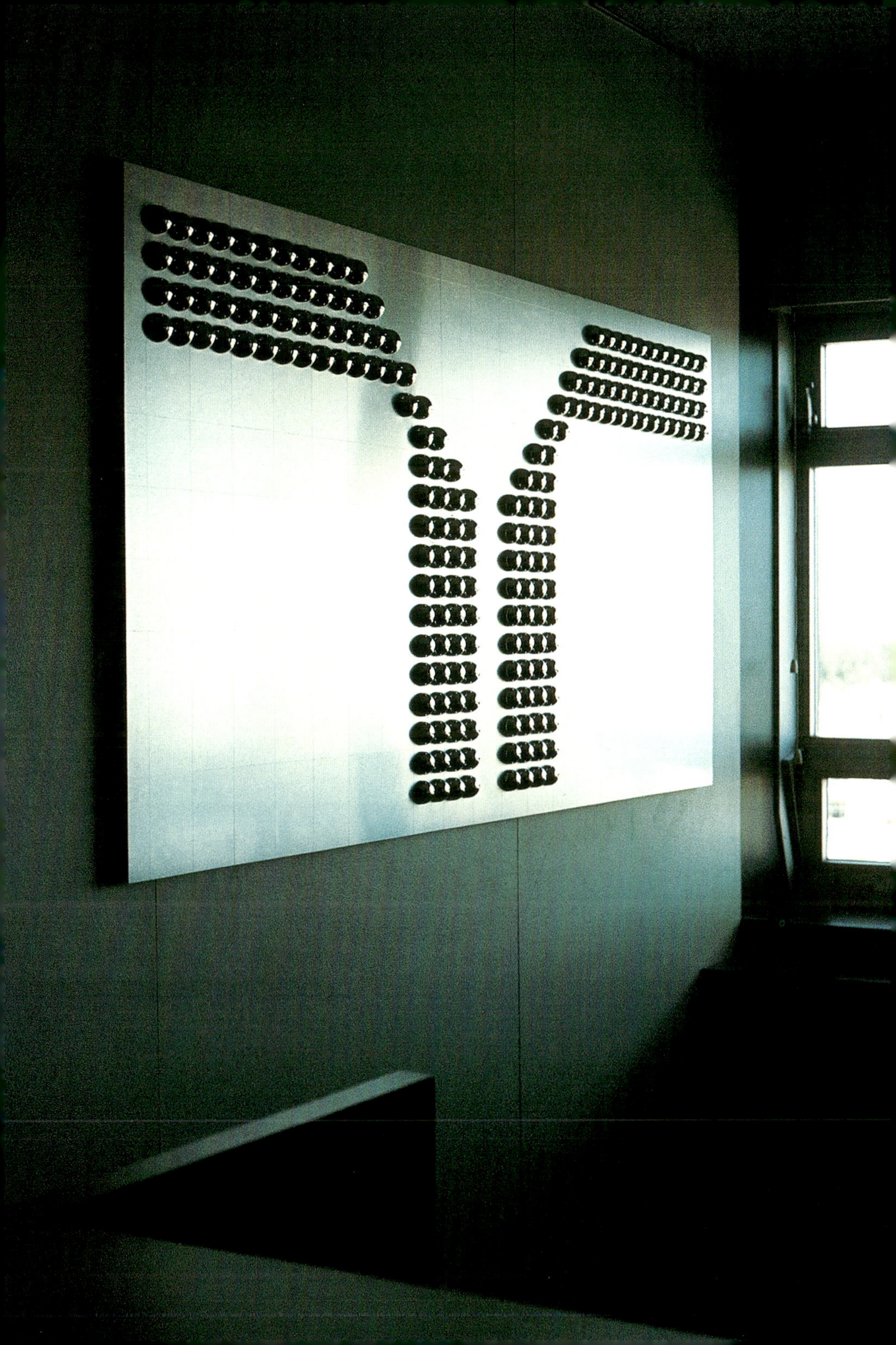

1975
Routing system
The Hague branch office

1975
Art object
Amsterdam branch office
In collaboration with
Zdena Sernets

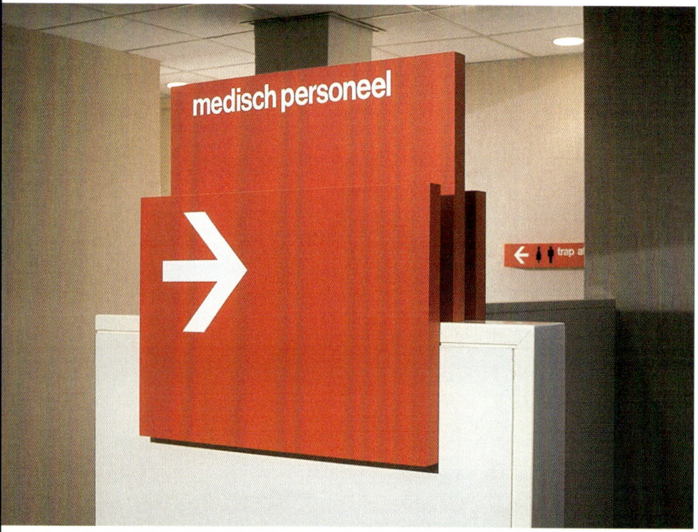

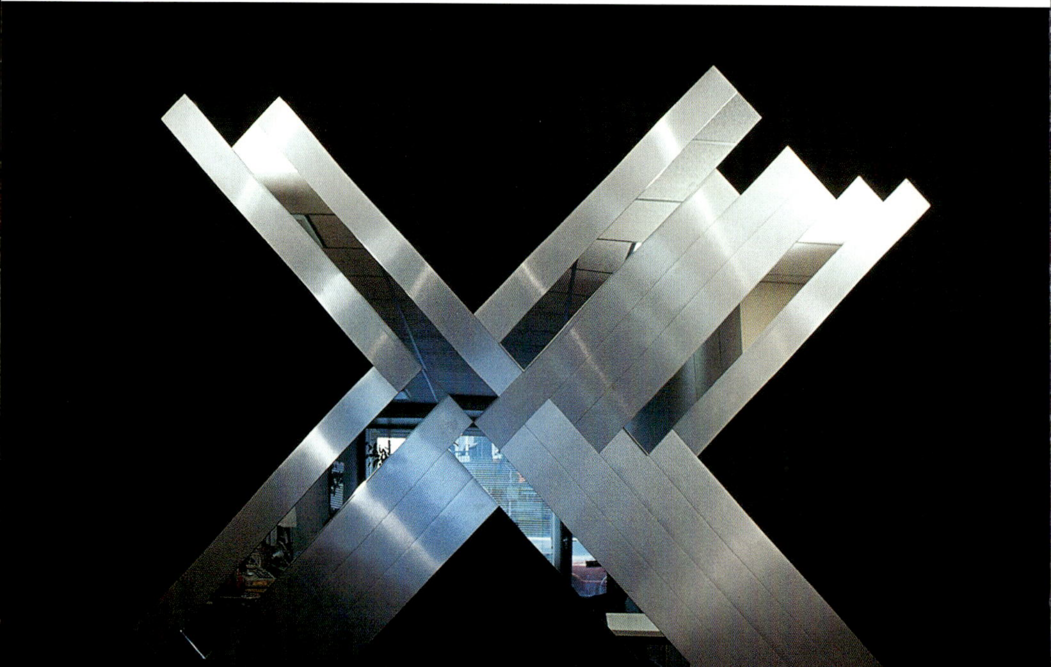

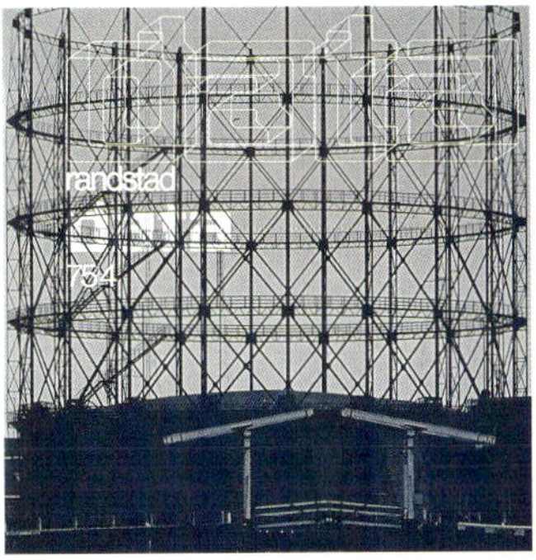

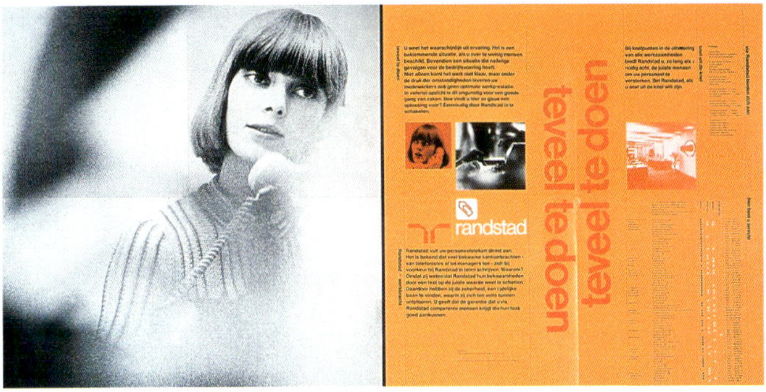

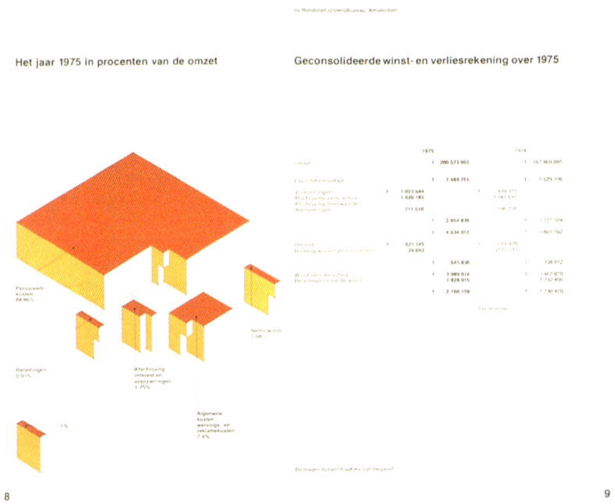

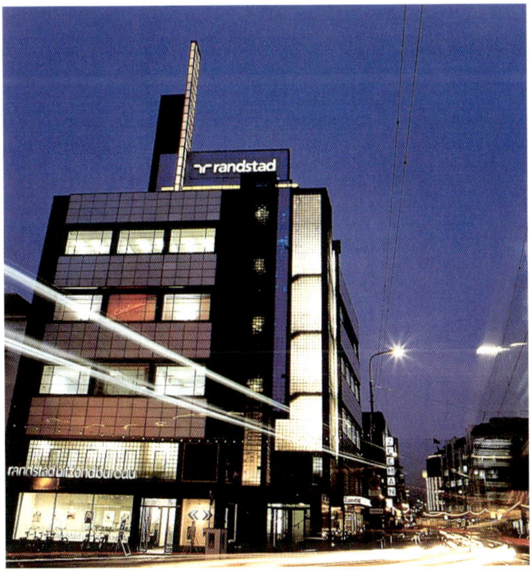

1975
'Randstad Data'
Quarterly magazine
Photography by Aart Klein

1975
Folding sheet
Photography by Peter Marcuse

1976
Diagram
Annual report 1975

1976
Interior design and architectural lettering
Branch office on Grote Markt square, The Hague

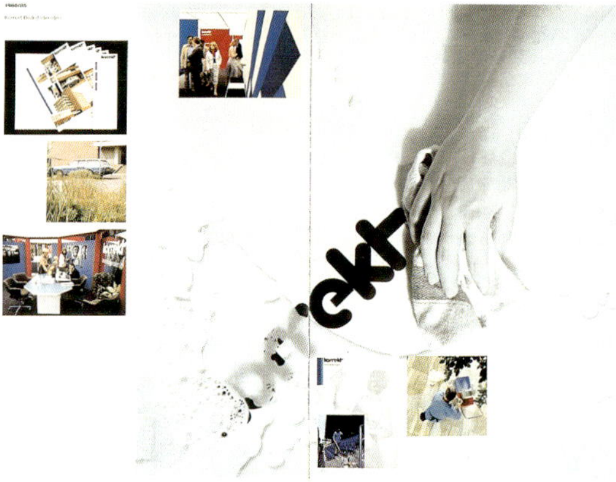

1985
Annual report Randstad

1983/1987/1989
Stands
RAI cleaning industry trade fair Amsterdam

korrekt

1976-1989
Korrekt bedrijfsdiensten
A Randstad subsidiary

Randstad subsidiary Korrekt was founded in 1976. The company was originally designed to provide a wide range of services. In addition to cleaners it supplied catering and security staff, among others. However, this set-up was soon abandoned. It was slimmed down to a cleaning company that developed into a sizeable enterprise. The collaboration with Bos lasted for twelve years. Commissions included the corporate identity, the exteriors of its branch offices, company brochures, fleet marking and stands for the RAI trade fair. After a reorganisation the company was continued by Randstad daughter Lavold.

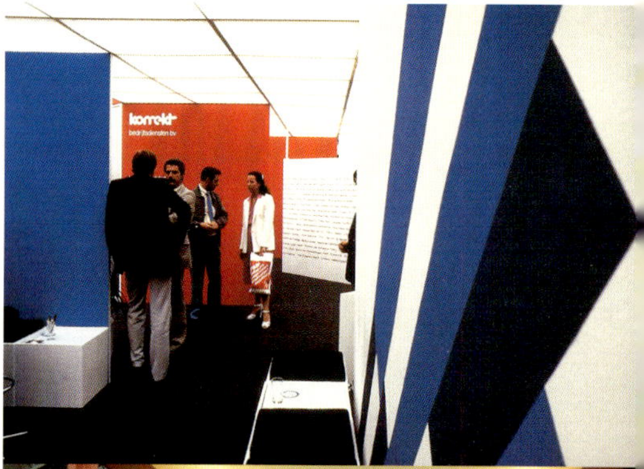

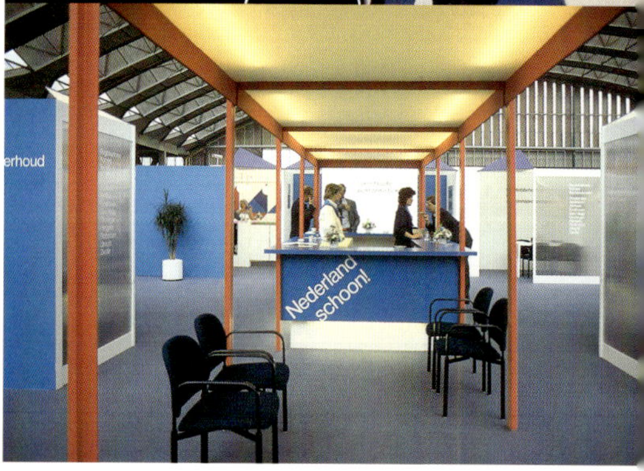

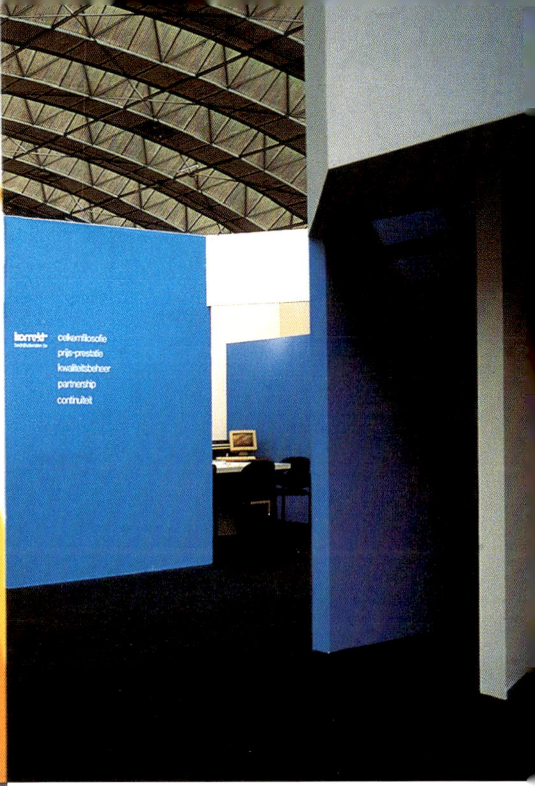

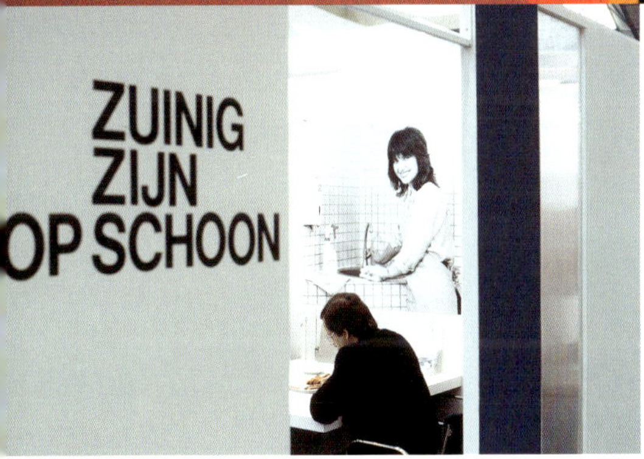

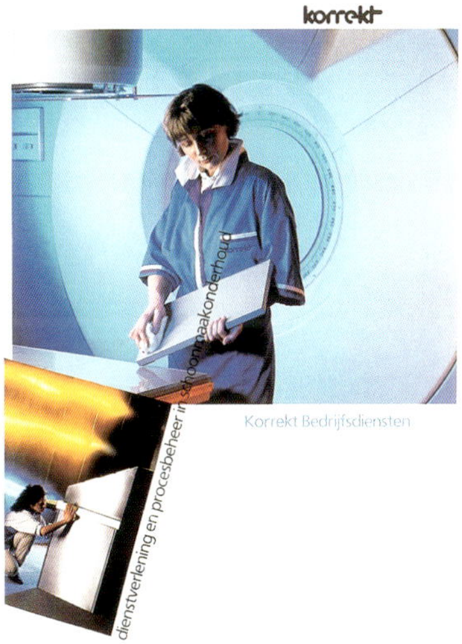

1987
Brochure
Photography by Jan van der Horn

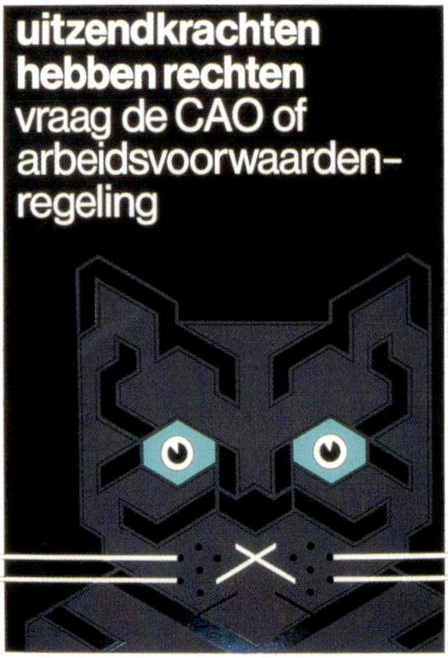

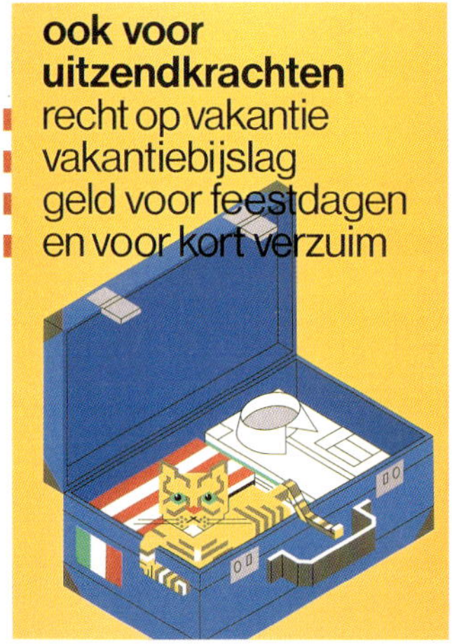

1977
Posters

1977
Calendar

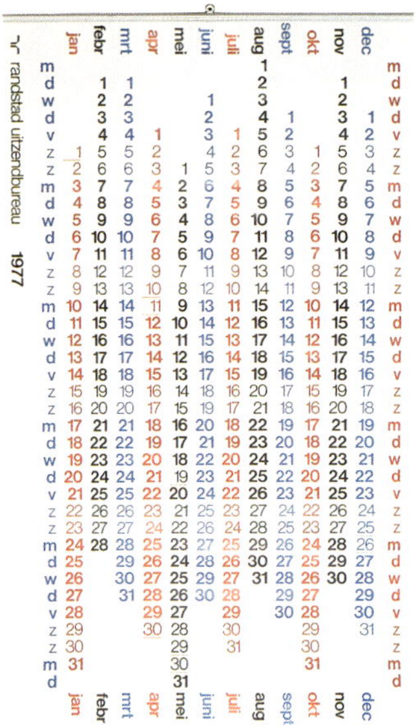

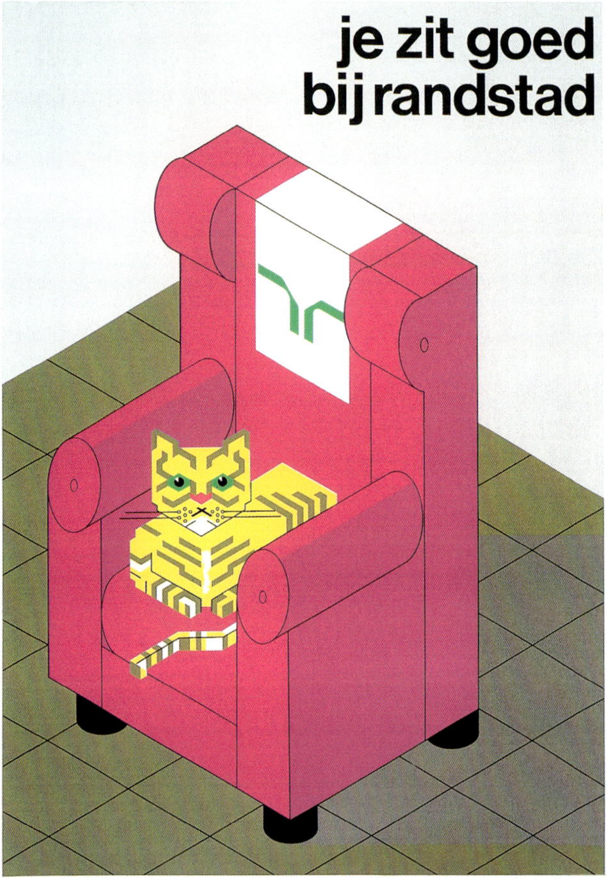

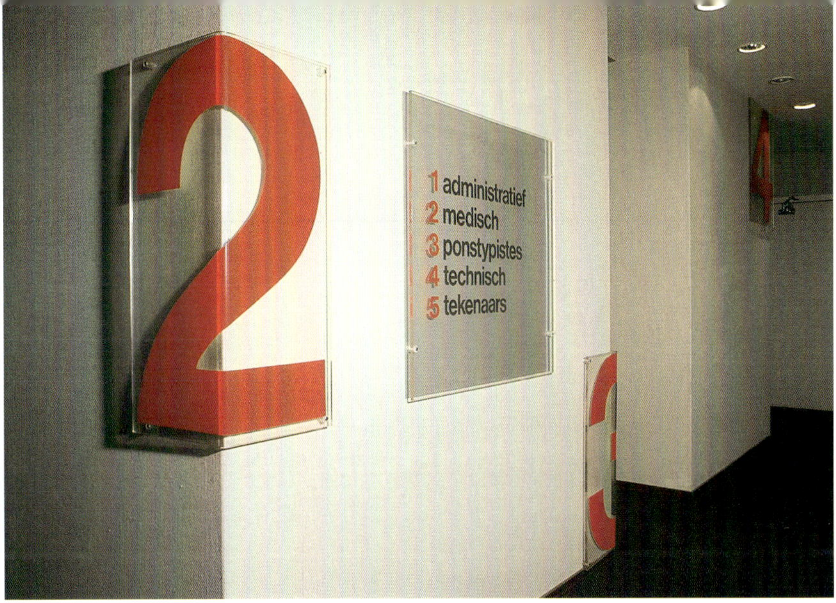

1978
Routing system
Branche office Dam, Amsterdam

1979
New Year's poster
Photography by Marcel Minee

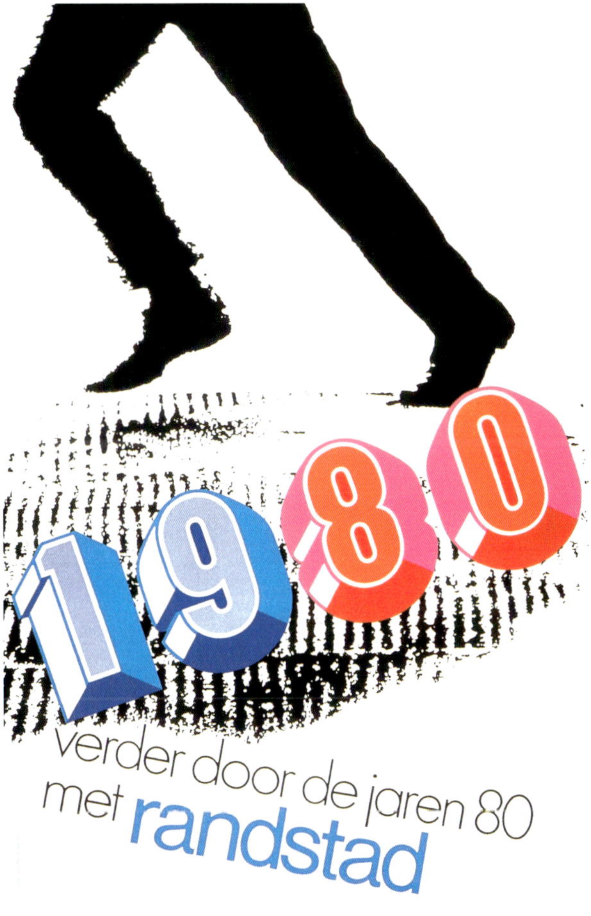

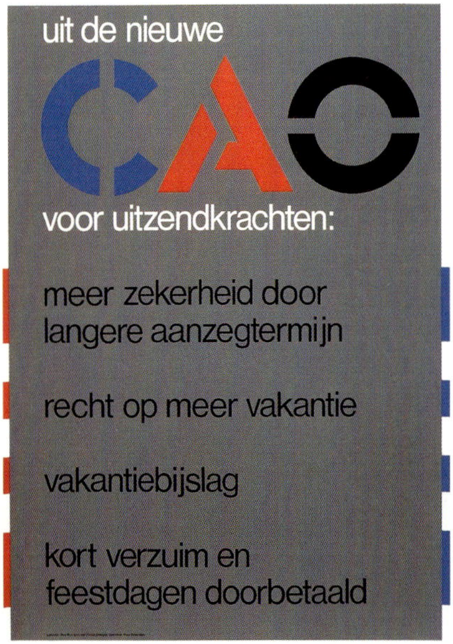

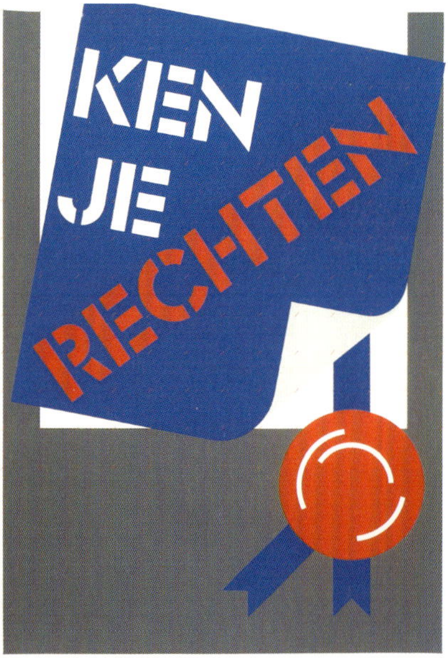

1980
Posters on the rights of temporary workers

1980
Logo and corporate identety GSI Groupe Services Industrie
Cleaning company, Paris
A Randstad subsidiary

1982
'Randstad Data'
Quarterly magazine
Photography by Ben Bos

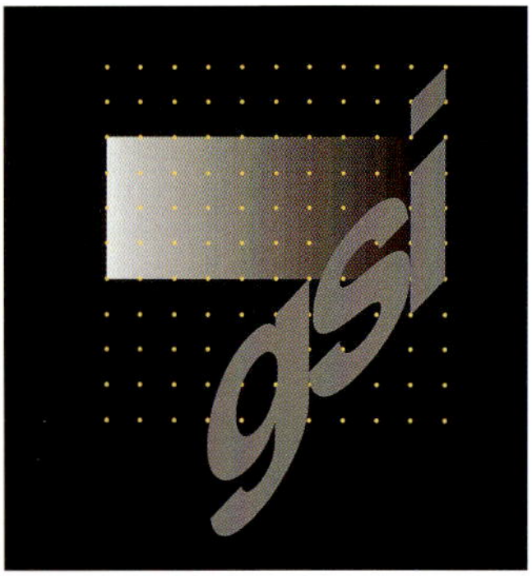

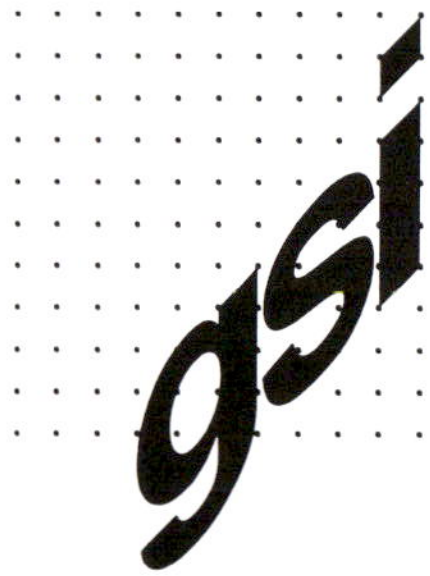

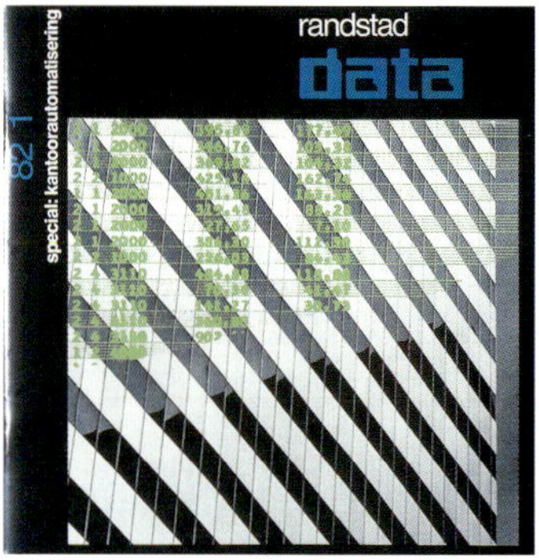

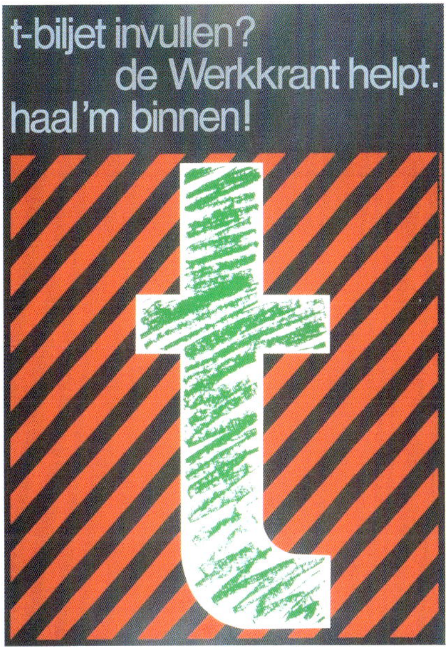

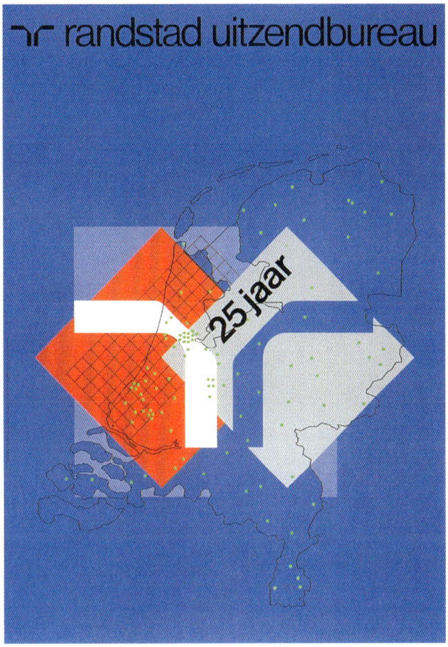

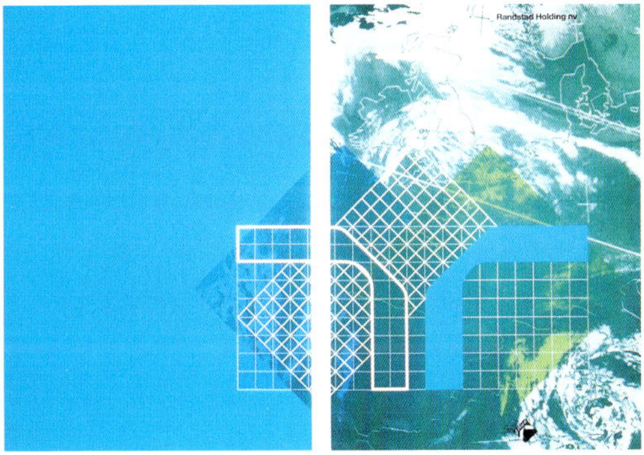

1982
Poster on taxes

1985
Poster commemorating 25 years of Randstad

1985
Cover of annual report
In collaboration with Wim Verboven
and Joost Klinkenberg
Jubilee logo by Ben Bos

1986
Cover and diagram from annual report 1985

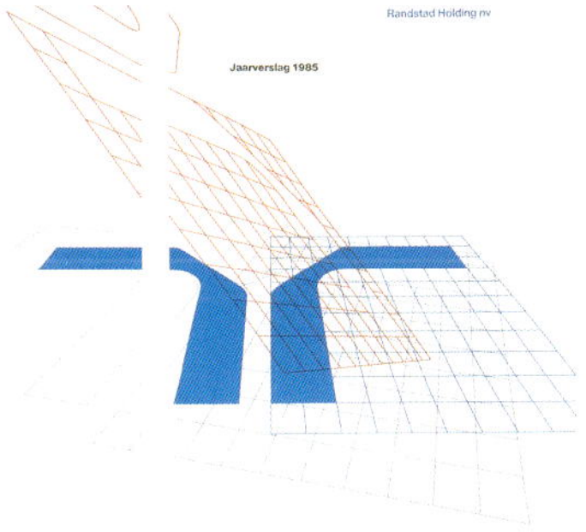

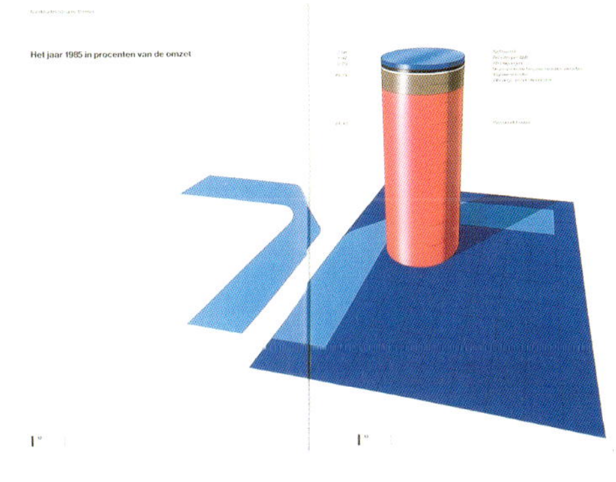

1986

Poster series on the topic ‘yes’

Distributed in the Netherlands and Germany

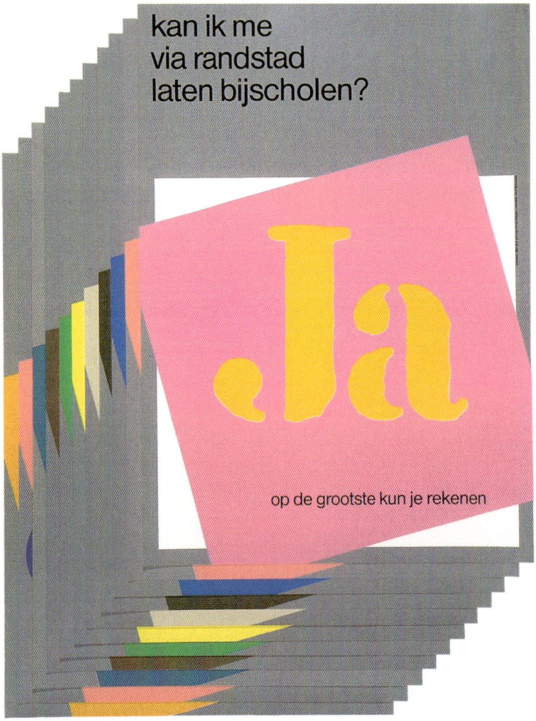

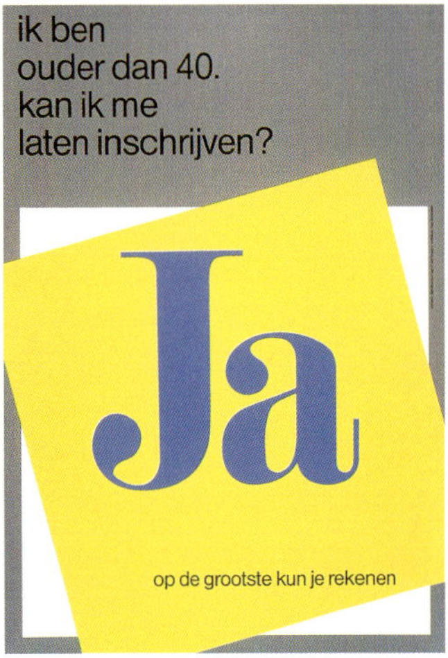

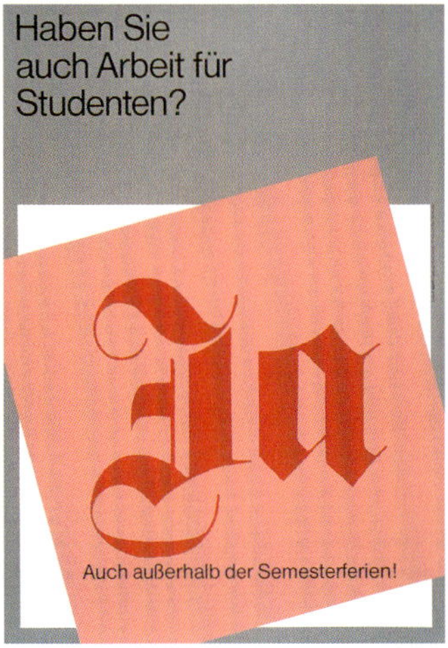

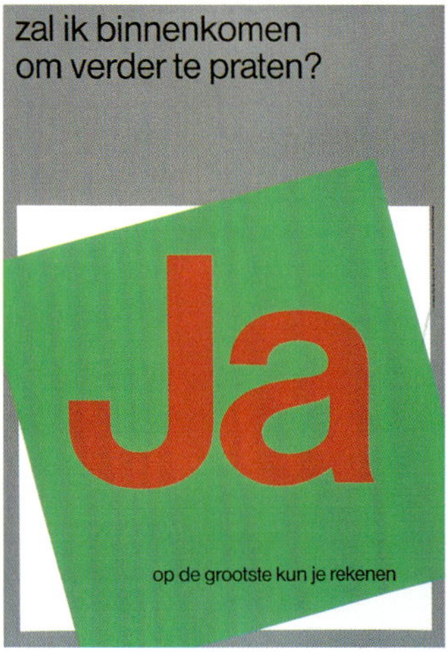

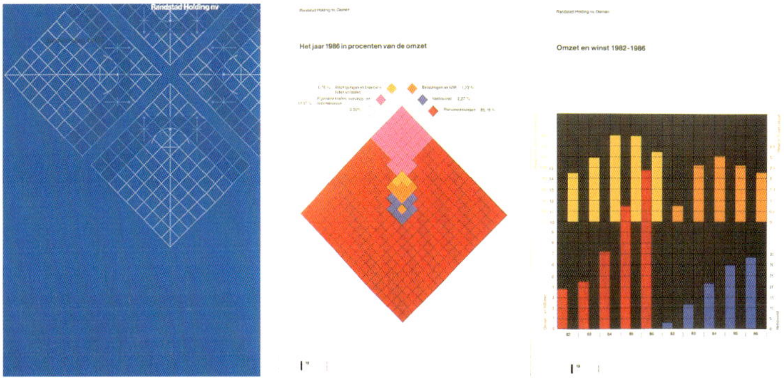

1987
Cover and diagrams annual report 1986

1987
'Wrapping' of five floors of Art Deco housefront
During the restoration of the Utrecht branch office

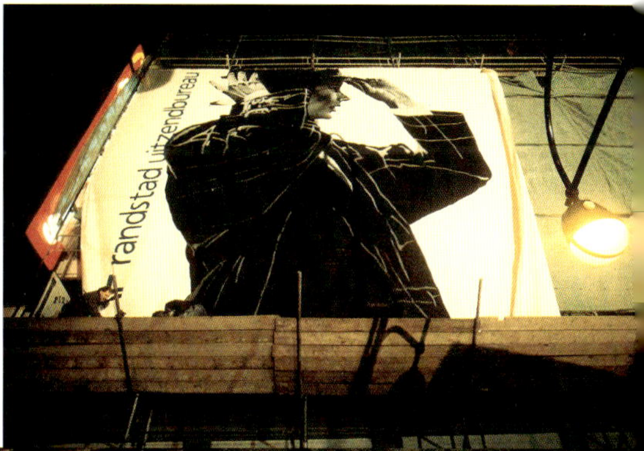

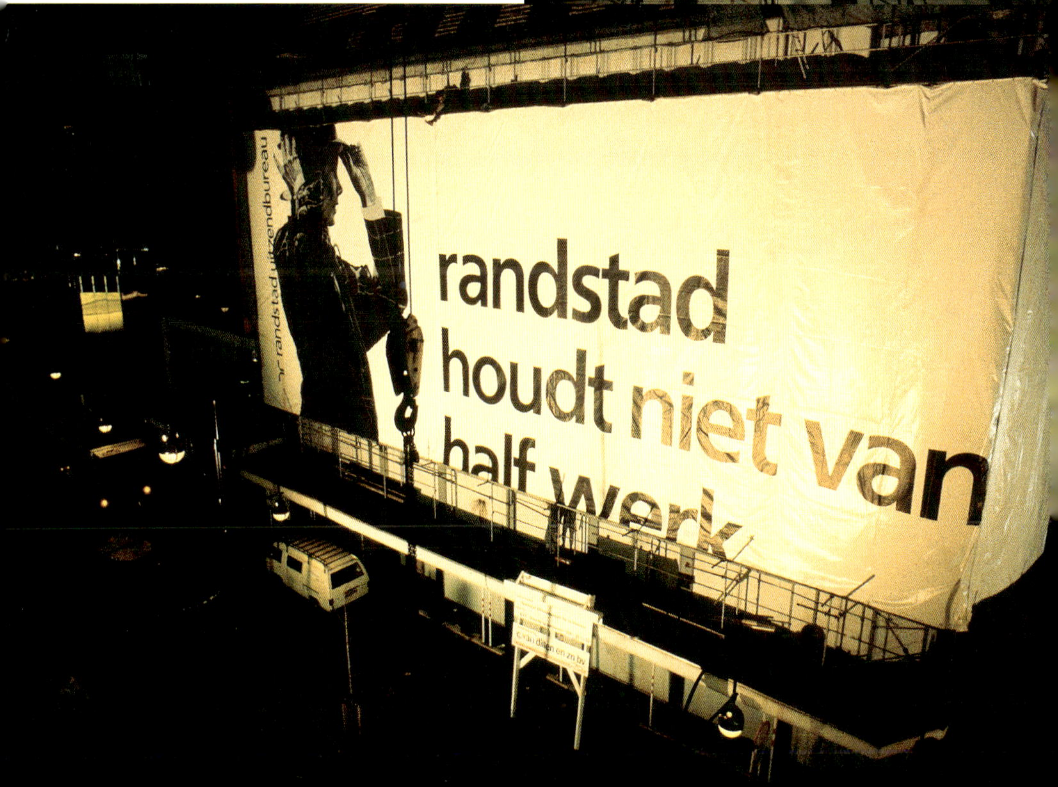

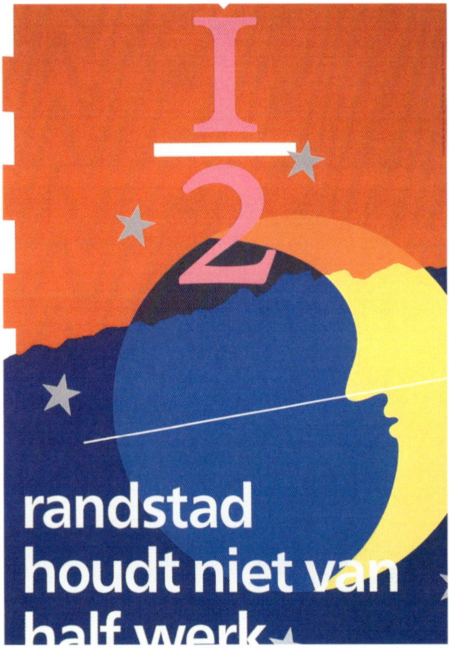

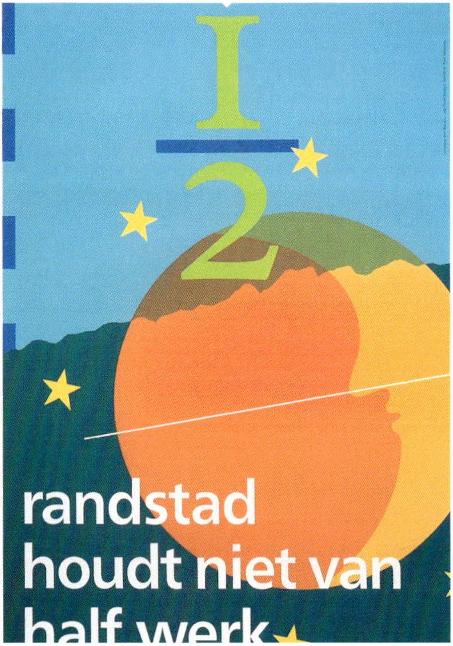

1988
Posters

1988
Routing system
Head office, Diemen

1988
Architectural lettering
Head office, Diemen
Architect Wim Quist

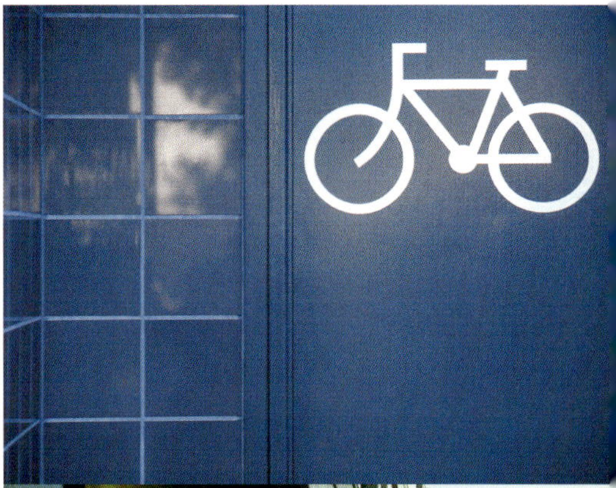

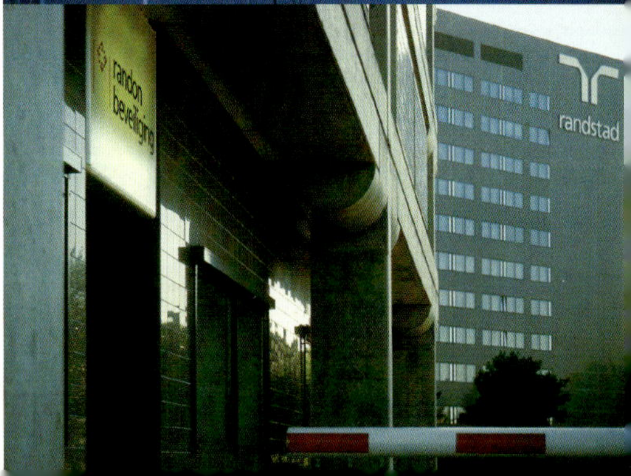

A fighter

Wim Verboven started working for Total Design in 1974 and left in early 1992, briefly after Ben Bos. He had gained experience as a draughtsman at a design studio. However, before long Bos decided that Verboven had much more to offer and promoted him to assistant designer. Verboven currently is manager of Design Connection in Amsterdam.

In Ben's team I did a lot of work for Randstad. Although I did work under his direction, my position became increasingly independent. If Ben put confidence in you, you gradually got more opportunities for doing things on your own. He never pressurized me. He was quite emotional and had many moods, but that didn't bother me. I gradually bonded with him and that bond is still there.

At the end of his Total Design period Ben was no longer allowed to interfere with policy and that came as a big blow to him. Anyway, Total Design was already past its prime then. The seventies had been its greatest period.

The clients did not yet know a lot about design and were persuaded by the designers of the importance of giving their company an identity. The attitude of clients began to change then.

There were two 'houses' at the Herengracht, the old one and the new one, between which there existed a certain amount of rivalry. We were in the second house. A lot of hard work was done there and Ben earned the money for Total Design. The old house concentrated on the cultural projects, which weren't quite so profitable. Nevertheless we operated in the shadow of the Crouwelites and Ben was quite sensitive about that. Still, he was a fighter, as tenacious as a terrier and he stayed put. The arrival of the Aesthedes caused many internal changes. It sort of upset everything. It was also a period of discussion on principles. That caused tension, while there also existed tension in other areas. Ben en Anthon Beeke did not get along, for instance. They threw pencils at each other during heated arguments and for a long time there was an ink stain on a wall as a silent witness to one of those vehement discussions.

The aims of Jelle van der Toorn, the new deputy manager, were really at odds with the Total Design philosophy: lucidity in design. The Aesthedes that he so fervently advocated was really just a new toy: look what wonderful tricks the computer can do. That sometimes was at the expense of the message. The older generation had difficulty accepting that, and so did Ben. He was a great admirer of Pentagram, where they didn't use computers either at that time. Ben is a real craftsman, someone who uses his hands. On top of that, his views differed from Crouwel's. He was more humane, partly as a result of his temperament and commitment. That was Ben's forte and that was reflected in his designs, which nevertheless were always lucid and full of contrast.

He also was quick at finding solutions. When he left a meeting in which he had been given a commission, he already started preparations in the car on the way back. At the studio he quickly outlined the design on paper. He is able to see through certain problems and propose solutions at great speed. That was a very useful lesson to me. When he had thought up something, he passed the commission on to me and let me work it out. He didn't interfere from that point onwards.

Ben did have certain principles, like about dress code. I often wore a corduroy jacket on my visits to the Furness management. A photographer told me that Ben would say: 'Unbelievable that this boy goes to that meeting wearing a coalman's jacket. I don't get it.' But he didn't let you down. He could snort when you did a presentation and that used to make me very insecure. He was capable of unsettling people quite badly. I have seen many women in tears. Ben also had some prejudices. He believed that women couldn't draw perspective.

But he himself could also be unsettled. I remember a management meeting at the Nationale Investeringsbank. He had made a logo that had been approved by the management. We only had to show it to the chief typists, in a room filled with twelve women. One of the older ladies asked Ben: 'Did you make up that 'f' all by yourself?' Ben had no reply to such a lethal remark and passed the commission on to me. He never went back there.

He could also be authoritarian, not just towards the designers ('I can get ten others instead of you') but also towards clients. He would simply say: 'This is good.' In other words: Take it or leave it. In those days you got away with that. Such behaviour is no longer possible.

You didn't learn to do speak that way at the academy, you had to develop that by yourself. Ben set an example in that field, too. But I have also learnt a lot from Ben in other respects. His working methods have certainly left their mark on me.

PH

1989
Poster

1990
Book 'Fotografen aan het werk voor Randstad'
(Photographers working for Randstad)
Concept and design Ben Bos

1988
Relief wall
Utrecht branch office

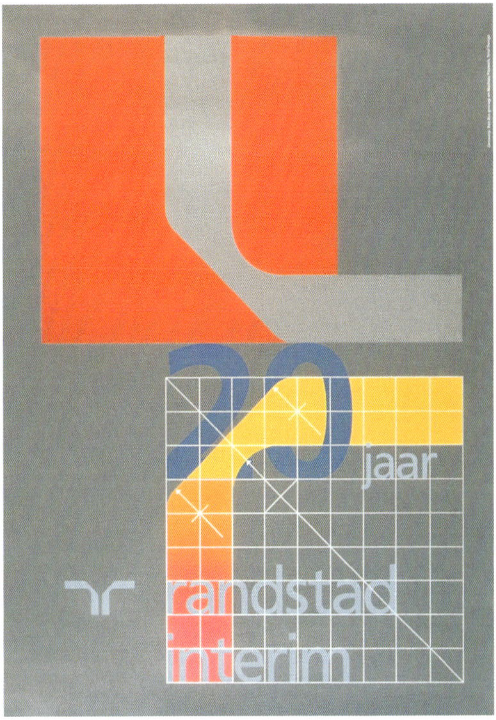

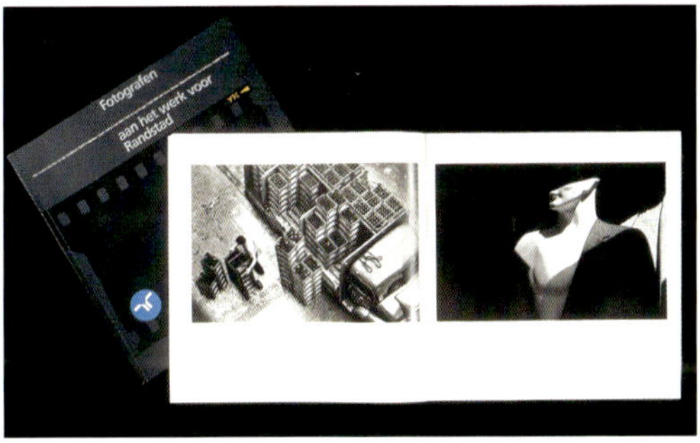

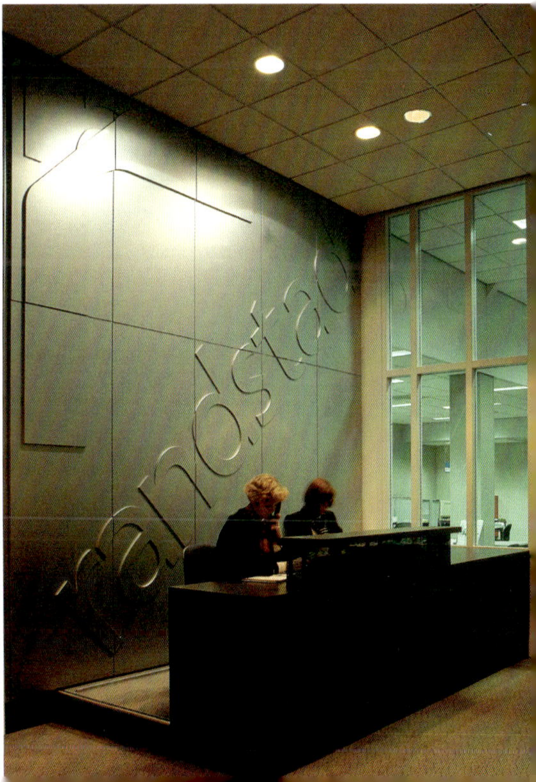

1994
Planning calendar
Randstad Staffing Services, Atlanta

1994
Wall panel Staffing Employee of the Month Award
USA branch offices

1995
Design Manual
In collaboration with
Wim Verboven and Olga IJspeert,
Design Connection bv

randstad
staffing services

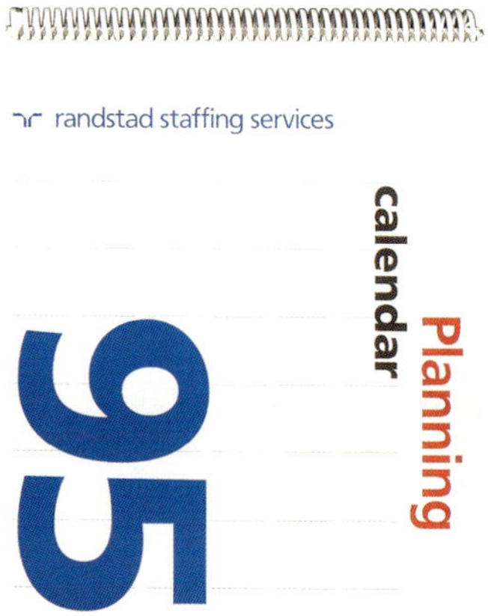

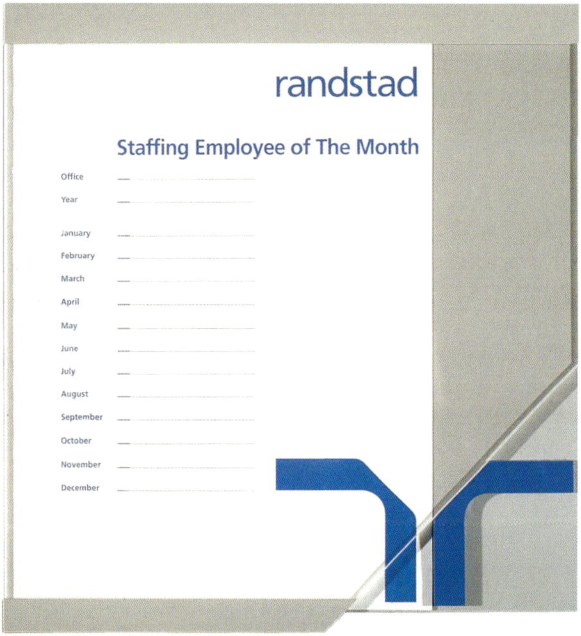

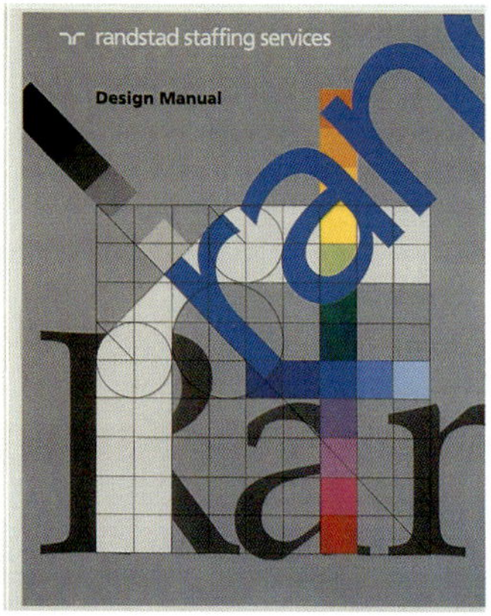

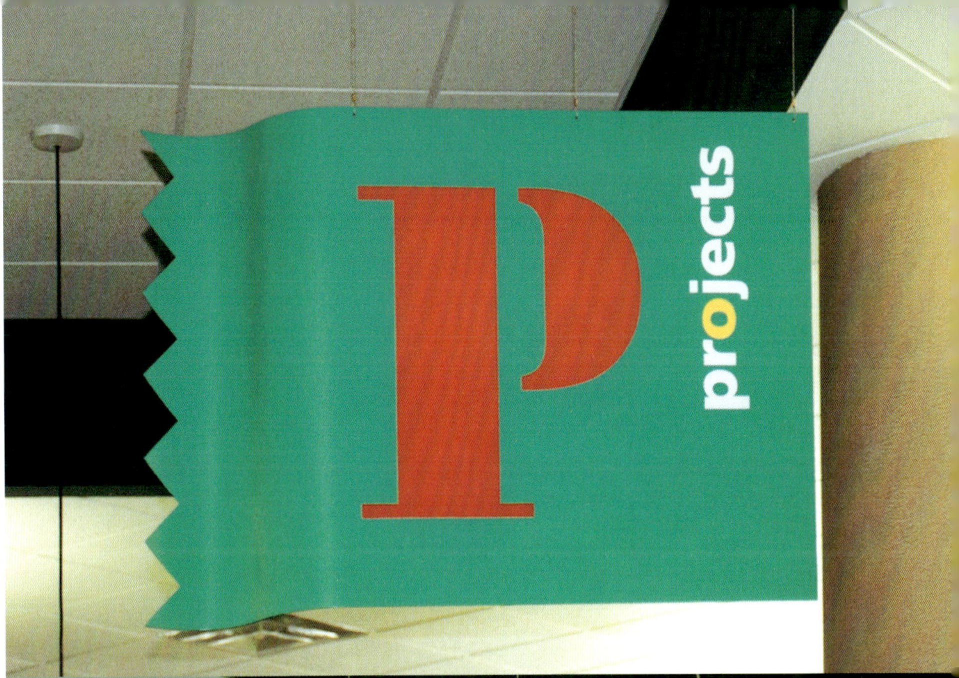

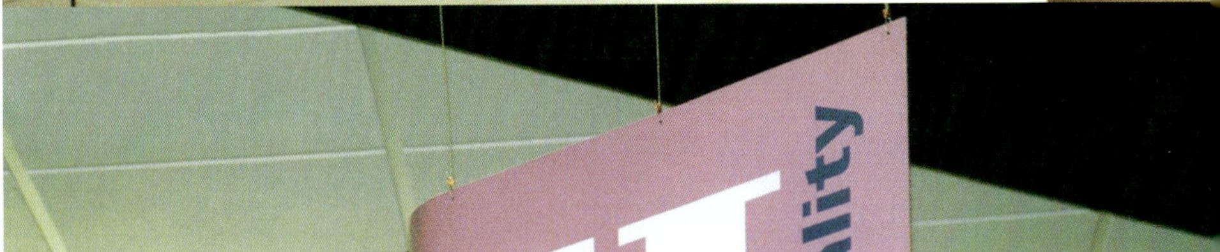

1996
Interior design and routing system
Atlanta

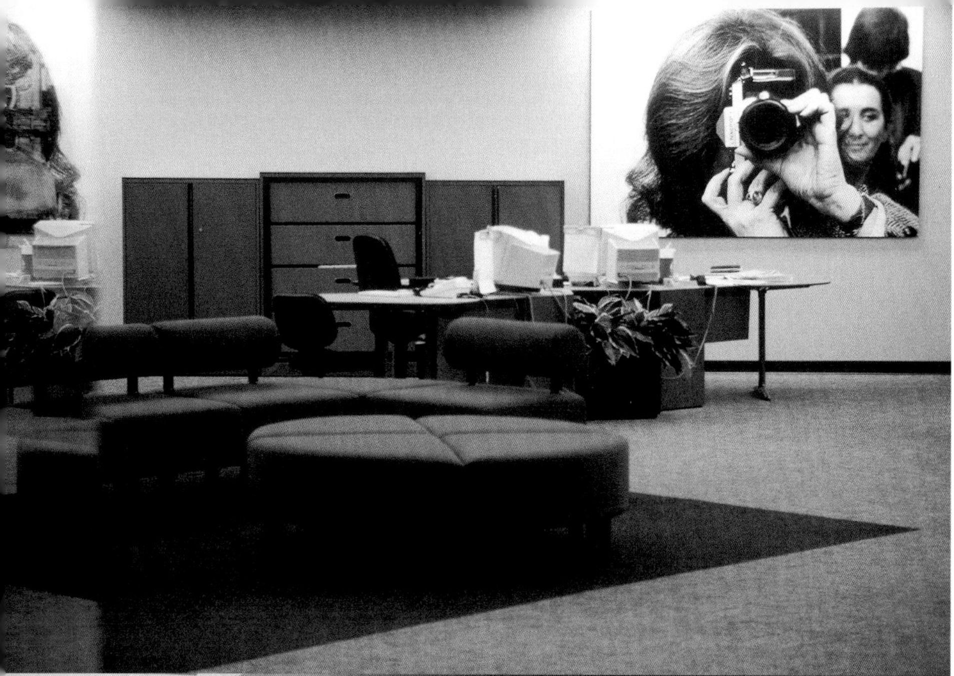

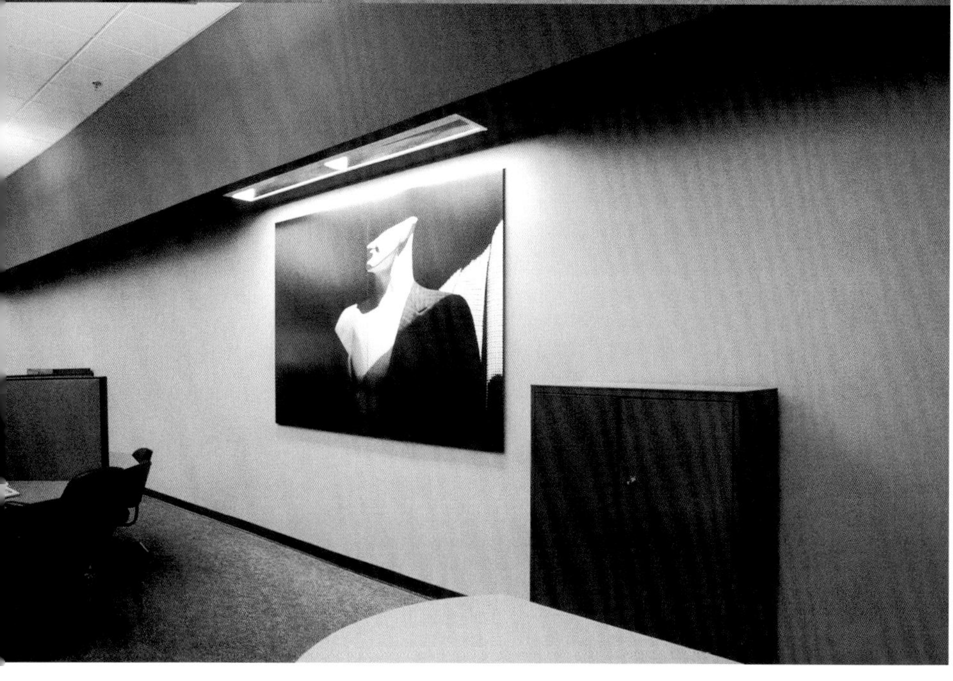

1996
Interior design and routing system
Atlanta

Other projects
1958-2000

1958-1963
Fraay & Korper
Wholesale trade in electronics
and light fittings
Amsterdam

Logo, corporate design,
washing machine brochure

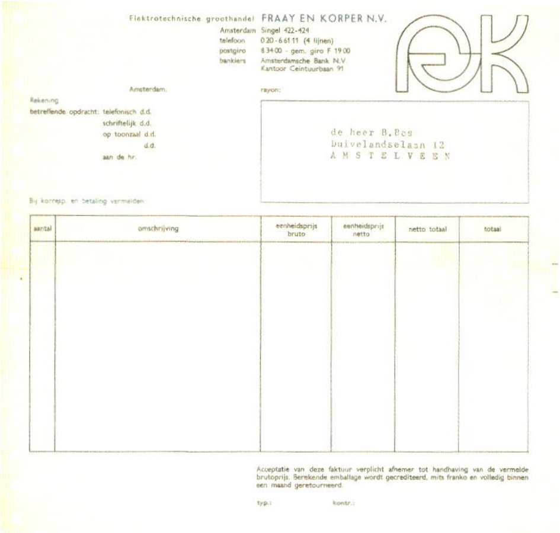

Flektrotechnische groothandel FRAAY EN KORPER N.V.
Amsterdam Singel 422-424
telefoon 020-66111 (4 lijnen)
postgiro 83400 - gem. giro F 1900
bankiers Amsterdamsche Bank N.V.
Kantoor Ceintuurbaan 91

Amsterdam, rayon:

Rekening
betreffende opdracht: telefonisch d.d.
schriftelijk d.d.
op toonzaal d.d.
d.d.
aan de hr.

de heer B. Bos
Duivelandselaan 12
AMSTELVEEN

Bij korresp. en betaling vermelden

aantal	omschrijving	eenheidsprijs bruto	eenheidsprijs netto	netto totaal	totaal

Acceptatie van deze faktuur verplicht afnemer tot handhaving van de vermelde brutoprijs. Berekende emballage wordt gecrediteerd, mits franko en volledig binnen een maand geretourneerd.

typ.: kontr.:

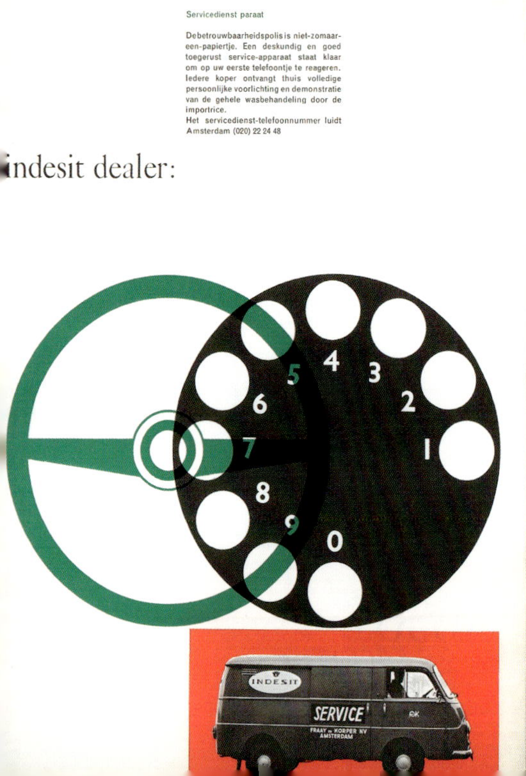

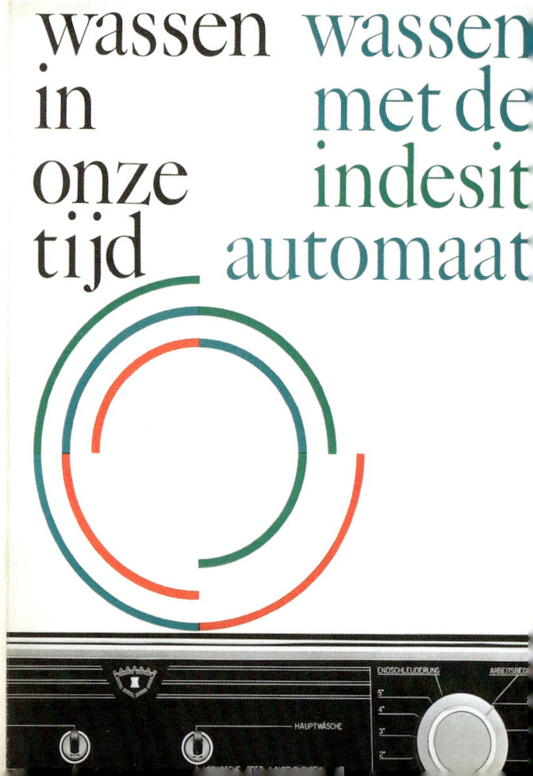

1960
Bureau Van Lee
Insurance consultant
Alkmaar

Logo, corporate design

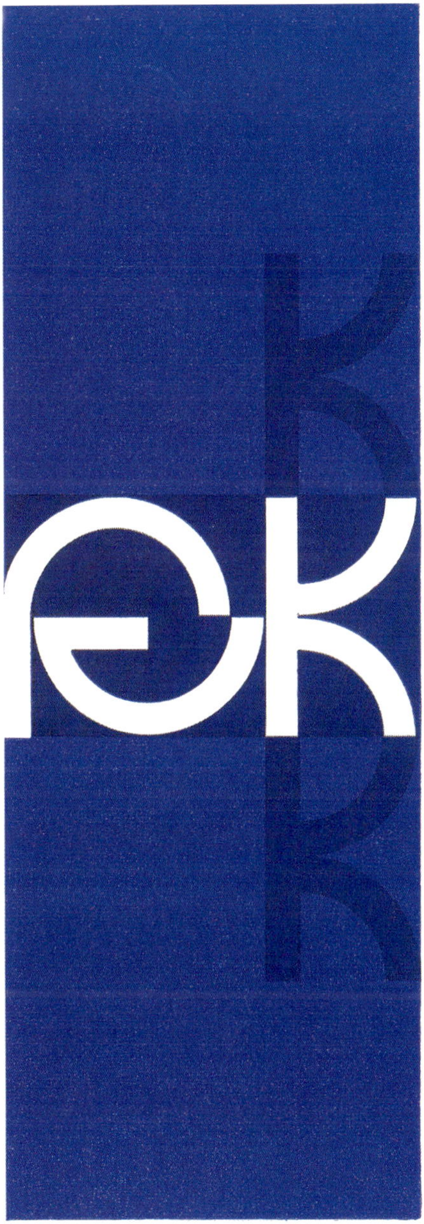

een ander dak
een nieuw jasje

BUREAU VAN LEE (onafhankelijke verzekeringsadviseurs)

is onlangs verplaatst naar het pand*
Jan de Heemstraat 5, Alkmaar.
Het nieuwe postadres luidt: postbus 168 Alkmaar,
het nieuwe telefoonnummer (02200) 15200,
privé-nummer J. J. van Lee (02200) 12273

Terzelfdertijd is ons 'vogeltje gevlogen'
en hebben wij ons een nieuw vignet laten aanmeten
dat wij gaarne bij u introduceren:
het doolhof van mogelijkheden in het verzekeringsbedrijf,
waarin wij u graag tot gids zullen blijven.

*gebouw B.V.A.B., Bedrijfsvereniging voor het Agrarisch Bedrijf
kantoortijden 8.15 - 12.15, 13.15 - 17.15 uur, 's zaterdags gesloten.

1957-1991
Hulp voor Onbehuisden
(Aid for the Homeless)
Amsterdam

Logo, 1969

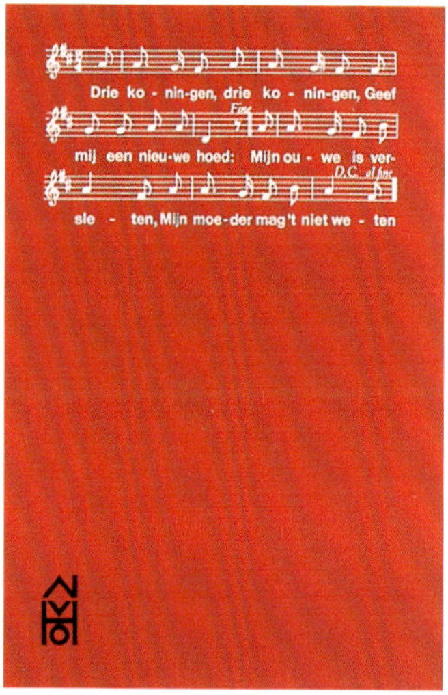

Hulp voor Onbehuisden
For this organisation Bos produced the members' magazine and the annual reports. Several times annually he also produced the 'begging folders', which he both wrote and designed.
He occasionally did special projects, such as the interior design of director Onko Heldring's office and the information desk at the head office. From the bottom of the stairs a rainbow appears to be spanned on the wall behind the desk. However, on reaching the top of the stairs the visitor sees it is the top of a big question mark.

Bos also participated in the action for the Mothers' and Children's Shelter in the Roggeveenstraat which the city refused to fund: 'We placed scaffolding against the front, filled it with dilapidated prams and put Heldring's own bed behind the front door. He spent a couple of nights there, until the publicity which this generated made the municipality change its mind.'

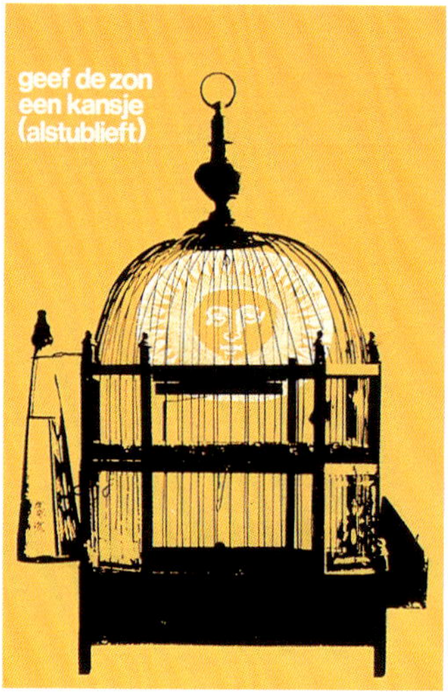

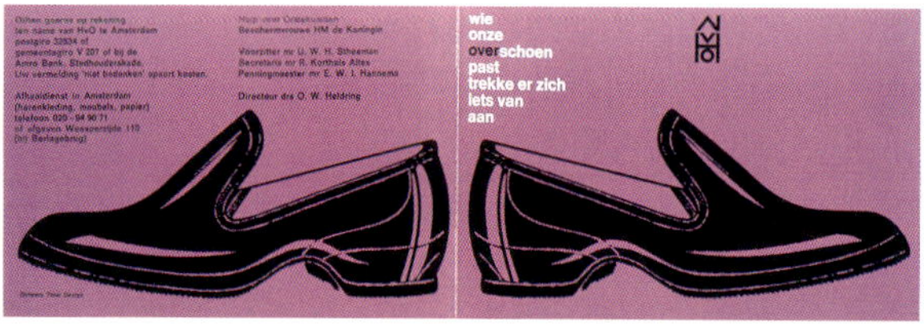

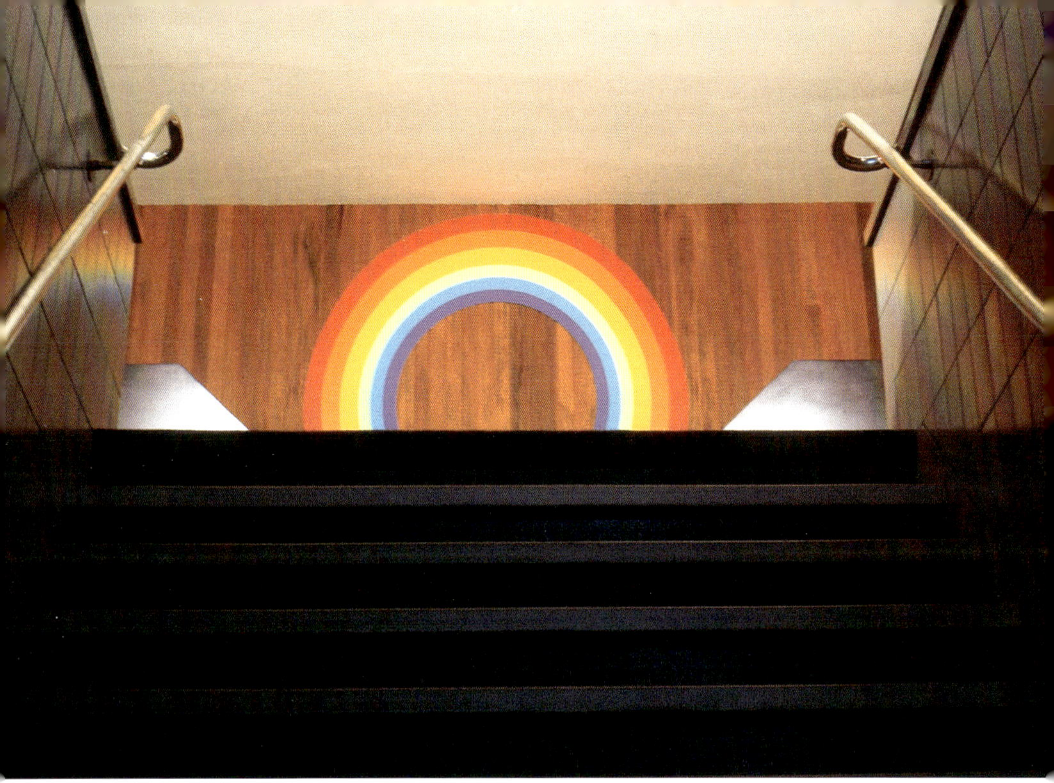

de beenruimte
in het vliegtuig
naar Dar es Salaam
is ons
beslist te krap

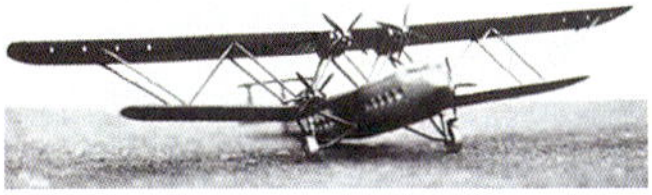

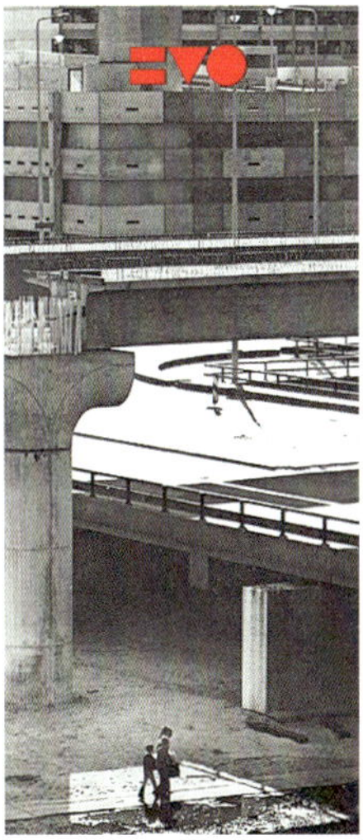

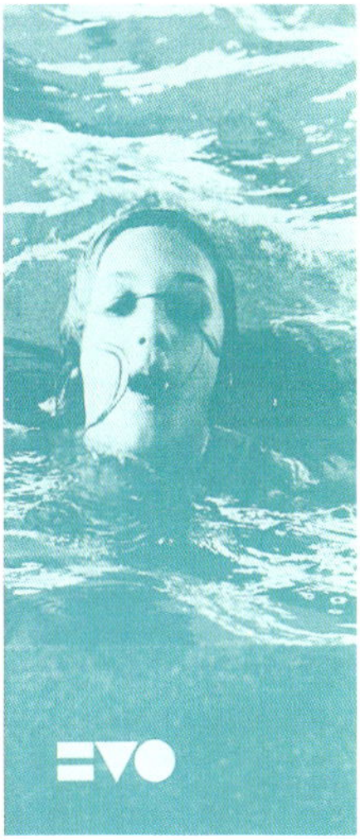

1957-1991

Hulp voor Onbehuisden

Amsterdam

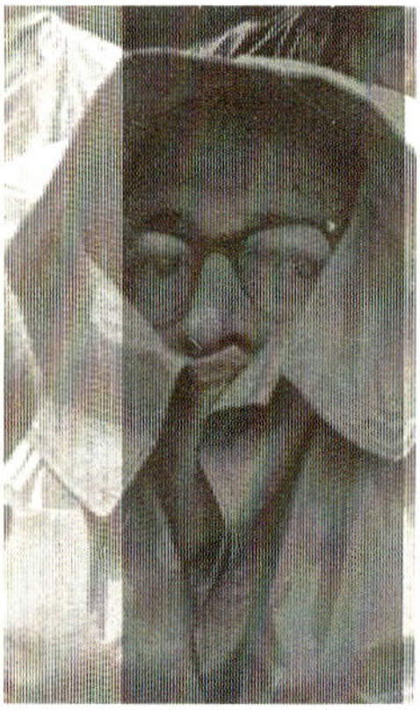

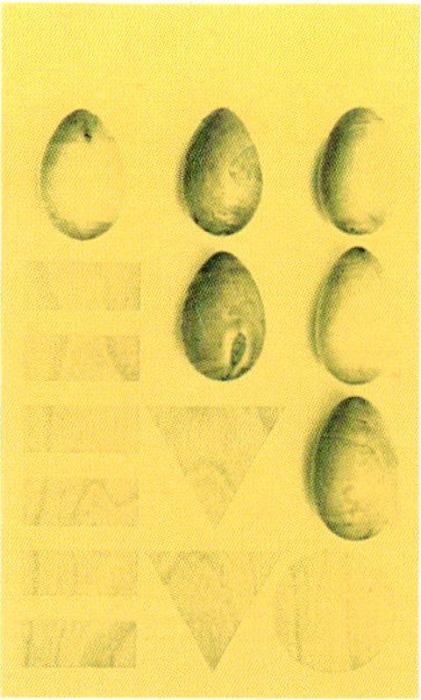

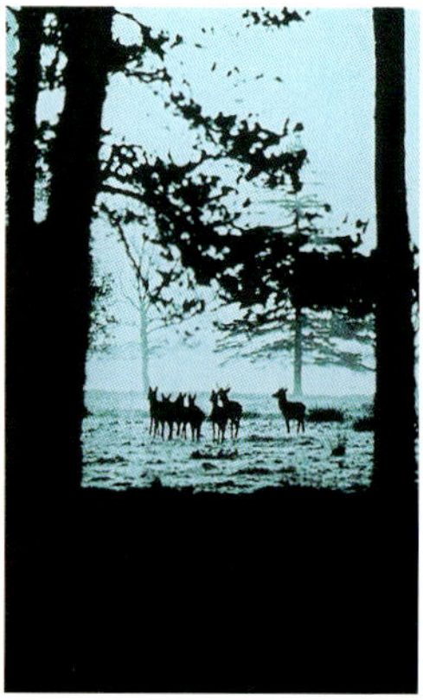

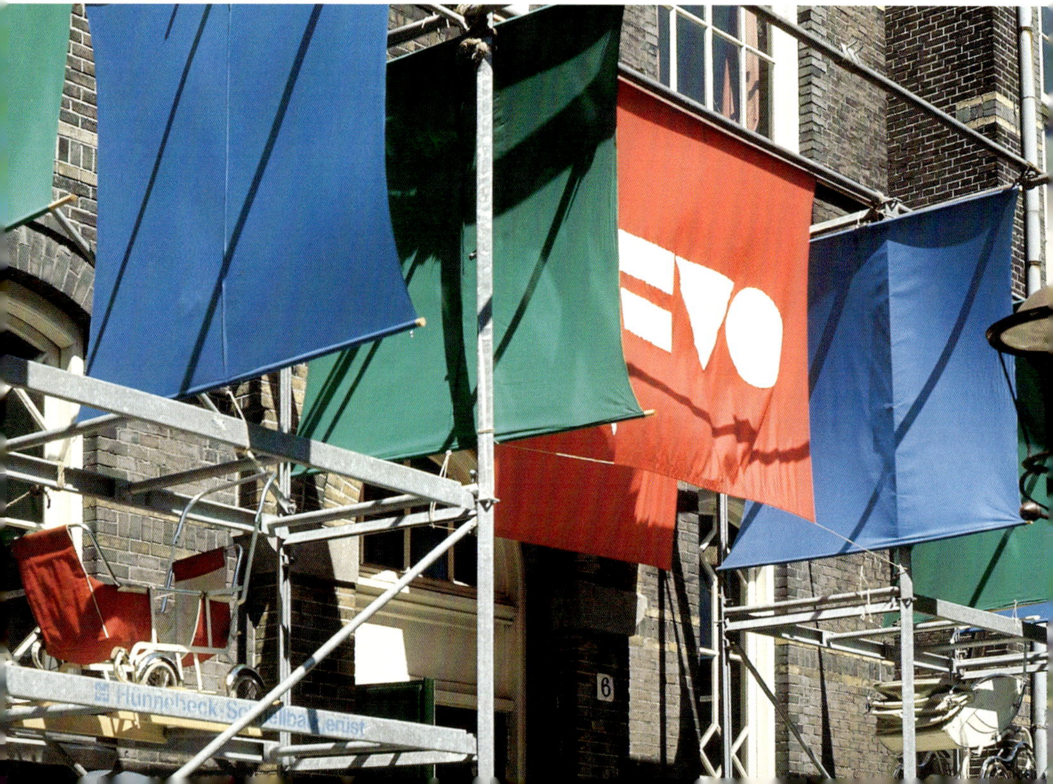

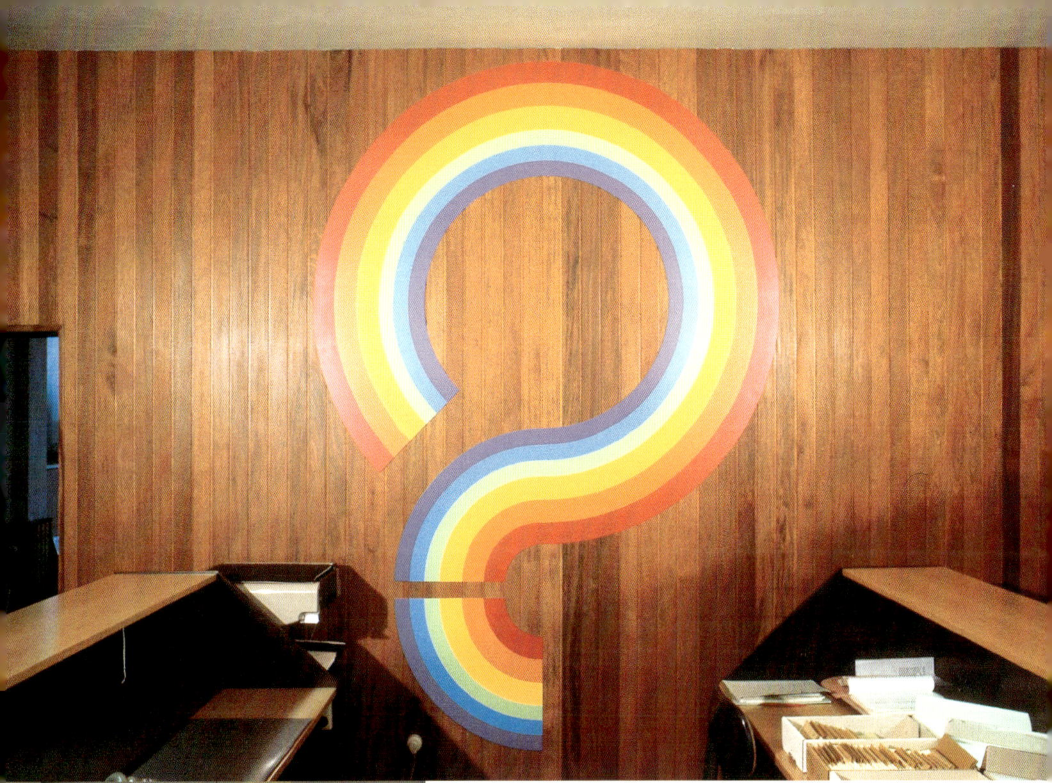

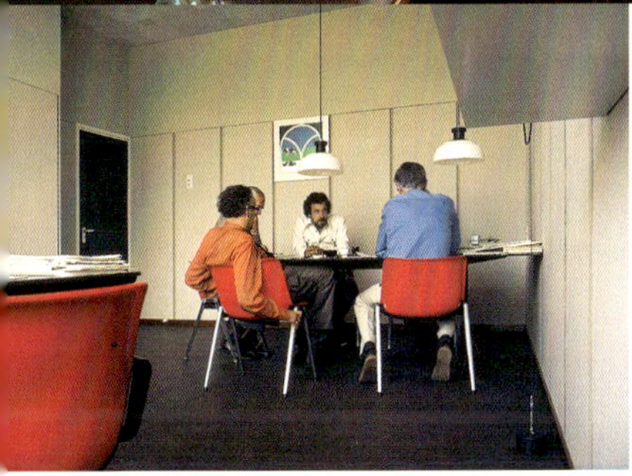

1975
Interior design of manager
O.W. Heldring's office

1960

Calendar for 1961

Drukkerij Erven E. van de Geer

Amsterdam

Texts by Ben Bos
Design by Wim Crouwel
Photography by Eddy Posthuma de Boer

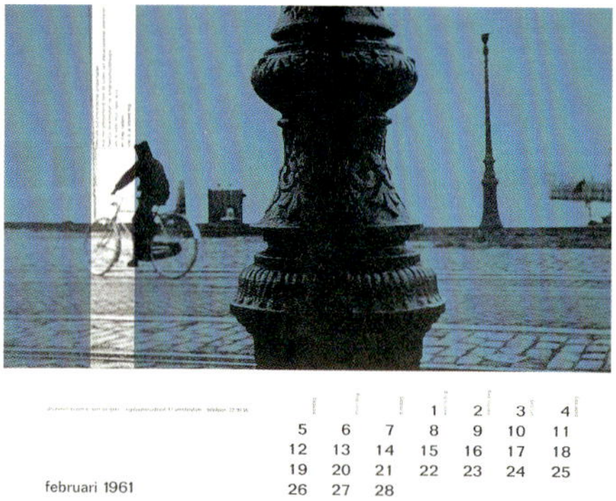

1963

Change of address card

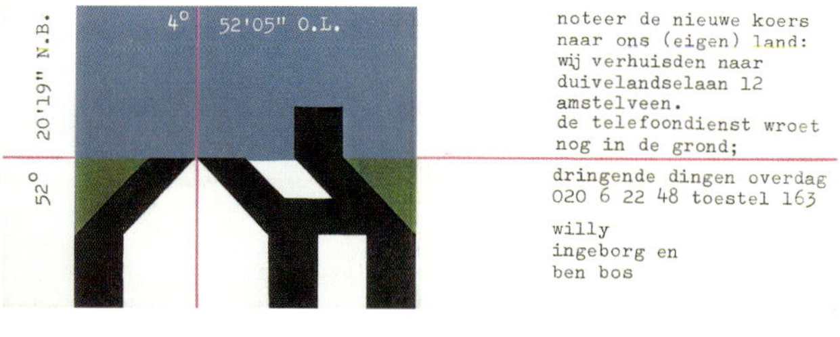

january

when all the wheels
hurtle out of central station
the father in the pulpit falls silent
only to continue
when the sign is at clear
and the voice triumphs over the monster

june

the man who said
that exams should be taken in june
never slept under a tin roof
that had felt the weight
of a high-pressure area

august

on easter monday my dad always took me to the barber
and one year
the man soaped up my face too
and with the steel he cut
more than the hairs on my chin

october

one day
we suddenly feel
how cold the steel
of the moped is
and of the bridge
and of the lamp
and of the sign warning for the man across the street -
and we know this is called october

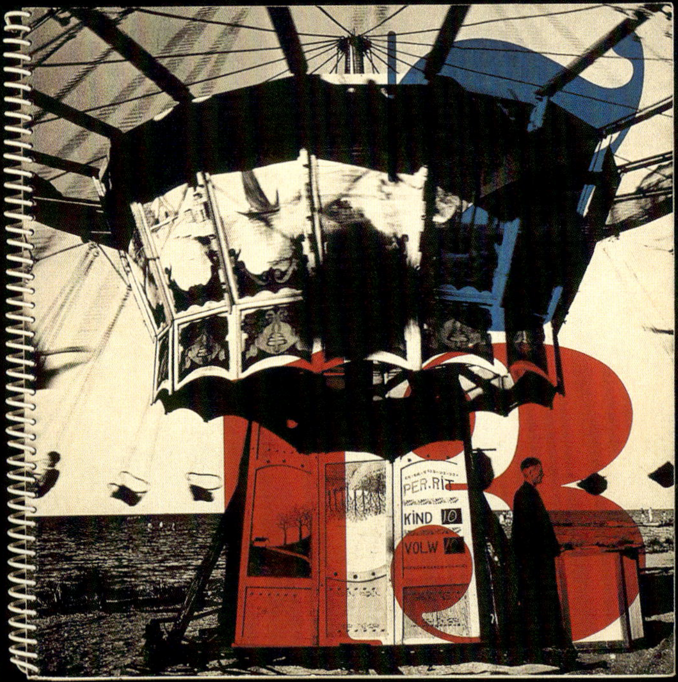

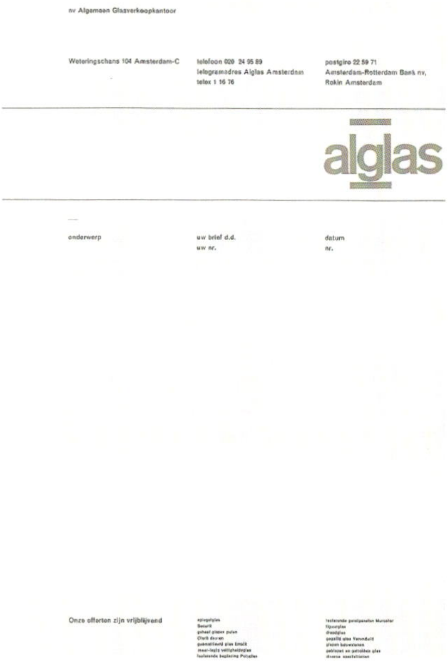

1964
Raad voor het Grootwinkel-bedrijf
(Wholesale Trade Council)
Amsterdam

Book on the introduction of the five-day working week
Photography by Carel Blazer

1964
Alglas
Wholesale trade in construction glass
Amsterdam

Logo, corporate design

1963-1972

Alarma '33

Security and communication
Amsterdam

Logo, printed matter,
product folders and
trade fair stands

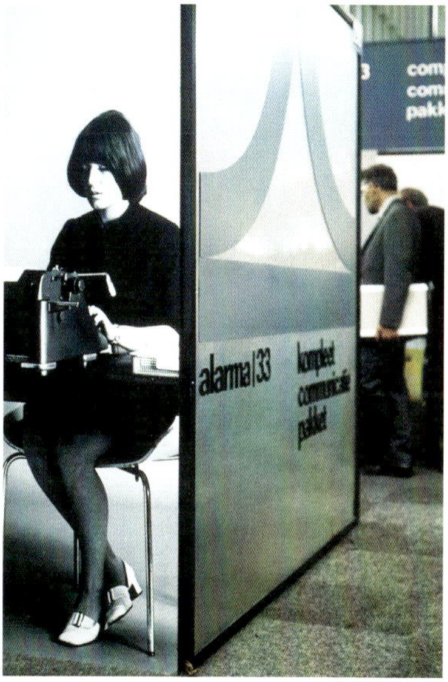

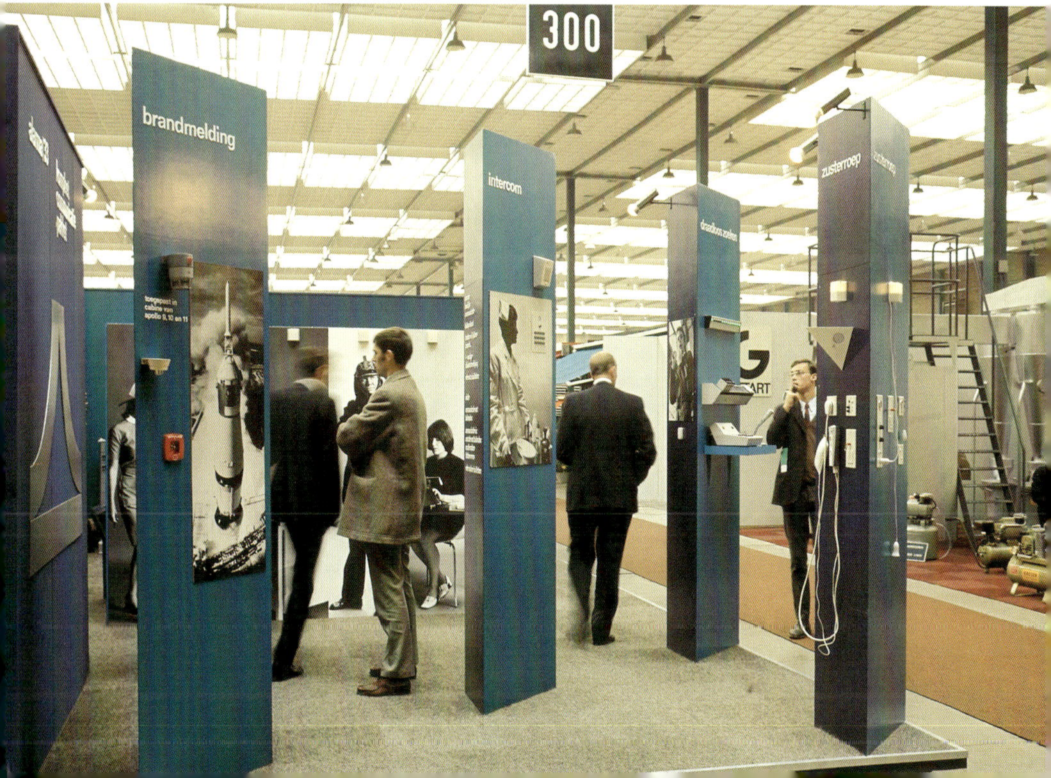

1963-1970

De Bijenkorf

Department store with branches in Amsterdam, The Hague, Rotterdam en Eindhoven

From 1964 to 1970 Ben Bos designed the monthly, abundantly illustrated staff magazine on the basis of a 28 unit grid. On top of this he realized commissions such as photography and film guides, the camping guide, wine specials, the book and record magazines, packaging, clothing labels, a price tag system, information labels, logos, campaign posters. His greatest challenge was the development of an introduction campaign and all of the festive printed matter for the opening of a new branch of De Bijenkorf in Eindhoven in 1969.

1967

Wine catalogue

1965

Mother's Day poster

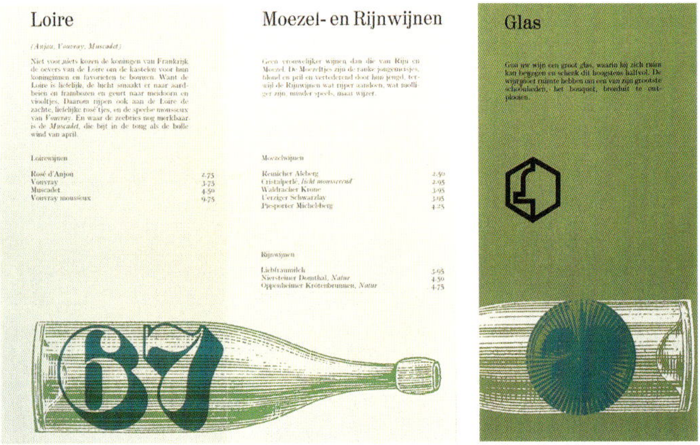

A genuinely instrumental designer

In the late seventies Anthon Beeke joined Total Design to act as a counterbalance to the studio's 'severe appearance'. He already knew Ben Bos from the Instituut voor Kunstnijverheidsonderwijs that they had both attended. Soon after, Beeke would set up his own studio.

Even during his studies Ben was already highly experienced. I was just a youngster, a dirty little dog, really. When I joined Total Design he had his own team, and this team made the money that kept Total Design afloat. Ben was certainly no dreamer. He was the one who had to make sure that everything was finished at full speed.
He was absolutely a professional designer, not an 'artisan.' He was a hard worker, an excellent organiser and a good talker. He was an expert communicator.
Ben was a great admirer of Crouwel, but also held the Swiss typographers in high esteem. He often visited Switzerland. It was a clean, well-organized, well-designed country. That was quite unusual in those days.
With the clarity of his designs Ben Bos carried on the ideal of Total Design and really put into practice the gospel that the studio preached. That is to say, he did not work as an artist, but as a genuinely instrumental designer. Ben was worth his weight in gold to Total Design.
PH

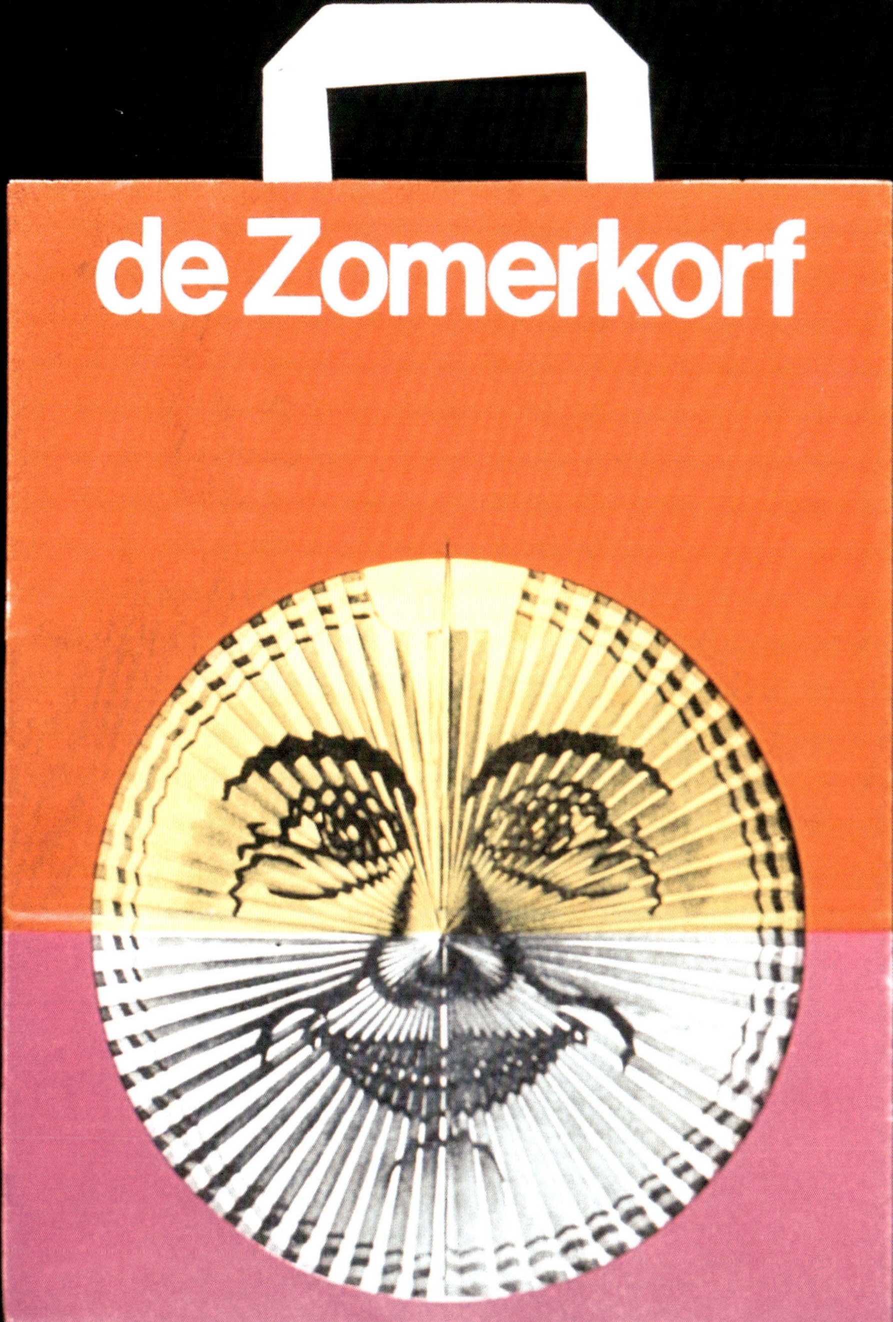
de Zomerkorf

1963-1970

De Bijenkorf

1966/68

Camping product guides

1970

Product information system

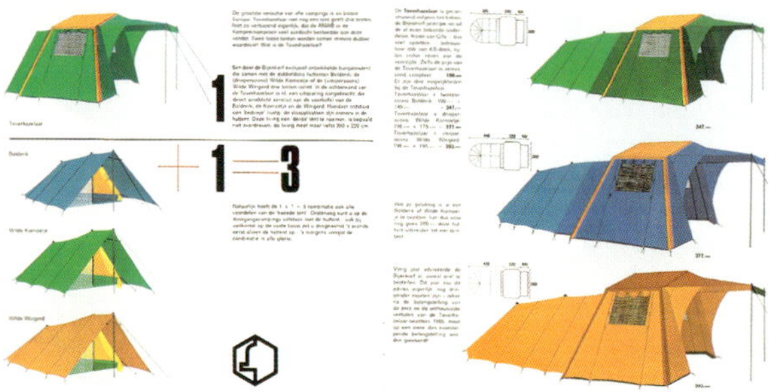

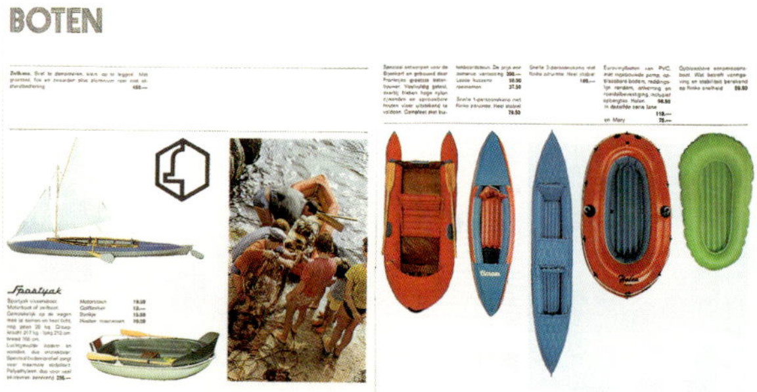

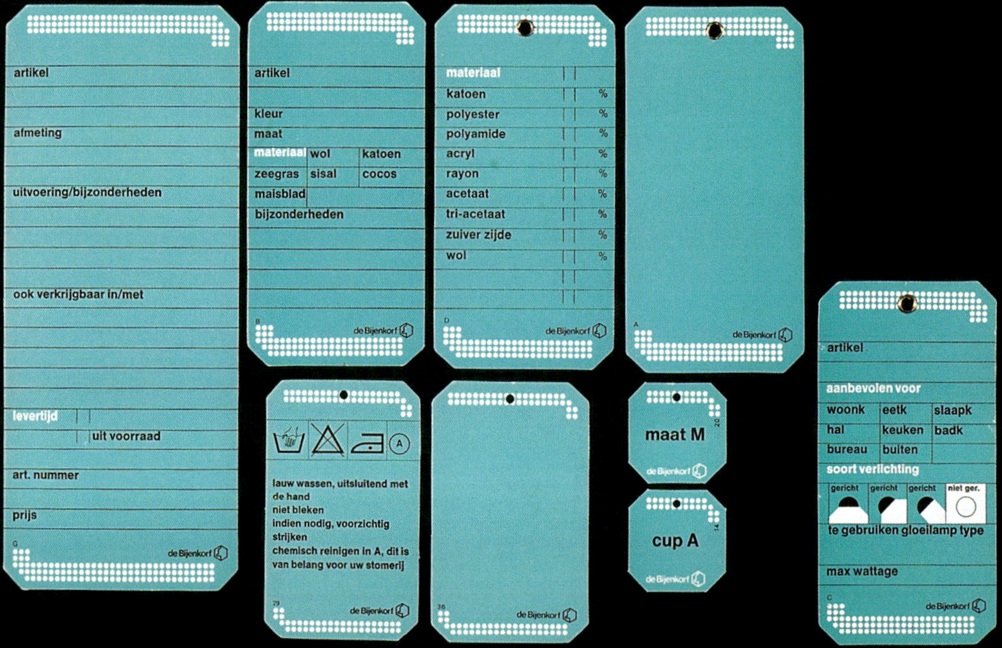

1969
Campaign for the opening of
the Eindhoven branch

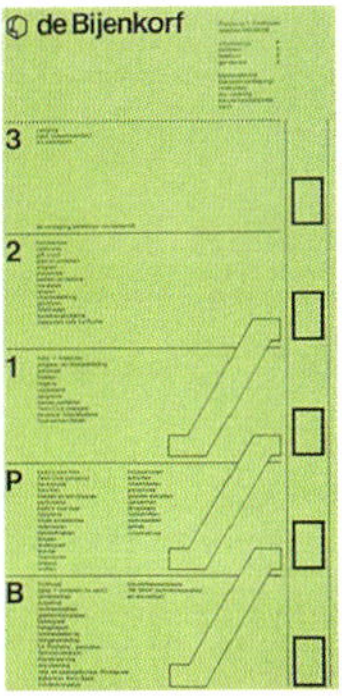

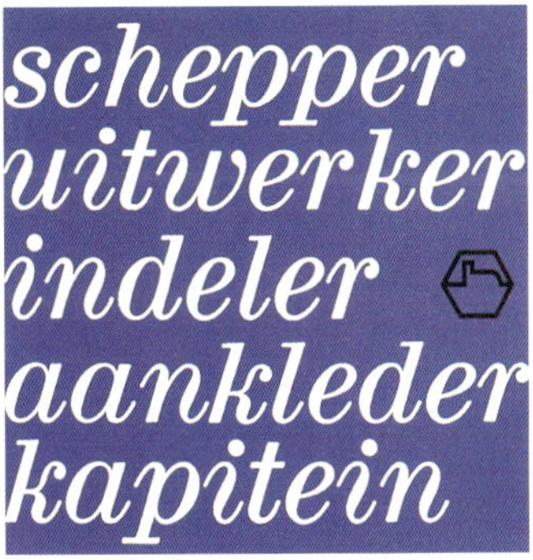

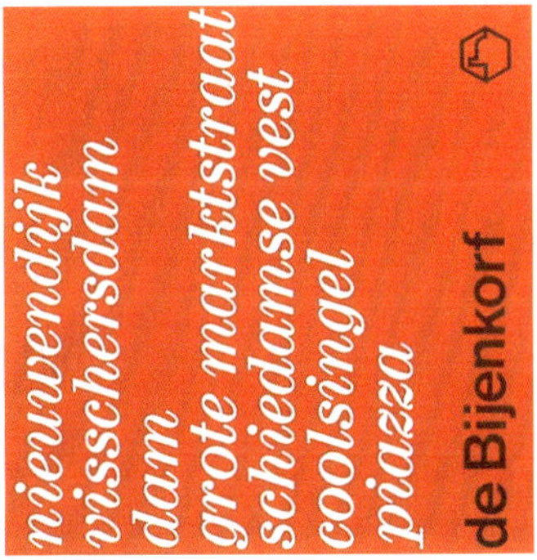

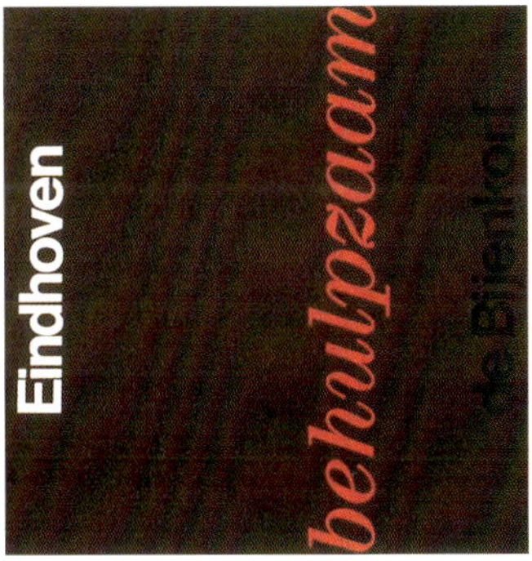

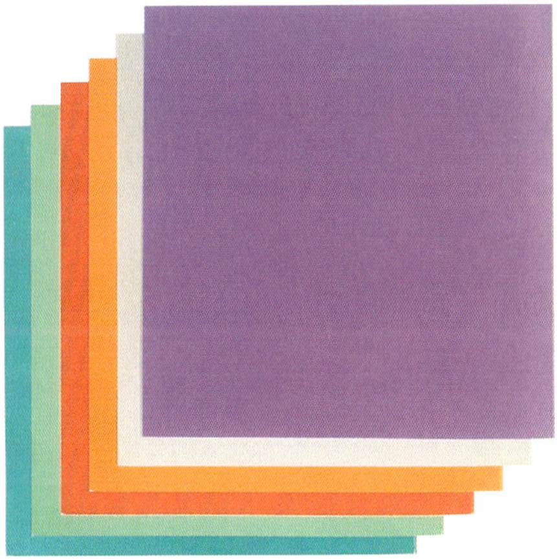

De directie van n.v. Magazijn de Bijenkorf heeft het genoegen
u uit te nodigen
voor een ontvangst op maandag 17 maart a.s. om 9.30 uur
ter gelegenheid van de officiële opening van de nieuwe Bijenkorf in Eindhoven
op 18 maart 1969.
U kunt het gebouw betreden via de ingang aan de piazza.
De heer J. H. Polak
directeur inkoop van n.v. Magazijn de Bijenkorf
zal de bijeenkomst inleiden,
waarna een rondgang door het gebouw zal worden gemaakt.
Na het gebruiken van een aperitief zal de ontvangst
te ongeveer 12.00 uur worden besloten.
Gaarne vernemen wij door middel van bijgesloten antwoordkaart
zo mogelijk voor zaterdag 1 maart a.s.
of op uw aanwezigheid bij deze ontvangst mag worden gerekend.

1963-1970
De Bijenkorf

1967
Logo for Bijenkorf gift services

1967/1969
Carrier bags for wine and records departments

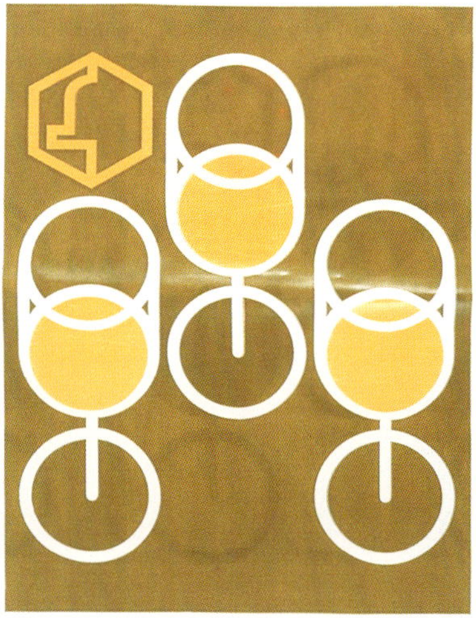

de Bijenkorf

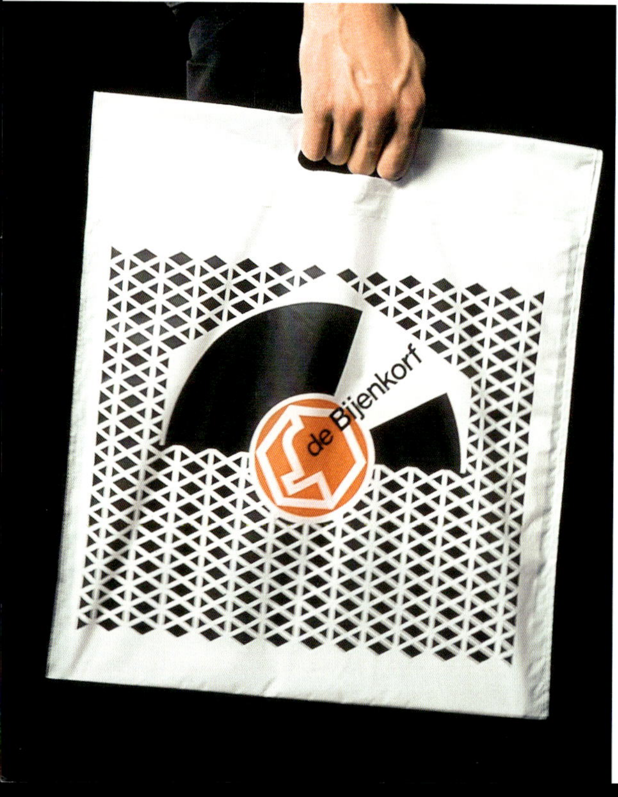

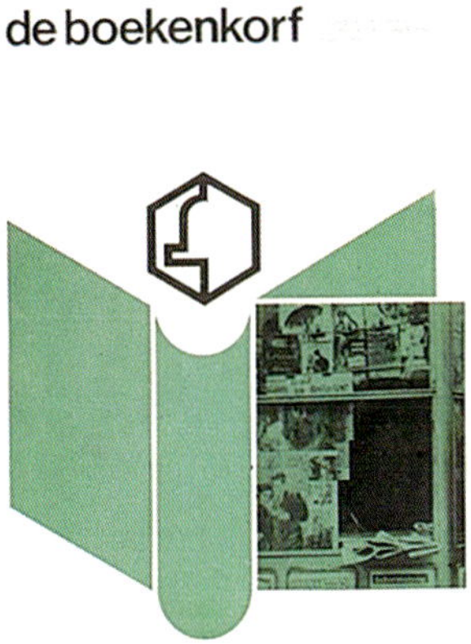

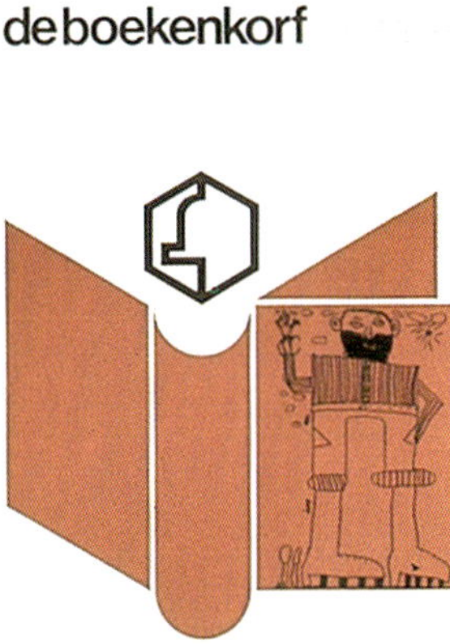

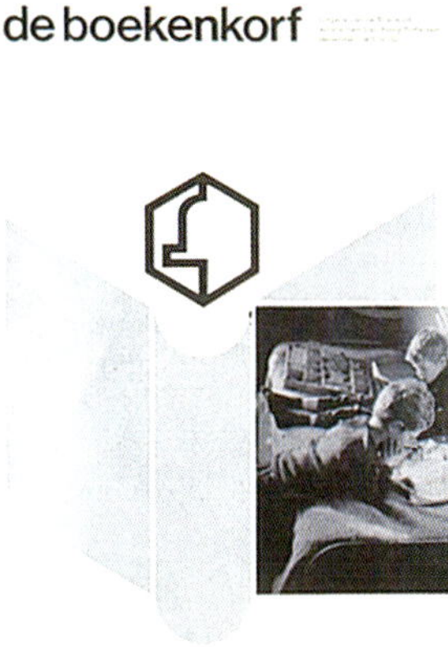

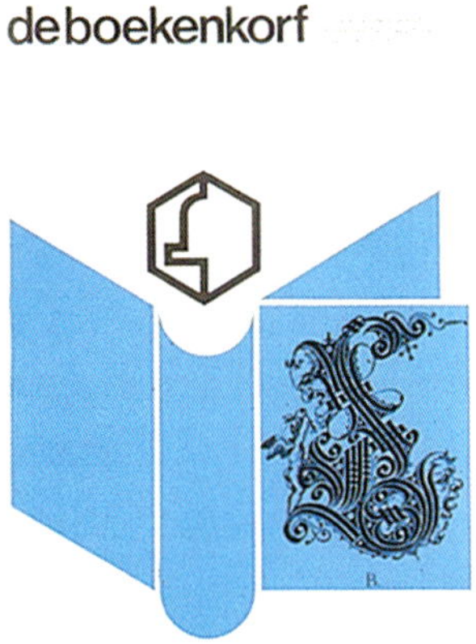

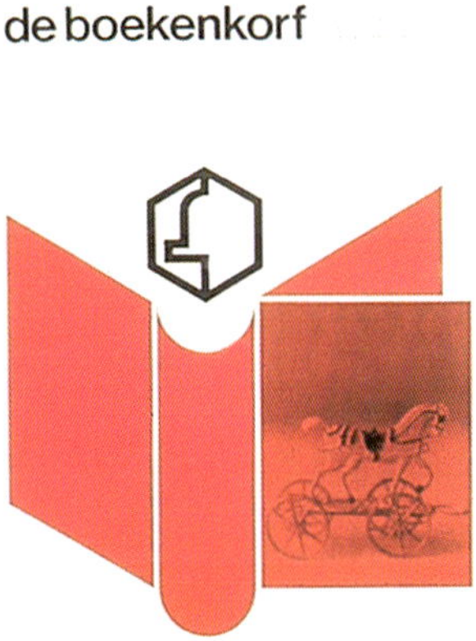

1967
'De Boekenkorf'

BYE
BYE
BIJ

1963-1978
Stichting Kunst & Bedrijf
(Foundation Art & Industry)
Amsterdam

1967
Logo

1971
Book on technology in the visual arts

Book on sites under construction
Photography by Peter Marcuse

1964-1970
Quarterly magazines

From 1963 to the late seventies Bos designed quarterly bulletins and occasional monographs for this organization. The new logo and the visual identity based on it date from 1978.
The early covers reveal the influence of Richard P. Lohse and Joseph Albers, whom Bos greatly admired.

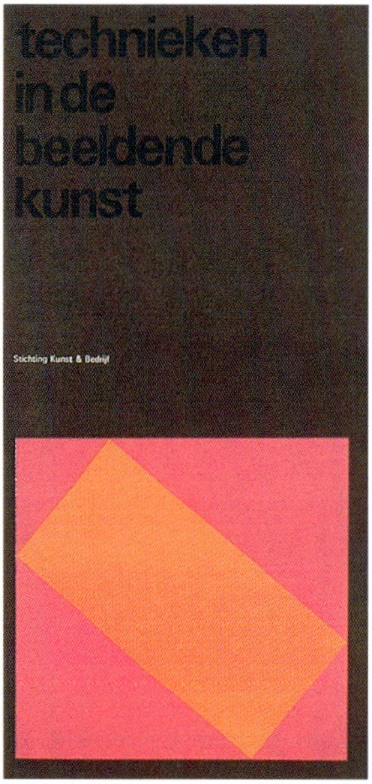

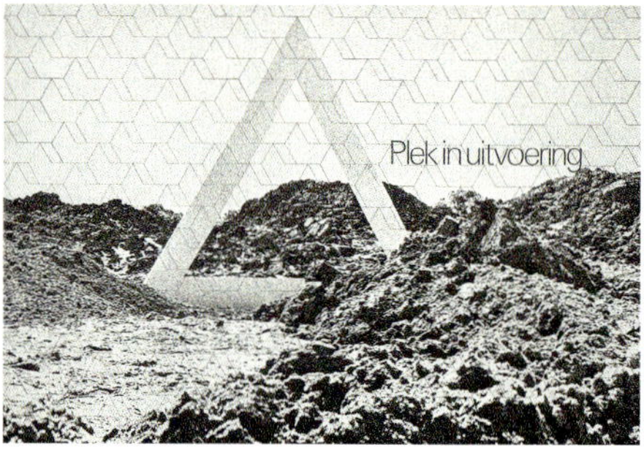

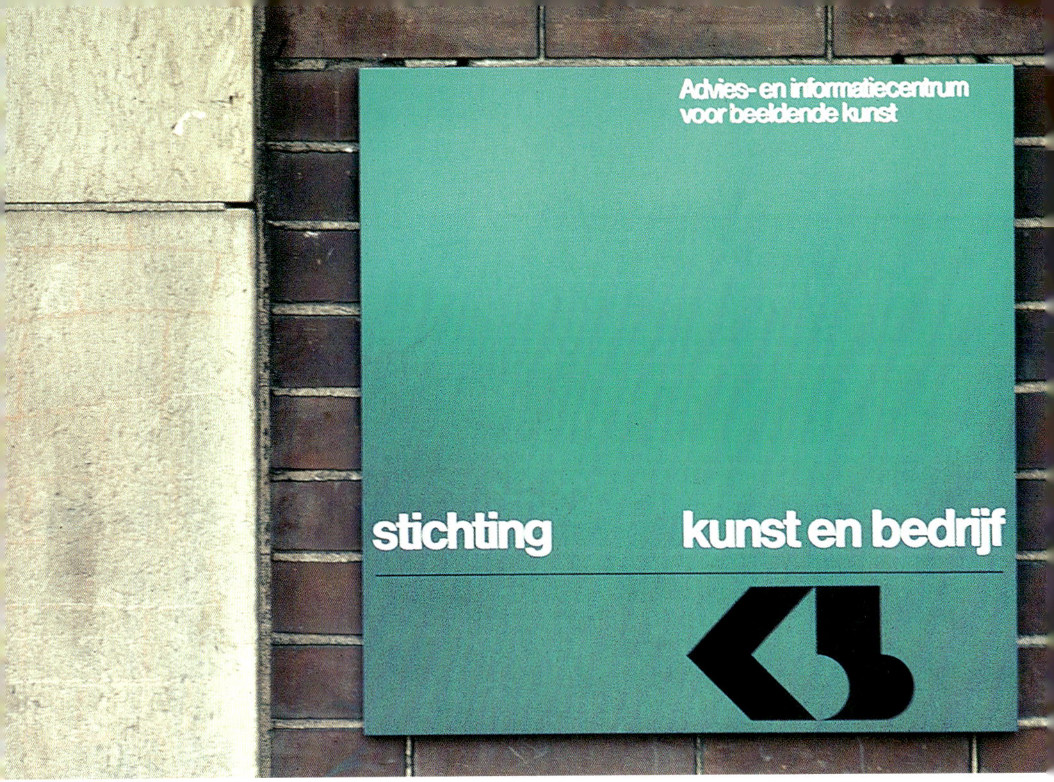
Advies- en informatiecentrum
voor beeldende kunst
stichting
kunst en bedrijf

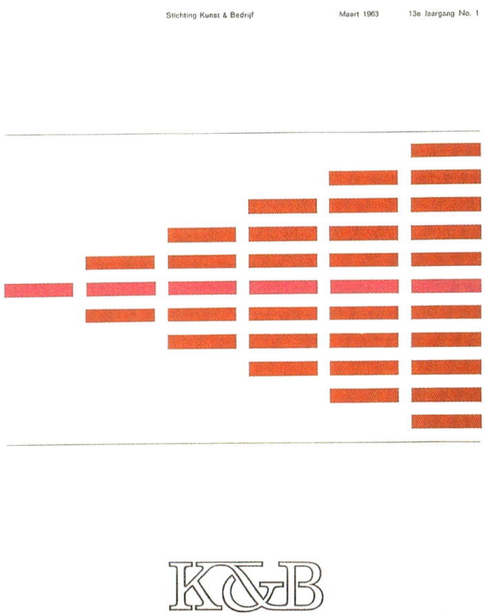
Stichting Kunst & Bedrijf
Maart 1963
13e Jaargang No. 1
K&B

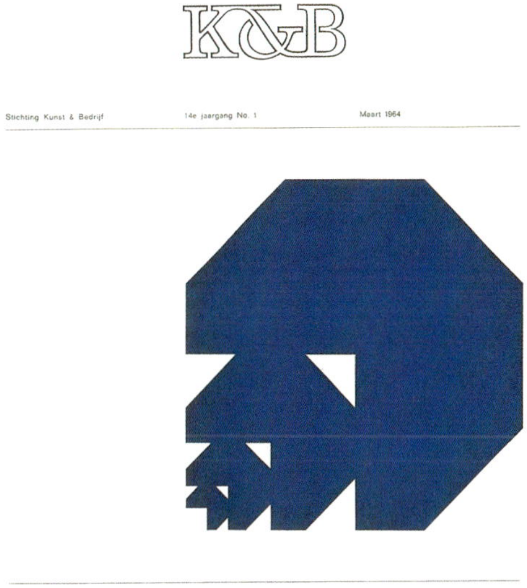
K&B
Stichting Kunst & Bedrijf
14e jaargang No. 1
Maart 1964

1963-1978
Stichting Kunst & Bedrijf

1964-1970
Quarterly magazines

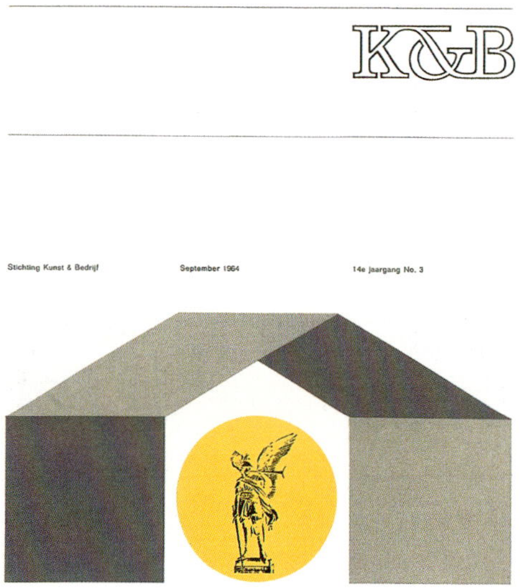

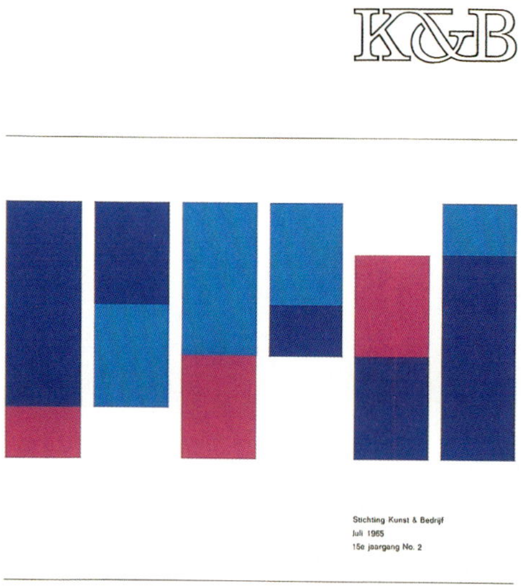

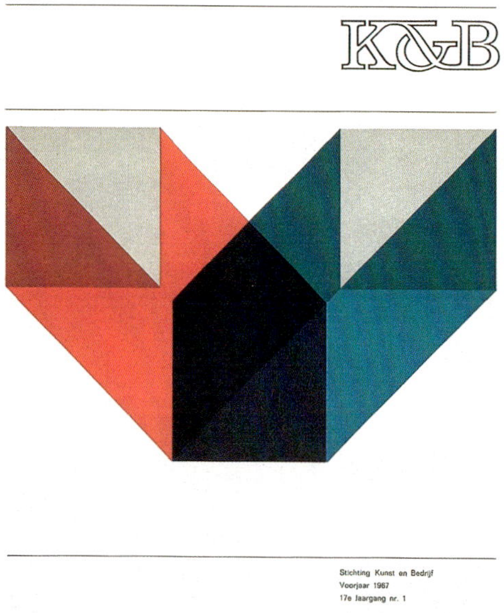

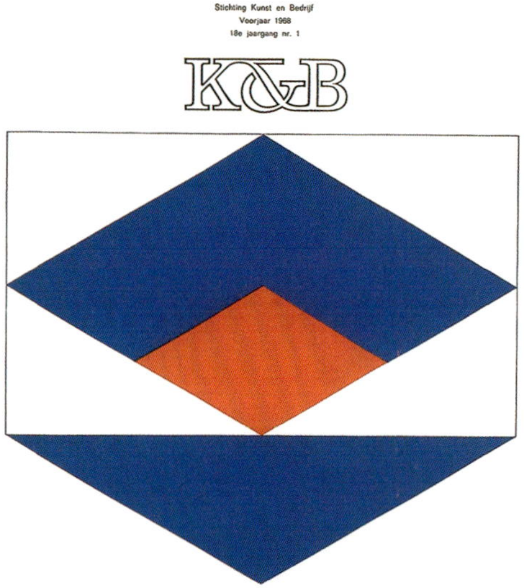

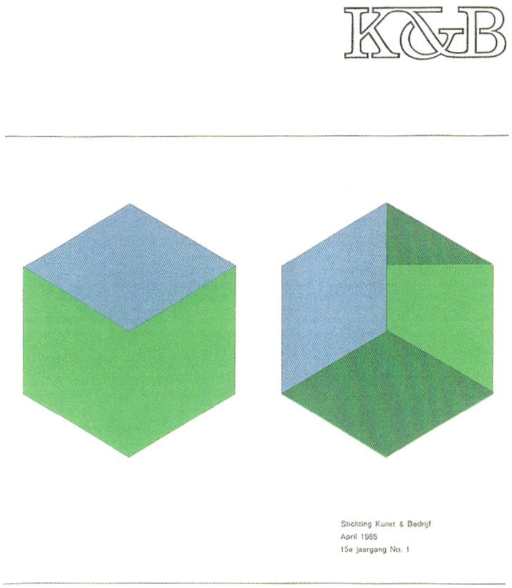
K&B
Stichting Kunst & Bedrijf
April 1965
15e jaargang No. 1

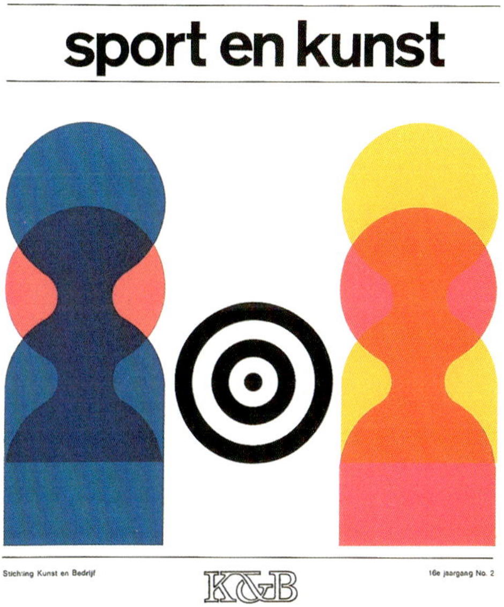
sport en kunst
Stichting Kunst en Bedrijf
K&B
16e jaargang No. 2

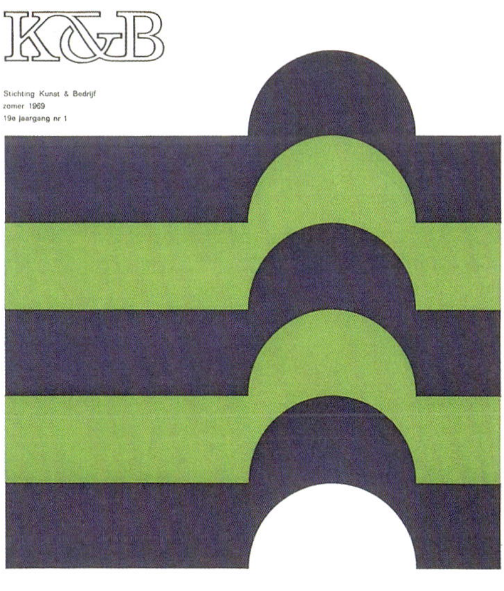
K&B
Stichting Kunst & Bedrijf
zomer 1969
19e jaargang nr 1

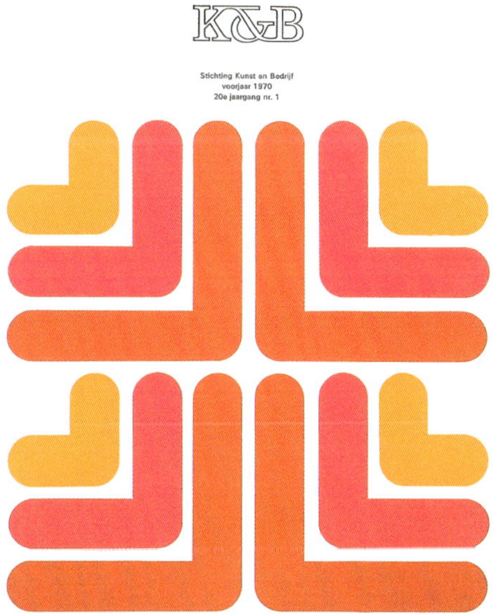
K&B
Stichting Kunst en Bedrijf
voorjaar 1970
20e jaargang nr. 1

1968
Philips Phonogram

Record and cassette subscription campaign

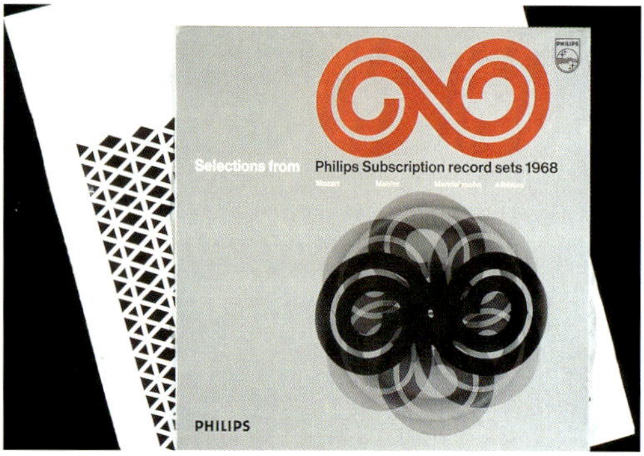

Campagne de Souscription Philips 1968

4 collections — 25 disques 30 cm

PHILIPS

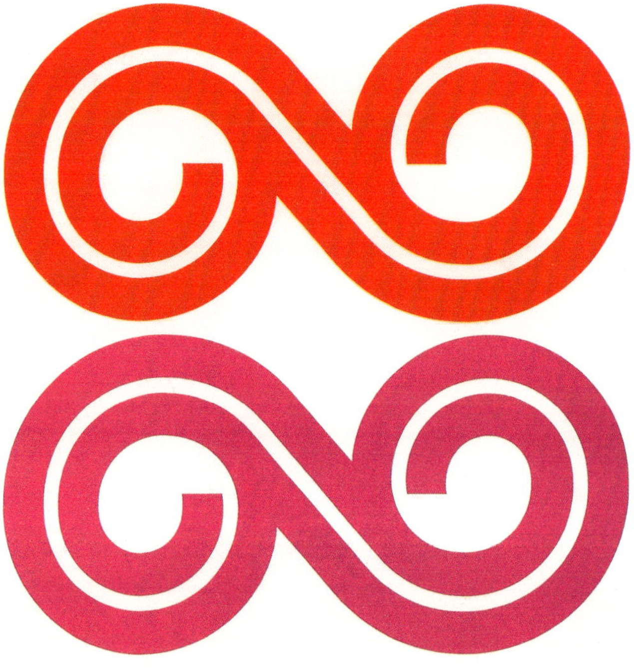

1969
Tweka Swimwear
Geldrop

Product logo

1968
Struktuur 68
Ceramic studio, The Hague

Logo

struktuur 68

1968 - 1972

Kluwer printers and publishers

Deventer

Logo, corporate design

In 1968 Bos designed a corporate identity for these publishers and printers. The logo is still used today. In spite of repeated urgings, Bos has never succeeded in persuading the various Kluwer publishing companies to consistently use a corporate identity.

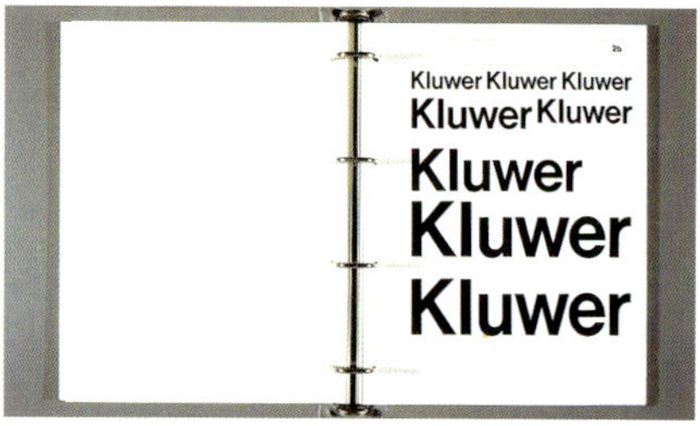

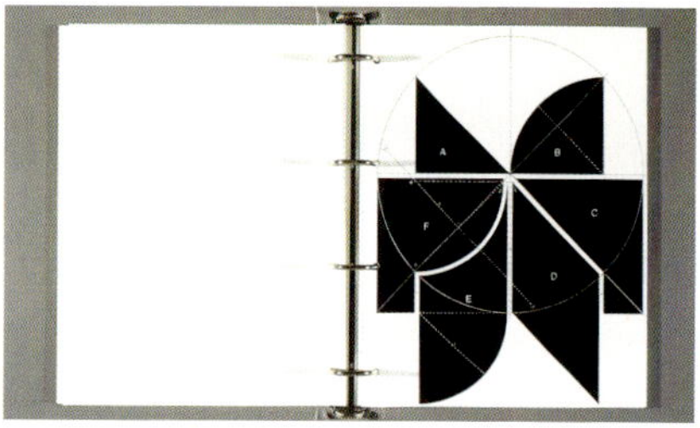

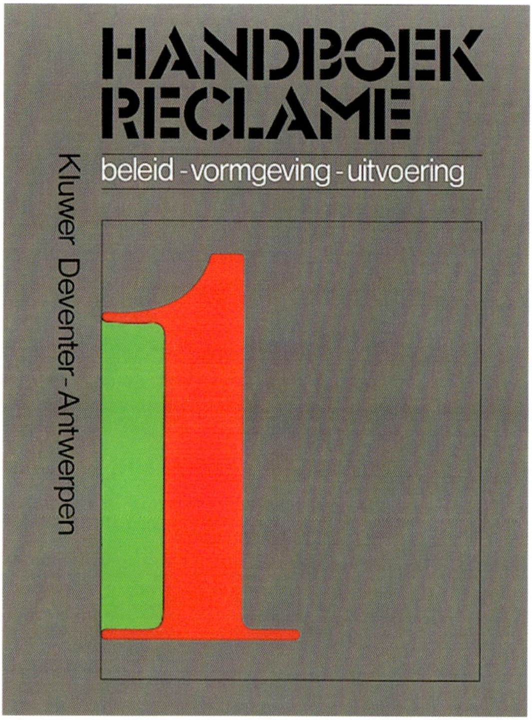

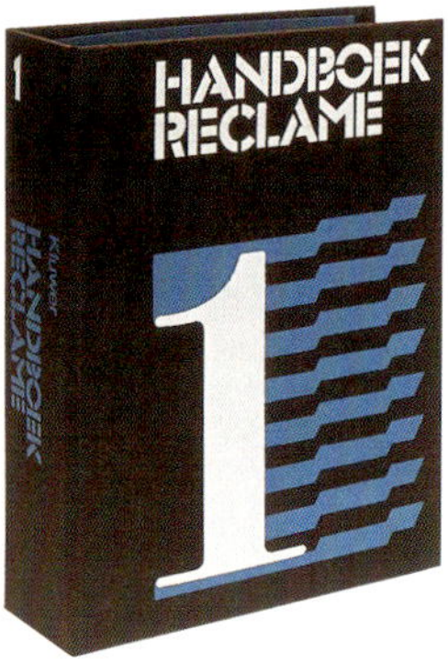

1972

Advertising handbook

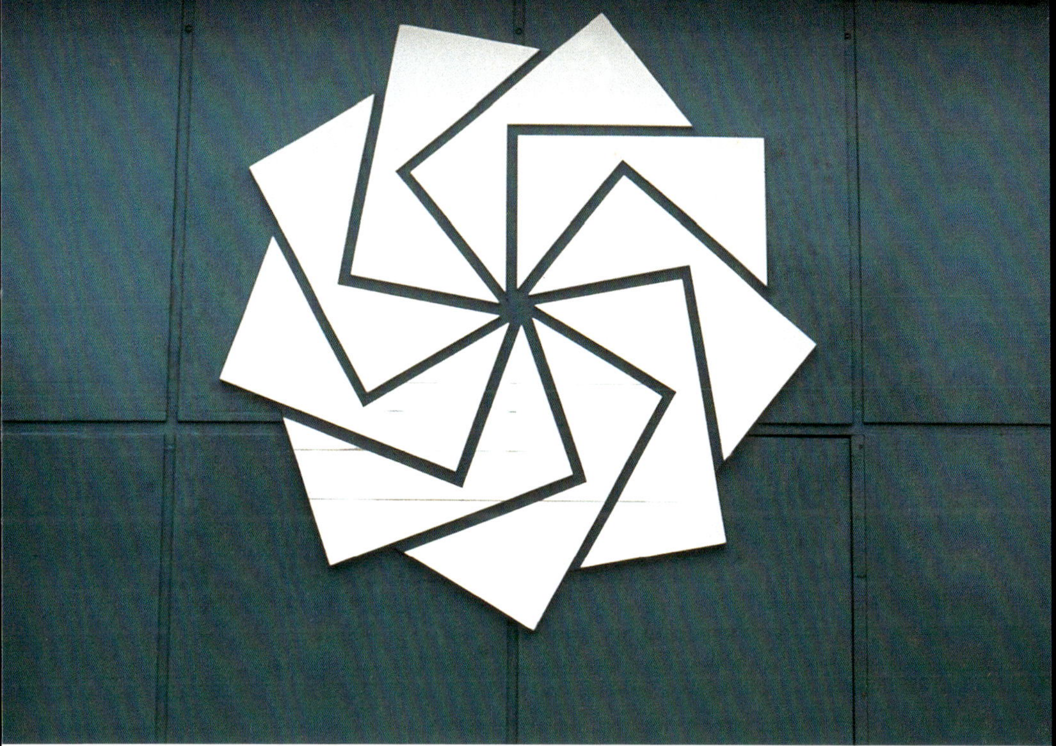

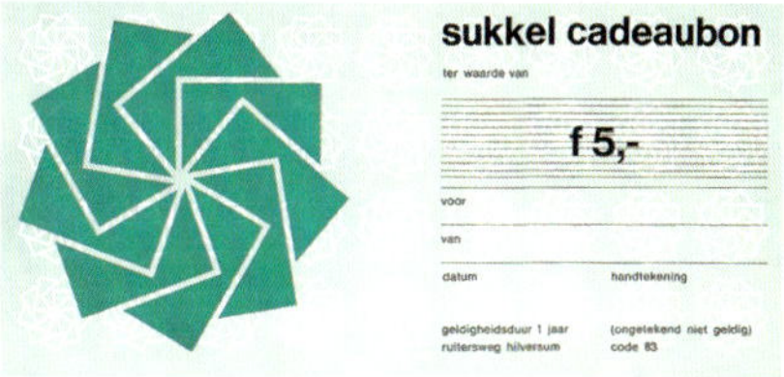

sukkel cadeaubon

ter waarde van

f 5,-

voor

van

datum

handtekening

geldigheidsduur 1 jaar
ruitersweg hilversum

(ongetekend niet geldig)
code 83

1968

Sukkel

Glass and paint shop
Hilversum

Logo, corporate design

Voucher

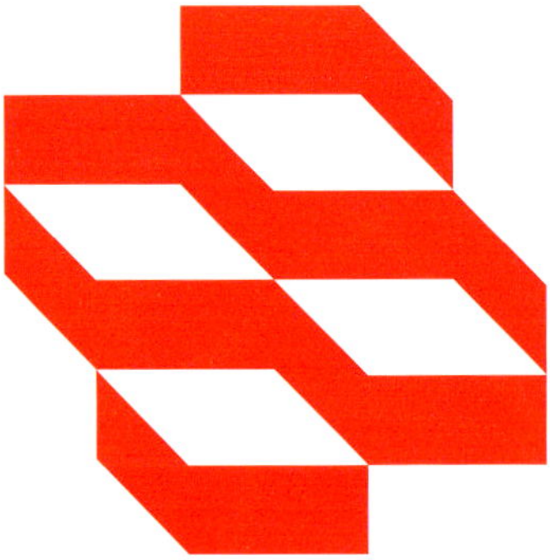

1969
Van Heeswijk
Boxtel
Contractors

Logo, corporate design

Silkscreen prints as promotional gifts

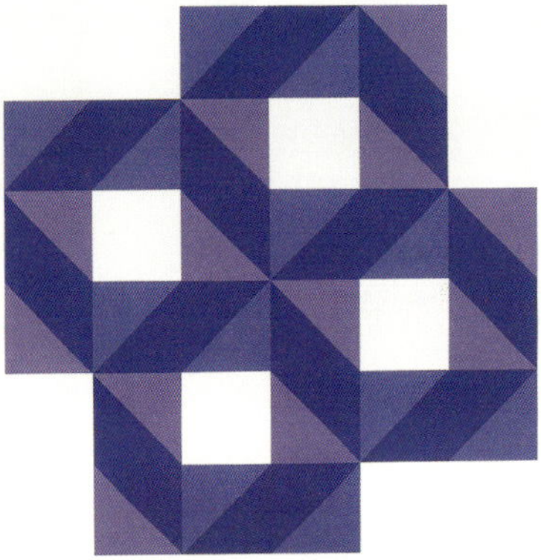

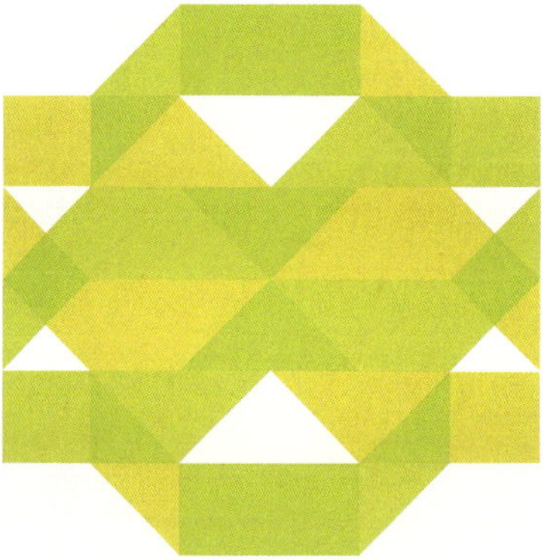

1968-1993
Furness
Rotterdam

Logos, corporate design

Logos for the holding and its subsidiaries Harbours, Shipping Company, Ship Brokers, Road Transport, Insurance, Dealer Companies and Real Estate.

A concern of Rotterdam harbour barons that set up subsidiaries in the seventies such as international road transport, stevedore and ship broker companies, insurance, real estate, a shipping company and a car dealer.
In 1968 Bos designed a brochure and an annual report for this concern. Subsequently he developed a wide-ranging corporate identity for the holding and its various subsidiaries around the world.
The holding's logo was the starting point for a whole series. Bos got the idea for it in late August 1968, on the morning on which the Russians invaded Prague, while the world-wide designers association Icograda was conducting a conference at the Technical Polytechnic in Eindhoven. He drew eight maritime flags in a (holding) circle on the back of the conference programme. On this he based a whole series of divisional logos, each with its own colour, that symbolize freedom-in-restraint.
The logos were featured on ships, cranes, sheds, trucks, internal transport vehicles, various printed matter, illuminated advertising, flags, ties and belts.

Until today the eight little flags have survived all reorganisations and economy measures. In 2000 Furtrans expedition company still sports the four flags of the four winds.

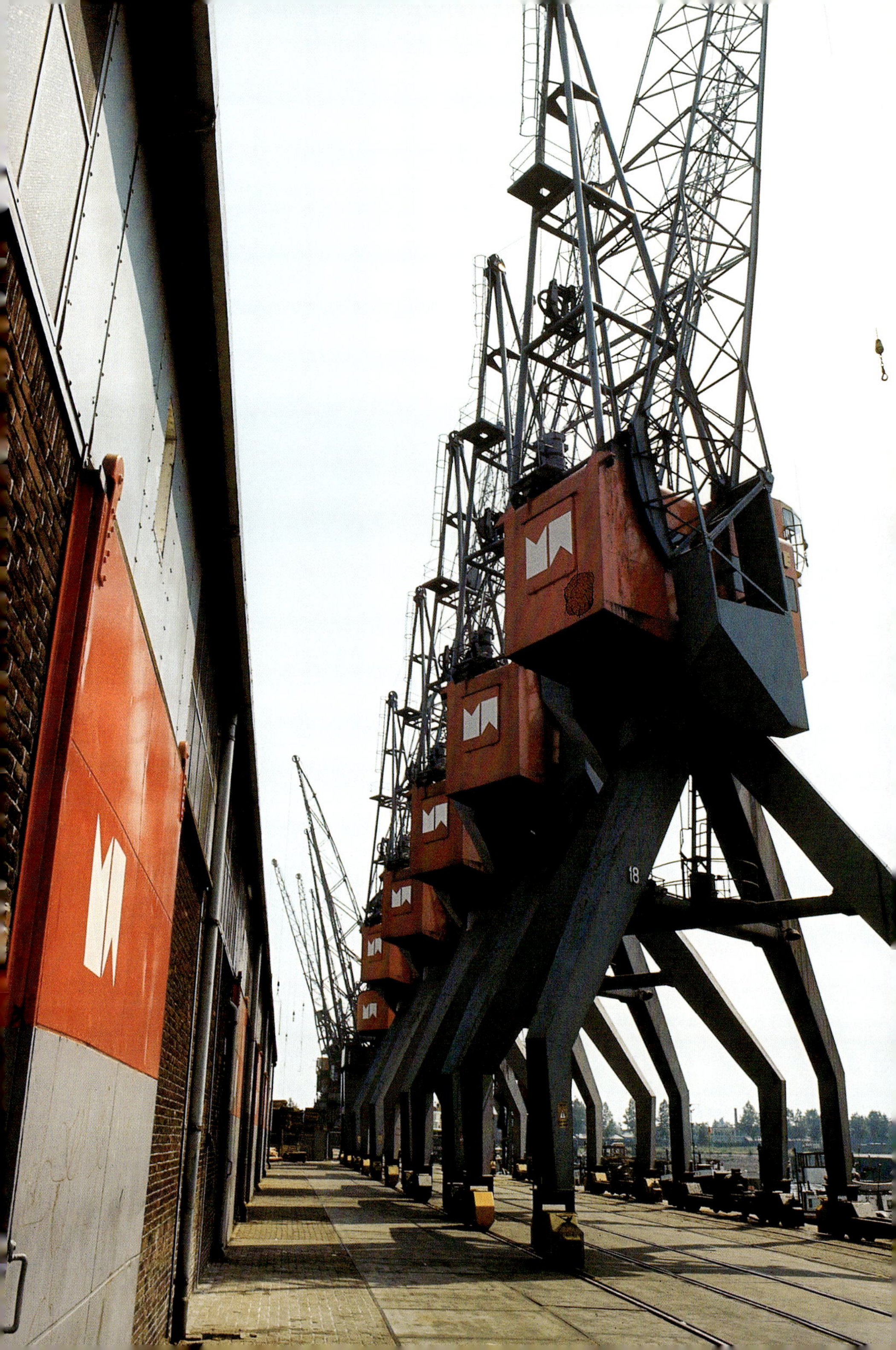
18

Ben was simply Ben

For five years, from 1981 to 1986, Paul Mijksenaar combined part-time employment at Total Design with his position of staff member at Delft Technische Hogeschool. In 1986 he resigned from both jobs to set up his own business. In addition to running his own Bureau Mijksenaar he has been professor of Visual Information Design at the Industrial Design department of Delft Technical University for many years.

I still remember how I went to Ben Bos to give him my notice. To my considerable surprise he told me he was not at all surprised. So he knew me better than I knew myself.
That was rather odd, because I rarely spoke to Ben, like all people who weren't members of his group. His team was a tight-knit and disciplined but impenetrable bastion within Total Design. You didn't enter their rooms just for social chat or for trifles. This was a place where people worked and money was being earned. Ben's team could afford to be so aloof because it worked for Randstad, Total Design's biggest account. Its position was unique in that it could actually charge all of its working hours. None of the other teams had that luxury. That was also invariably insinuated during the annual discussion of the accounts. We – the members of the other teams – naturally considered that extremely unfair.
What was Ben like? Well, I really can't say much more than: Ben was simply Ben. You were a bit on your guard with him, you were cautious. To be on the safe side, laughing, sniggering and other types of hilarity were abruptly stopped whenever Ben appeared.
I got to know the courteous, charming and loyal Ben Bos only many years after, when he accompanied Jantien to Saturday night visits to our house where we played Mah Yong. And of course that side of him came to the fore during our innumerable return visits to the Boses at Plantagekade 48. Those were occasions where Jantien proved herself to be a past master. That was also the time when I discovered that Ben greatly respected me as a professional and also was very fond of me and Ellen personally, and made no attempt to hide it.
At that time Ben Bos made a powerful bid to attract a commission from Randstad in collaboration with Bureau Mijksenaar. I will never forget the Randstad officer who turned up at my studio to size up the situation. The first question that this brat asked was if I could explain why on earth Randstad would go to the trouble of cooperating with Bureau Mijksenaar... Only my respect for Ben Bos withheld me from jamming the head of this temp agency nitwit between our file cabinets on wheels.
PH

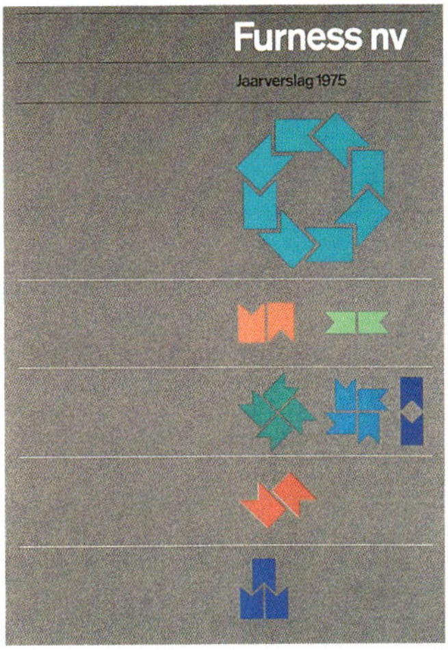

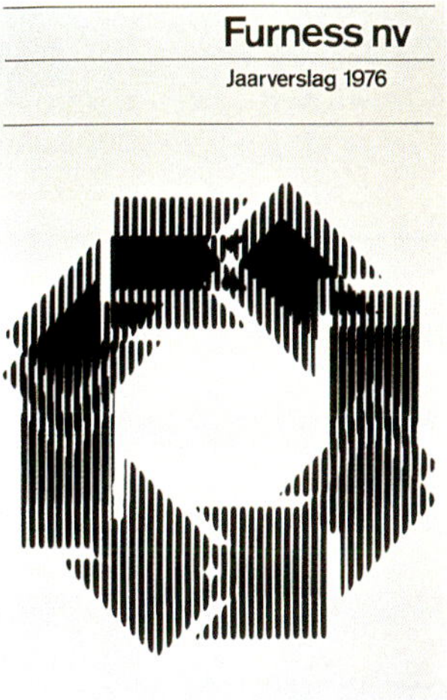

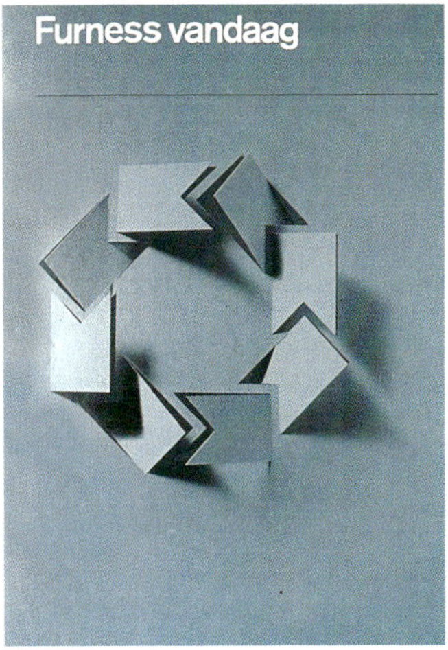

1975 / 1976
Annual reports

1977
Company brochure

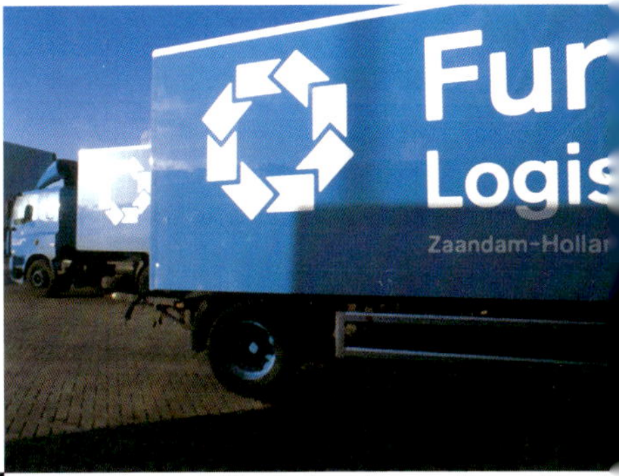

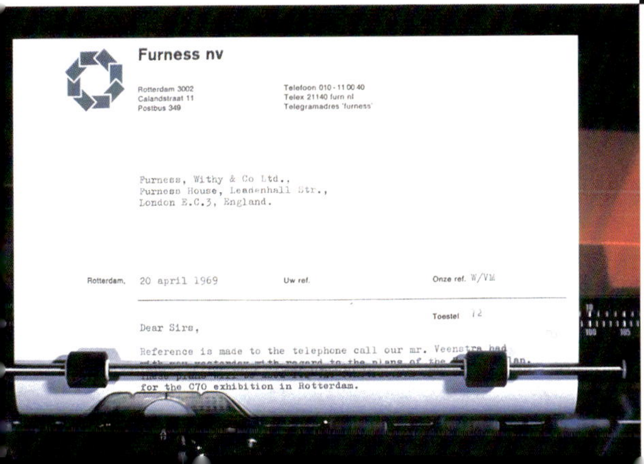

1972
Company brochure

1976
Diagram from annual report

1970
Shipping company

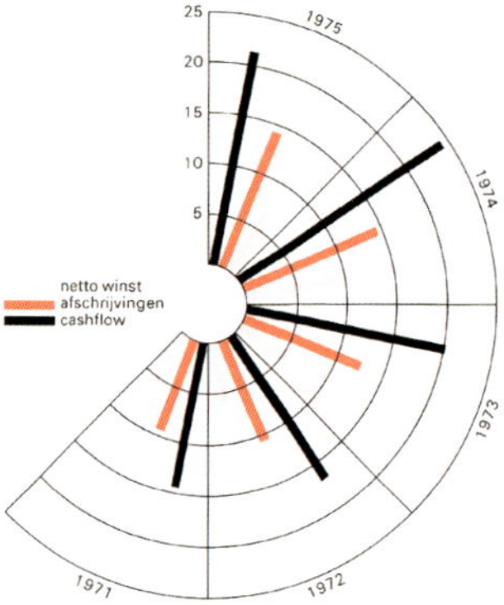

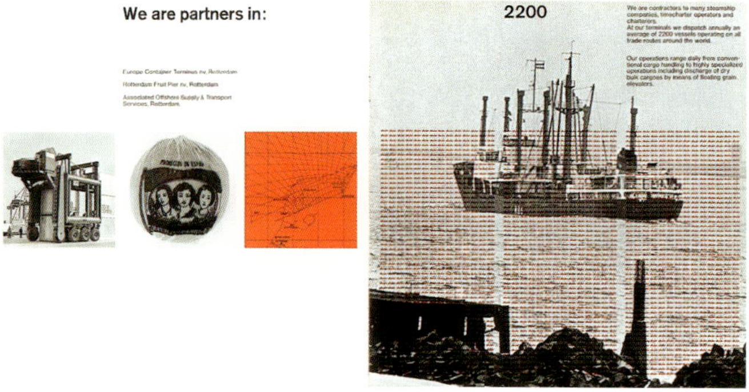

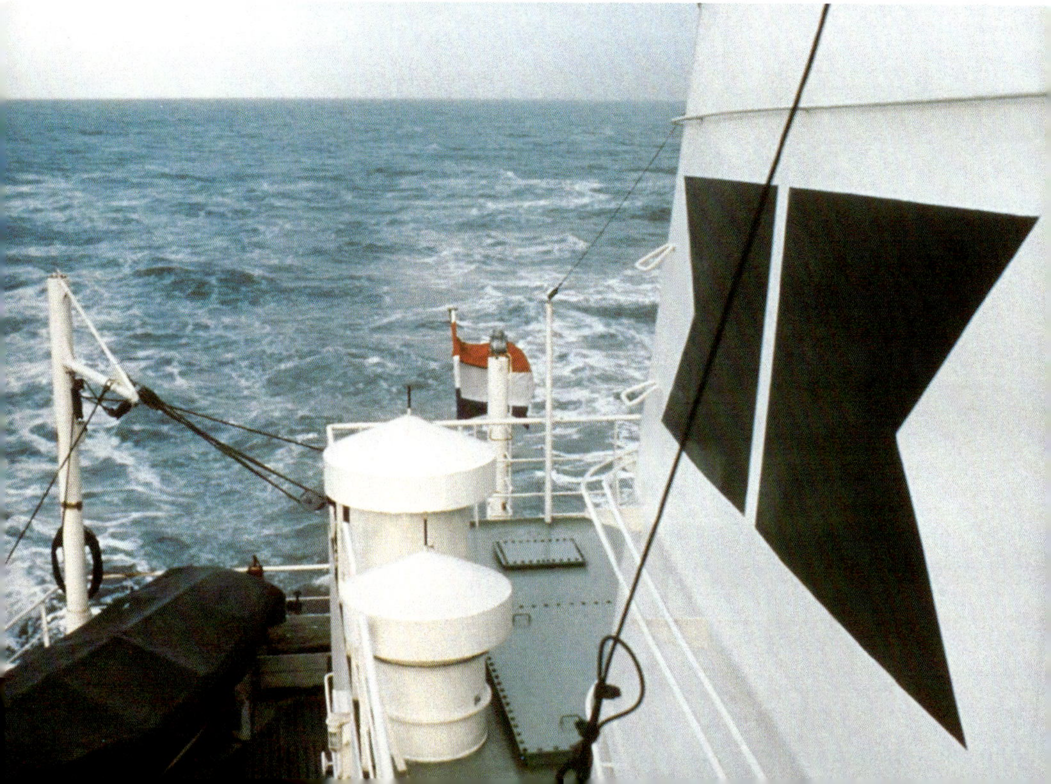

1969
Aannemerscombinatie Bouw Binnenziekenhuis
(hospital building contactors combination)
Eindhoven

Logo, corporate design

1970
Cisca cultural ticket office
Amsterdam

Logo, corporate design
Programme for arts festival

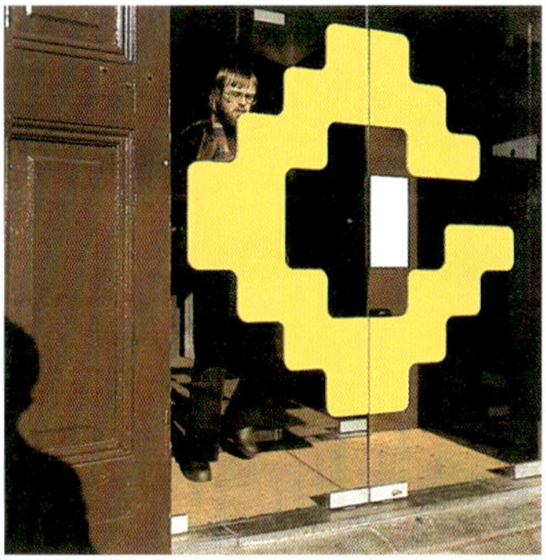

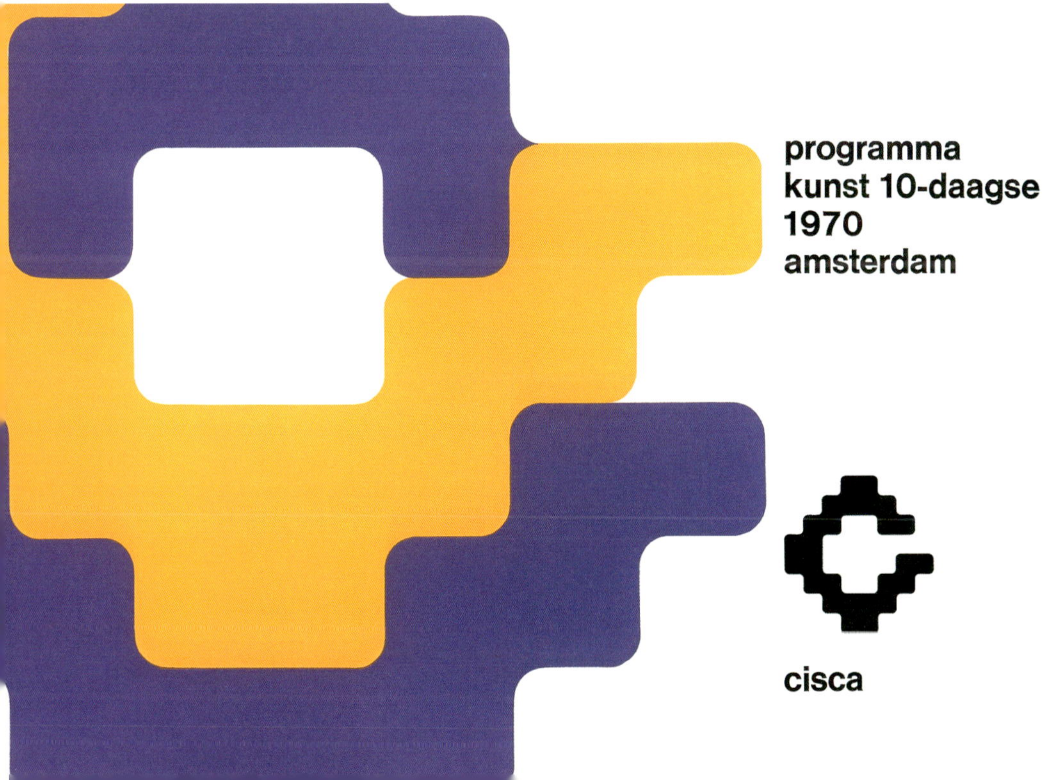

1970
PTT Nederland
The Hague

Postage stamp Interparliamentary Union
Postage stamp 25 years of the United Nations

In 1970 the silver jubilee of the United Nations (in Dutch: Verenigde Naties – VN) coincided with the 25th anniversary of 'Vrij Nederland' weekly (also VN). That is why Bos resorted to the English acronym UNO. The Inter-parliamentary Union is a world-wide organization for parliaments.

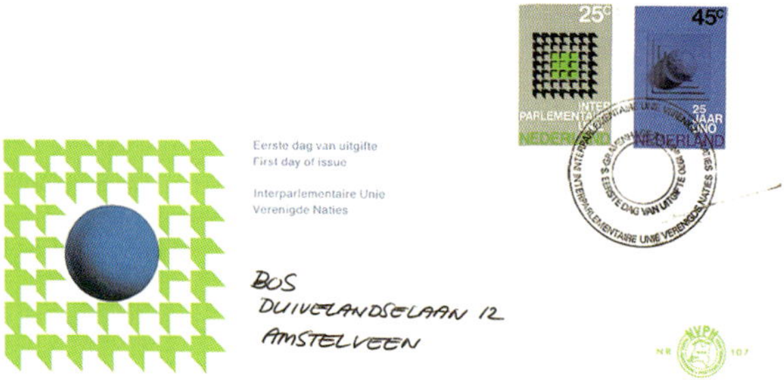

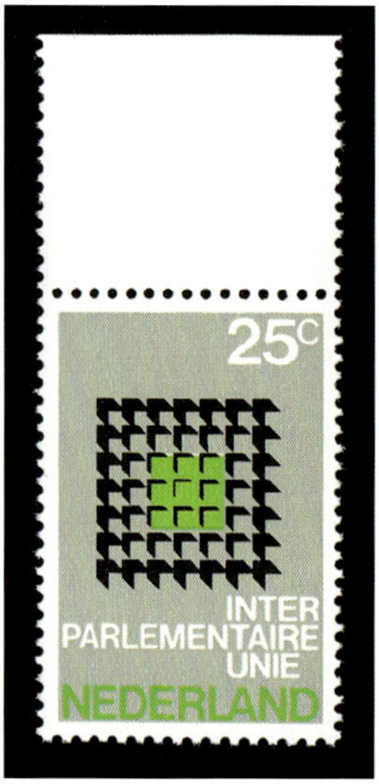

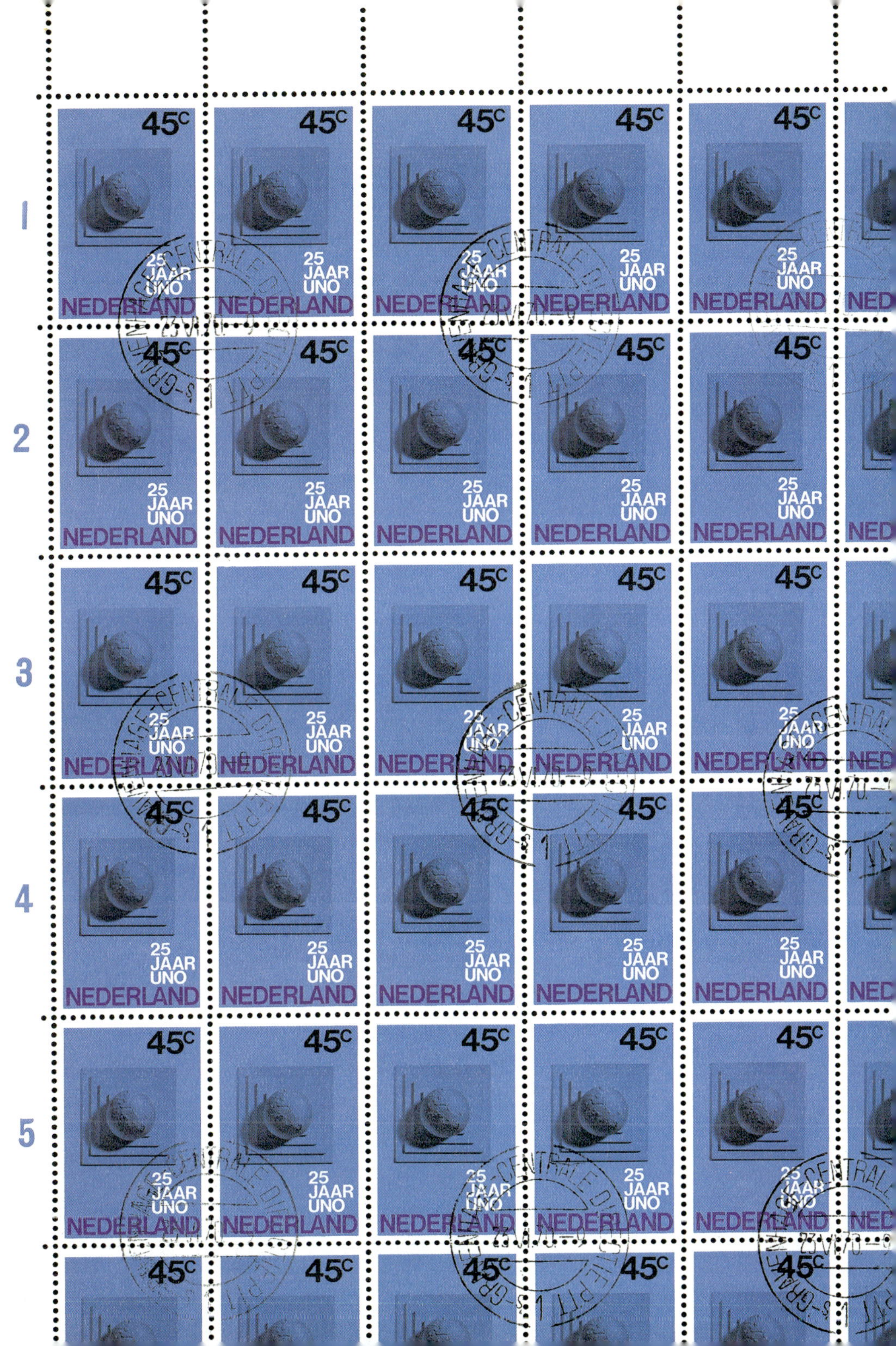
1
2
3
4
5
45c
25 JAAR UNO
NEDERLAND

Daily newspapers

Bos's active interest in journalism, which was demonstrated i.a. by his many years of activity as teacher and designer in corporate journalism, received a new impulse in 1970 in the form of a commission to re-design 'Algemeen Handelsblad', which was then struggling with poor circulation.
The page structure was divided into blocks, while the regular features were given their own spot. The choice of another typeface was not a simple matter in those days of lead typesetting. Theoretical lay-out schemes needed to be produced, both for days 'when the world ended' and for days in the silly season.
To avoid startling the readers too much, the sanserif bold letters were introduced in chapeaus and subheadings in addition to a Clarendon-like letter. These typefaces could later switch roles.

As a next step in the general layout Bos proposed to divide the page into four parts, which would facilitate the readers' ability to manage their paper in small spaces when travelling by tram, train or plane.

'Algemeen Handelsblad' did not get much time to learn to use the new design. Briefly after its introduction the paper merged into NRC-Handelsblad. For this Bos was merely allowed to design the masthead. The design and new lettering for the Handelsblad quietly went under.

The quartering of the front page got a second chance when in late 1983 Bos and his assistant Melle Hammer were requested by publisher Hollander and editor Wouter Gortzak to restyle the design of 'Het Parool'.
Among other things, this led to the most important new items being discussed in the top right quarter of the front page.

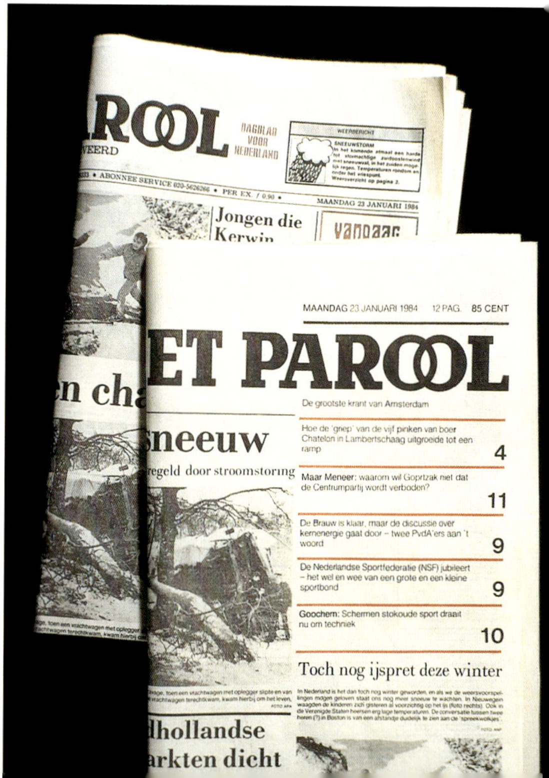

1984
Het Parool daily newspaper
Amsterdam

Re-design
In collaboration with
Melle Hammer

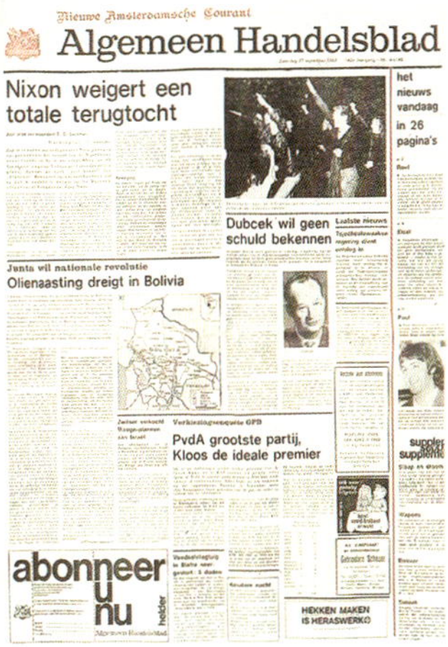
Nieuwe Amsterdamsche Courant

Algemeen Handelsblad

Nixon weigert een totale terugtocht

het nieuws vandaag in 26 pagina's

Dubcek wil geen schuld bekennen

Laatste nieuws

Junta wil nationale revolutie

Olienaasting dreigt in Bolivia

PvdA grootste partij, Kloos de ideale premier

abonneer u nu

HEKKEN MAKEN IS HERASWERK

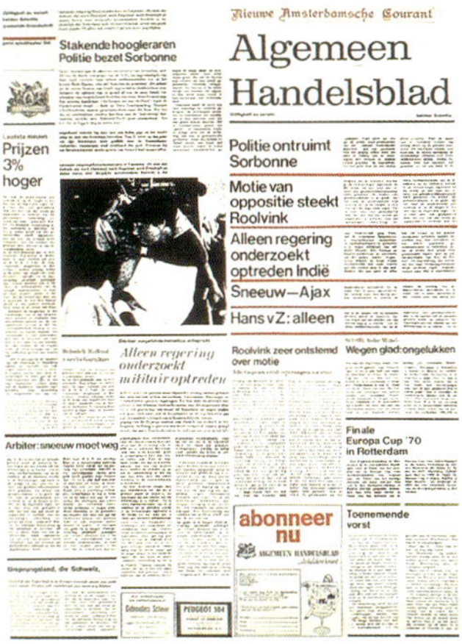
Nieuwe Amsterdamsche Courant

Algemeen Handelsblad

Stakende hoogleraren Politie bezet Sorbonne

Prijzen 3% hoger

Politie ontruimt Sorbonne

Motie van oppositie steekt Roolvink

Alleen regering onderzoekt optreden Indië

Sneeuw—Ajax

Hans v Z: alleen

Alleen regering onderzoekt militair optreden

Roolvink zeer ontstemd over motie

Wegen glad: ongelukken

Arbiter: sneeuw moet weg

Finale Europa Cup '70 in Rotterdam

Toenemende vorst

abonneer nu

1970

Algemeen Handelsblad daily newspaper

Amsterdam

Re-design in consultation with Wim Crouwel

Lay-out instructions for the first page of the second quire

1971

NRC-Handelsblad daily newspaper

Rotterdam

Newspaper logo

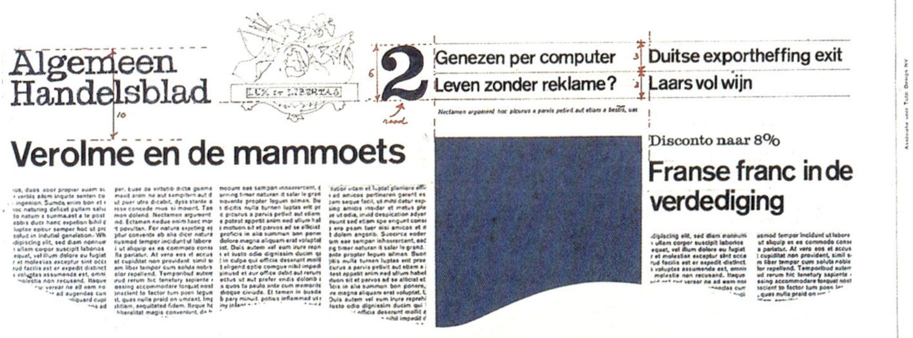

NRC HANDELSBLAD

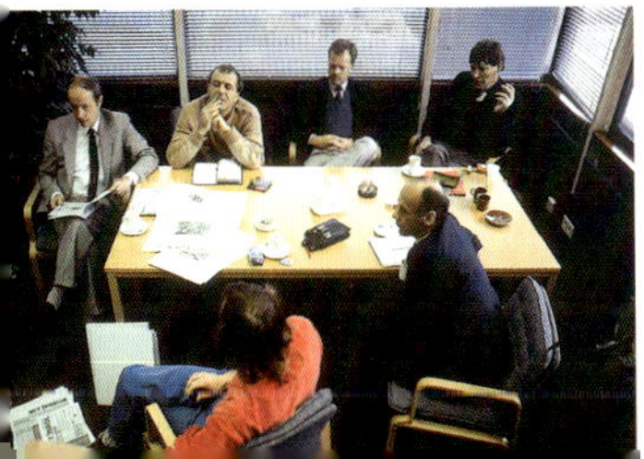

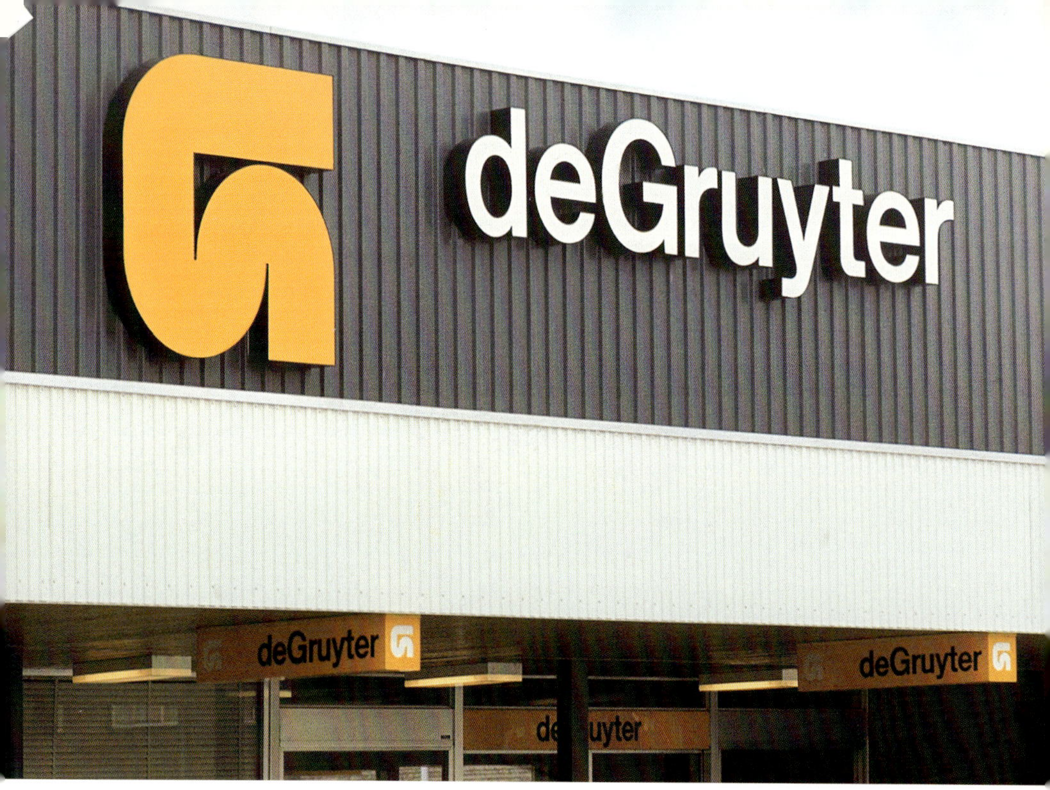

1971-1972

De Gruyter

's-Hertogenbosch

Corporate design and packaging

In collaboration with
Wim van der Weerd (logo) and
Peter Marcuse (photography)

The old family business P. de Gruyter & Zonen had waited too long with the switch to self-service, the sale of national A brands from other manufacturers and the creation of a supermarket chain. After the takeover of De Gruyter by SHV (a major client of Total Design), its corporate design was radically revised. However, further management blunders led to De Gruyter's demise.

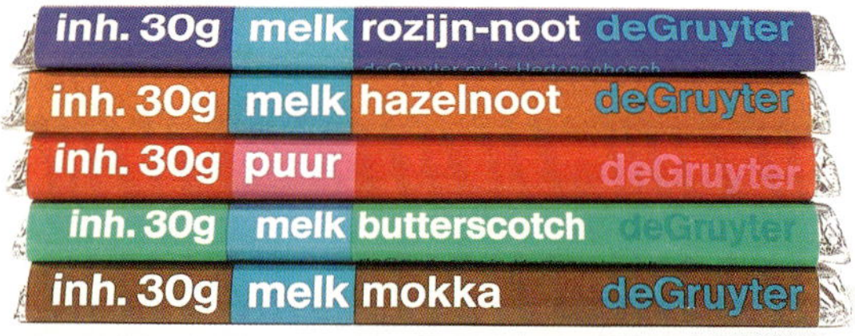

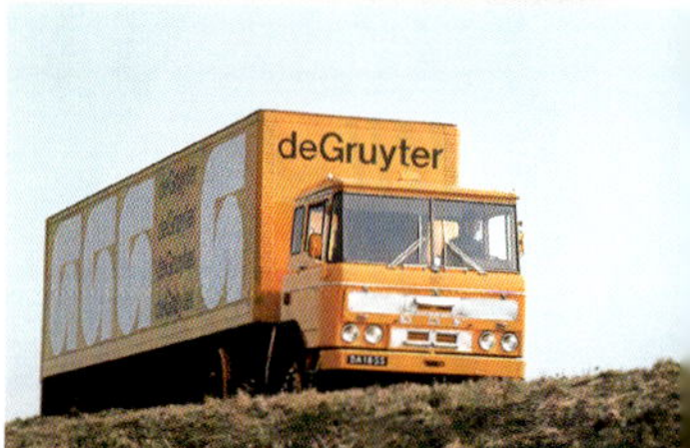

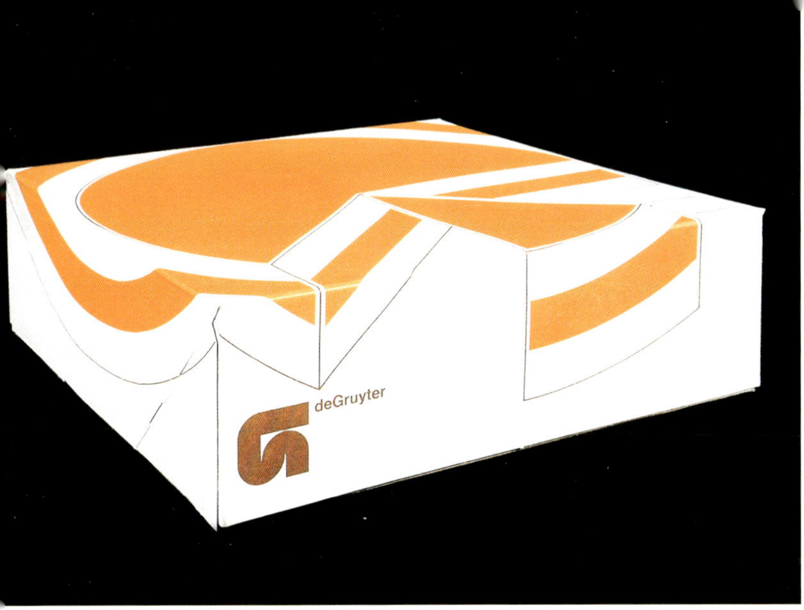
deGruyter

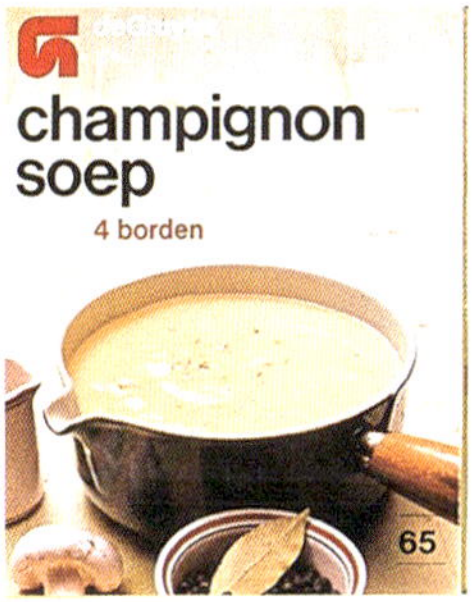
champignon
soep
4 borden
65

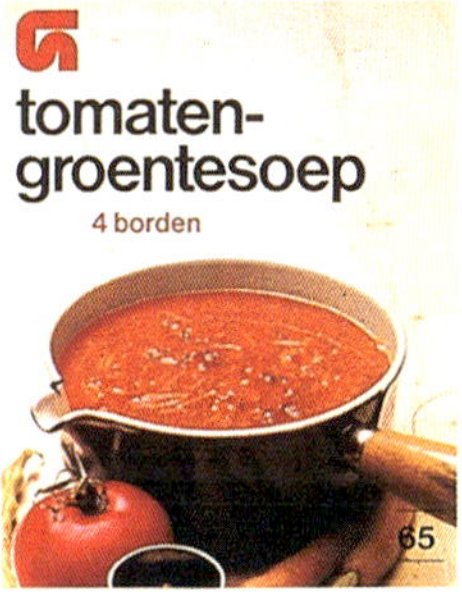
tomaten-
groentesoep
4 borden
65

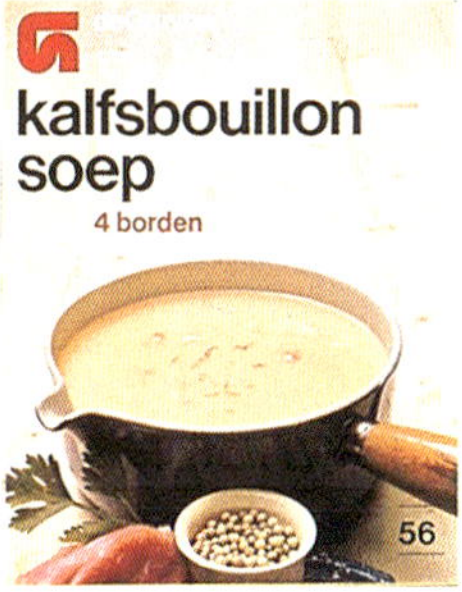
kalfsbouillon
soep
4 borden
56

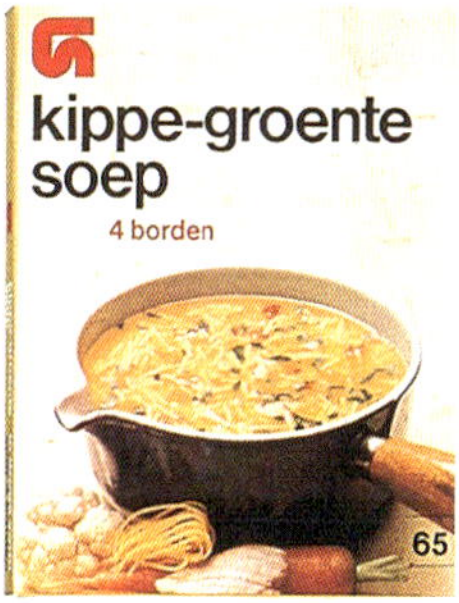
kippe-groente
soep
4 borden
65

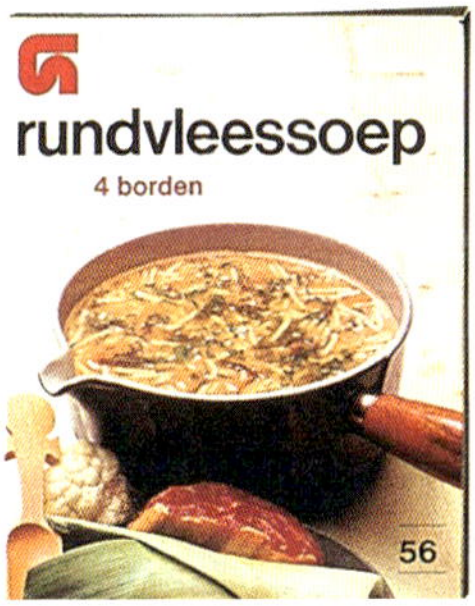
rundvleessoep
4 borden
56

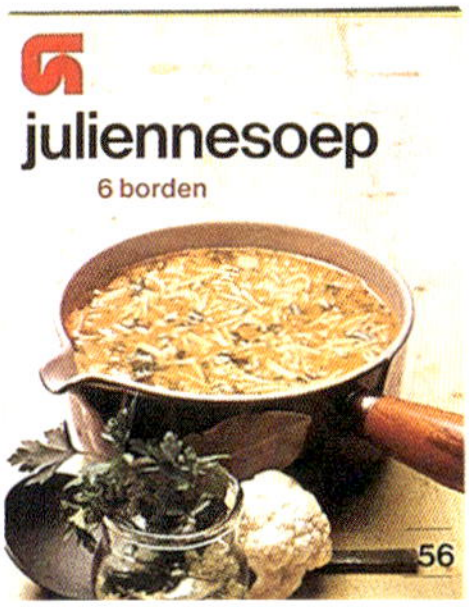
juliennesoep
6 borden
56

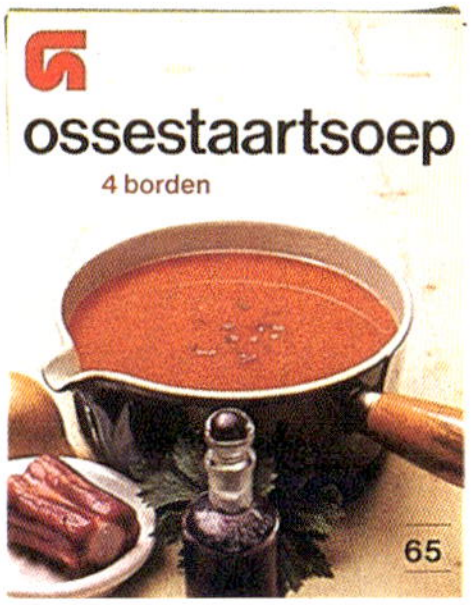
ossestaartsoep
4 borden
65

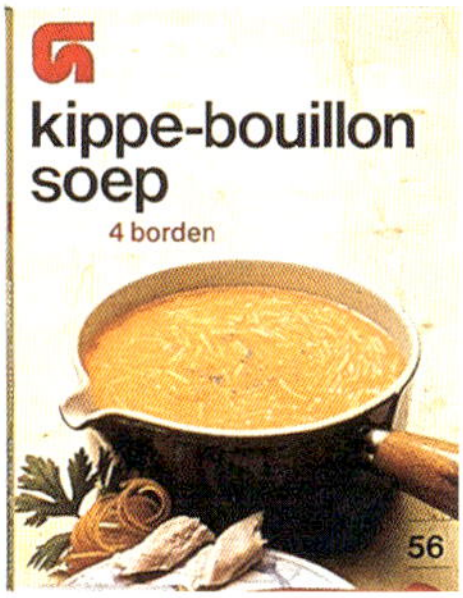
kippe-bouillon
soep
4 borden
56

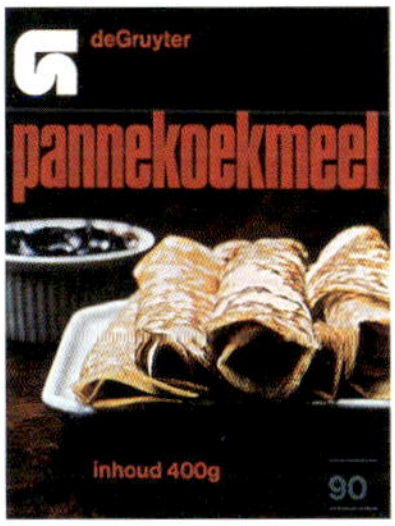
deGruyter
pannekoekmeel
inhoud 400g
90

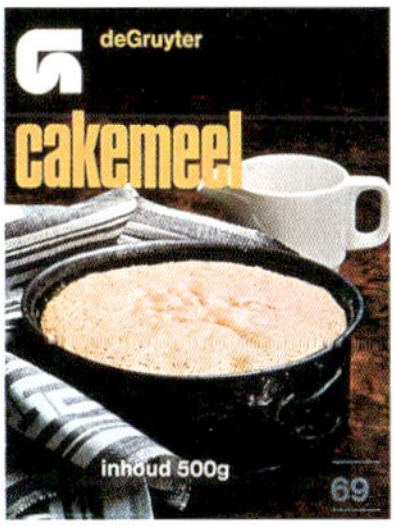
deGruyter
cakemeel
inhoud 500g
69

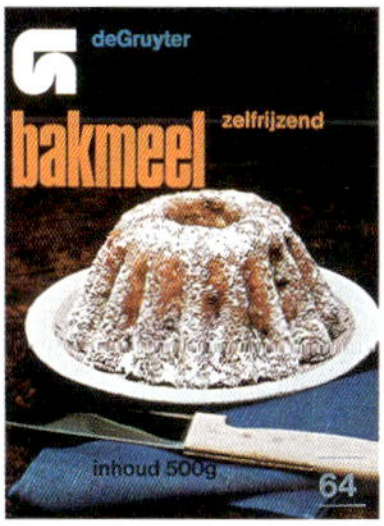
deGruyter
bakmeel
zelfrijzend
inhoud 500g
64

deGruyter

no. 1 - januari 1972

Uitgave van deGruyter
Redaktie:
Postbus 314, Den Bosch

nieuwe huisstijl

modern kommunikatiemiddel tussen klant en deGruyter

Een nieuwe huisstijl bij deGruyter. Dat wist u ongetwijfeld al, want het afgelopen jaar 1971 is er waarlijk wat gebeurd om uw deGruyter een nieuwe koers te doen inslaan.

Nu en dan ook een nieuwe huisstijl: een nieuw merkbeeld: de gestileerde letter G; een huiskleur oranje geel; nieuwe verpakkingen voor onze eigen produkten (ze komen geleidelijk in de winkels, die verpakkingen); nieuw beschilderde en beletterde vrachtauto's; een nieuwe aanpak van advertenties en winkelraambiljetten.
En straks ook nieuwe bedrijfskleding voor onze mensen in de winkels. Heeft deGruyter zoveel verdiend of zoveel geld over om al die vernieuwingen te bekostigen? Waarlijk niet. Het is ook voor ons hárd werken voor de kost.

Maar tóch: een nieuwe huisstijl.
Waarom dan?
Wel, u, als konsument, hebt er recht op te weten wie die leverancier van u is. Welke zijn gedragslijn is, hoe hij tegenover u staat. U moet hem kunnen herkennen, duidelijk en steeds weer. En als hij op een goed moment anders wordt, dan moet u als konsument dat goed kunnen vaststellen.
Duidelijkheid én eerlijkheid jegens de konsument, dat is ons grote parool geworden gedurende het afgelopen jaar. Kijkt u maar wat we inmiddels in onze winkels gedaan hebben. Daar waar het kon, ruimte geschapen, opdat u rustig en ongestoord uw inkopen kunt doen.
Prijsbulletins bij een groot aantal artikelgroepen, opdat u, uit de wirwar van merken en verpakkingsgrootten, goed kunt vaststellen waaraan u eigenlijk met de prijs per 100 gram, per liter, per 100 cc enz. toe bent.
Het aanbrengen van de gereduceerde prijs op artikelen die „in de reklame" zijn.

Tussen al dat nieuwe, dat betere, bestaat verband. Het zijn evenzovele uitingen van onze wil om ons als een „nieuwe deGruyter" aan u voor te stellen.
Dat is een vorm van kommunikatie waaraan u en wij behoefte hebben. En die kommunikatie krijgt nu zijn „bezegeling", zijn afronding in de nieuwe huisstijl van deGruyter.
Een huisstijl die u mag zien als ons visitekaartje jegens u.
Als ons „wij tekenen ervoor", dat wil zeggen: we blijven er voor instaan. Zoiets als een handtekening onder een kontrakt. Héél sterk gezegd: een vorm van adel die verplicht.

Maar uiterlijk vertoon leidt tot niets als er geen inhoud achter schuil gaat.

En die inhoud gaat iedere man en vrouw, iedere jongen en ieder meisje in onze winkelorganisatie aan die huisstijl geven. Ze zijn bijeen geweest, al die 4.000 winkelmedewerkers en -medewerkers van deGruyter.
Op de avond van de 4e januari op 15 plaatsen in het land.
Om zelf als eersten te horen over die nieuwe huisstijl van hun bedrijf. Om daaruit de bezieling, de inspiratie te putten om die huisstijl inhoud te geven.
De inhoud van hún service jegens de konsument, van de kwaliteit van hun

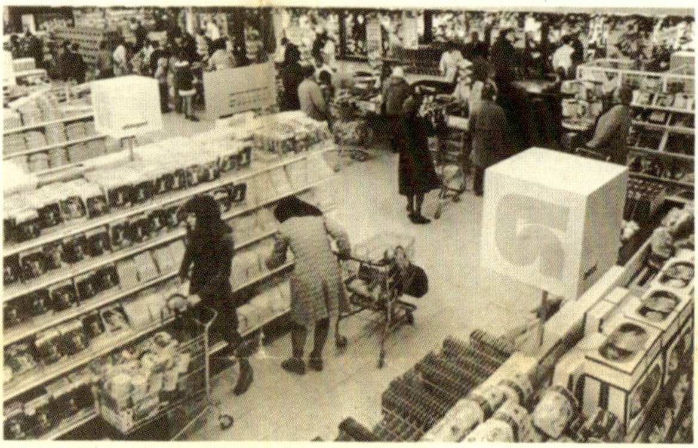

prestatie in de winkel en van al dat andere dat nodig is om u, als konsument, te doen zeggen: inderdaad, een nieuwe deGruyter.
Kijk, je kunt nieuwe dingen ondernemen, maar als dat incidenten zijn, kortstondige explosies zonder blijvende nawerking, schiet - op de lange termijn - niemand er veel mee op.
Wij van deGruyter hebben in 1971 nieuwe initiatieven genomen en zullen er in 1972 andere aan toevoegen.
Om het u zo goed mogelijk - en als het kan helemaal - naar de zin te maken. Maar we hebben er duidelijk geen incidenten mee beoogd. Geen kortstondige akties.
We hebben er onze nieuwe stijl van werken jegens u mee willen aantonen. Waarmee we zullen dóórgaan, ook in 1972 en daarna.
Van nu af gaan we dat doen onder een nieuwe vlag, met de gestileerde letter G tegen een oranjegeel fond.
Vroeger schreef een adverteerder onder zijn advertentie: beleefd aanbevelend. Dat is al lang uit de tijd.

U wilt geen loze kreten meer. U wilt inhoud.

Die inhoud geven wij van deGruyter aan onze houding jegens u. En ook uiterlijk duidelijk herkenbaar als een nieuwe deGruyter. Wij wensen u een voorspoedig Nieuwjaar.

je ziet aan de buitenkant dat er binnen wat te koop is

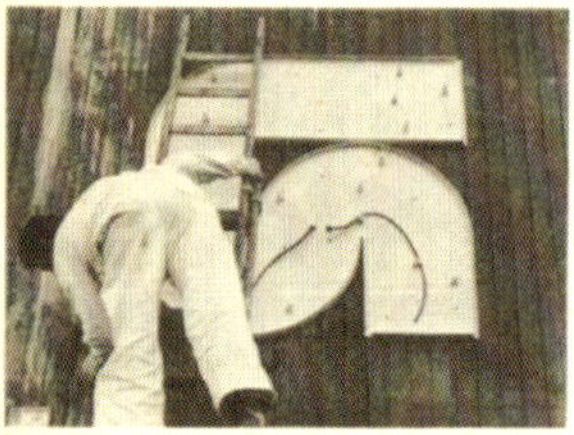

Dit beeld komt u vast wel bekend voor. Koortsachtig is en wordt er de laatste tijd gewerkt aan de vernieuwing van de buitenkant van deGruyter supermarkten. Uiteraard is er eerst aan de tekentafels berekend, hoe de letters van deGruyter eruit moeten zien en in welke afmetingen zij moeten worden aangebracht? Er is gestoeid over materialen en kleuren. Nu ziet u al op veel supermarkten het resultaat van al dit kreatieve denken en werken.

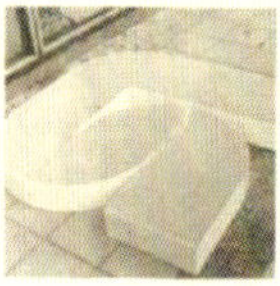

Hier wordt het nieuwe beeld duidelijker. Dit is de lichtbak van het G-beeldmerk, die op de grondplaten wordt gemonteerd. De lichten achter deze oranjegele letter zullen straks het illustrerende werk moeten doen.

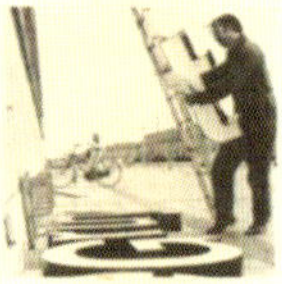

De puzzel is opgelost. De gele G zit er al op en de witte naam deGruyter ligt keurig gerangschikt klaar om gemonteerd te worden. Het is alleen nog een kwestie van draden, schroeven, lampen, trap op en trap af. Felle lampen als inhoud zorgen voor de finishing touch.

De overdekte passages worden niet vergeten. Ook daar is voor verlichting gezocht in een vorm, die aansluit bij de nieuwe huisstijl. De oranjegele lichtbakken laten hier de -G- in wit oplichten, terwijl de naam deGruyter in een strakke zwarte letter aan duidelijkheid niets te wensen overlaat.

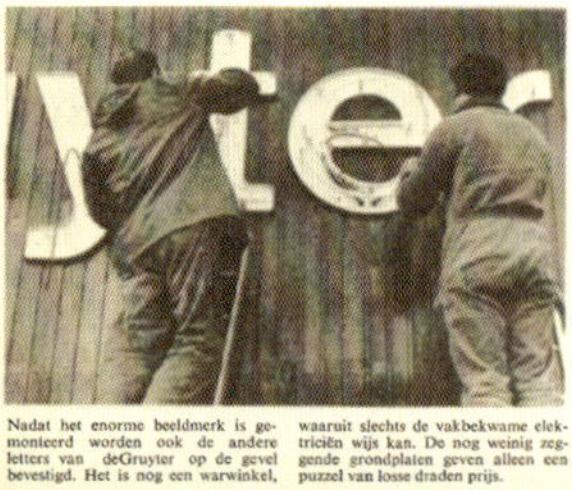

Nadat het enorme beeldmerk is gemonteerd worden ook de andere letters van deGruyter op de gevel bevestigd. Het is nog een warwinkel, waaruit slechts de vakbekwame elektriciën wijs kan. De nog weinig zeggende grondplaten geven alleen een puzzel van losse draden prijs.

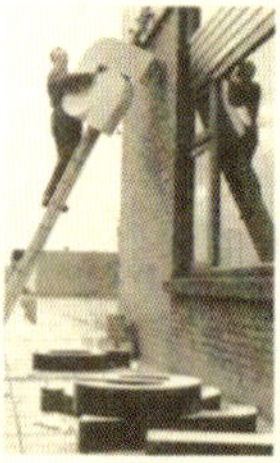

De lichtreklame-jongens hebben de nodige letters in voorraad om zo de boodschap in zijn totaal op de gevel te kunnen plaatsen. Rekening houdende met het architektonische klimaat er omheen, zal op de ene supermarkt de naam in losse blokletters worden geplaatst, terwijl men in een ander centrum grote lichtbakken zal gebruiken.

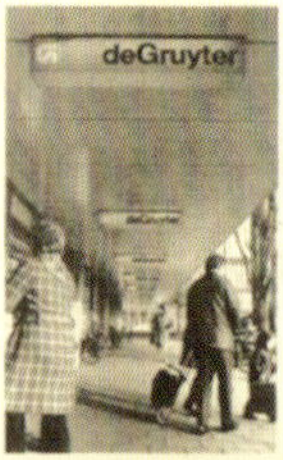

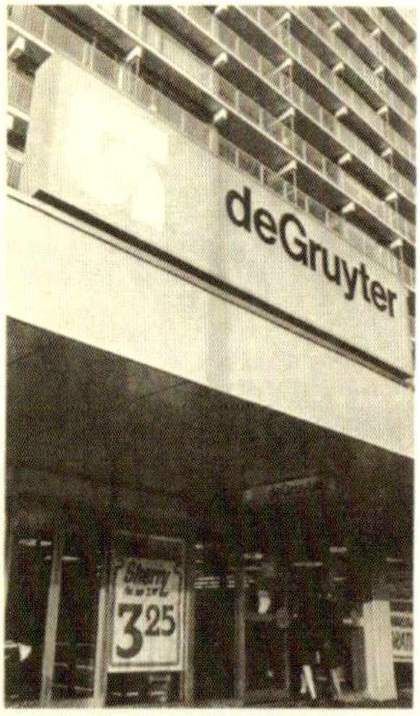

Of het nu de losse 'blokletters' zijn, of het is een grote lichtbak; de nieuwe lichtreklames ontworpen volgens huisstijlprocedure, laten aan de buitenkant duidelijk zien dat er aan de binnenkant wat te koop is bij deGruyter.

in dit nummer o.a.

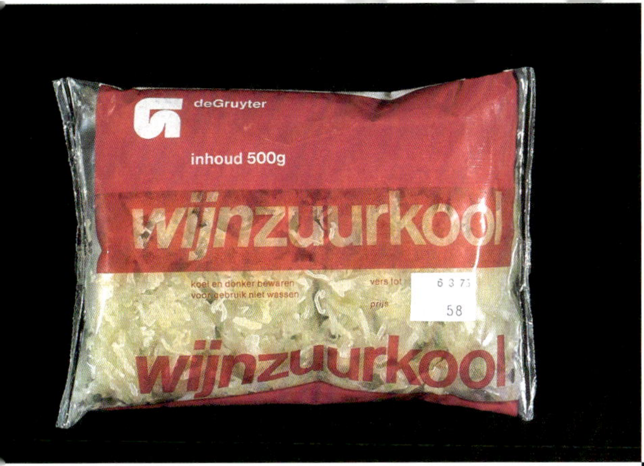

1971-1972
De Gruyter

Corporate design and packaging

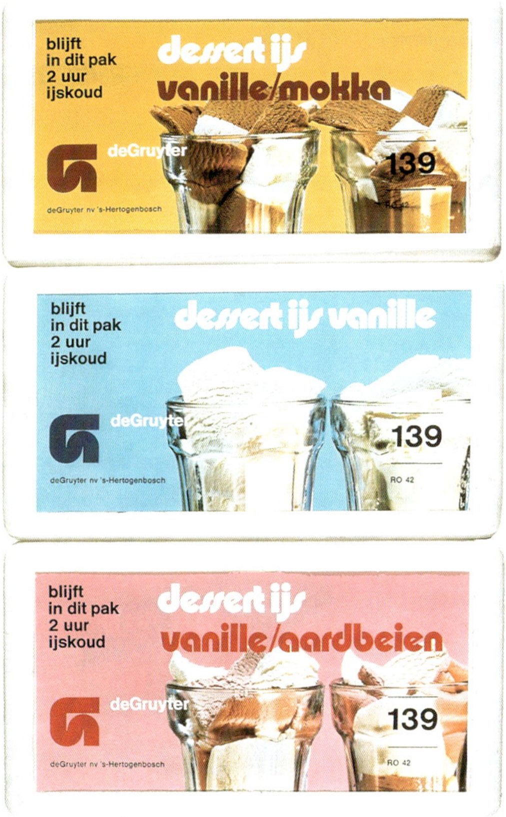

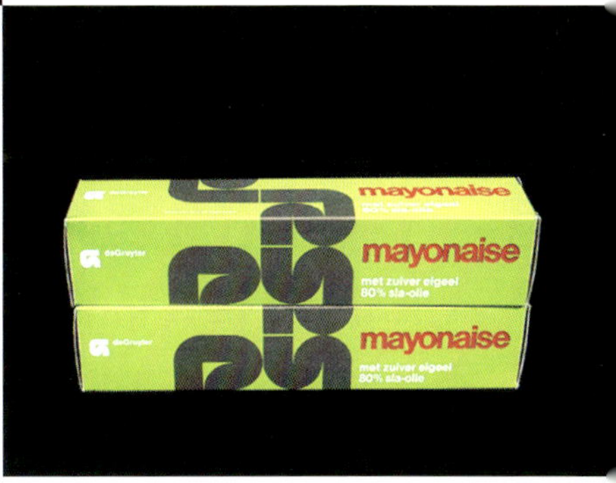

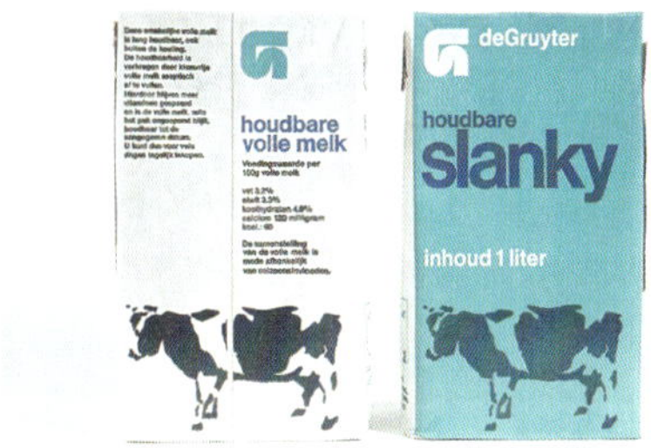

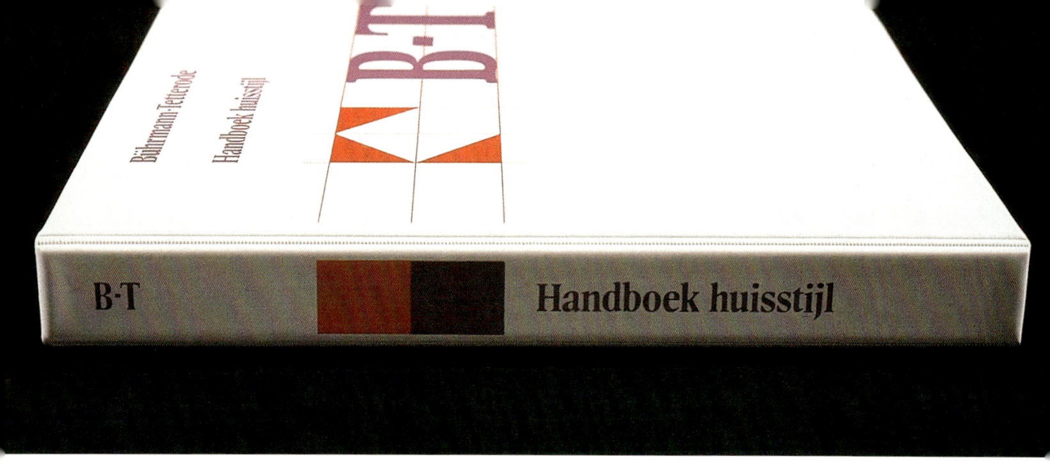

1975
Bührmann-Tetterode
Amsterdam
Wholesale trade in paper and graphic supplies

Corporate design, annual reports

Proposed logo for subsidiary BeauToy (not used)

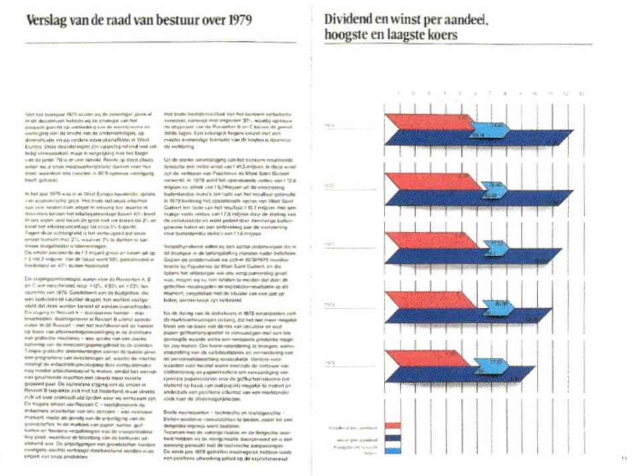

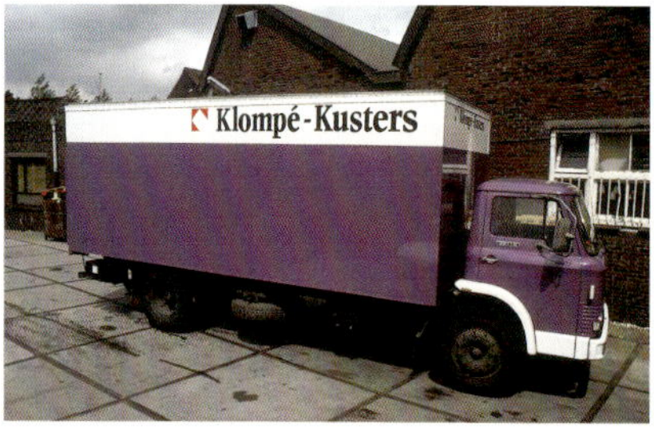

BeauToy

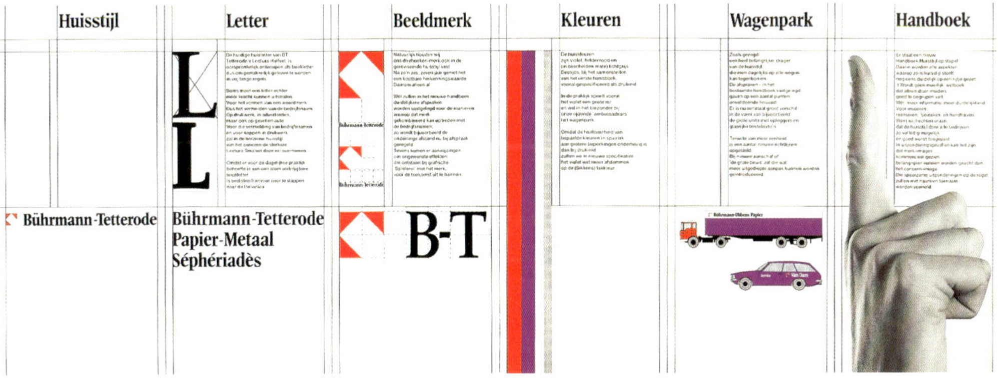
Huisstijl
Letter
Beeldmerk
Kleuren
Wagenpark
Handboek
Bührmann-Tetterode
Bührmann-Tetterode
Papier-Metaal
Séphériadès
B-T

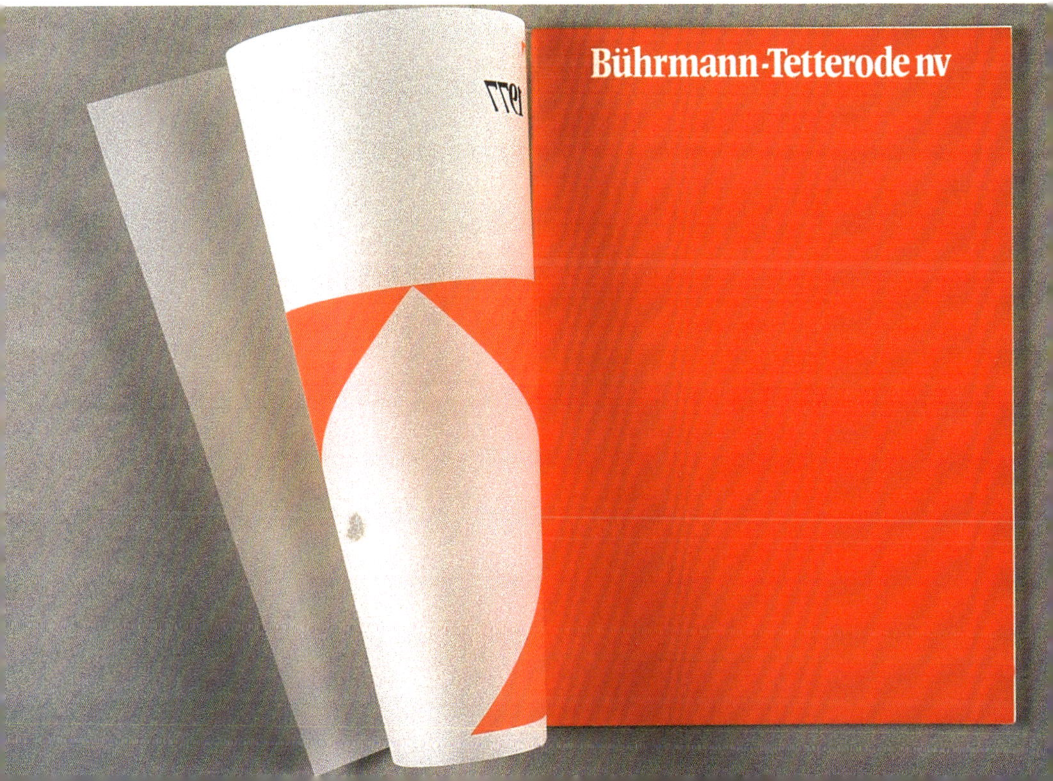
Bührmann-Tetterode nv
1977

1972
Amsterdam Creative Team

Logo, corporate design

1972
VNU publishers
Bloemendaal

Company brochure
Photography by Dolf Kruger

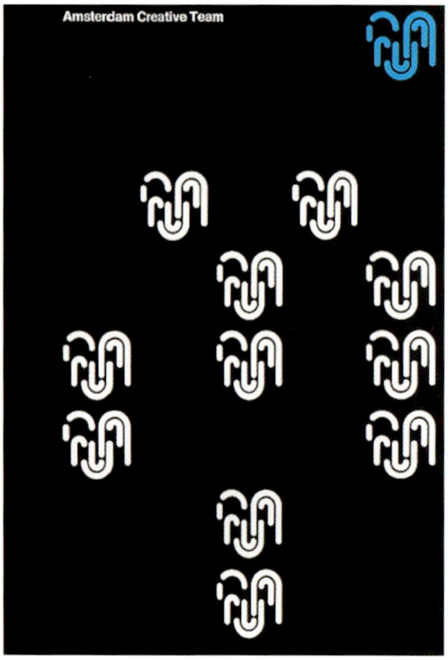

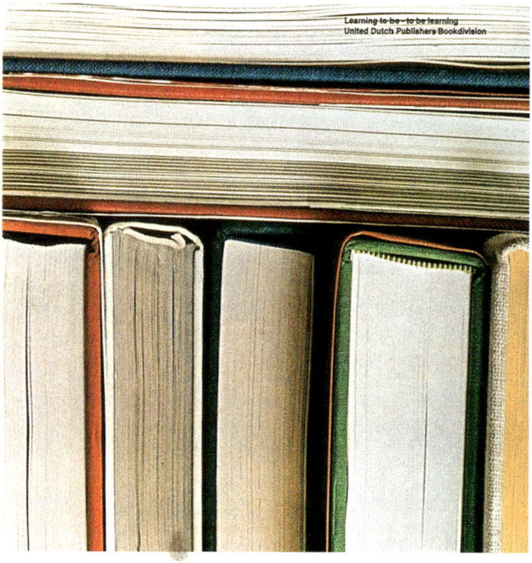

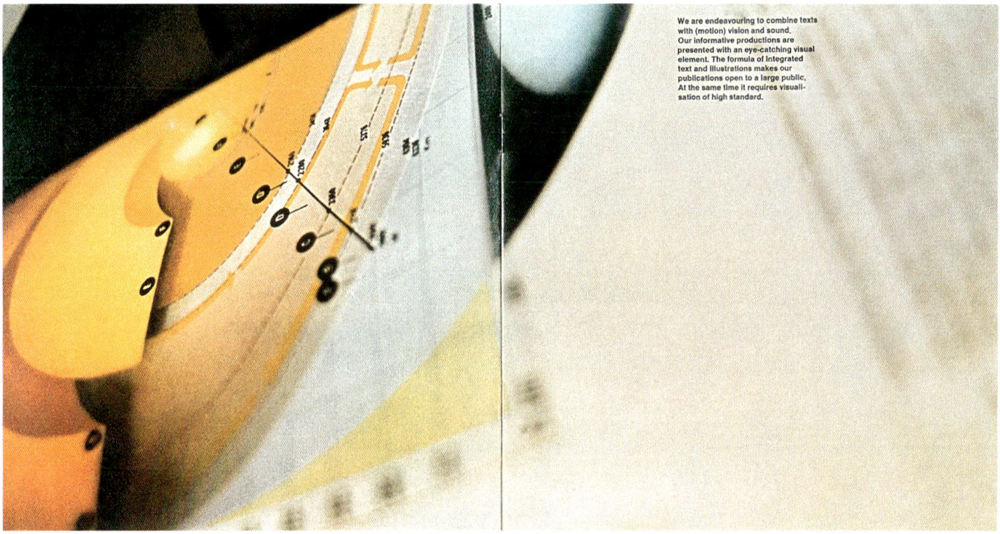
We are endeavouring to combine texts
with (motion) vision and sound.
Our informative productions are
presented with an eye-catching visual
element. The formula of integrated
text and illustrations makes our
publications open to a large public.
At the same time it requires visuali-
sation of high standard.

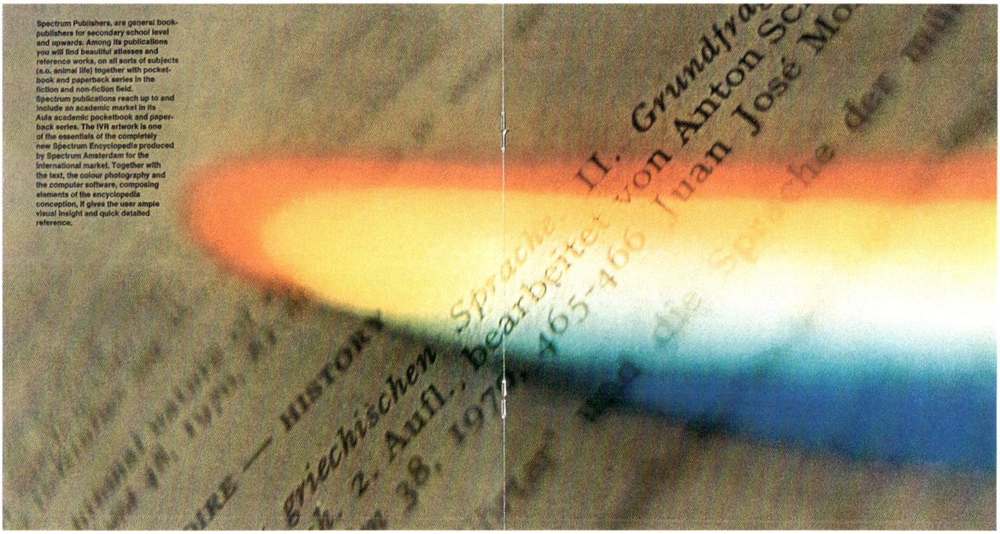
Spectrum Publishers, are general book-
publishers for secondary school level
and upwards. Among its publications
you will find beautiful atlasses and
reference works, on all sorts of subjects
(a.o. animal life) together with pocket-
book and paperback series in the
fiction and non-fiction field.
Spectrum publications reach up to and
include an academic market in its
Aula academic pocketbook and paper-
back series. The IVR artwork is one
of the essentials of the completely
new Spectrum Encyclopedia produced
by Spectrum Amsterdam for the
international market. Together with
the text, the colour photography and
the computer software, composing
elements of the encyclopedia
conception, it gives the user ample
visual insight and quick detailed
reference.

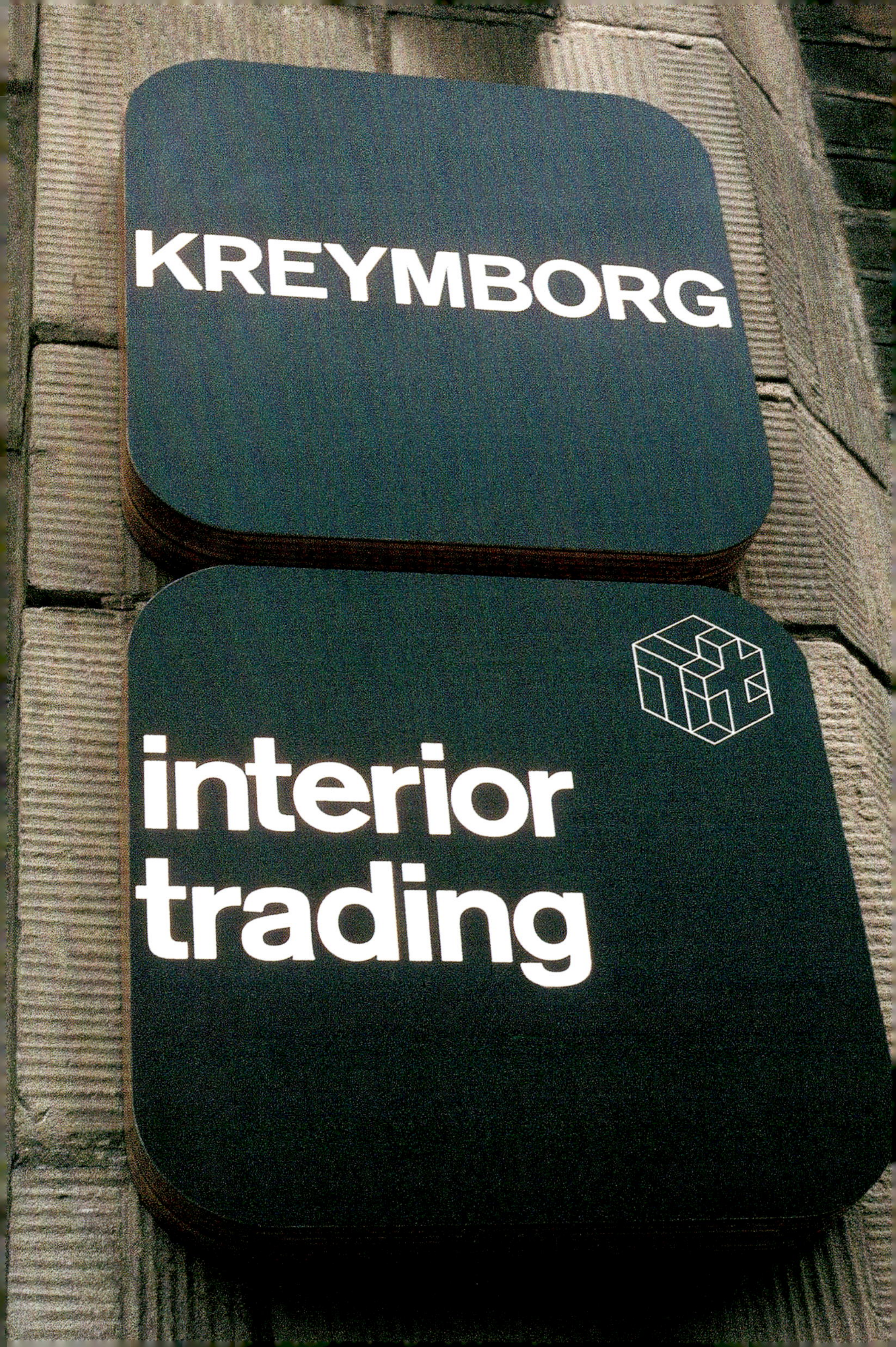
KREYMBORG
interior
trading

Push and shove

Prior to his appointment in 1982 as deputy manager at Total Design, Jelle van der Toorn Vrijthoff had headed the Sdu design department for six years. At this moment he is the manager of Total Design International Holding.

In the late seventies Total Design experimented with the recruitment of designers of an outspoken persuasion that strongly deviated from the TD culture. The point of these experiments was to give new creative impulses to the existing design practice. This policy can hardly be called a success. Anthon Beeke for instance, the most imaginative designer of these, was a loner, stuck to his own working hours, took no interest in other people and did not leave behind a permanent legacy at the studio in the sense of a visionary policy. This made Wim Crouwel realize that he did not just need a good designer, but someone who could lead the studio after he left. At the Sdu I had gained experience within the relatively protected/environment of a government institution with matters that had some resemblance to commercial activity: I could deal with staff, draw up an annual budget, introduce a policy... All of these were qualities that Total Design needed at that time. In 1982 I was appointed as deputy manager. At that time the management was composed of Wim Crouwel, Ben Bos and Loek van der Sande.

It certainly wasn't easy for me to join Total Design. In my opinion the company's products had created something of an expectation pattern. When a client commissioned Total Design he knew more or less what to expect. I believe that Crouwel thought it was about time that the 'old values' which he had introduced and to which he himself had strictly adhered should be abandoned and I wanted to get rid of that predictability, too. Moreover it was a period when other values were beginning to play a role in design, anyway. Total Design's rationality had found a foil in the successful emotionality of Gert Dumbar. The dry-as-dust and humourless functionalist designs which Total Design churned out by the truckload were simply becoming old hat. And although I had personally been influenced by functionalism, my approach was much more illustrative than Crouwel's. I think he suspected that that side of me could also have a 'redemptive' effect on the attitude towards the old design values of the 'Total Design institute'. I do not believe that Ben Bos, who was also very illustration-minded, objected to innovation in that direction. At least I cannot remember that he ever opposed it.

However, he did have strong reservations about the influence of the Aesthedes, the design computer that Total Design started using in 1984, as one of the first j1 design agencies. Suddenly our options multiplied, new shapes could be invented – like typesetting text in a circle in perspective, something that is nearly or wholly impossible to do by hand. However, the new forms also had their drawbacks: sometimes the design process became rather too technology-driven. Ben really hated that. However, I believed you shouldn't run away from technology, although I admit

it did occasionally lead to excesses in the initial stage. Moreover I was very ambitious. I looked ahead to the future and wanted to put my personal stamp on that development. In doing so I occasionally lost sight of the fact that the old values also have their merits. And Ben was unmistakably a representative of those, especially after Crouwel left in 1985. Unfortunately, that inevitably led to friction.
Ben Bos had to carry on at a design agency that was going through a transformation and at some point I think it all became too much for him. When Ben was 56 we had agreed that managers would step down at 60. This agreement also entailed that, in anticipation of this, Ben would gradually withdraw while my role would gradually become more dominant. That is the normal run of things: someone approaching retirement age no longer needs to put his stamp on decisions that concern the future of a company. However, it didn't really work out that way for Ben. Even at sixty he was unable to relinquish his leading role. He just hadn't reached the point where he could confidently hand over the baton. And my fellow manager Dirk-Jan van Haren Noman and I needed to force his hand. That involved a lot of push and shove, which created a certain distance between us. Ben was unhappy and disillusioned and one sad day he gave us his notice.
I have always regretted that. Ben is a gifted designer, not a revolutionary, but still someone who has consistently produced work of a very high standard. He was also a gifted studio worker, as steady as a rock, who always made sure that we worked at a profit. I thought then, and I still do, that his knowledge and expertise should have been preserved for the studio. I also think that at Total Design he could have had a much more valuable 'extension' of his career than the one he had at 2D3D. After all, he didn't really come into his own there. Fortunately he managed to live that down with the expansion of Randstad in America.
I have certainly not tried to sweep Total Design clean of the old design values, let alone that I tried to get rid of Ben, who was strongly identified with those values. I have always considered it a good thing if people from outside the design agency, even many years after Ben left, sensed that these values – analysis, precision, severity – were still present in our work. That Ben left us was the outcome of an emotional conflict. His subsequent attitude towards us was also quite rancorous and critical. But I can't turn back time. Everyone responds differently to events. I don't hold Ben's reaction against him.
DvG

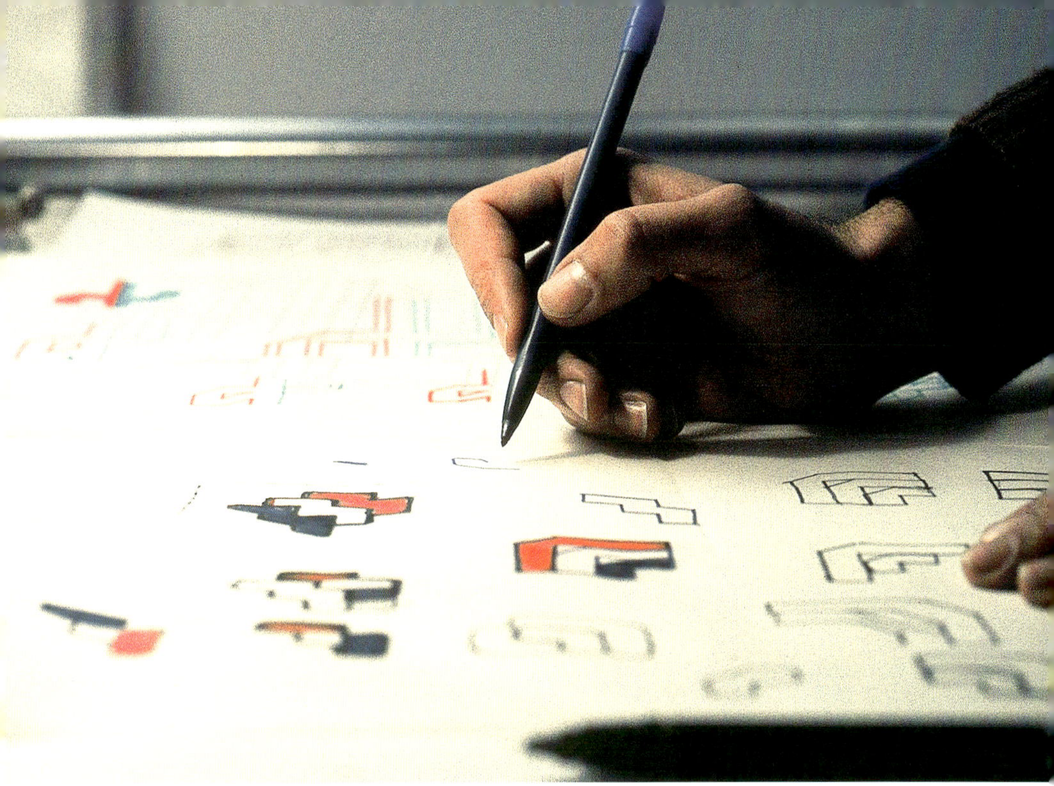

1975
Kreymborg and Interior Trading
Amsterdam

Logo, wall plates

1974
De Nationale Investeringsbank
The Hague

Logo, corporate design

De
Nationale
Investeringsbank
NV

1975
Arch
Waddinxveen
Architects and builders

Logo, corporate design

1975
Dronten municipality

Logo, corporate design

In 1975 Dronten, a city in the new land, the Flevo Polder on the former Zuiderzee bed, was one of the first Dutch municipalities to acquire a visual identity.
The commission was restricted to the initial work. The further realization was performed in-house.
In 2000 this visual identity is still in use.

1975
Folder
Photography by Aart Klein

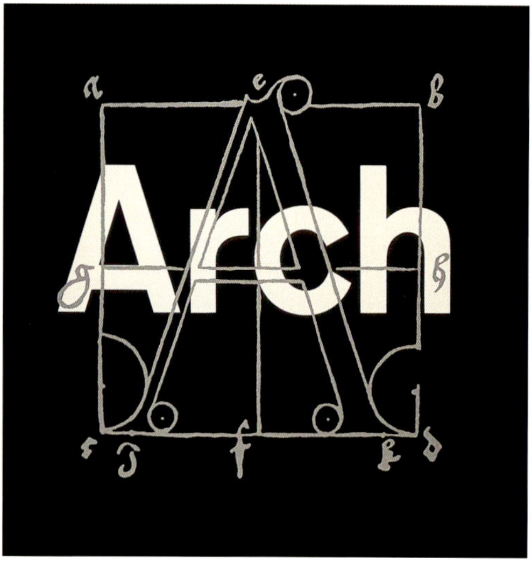

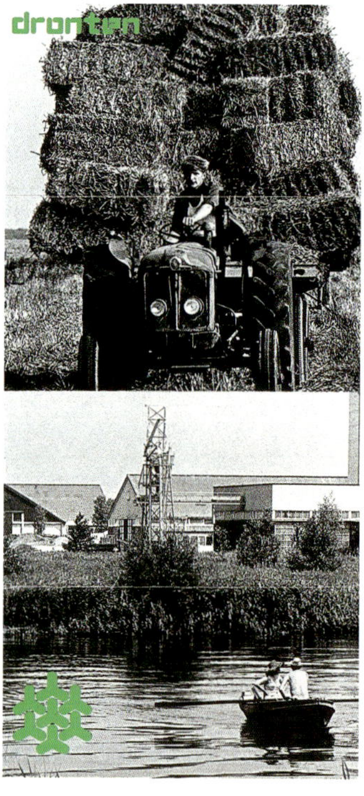

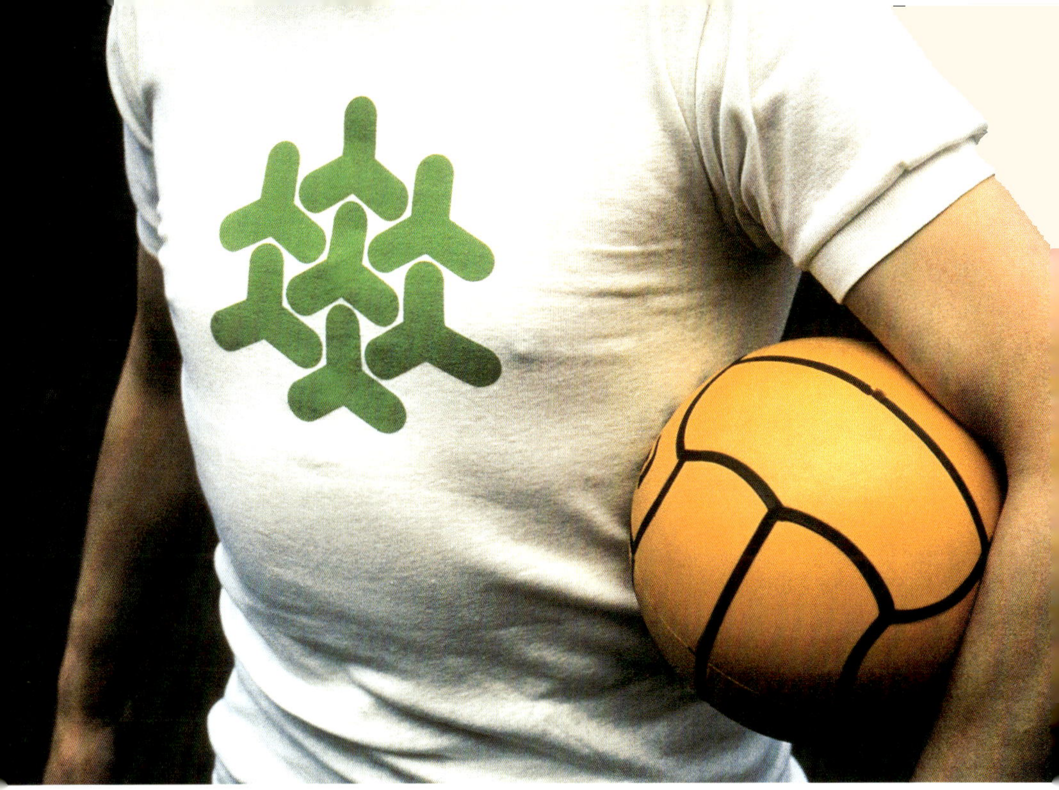

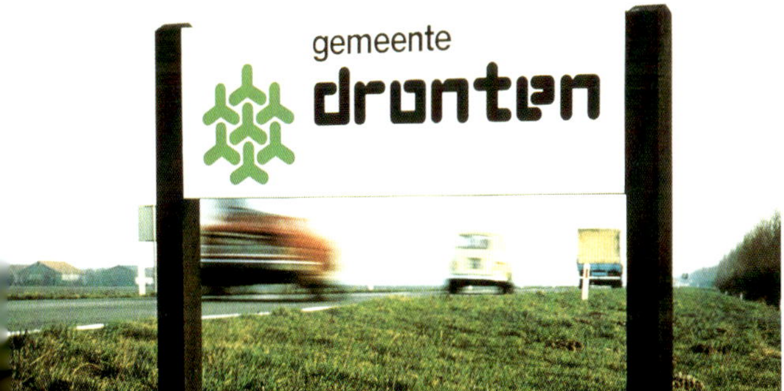
gemeente
dronten

1976
Jantje de Goede Banket
Mijdrecht

Jantje de Goede produces semi-finished products for confectioneries and restaurants.

Logo, corporate design

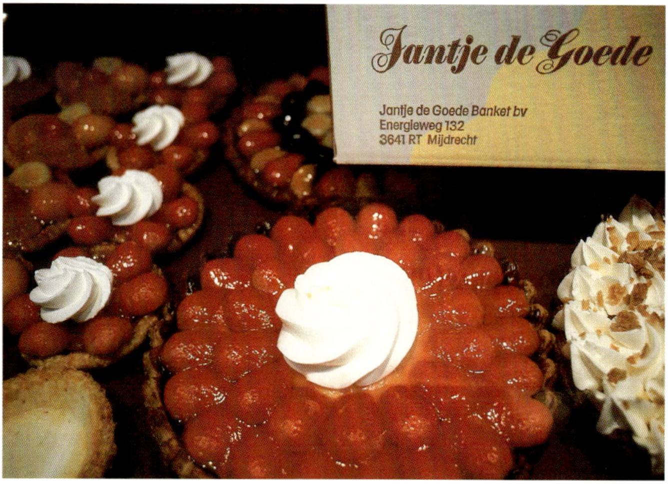

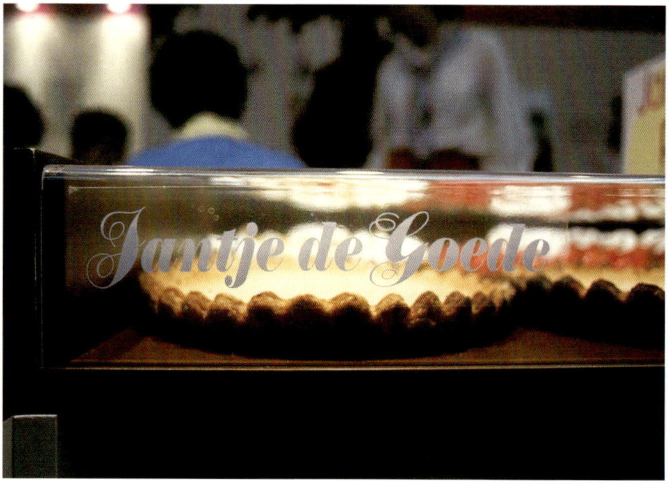

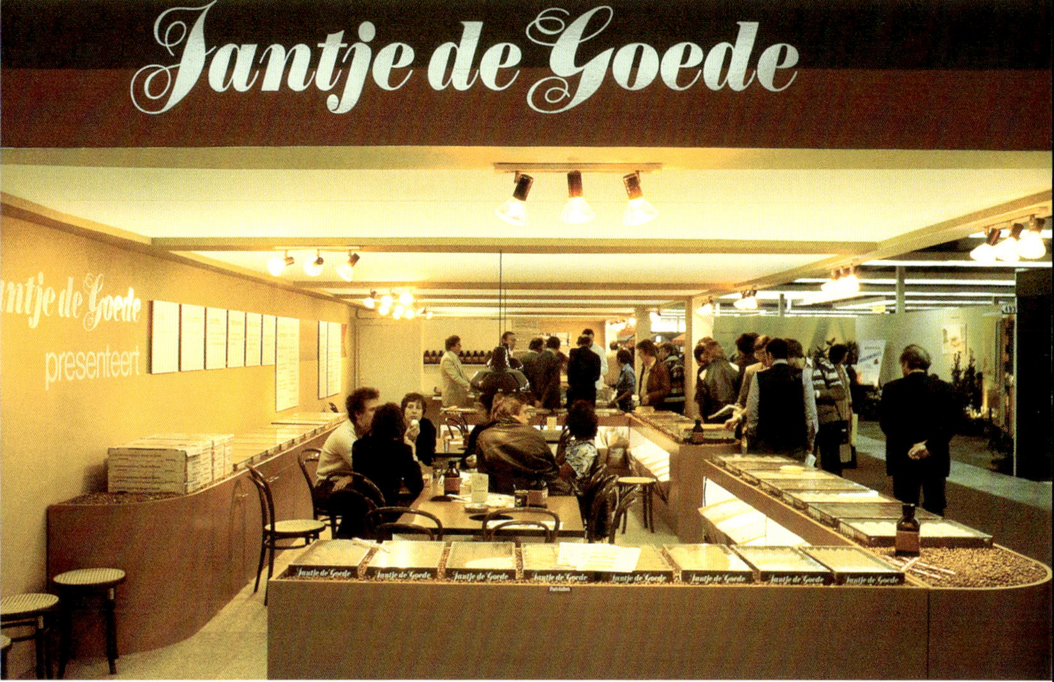

Nota nr.

Jantje de Goede Banket bv

Jantje de Goede

Energieweg 132
Mijdrecht
Postbus 113
Telefoon 02979-5750

Postgiro 50 49 48
Bankier: Banque de Paris et des Pays-Bas, Haarlem
Banknr. 63.35.27.068

Turko hazelnootgebak
Halffabrikaten
40 maal bekroond

Faktuurdatum

datum	aantal colli	omschrijving	per eenheid	totaal

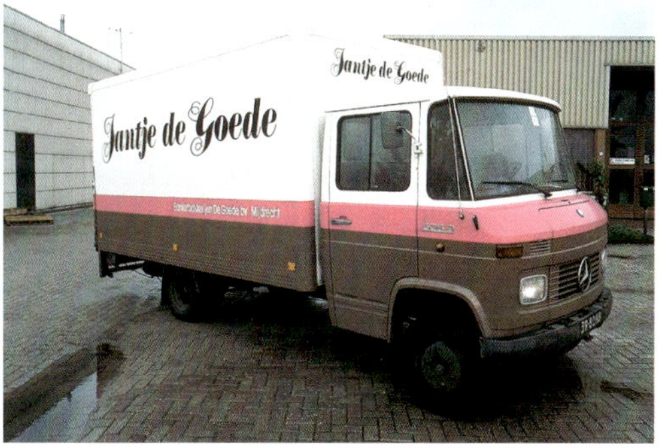

1980
Trade fair stand

>
1981
Colour scheme for machines developed in-house

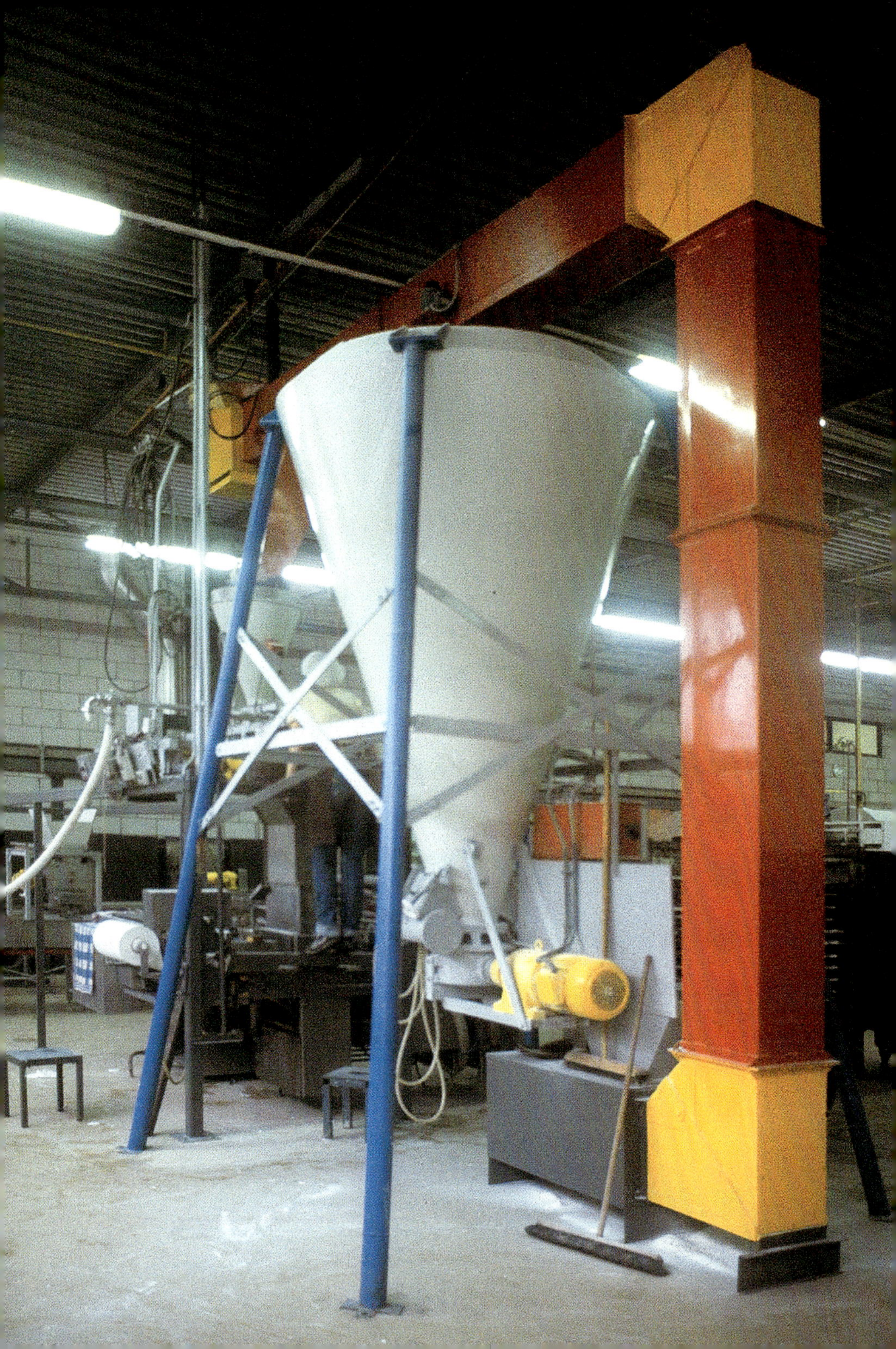

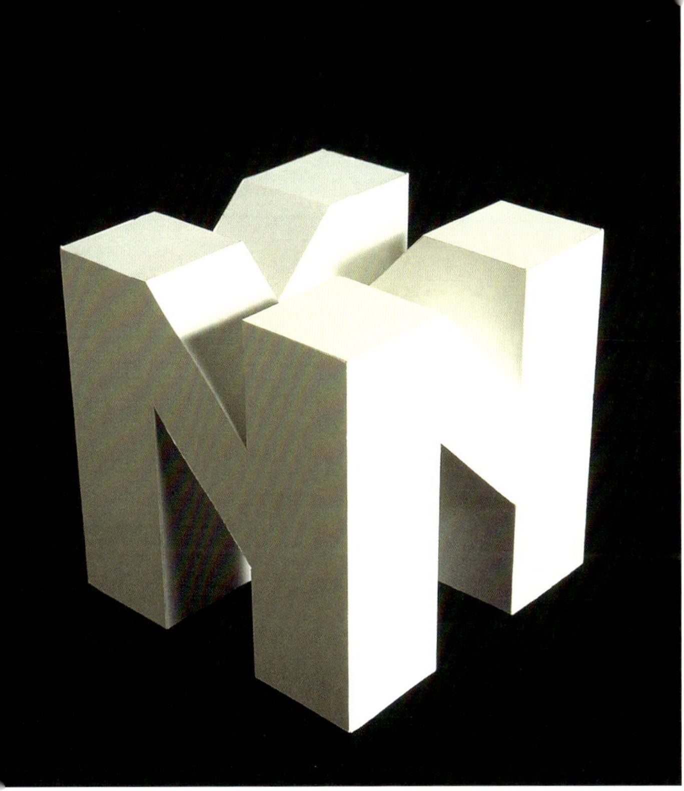

1976
Netwerk 3
Diemen
Security
(subsidiary of the Randstad Groep)

Logo, corporate design

1976
Vedior Holding
Amsterdam
Cleaning services

Logo, corporate design

vereniging van zieken-
bejaarden- en andere
huisomroepen
hilversum
postbus 645

1977
Ziekenomroep Nederland
(Dutch Hospital Broadcasting)
Hilversum

Logo, corporate design

1977
Chase International
Shipping company Europe-Canada
Antwerp

This shipping company intended to sail container ships between Europe and Canada. That is reflected in the corporate design. In the logo the Canadian maple leaf is combined with two arrows: one moving west and one moving east. The project stranded when the enterprise was rounded up by the Dutch Ministry of Justice.

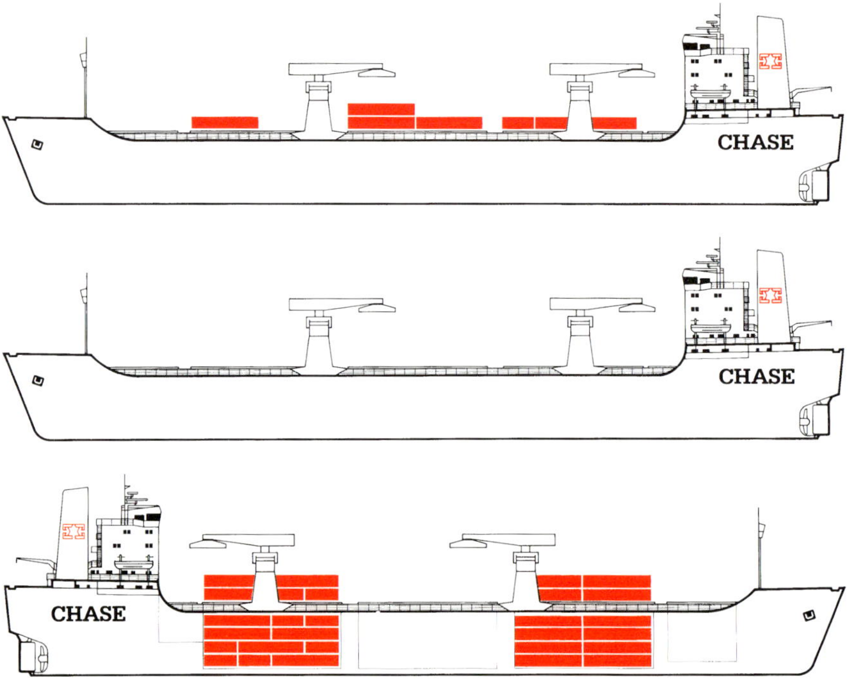

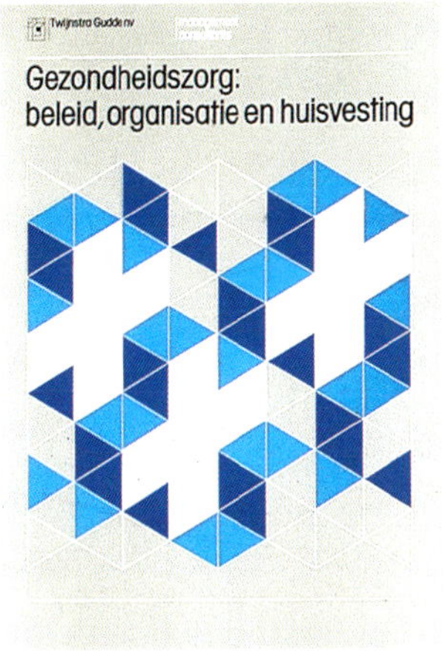

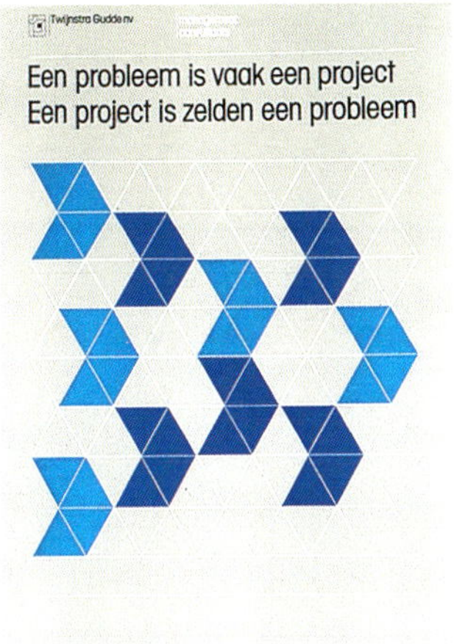

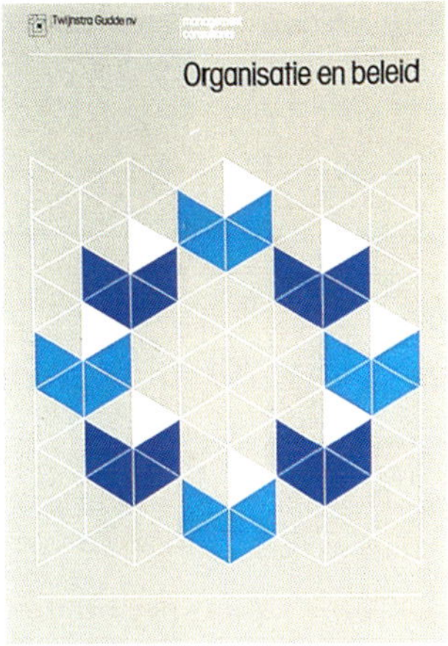

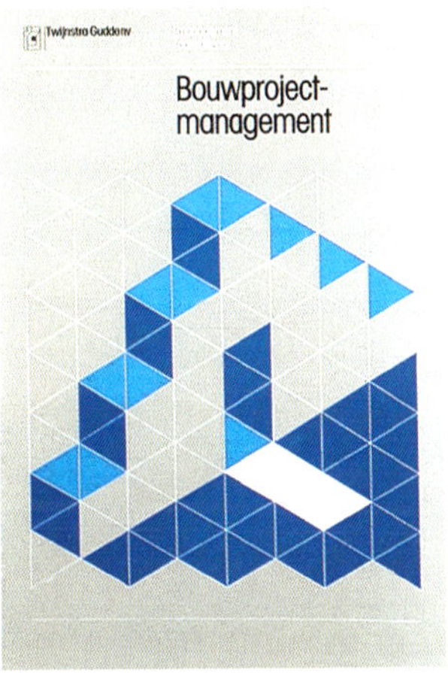

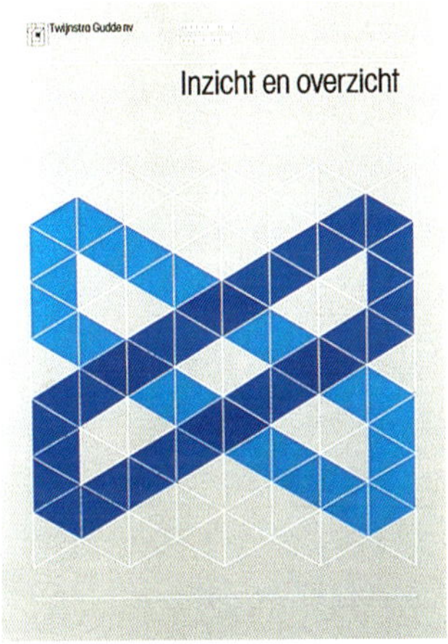

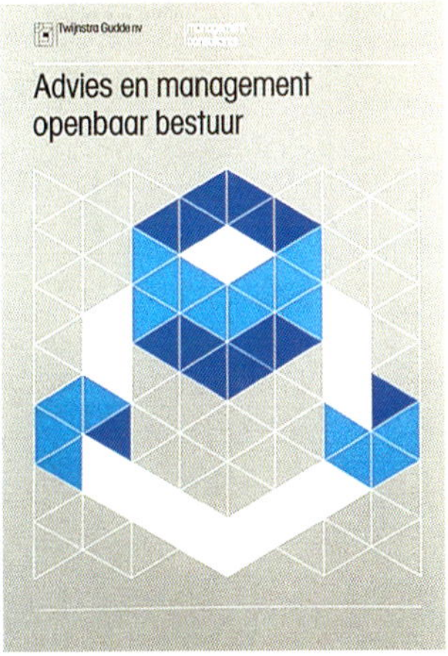

1977
TwijstraGudde
Management consultants
Deventer

Logo, corporate design
Product brochures

1977

Lecturis Eindhoven

Printers and publishers

Publication 'Indruk in Druk'

Text, editing, design

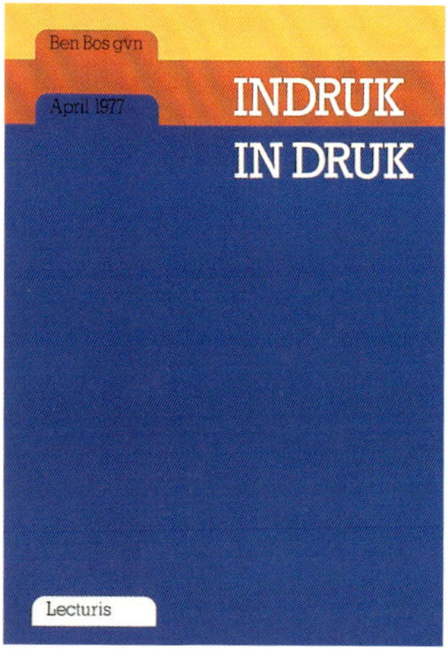

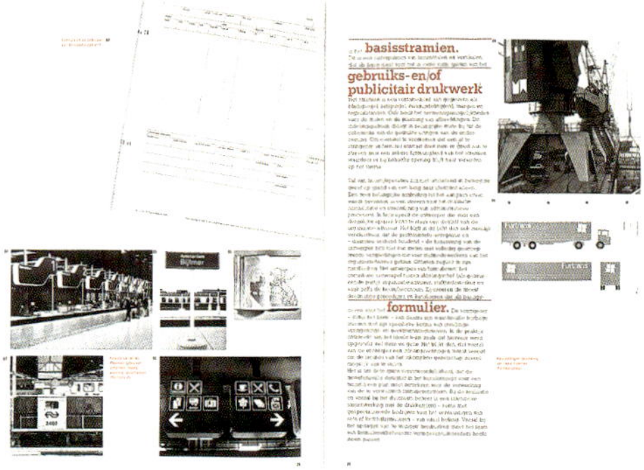

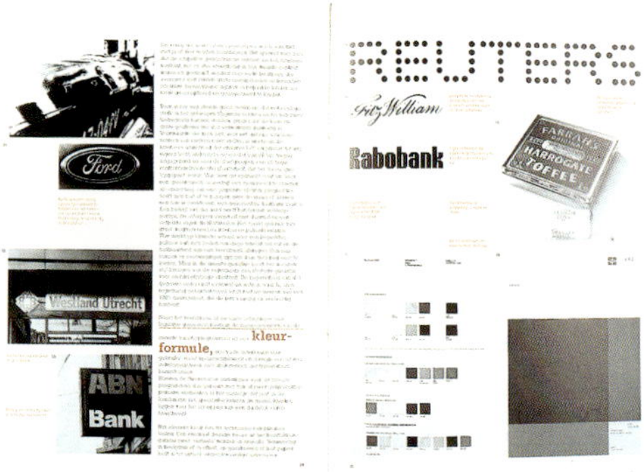

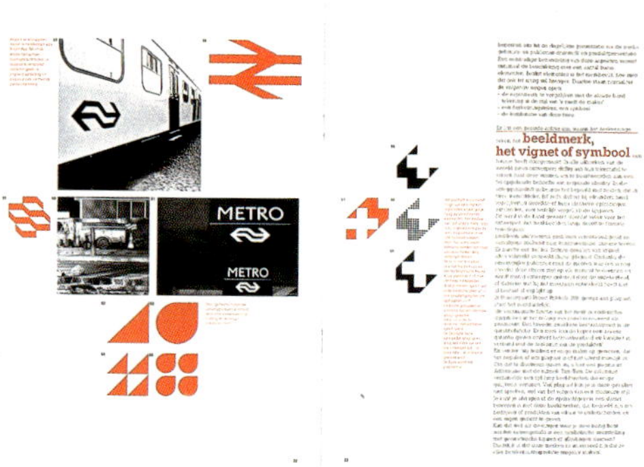

1992

Bis Publishers

Amsterdam

Publication 'Design, de onworpen meerwaarde' (Design, the designed added value)

Text and design

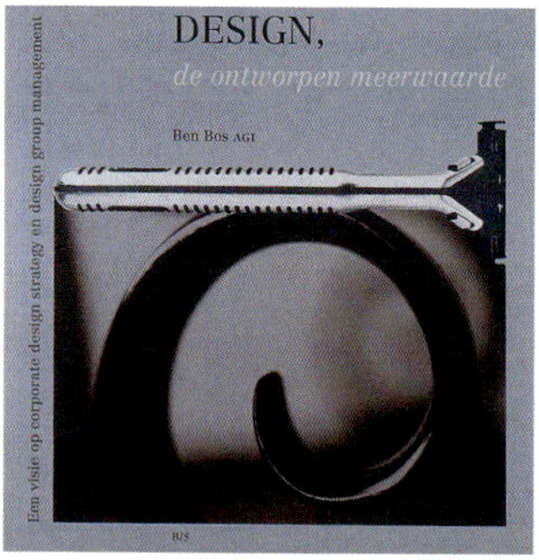

1978

B&G Hekwerk

Best

Fencing manufacturers

Logo, corporate design

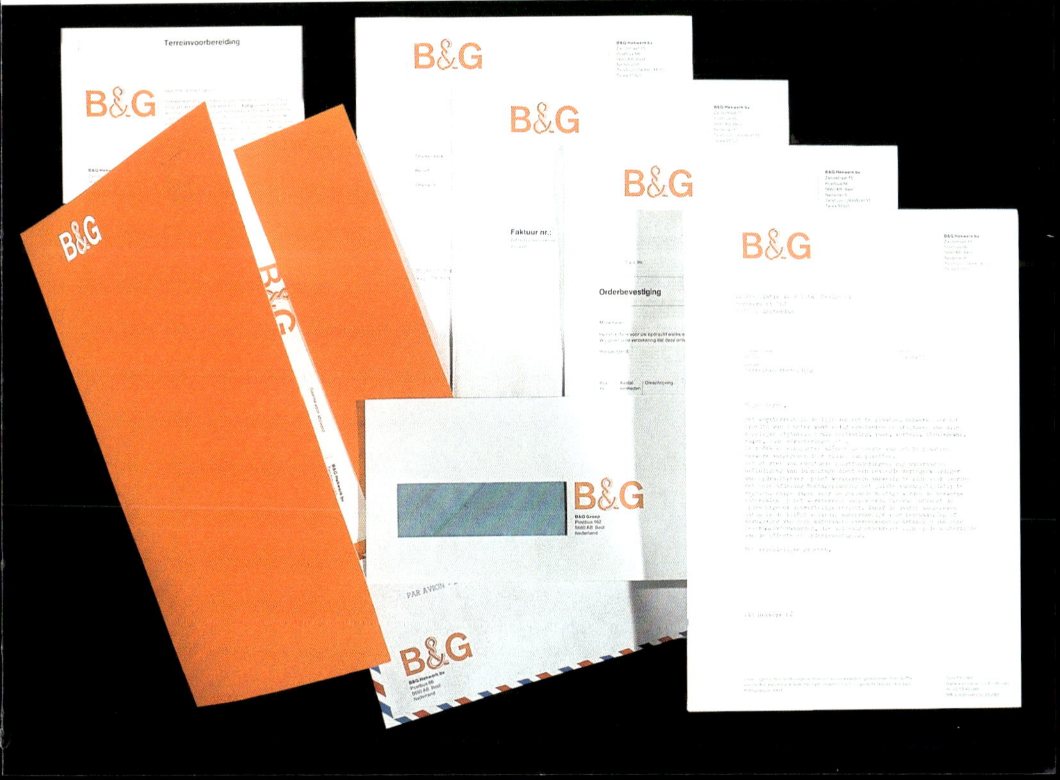

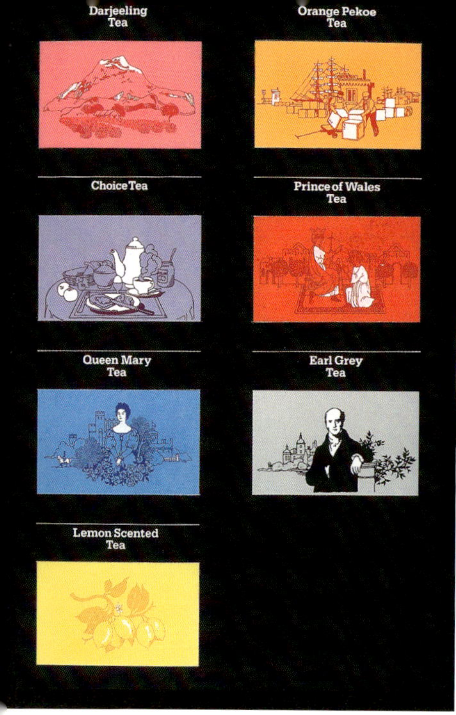

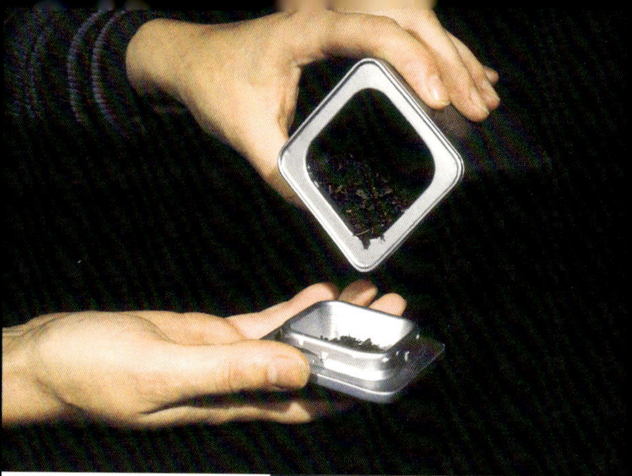

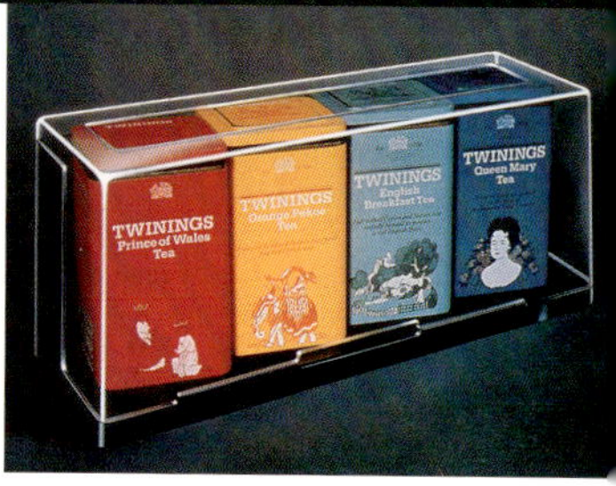

1979

Twinings Tea for Japan

Tokyo

In Japan tea is a luxury gift item. The tea gift is placed on a prominent spot in the room to display the beautiful gift that was received. It is intended for showing off, not for the tea pot. Accordingly, the tea comes from Europe, from England to be precise.
All major brands pack their tea in cubic cans with a lid on which you break your nails. They are executed in the classic colours for the various flavours and with a more or less identical typography, regardless whether the brand is called Lyons, Lipton's or Twinings. They are indistinguishable, certainly if you can only read Japanese characters.
Twining importer Kataoka did not reach his targets and wanted a new design from Europe. After all, that was where this tea came from.
Ben Bos and Wim Verboven were assigned Masaharu Noguchi (of GK Design, Tokyo) as a special assistant.
They developed a new concept in collaboration with industrial designer Hans Kraayenhof.
The new box is not cubic but high and narrow and can be stacked.
It has the same click-on lid as small shoe polish pots. The lid has a hollow for dosing the tea.
They used the Japanese printing ink colours of Dai Nippon Ink, which are much more refined than the standard PMS colours. The text was typeset using letters designed by Adrian Frutiger, while illustrations of Earl Grey, the mountains of Darjeeling, Orange Pekoe en Queen Mary were also used.

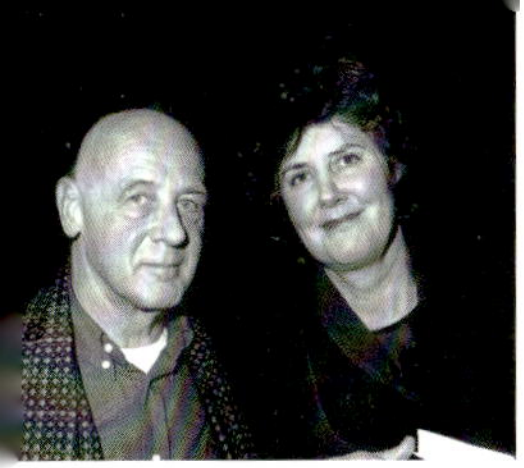

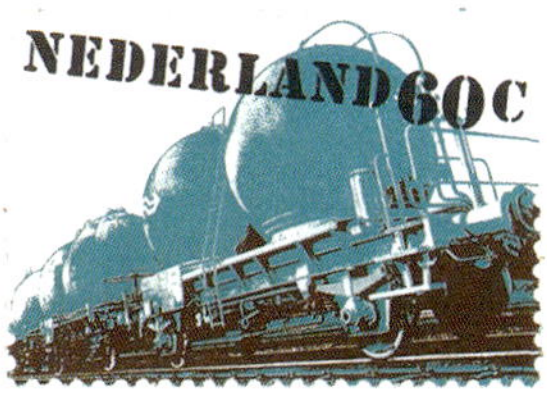

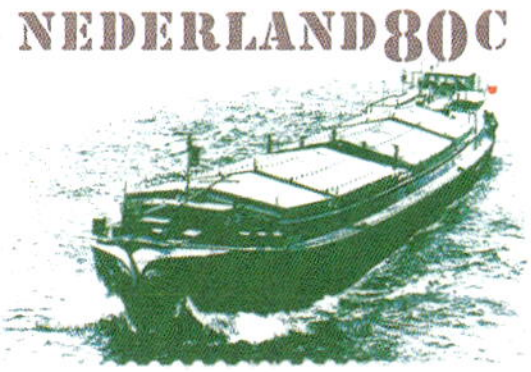

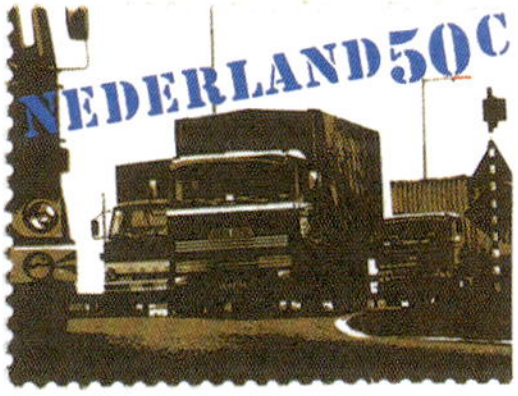

1980
PTT Nederland
Den Haag

Postage stamps series

The topic of the series was ‘Holland transport country’. To Bos’s great disappointment air transport was not included. During the presentation, director-general Leeman of the PTT objected to the legibility of the car brands (DAF and Ford) and the number plate on the road transport stamp. By means of minimal retouching Ben Bos changed the number plate into the telephone number of his girlfriend Jantien.

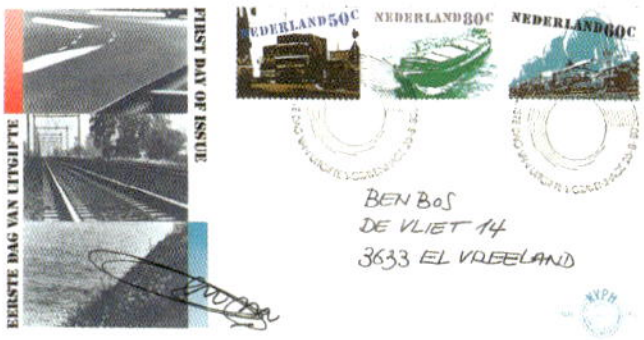

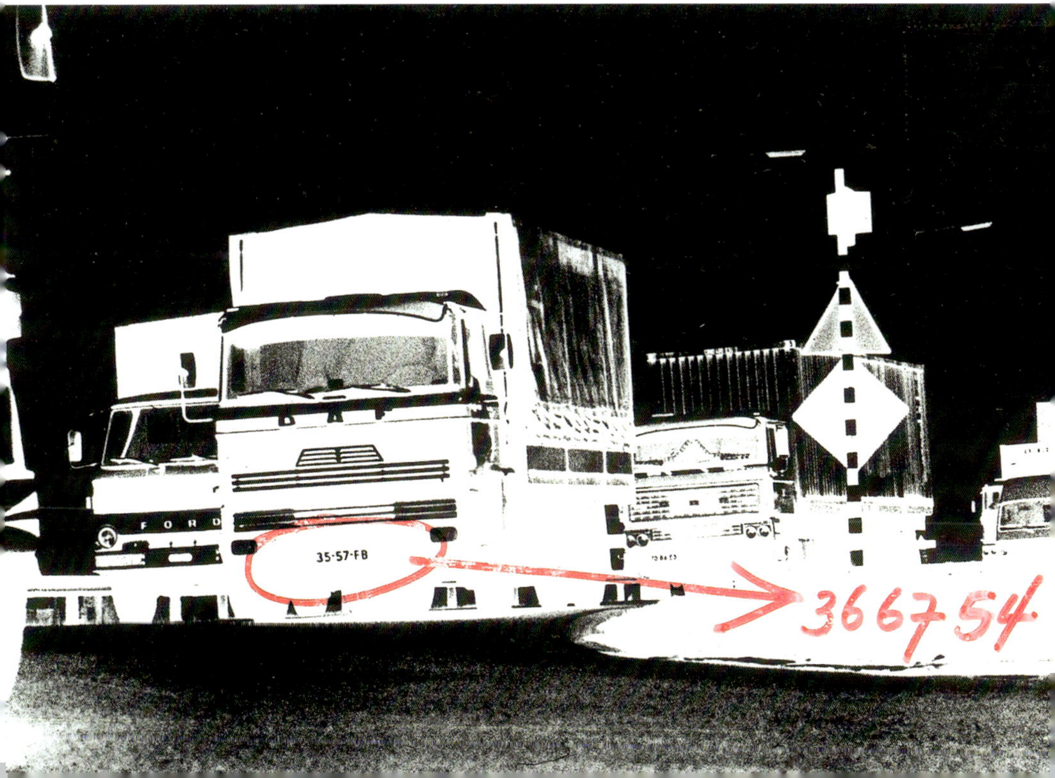

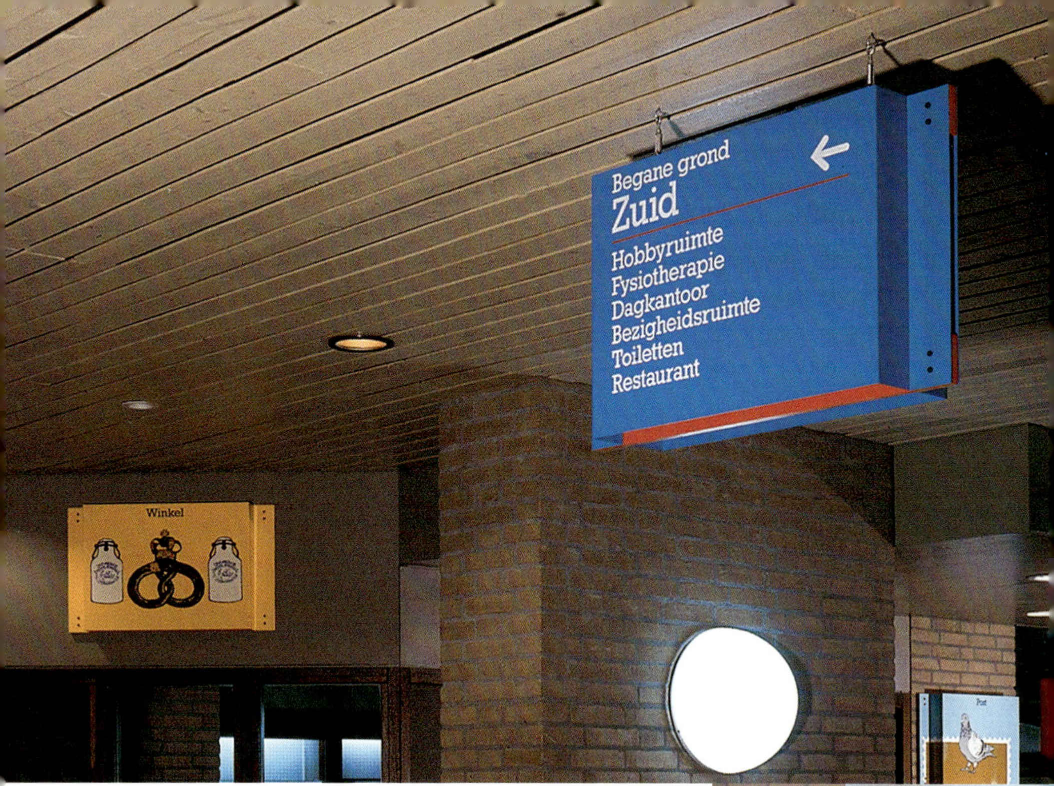

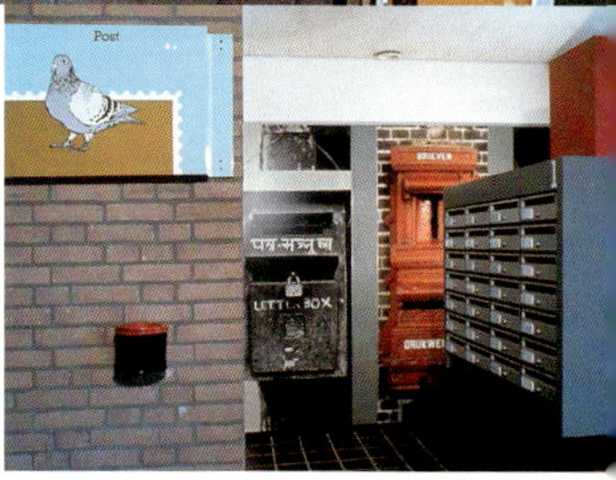

1980
Nieuw Vredenburgh
Old people's home
Amsterdam

Corporate design, interior design consultancy
In collaboration with
Wim van der Weerd and
Frans Lieshout

The St Augustinus Church at the Postjesweg had become too large for its parish, while the Vredenburgh old people's home near the Amsterdam red light district was long past its prime. The Stichting Vredenburgh saw an opportunity for constructing a new future at the Postjesweg for the church and the home.
Architects Van Gendt en Mühlstaff had already built several old people's homes.
Ben Bos was added to the team that would define the requirements that the new building had to meet while he would also design a routing system for the new complex. In response to the dull home in the village of Castricum where his mother lived Bos was anxious to contribute to the creation of a home that the occupants would experience as a warm place that their children and grandchildren would also be happy to visit.
The solution was sought in better colours, a real Amsterdam brown café, a stylish and fresh hairdresser's salon, a real shop instead of the standard supermarket, a pleasant telephone booth that was accessible for wheelchairs, a colourful routing system that was both pictorial and legible, and a cheerfully decorated pigeon-hole space. Bos called it 'one of my most satisfying commissions.'

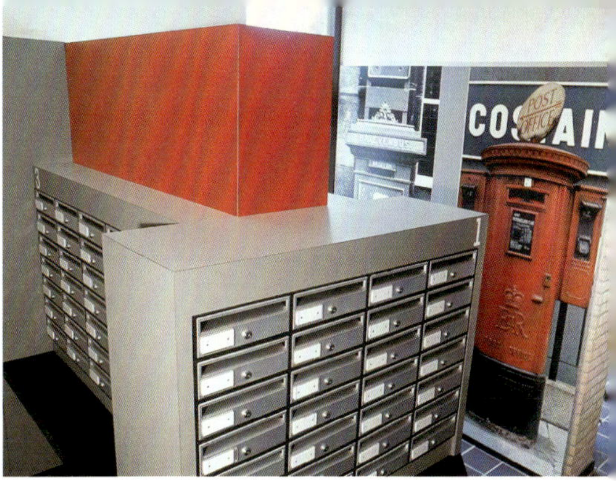
POST OFFICE

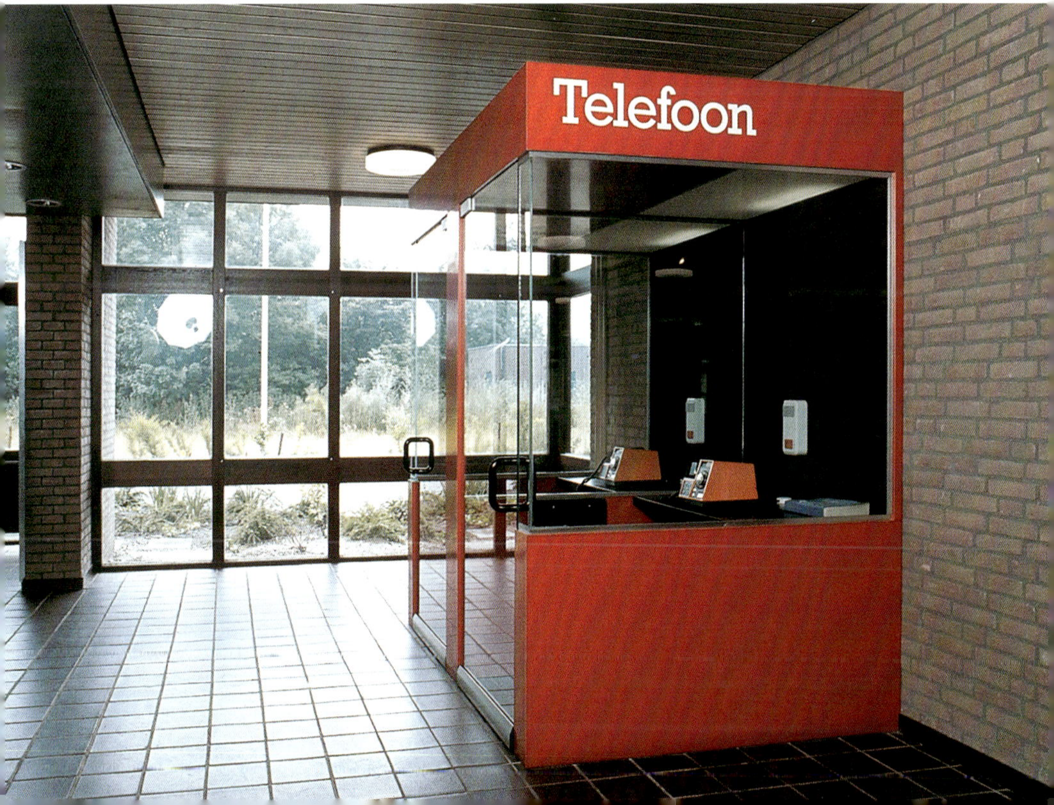
Telefoon

1980

Capelle aan den IJssel municipality

Logo, corporate design

Model of garbage truck
Routing system for temporary city hall

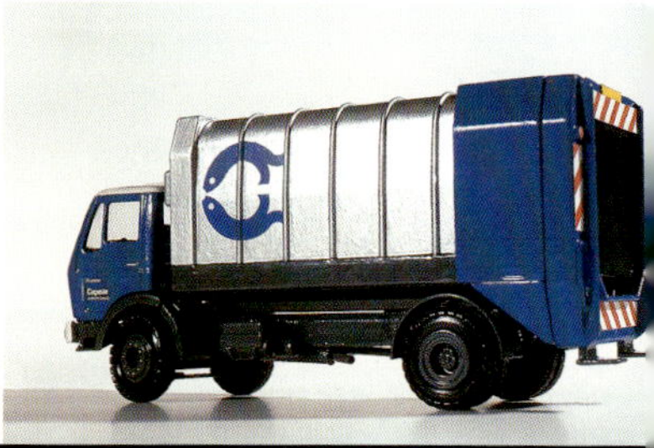

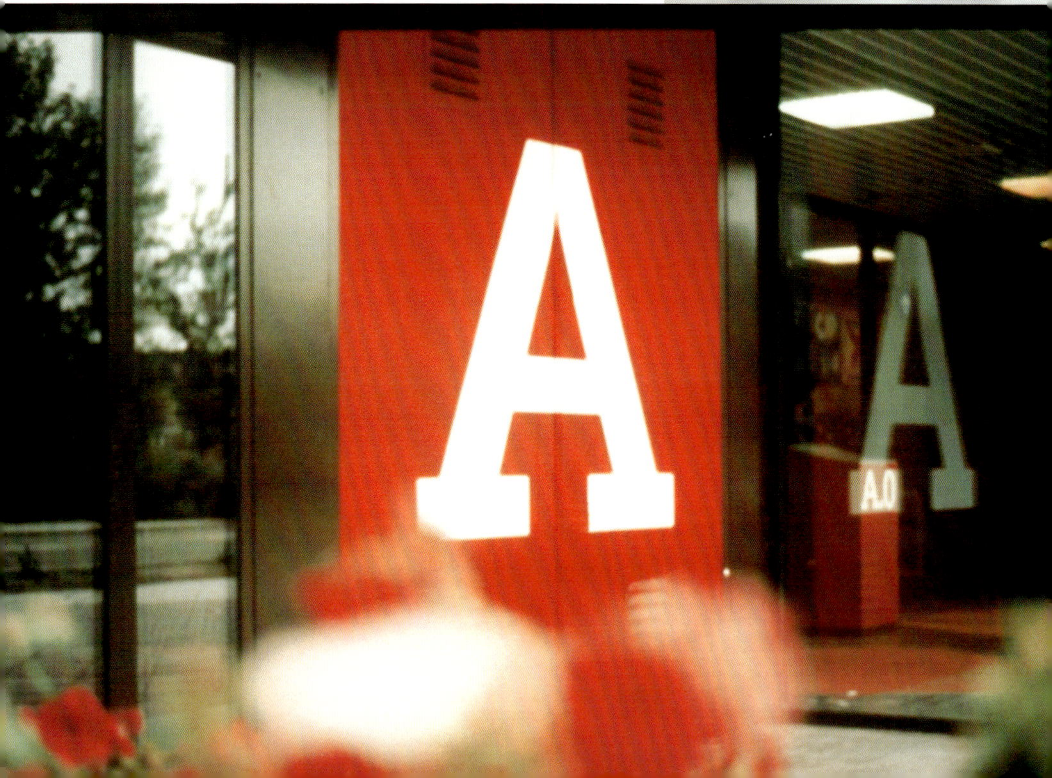

Ben's little backpack

From 1990 to 1996 Peter Boelsma was the only non-designing partner at 2D3D design studio. He was responsible for finances, automation, new business, personnel and future policy. Boelsma currently works as a consultant at New York design recruitment agency Janou Pakter Inc.

When I joined 2D3D it was a medium-size design studio strongly rooted in The Hague. Its clients were mainly public institutions and non-profit organisations like museums. 2D3D's core activities were the development of corporate identities and related activities such as designing brochures and annual reports. However, the studio aimed to become better, stronger and bigger. We wanted to rise above our regional ties, i.a. by developing consultancy activities for commercial clients. After all, you have to have several irons in the fire if you want to be a healthy and strong studio, especially at a time of government cuts. At some stage we heard that Ben Bos was not feeling happy at Total Design. He was 61 at the time. So we approached him.

An important motive for seeking cooperation with Ben was our wish to increase our credibility in the eyes of 'the outside world'. If Ben joined us we hoped to attract many years of experience, an extensive network, name familiarity and perhaps a couple of clients. Among ourselves we spoke of 'Ben's little backpack' that contained all of these things. We hoped that the contents of this backpack would generate new commissions.

To some extent these expectations proved justified. A number of clients became aware of 2D3D, simply because Ben had joined us. Other expectations were not realized. It is hard to pinpoint the precise reason for this, but it is a fact that in the end the cooperation did not work out the way we had all hoped. Due to various factors the cooperation ran aground.

2D3D was an egalitarian studio. Every designer partner was responsible for a team of which the members, including the junior designers, enjoyed considerable freedom. Sometimes the studio seemed to be made up of several small companies, each with its own subculture. I think Ben had difficulty dealing with that. In our studio he had the role of autonomous consultant. Ben acted as an advisor to our clients and had to translate their wishes into creative products. But for the realization of these he depended on the teams that already existed. And that was hard. I believe he felt a need to compete with the partner in charge of such a team. That was a cultural gap which we underestimated.

Ben was not a partner, but that was never his aim. We had an understanding that he would work with us for a limited number of years. We thought: Ben still has a few active years left before he retires. We want him to work here so that we can absorb his experience and the know-how that he has acquired over the years and be the guardians of his heritage after his retirement. We have always discussed this with

him in those terms. He would hand over the contents of his little backpack to us. He stayed with us for over two years and then decided to call it quits. That was a great disappointment to us, also financially, because he did not exactly come cheap. We had made an investment in the hope of making a return on it. But it didn't work out that way. When he left he just took his well-filled backpack with him. From his point of view that is quite understandable, but we greatly regretted it.
DvG

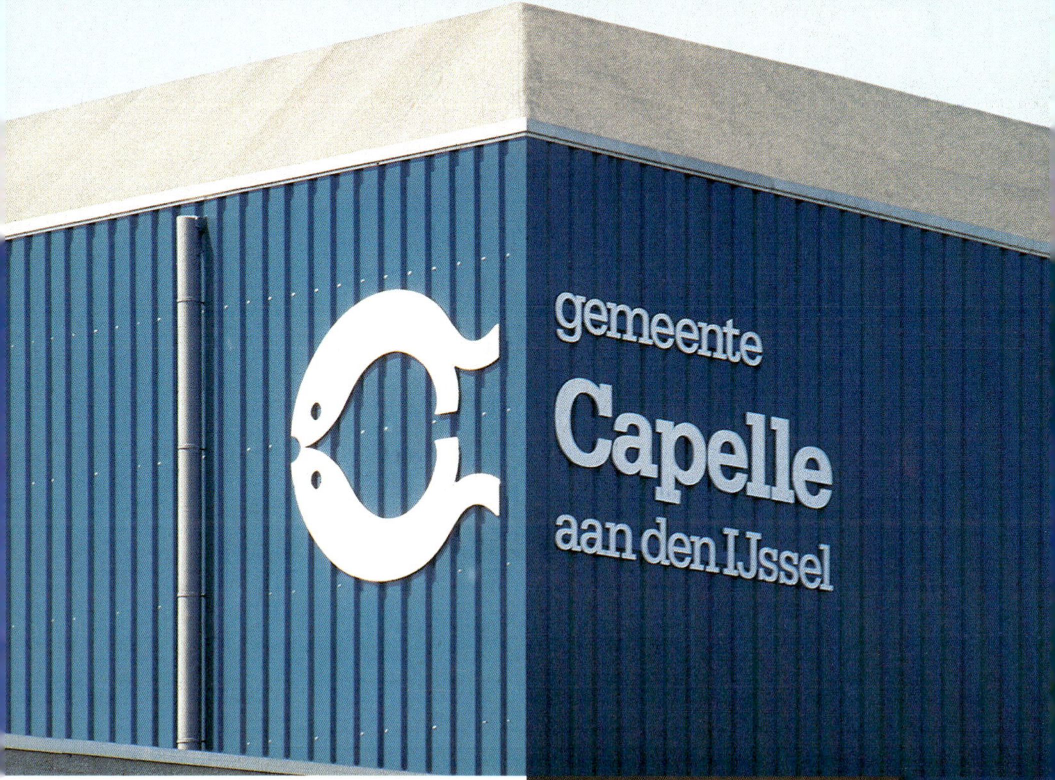
gemeente
Capelle
aan den IJssel

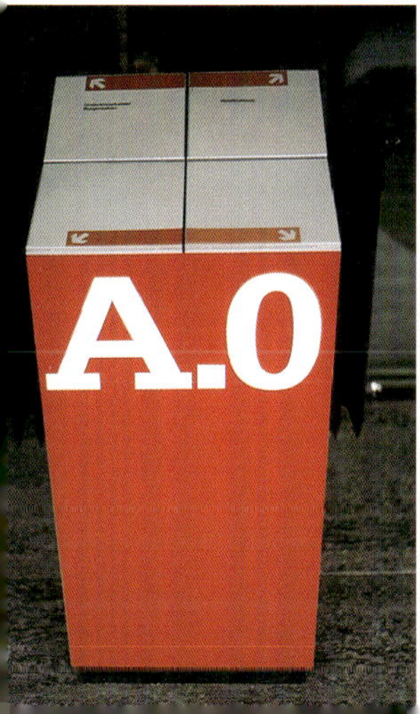
A.0

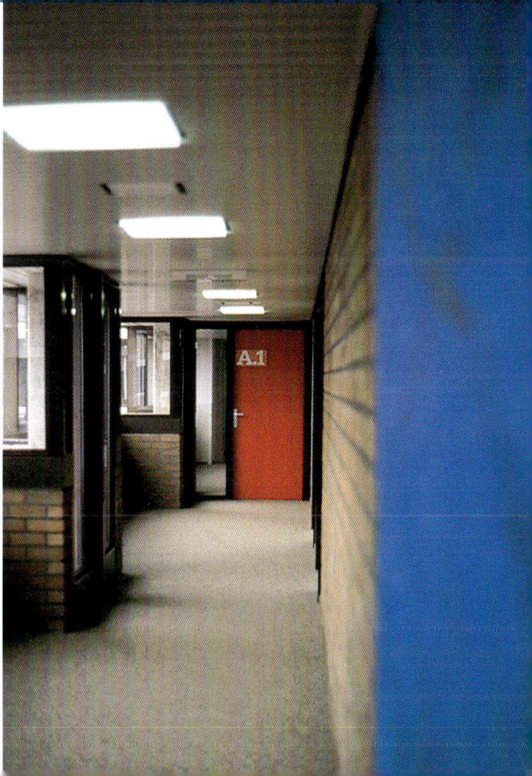
A.1

1982
Aurocontact
Geneva
Galvano technology

Logo

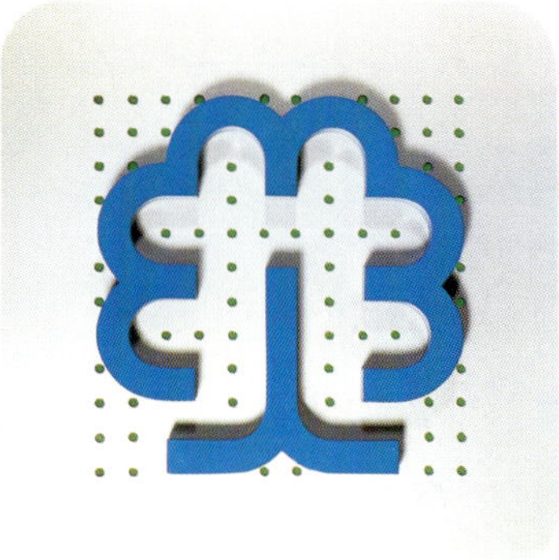

1982
Al Futtaim (Holding) Cy,
Dubai, United Arabian Emirates

Implementation of corporate design

1982
Middle East Bank

Logo (not used)
Interior design bank buildings
In collaboration with Ponzio & Cassati, Milan

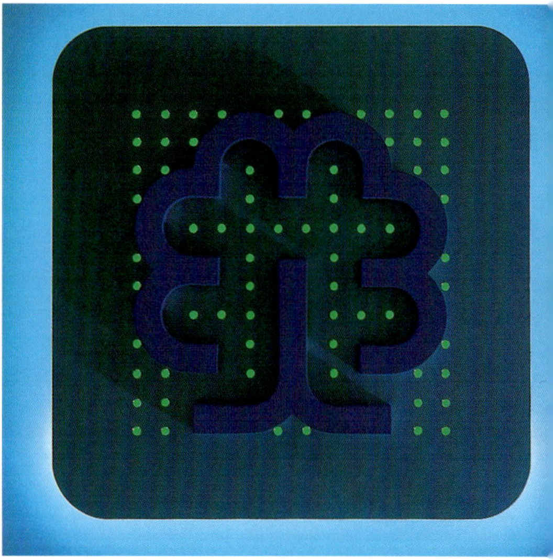

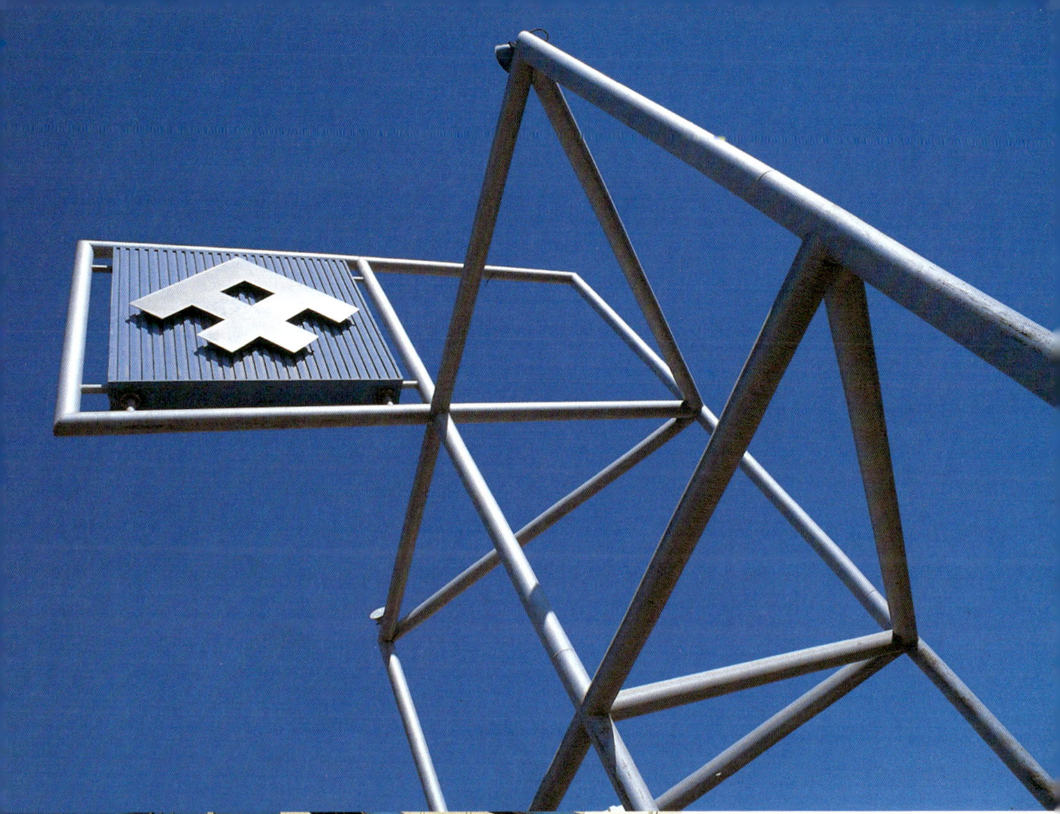

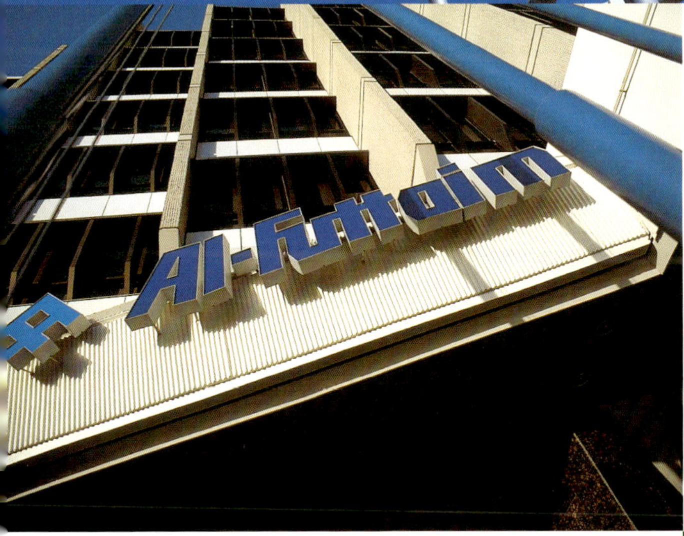
Al-Futtaim

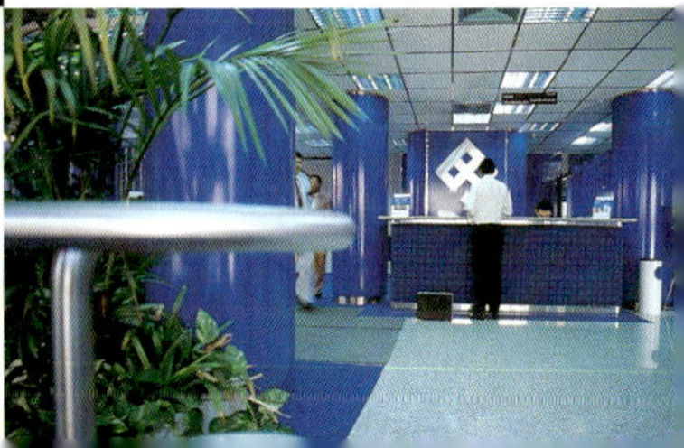

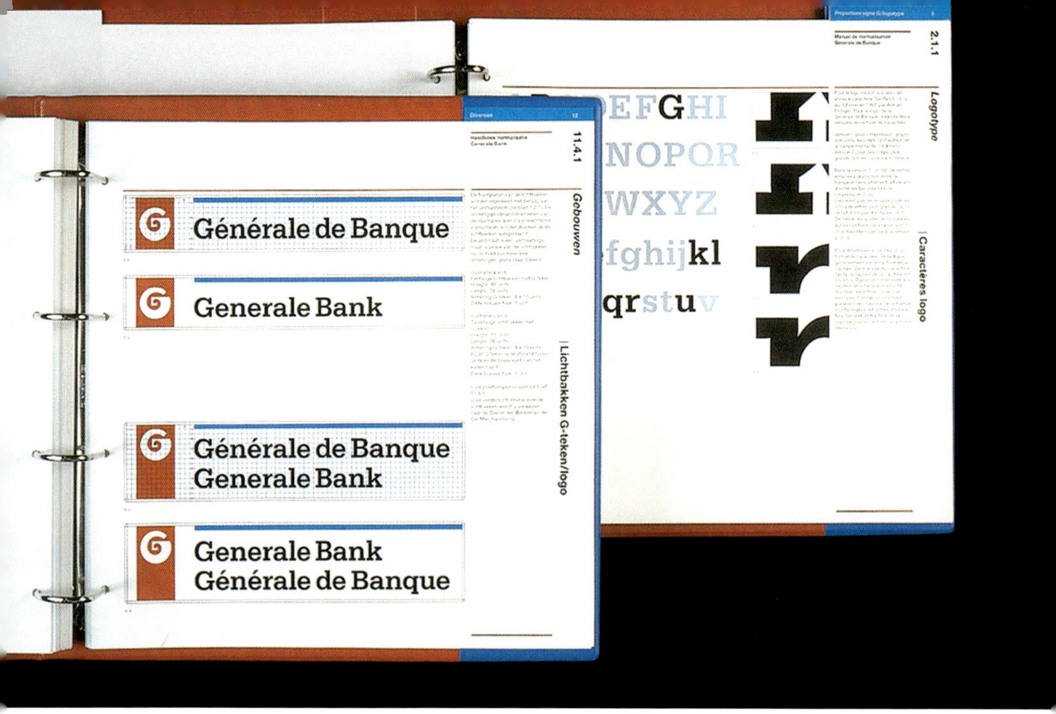

1987
Generale Bank
Brussels

Corporate design, letter logo
(visual logo by Jacques Richez)
Manual in collaboration with
Jan-Kees Visscher

Générale de Banque

Manuel de normalisation

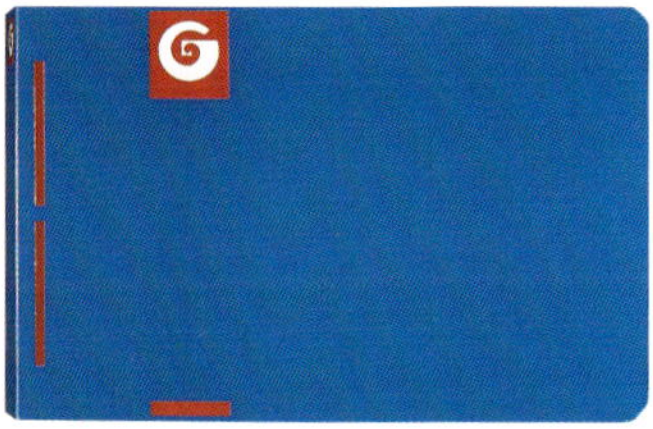

Generale Bank

1989
Koninklijk Instituut voor de Tropen
(Royal Institute for the Tropics)
Amsterdam

Logo, corporate design

1988
Credito Industriale Sardo
Cagliari, Italy

Logo
(international design competition entry)

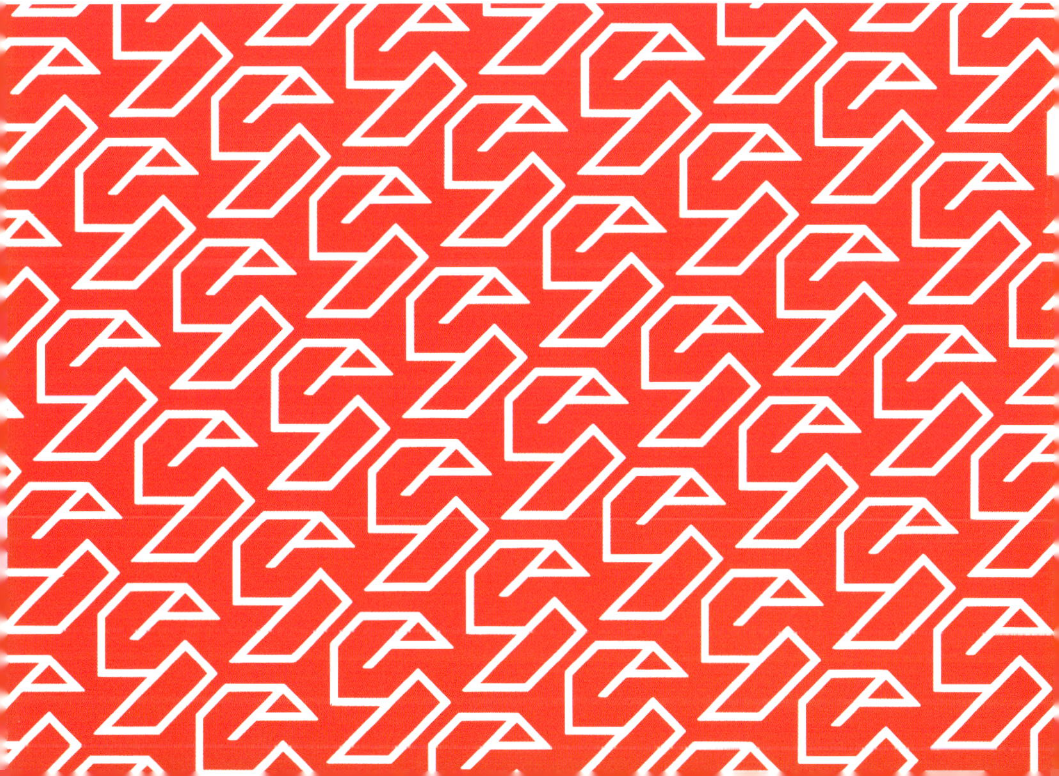

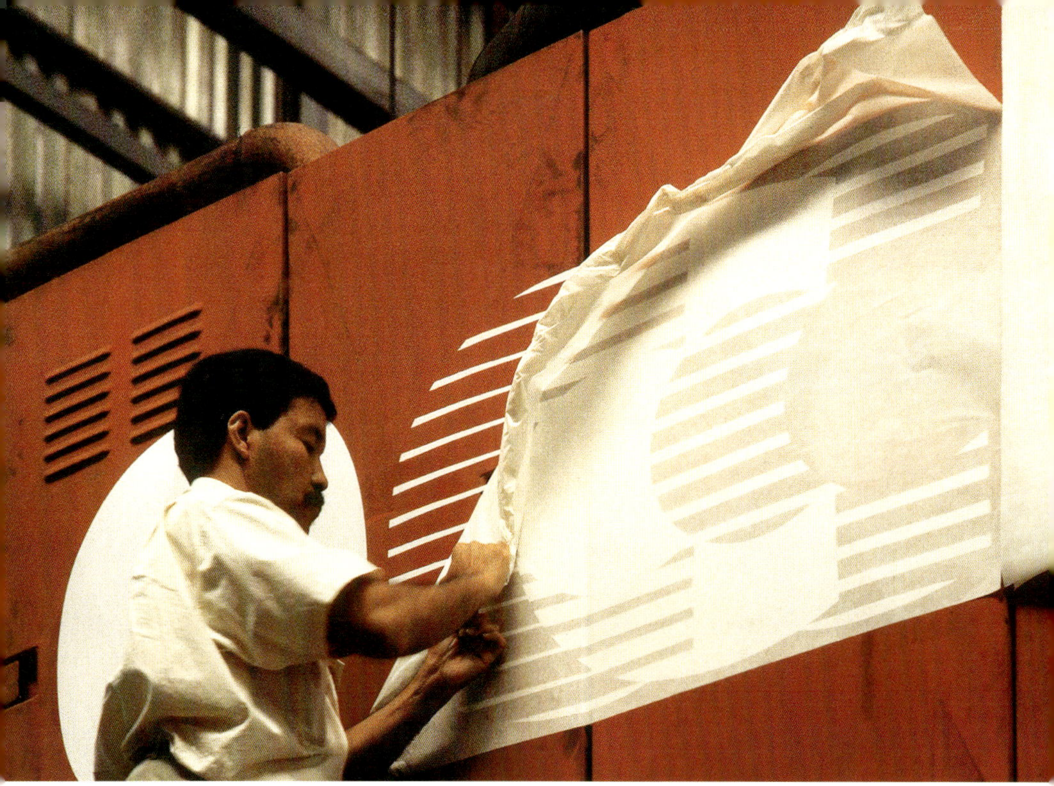

1989
European Combined Terminals
Rotterdam

Logo, corporate design

1989
European Banking Association
Amsterdam/Brussels

Logo
(The envisioned collaboration
between Amro Bank and Generale
Bank was called off.)

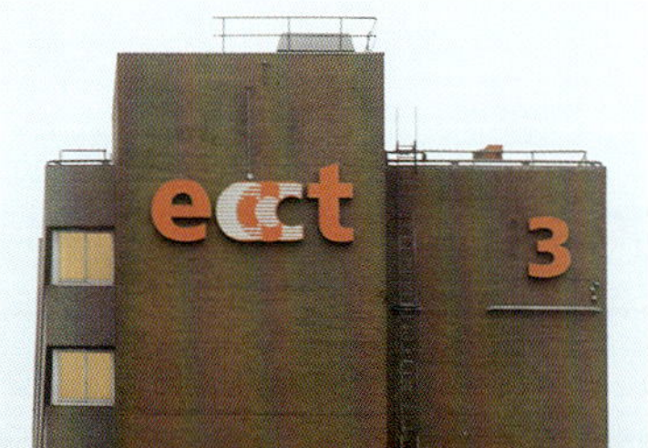

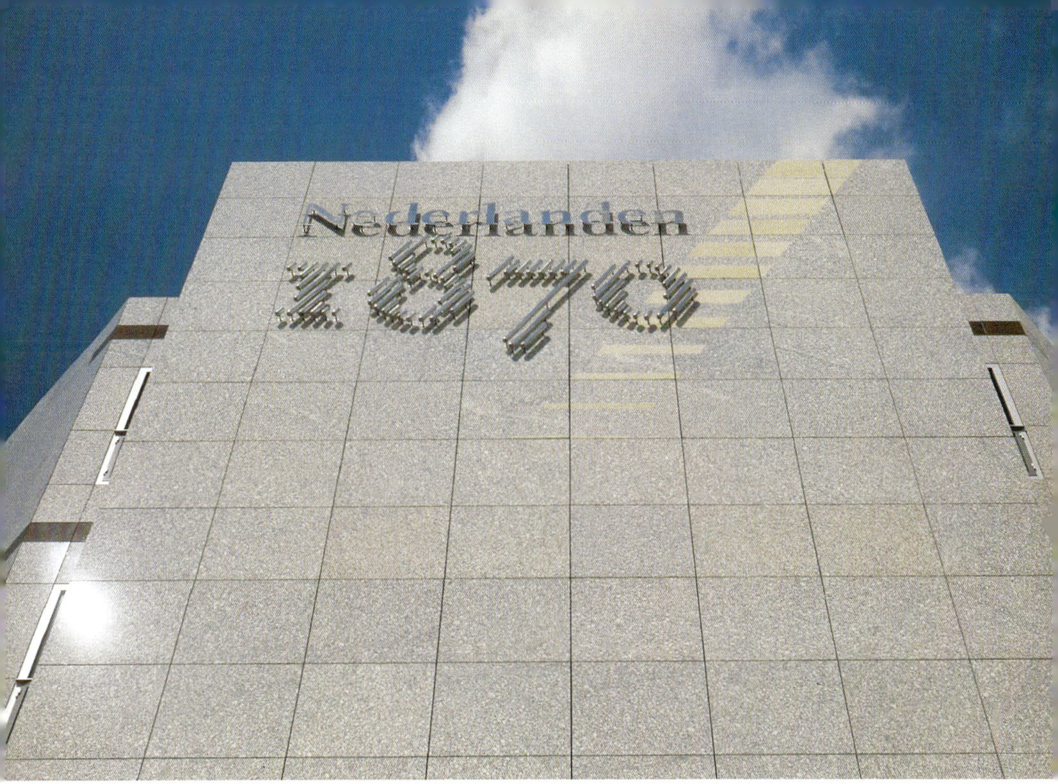

1990
Nederlanden van 1870
Diemen

Architectural lettering

1990
QL Management
Alphen aan den Rijn

Logo, corporate design

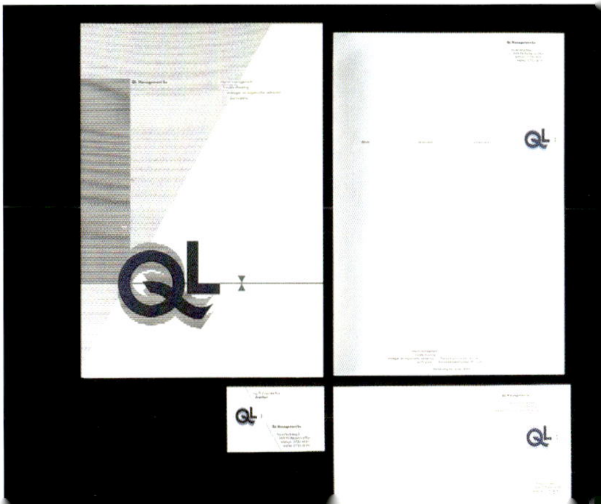

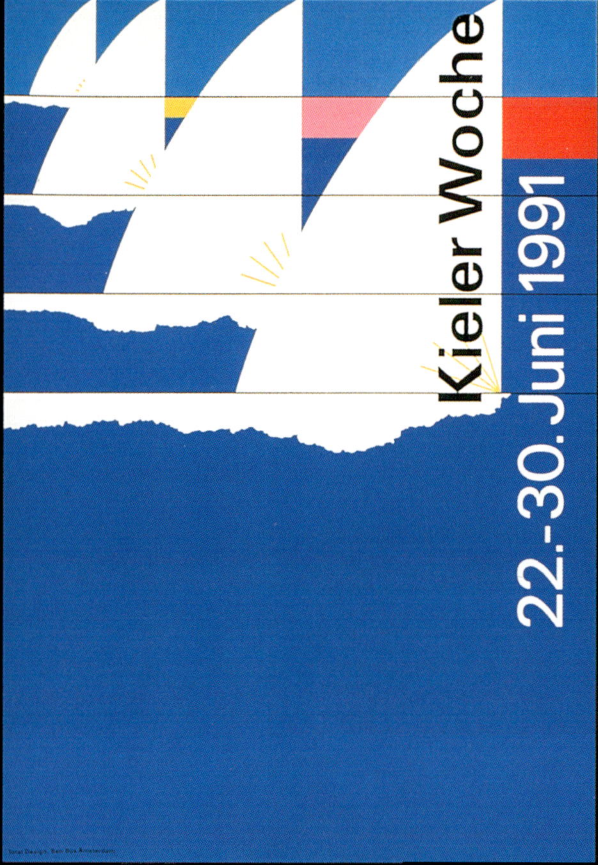

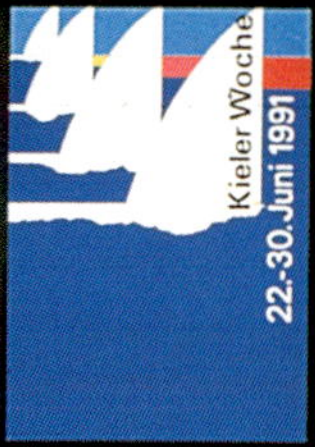

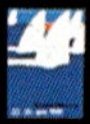

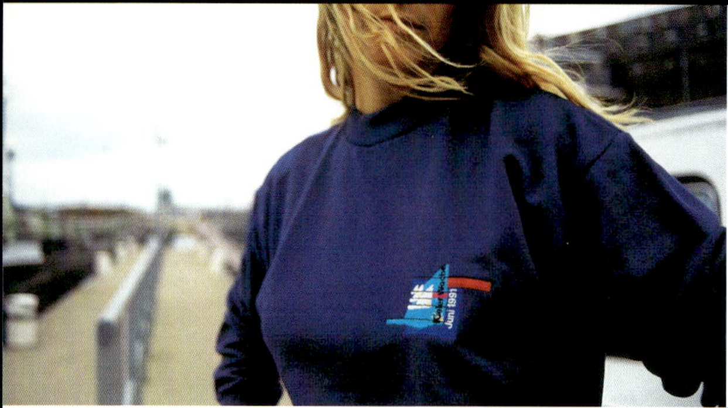

1991
Kieler Woche
Kiel, Germany
Annual sailing sports event

Event design
(international design competition)

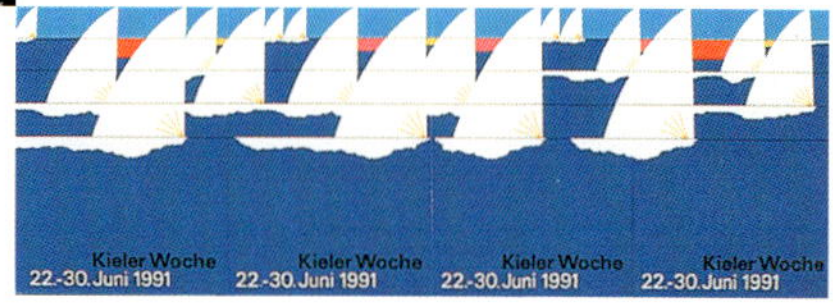

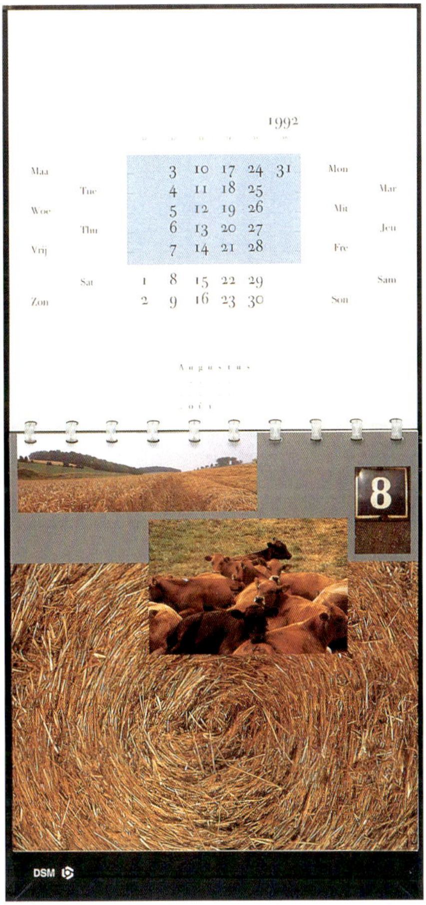

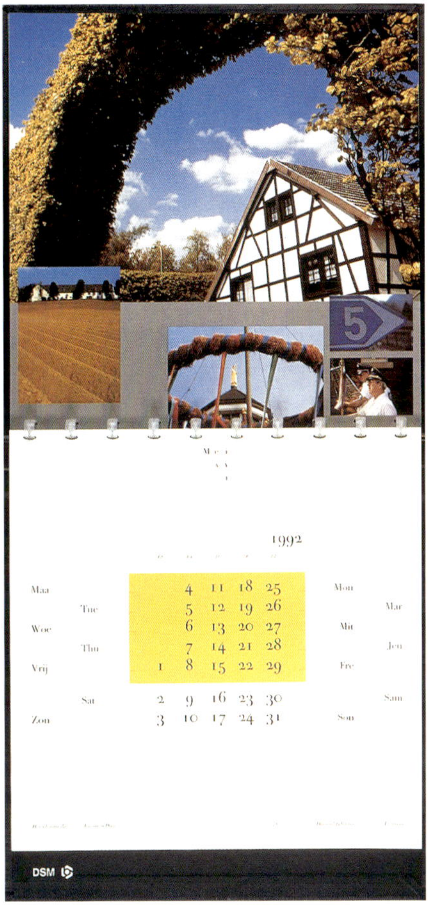

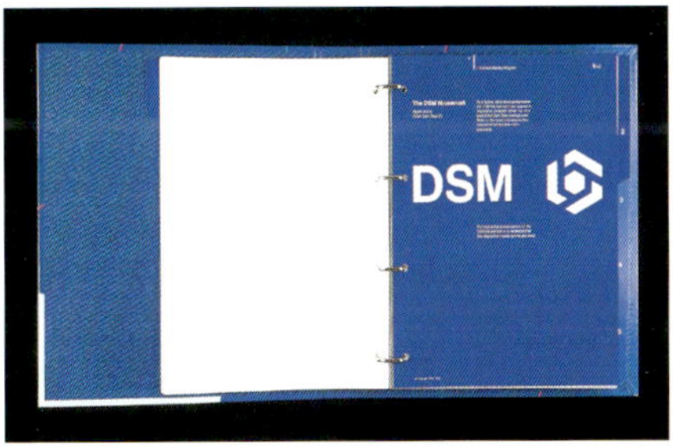

1990/1992
DSM Chemie concern
Heerlen

1992
Calendar/book
In collaboration with Karin Janssen
Photography by Peter Marcuse

1990
Restyling of corporate design
Design manual produced by DSM's
in-house studio

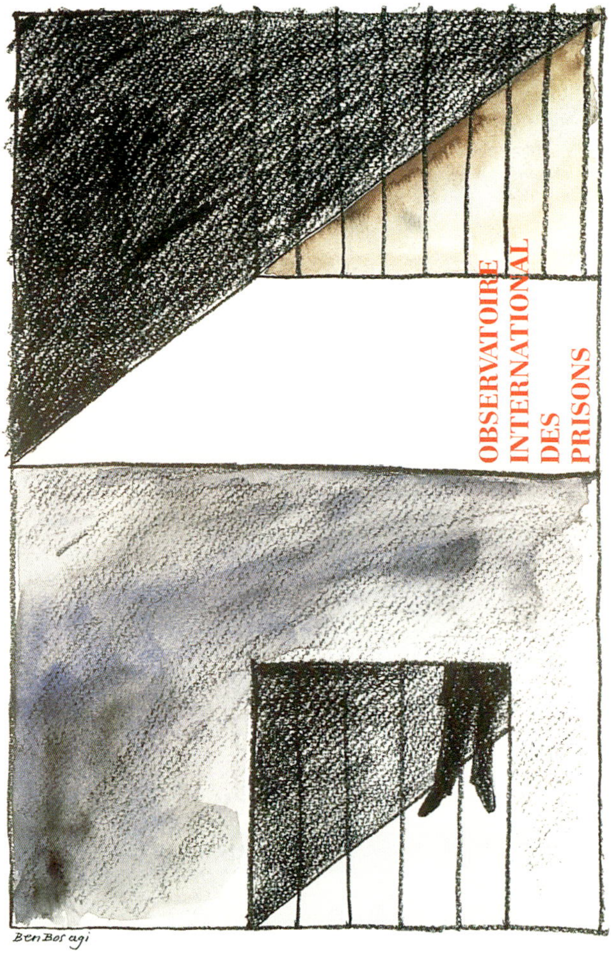

1992
Poster 'Observatoire International des Prisons'

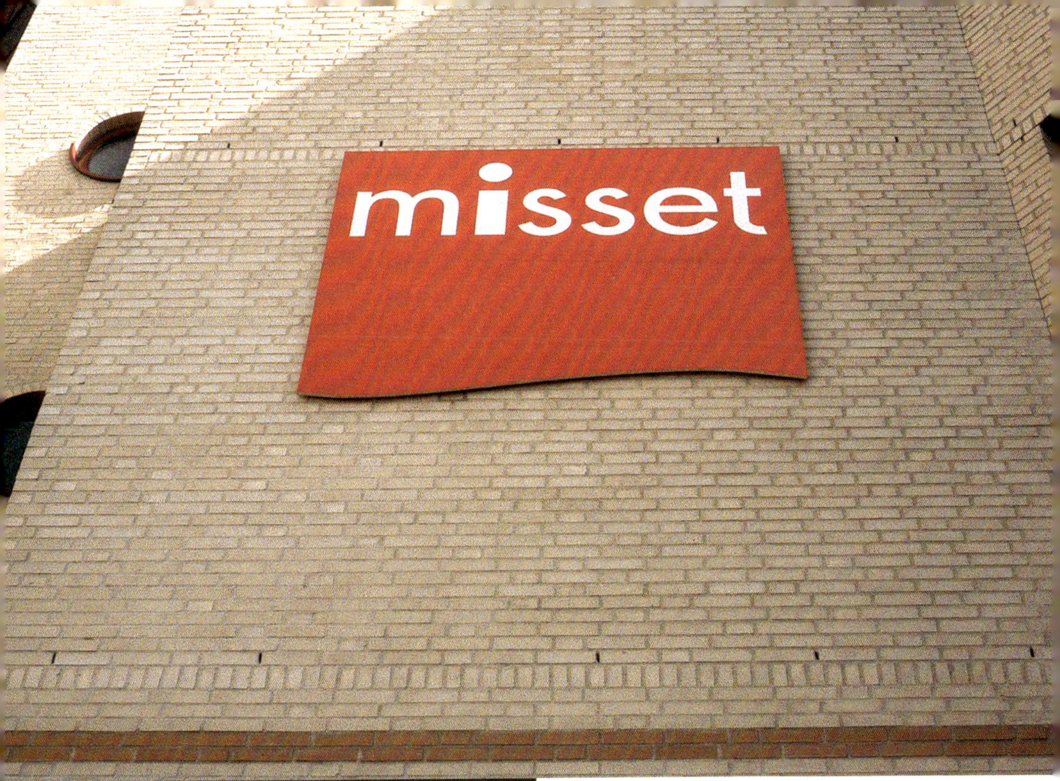

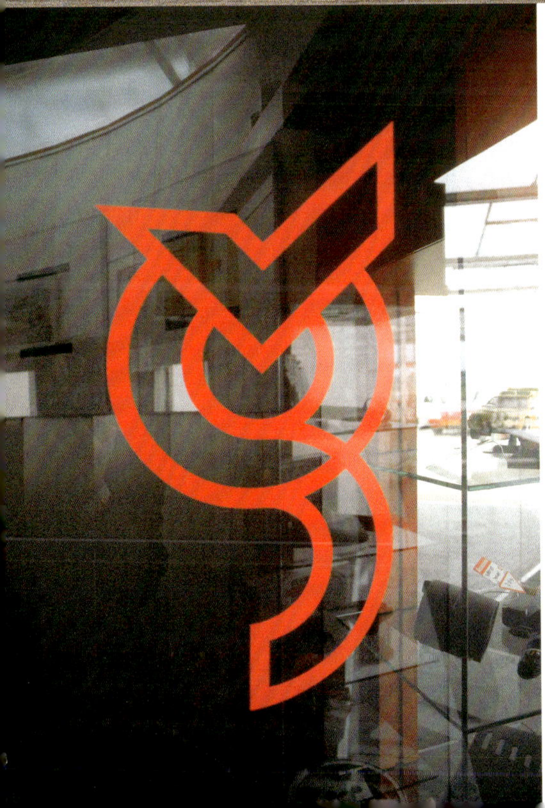

misset

1993
Misset publishers
Doetinchem

Logo, corporate design

1994
Vos car dealer
Genderen

Logo, corporate design

1994
PTT Nederland
The Hague

Series of postage stamps about Fepapost

Fepapost '94 was a kind of world exhibition for philately in The Hague. Bos was asked to do something with endangered bird species. In response to the overfilled and frequently illegible stamps (with 2-point letters) Bos tried to design clear, 'blank' stamps.
The organisation of Fepapost also commissioned him to design all of their printed matter.

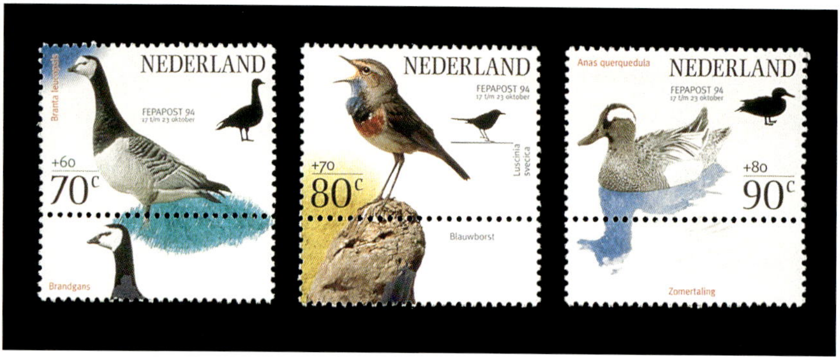

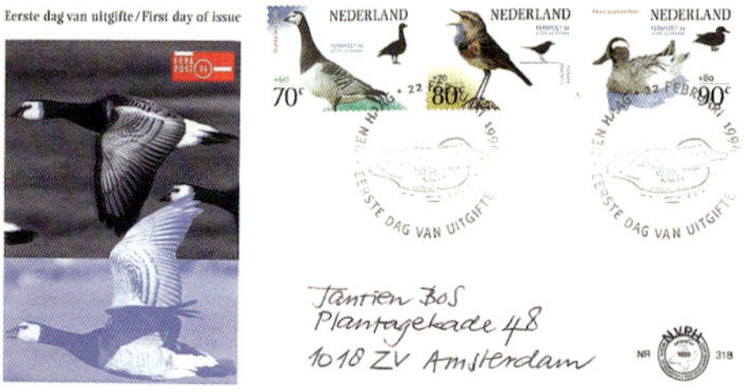

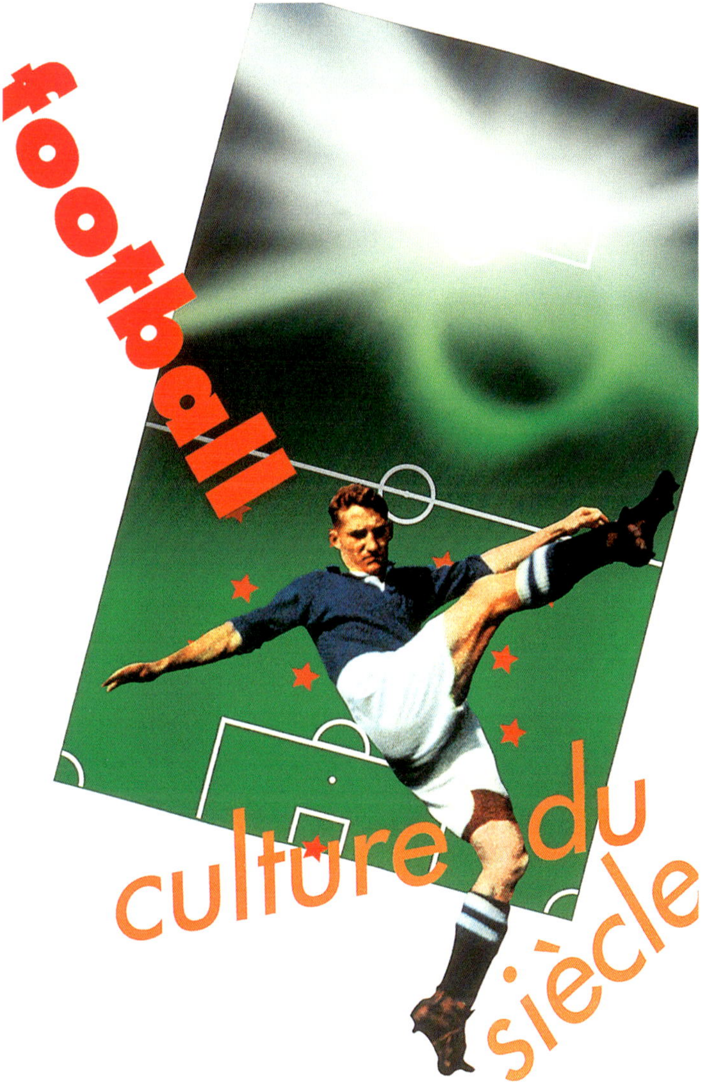

1996
Poster 'Football, Culture du Siècle'

Competition entry

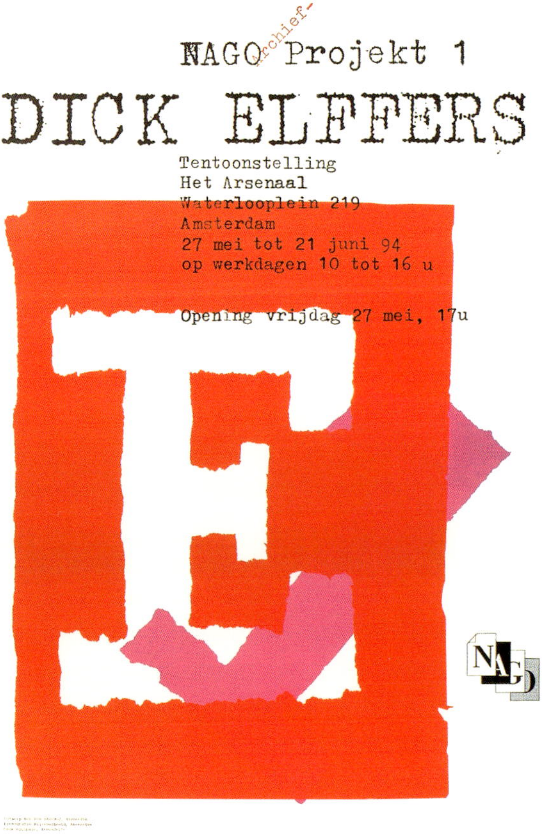

1996
Nederlands Archief Grafisch Ontwerpers
(Dutch Graphic Designers Archive)

Logo, corporate design

In 1993, on the initiative of Ben Bos, the Nederlands Archief Grafisch Ontwerpers (NAGO) was founded.

1994
Poster 'Dick Elffers'

1996
Poster 'Het Gezicht van Nederland'

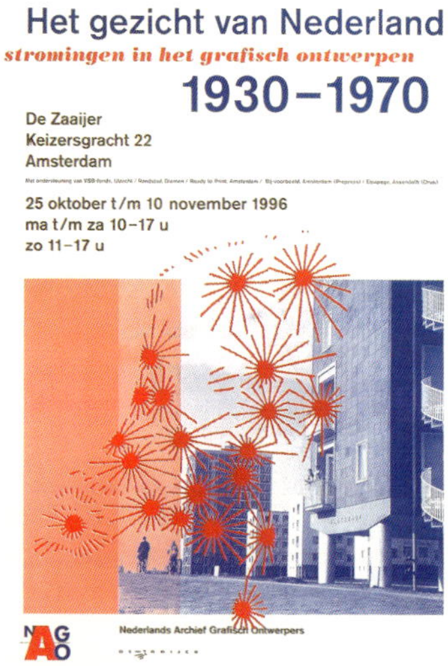

1995
Poster commemorating 50 years Hiroshima

1982
Poster for a dance programme Amsterdam

1999
Poster for kite-flying festivity Spaarnwoude

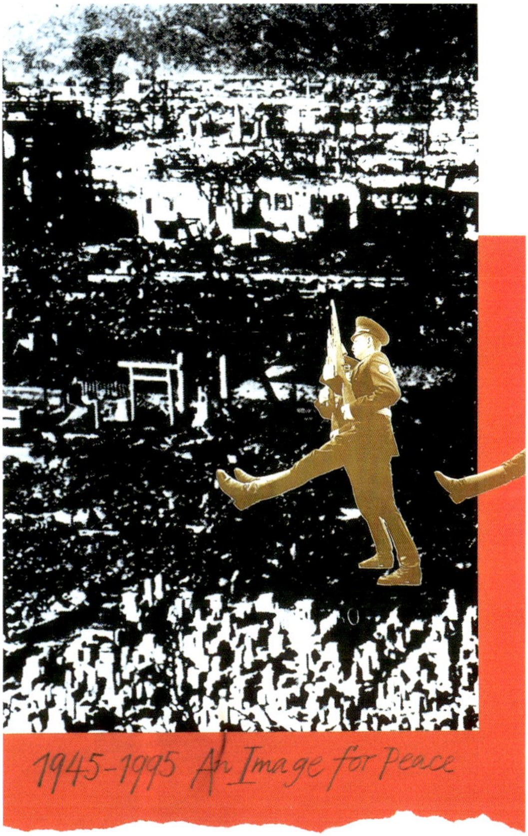

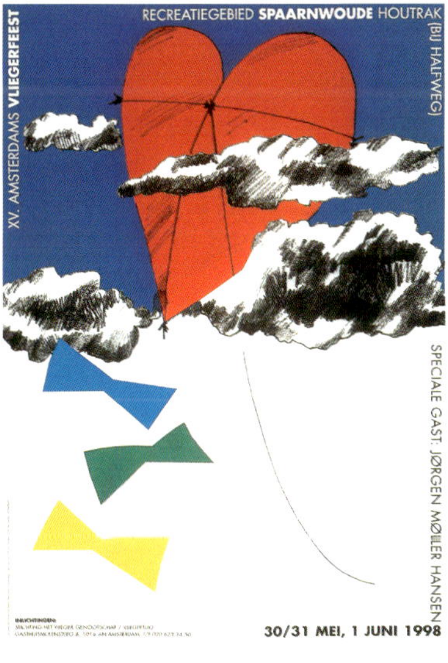

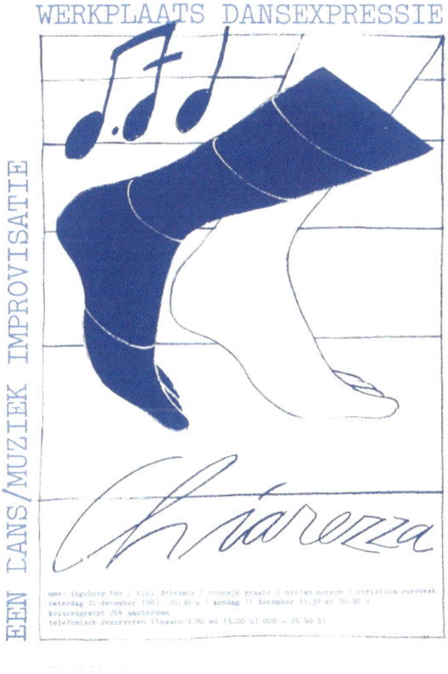

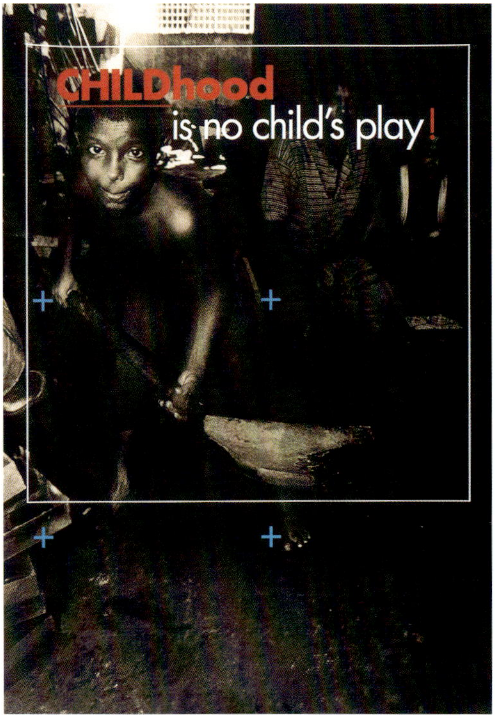

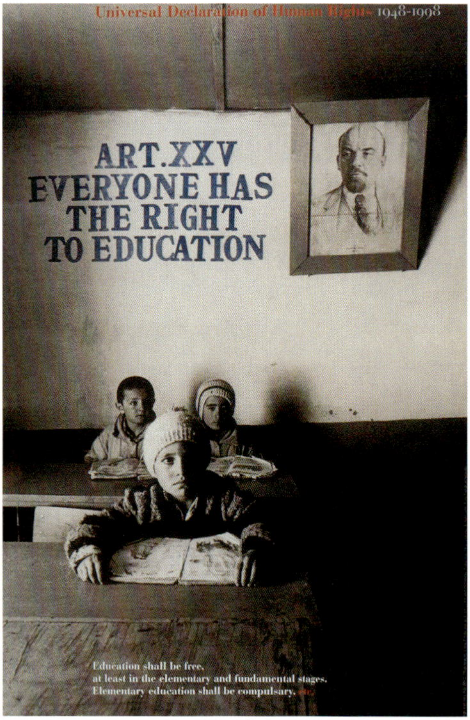

1998
Poster campaign against child labour
Deutsches Plakkatmuseum and
Plakatkunsthof Rüttenscheid
Essen
Photography by Eddy Posthuma
de Boer

1998
50 years Universal Declaration of Human Rights
Le Mouvement de la Paix
Paris
Photography by Eddy Posthuma
de Boer

2000
Logo Marijke de Goey
Visual artist
Amsterdam

Biography

1930 born in Amsterdam
1952 correspondence course in journalism at LOI
1953 copywriter/advertising assistant at nv Wed. J. Ahrend en Zoon; continues to work there until 1963, i.a. as corporate journalist, designer and art director
1954-55 attends evening classes in Layout, Amsterdam Graphic School; graduates with distinction
1956-61 attends evening study programme in Design at the IvKNO in Amsterdam (the later Gerrit Rietveld Academie); graduates with distinction
– runs a small freelance studio
1961-62 receives annual prizes from the Genootschap voor Reclame for advertisements and *Facetten* magazine for Ahrend
1963-66 studio manager and later designer/team leader at TD Association for Total Design nv, Amsterdam
1963-77 teaches design and corporate journalism (CSWV/VNO)
– teaches graphic design at LOI
1966-91 appointed as (creative) manager at Total Design; as of 1990 also director of Total Design Brussels
1966/1969/1971 awards from the Thieme-fonds for calendars and annual reports
1964 joins the GKf, a professional association of graphic designers
1966 start of his consultancy and design activities for Randstad Uitzendbureau and its subsidiaries
1967 design and realization of film *Straminologie* in collaboration with Dick Schwarz
1968 bronze medal at the World Exhibition for Youth in Sofia
– guest lecturer and consultant of Ravensbourne College of Art & Design, Bromley (UK)
– starts working for Furness group
1968-70 member of the Applied Arts committee for the city of Amsterdam
1969 receives three awards at Typomundus 20/II, Stuttgart
1969-88 joins the professional association GVN; later also a member of its Supervisory Board, board member and liaison officer to Icograda
1970 bronze medal at the Biennale in Brno (CSSR)
– series of postage stamps about 25 years of UN and Interparliamentary Union
– re-design of *Algemeen Handelsblad*
1973 receives Frans Duwaer Prize for typography, Amsterdams Fonds voor de Kunsten
– honourable citation at Industrial Design Biennale, Ljubljana (Yugoslavia); same in 1977
– guest lectures at academies in Amsterdam, The Hague, 's-Hertogenbosch, Ravensbourne, TH Delft, Wuppertal
1976-80 external examiner at academies in Amsterdam, Breda, Eindhoven
1977 author/designer of Lecturis documentary *Indruk in Druk*
1978-79 teaches at Stichting Studiecentrum Tijdschriftpers and Rietveld Academie evening study programme in Graphic Design
1978 joins the Alliance Graphique Internationale (AGI)
1980 series of postage stamps about the Netherlands as a transport country
– first work for Capelle aan den IJssel municipality
1980-90 jury member professional journal prizes NOTU
1981 co-author of *Gemeenten, wapens, gemeentewapens* (publ. GVN)
1981-85 member of the Amsterdam Arts Council
1982 workshop for journalists in developing countries of the Dutch World Service
– lectures at Northern Illinois University, Dekalb, USA
1983-93 teaches corporate identity at SRM
1984 presentation at Icograda Student Seminar, London
– guest lectures at London School of Printing and Harrow School
– lectures at GK Design, Tokyo
– exhibition on Randstad Uitzendbureau, Waterland Museum, Purmerend
1985 chairman for the Netherlands of Alliance Graphique Internationale
1985 exhibition on Randstad Uitzendbureau's corporate identity, ioN, Rotterdam
1986 organiser of AGI conference and student seminar at the Rietveld Academie
1986 author of *Huisstijl, een expressie van kwaliteitszin* (publ. Van Loghum Slaterus, Deventer)
– guest lecture 'Identity of municipalities', Bielefeld (Germany)
– bronze medal Biennale Brno (Czechoslovakia)
1987 guest lectures at academies in Hasselt (Belgium), Leeuwarden, Jerusalem (Bezalel), Haifa
– speaker at conference on corporate identity, Amsterdam
– work included in exhibition 'Holland in Vorm', Stedelijk Museum, Amsterdam
– revision of Randstad Groep's corporate identity
1988 exhibition in De Beyerd, Breda: 'Ben Bos, 25 jaar Total Designer'
– one of the initiators and administrator of bNO professional association, design studios division

- **lectures on corporate identity to SVPr, bNO and NIVE**

1989 **author of 'Lifestyle', published in** De Gids, **Vol. 152, no 8/9**
- **author of** Ontwerpers m/v, visueel vertalers tussen producent and consument **(publ. Van Loghum Slaterus, Houten)**
- **wins design competition at Kieler Woche 1991, Kiel (Germany)**
- **member of steering group on increasing the level of expertise, bNO, BNI, KIO**

1990 **speaker at conferences/ seminars in London (PIRA: Design & Technology), Helsinki (corporate identity in an integrating Europe), Brno, Czecho-slovakia, (the identity of the Randstad Groep), Leiden University ('lifestyle')**
- **radio talks 'Lifestyle' on** Met het oog op morgen, KRO 50+ **and Radio West**
- **edits/designs book** Fotografen werken voor Randstad
- **editor of AGI Bulletin**
- **jury member Kieler Woche competition 1992**

1991 **jury member New York Type Directors Club**
- **external examiner Hoge-school voor de Kunsten, Arnhem**
- **jury member at examina-tions Ecole Supérieure des Arts Graphiques, Paris**
- **co-author of** The Image of a Company, **publ. Sdu, The Hague**
- **leaves Total Design**
- **joins design studio 2D3D in The Hague as design director**
- **lecture at PIRA conference, Copenhagen**
- **certificate 'Excellent Trademarks & Symbols', ITC Antwerp**
- **regular contributor on corporate identities to** Art View **professional journal**

1992 **author of** Design, de ontworpen meerwaarde, **publ. BIS, Amsterdam**
- **award for calendar/book DSM: Euregio Maas-Rijn**
- **speaks at academies in Utrecht and Arnhem, Ichthus HEAO Rotterdam; Symposium 'Mode en Strategie', Centraal Museum, Utrecht; Club Brabant, Eindhoven**
- **lecture and workshop at Rhode Island School of Design, Providence, USA**

1993 **participant on invitation to 100 posters for Observatoire International des Prisons, Lyon/Paris**
- **initiates the foundation of Nederlands Archief Grafisch Ontwerpers – NAGO; becomes its chairman**
- **lectures on Dutch Design, University of Hartford, Conn. USA**
- **jury member international prize for children's books, Bologna**
- **lecture 'Dyslexia in the Urban Visual Jungle', at conference Design, Architecture & Ville, Arc en Rève, Bordeaux**
- **lecture on 'Dutch Design' at Salisbury College, Bournemouth & Poole College and University of Plymouth (Exeter)**
- **Organiser/designer of exhibition on Benno Wissing (and Jan Bons), Stedelijk Museum Amsterdam**
- **author/designer of bNO brochure on Benno Wissing**
- **lecture on graphic design for government organiza-tions in Mechelen (Belgium)**
- **commission to design a series of postage stamps and stand for philately exhibition Fepapost '94 in The Hague**
- **jury member Deutscher Preis für Kommunikations-design, Design Zentrum Nordrhein-Westfalen, Essen**
- **jury chairman Jaarverslag Erkenning '92**
- **starts activities for Randstad Staffing Services, Atlanta, USA**
- **leaves 2D3D design agency and continues as a free-lance with his wife Jantien, in his own private company FORMatie2**

1994 **participant exhibition 'Coca-Cola Kultur', Essen**
- **guest lecture on design management at HKA Arnhem, 'Mode & Strategie'**
- **Randstad is awarded the Grafische Cultuurprijs 1994**
- **invited to participate in jubilee exhibition UPIDIV NoviSad; awarded 'Special Golden Forma'**
- **invited to participate in posters project Le Mouve-ment de la Paix, St Ouen, France**
- **co-author project** Meester/ Leerling, **publ. Tecno Forum**
- **author of** Je goeie gezicht, **(Walburg Pers/Bührmann Ubbens)**

1995 **made an honorary member of Les Amis d'Arc and Rêve, Bordeaux**
- **forum member Commu-nicatieclub Tilburg: 'de Rabo-huisstijl'**
- **discussion leader 'Design Management' at the Vormgevingsinstituut**
- **member of advisory committee of (graphic museum) De Beyerd, Breda**
- **SMAU Milan: lecture on computer aided design, 'A mouse behind the Dikes'**
- **jury chairman poster competition NOC/NSF**

1996 **adviser Ichthus Hoge-school Rotterdam, study programme Design management**
- **photography in postage stamp design: PTT Museum, The Hague**
- **'Merci M. Nièpce; intro-duction at the opening of this exhibition in Warsaw, Design Institute**
- **seminar speaker 'Vormgeving voor PTT organisaties'**
- **honorary member of Biennale (graphic design) Brno, Czechoslovakia**

- author of chapter on corporate identity in *Handboek Interne Communicatie*
- nomination at Unesco/Icograda poster exhibition, Paris
- hands out Oeuvreprijs to Benno Wissing, Stedelijk Museum, Amsterdam
- curator of exhibition 'De Vorm van Ahrend', De Beyerd, Breda
- author of *Design in Business*, publ. BIS

1997 jury chairman 'Karikatura II: Die Goldene Nase', Rostock, Germany
- member Individual Subsidies committee, Fonds voor Beeldende kunsten, Vormgeving en Bouwkunst, Amsterdam
- until 2000. Teacher Professional history, Ichthus Hogeschool Rotterdam
- reads from his own work at Hochschule Karlsruhe
- lecture 'To read or not to read', Wynkyn de Worde Society, London
- invited to participate in poster competition 'Football, culture du Siècle', Paris
- invited to participate in poster competition 'Childhood is no child's play', Deutsches Plakat Museum, Essen; is nominated, in collaboration with Eddy Posthuma de Boer
- initiates, designs and is curator of Ahrend Museum, Amsterdam,
- TV programme on Randstad's corporate identity, in Teleac-series *Nederlands Fabrikaat*
- member of Professional Field Committee (Design Management) Ichthus Hogeschool

1998 honorary member of bNO, the professional association of Dutch designers
- hands over the presidency of NAGO to Andrew Fallon
- World Logotype Award, ICT Antwerp
- lecture for New York Chapter of AIGA
- jury chairman (student) Packaging Designer of the Year, Aestron Foundation, Hilversum
- invited to participate in poster project Galerie l'Art et la Paix, Parijs: 50 years of universal human rights, together with Eddy Posthuma de Boer

1999 starts writing regular 'Logorama' column for *iM, Identity Matters*
- invited to participate in fax project 'Children are the Rhythm of the World', Deutsches Plakatmuseum Essen/Plakatkunsthof Rüttenscheid; is nominated
- involved in publications on 25 Years of Icograda Student Seminar, London
- invitation to contribute work to Design 2000, Beijing Design Museum

2000 invited to to participate in poster project 'Water for human kind', Paris
- participates in Triennale (posters) Trnava, Slovakia; poster Biennale Warsaw; 'World of Friends', tribute to Jan Rajlich Sr, Brno
- invited to participate in billboard project 'Co-Existence or No Existence', Jerusalem Museum of the Seam
- invited to participate in project 'Happy Birthday, Johannes: J. Gutenberg, Man of the Millennium', Mainz

Publications (partly) on Ben Bos

'Ahrend (Holland): Bird's eye view of its business activities', Idea **53, Tokyo, 1962, p. 58-65**

'Profiel van twee docenten', Kopij Genoeg, **April, 1964, p. 2**

Total Design BV, Idea **79, Tokyo, 1966, p. 40-61**

TD Amsterdam, **Interpress Grafik, Prague/Budapest, 1969, p. 2-16**

Crosby Fletcher Forbes, 3x Trademarks, **Total Design, Amsterdam; Chermayeff & Geismar, New York, 1969**

Keith Murgatroyd, Modern Graphics, **Studio Vista, London, 1969, p. 96-106**

Pieter Brattinga, Einflüsse auf die niederländische Plakatkunst in der ersten Hälfte des 20. Jahrhunderts, **Steendrukkerij de Jong & Co., Hilversum, 1970**

Walter Diethelm, Signet, signal, symbol, **ABC Verlag, Zürich, 1972**

Charles Jongejans, Letterbeelden, **Wolters-Noordhof, Groningen, 1971**

Hein van Haaren, 'De vormgeving van de Nederlandse postzegel', Maandblad voor philatelie, **October, 1973**

Rolf Mager, 'Duwaerprijs toegekend aan Ben Bos (Total Design) voor zijn wat subjectieve benadering van design', Ariadne **15, Amsterdam, 1973, p. 12-15**

'Priorité au programme', Crée **28, Paris, 1974, p. 56-61**

Walter Diethelm, form + communication, **ABC Verlag, Zürich, 1974**

Shigeru Watano, 'Total Design bv', Idea **131, special on International Advertising Art, Tokyo, 1975, p. 88-100**

Basic Design, Elements and their systems, **(Furness) B5, The CocoMas Committee, Tokyo, 1979, p. 42-51**

Peter Wildbur, International Trademark Design, **Van Nostrand Reinhold Cy., New York, 1979**

'"Het is een enorm gepriegel"; Vreelander ontwierp nieuwe serie postzegels', De Gooi- en Eemlander, **7 August, 1980, p. 17**

Willem Boom, 'Het kader van grafisch ontwerpers', Lecturis, **Eindhoven, 'Documentaire' series no. 10, 1980**

Pierre Hosman, 'Beeldmerken van gemeenten in GVN-bulletin' Adformatie, **24 September, 1981, p. 45**

Huib van Krimpen, Typos 1, **London School of Printing, 1981**

'Foto in vorm, Ben Bos', GKf Fotografen **5, Amsterdam, 1981, p. 6,7**

'Where Design is Total', Design **411, London, 1983, p. 62-63**

Rudolf van Wezel, 'Ontwerp: Total Design', Libris over Boeken, **Libris, Hoevelaken, 1983, p. 20-25**

'Dutch design in Total', Holland Herald **9, Amsterdam, 1983, p. 36-41**

Takenobu Igarashi, World Trademarks and Logotypes I, **Graphic Sha, Tokyo, 1983**

Kees Broos, Ontwerp: Total Design, **Reflex, Utrecht, 1983**

Gees-Ineke Smit, 'De filosofie van een uitzendbureau' in Industrieel ontwerpen in Nederland 5: Bedrijfsstijlen, **Uitgeverij 010, Rotterdam, 1985**

Rudolph de Harak, Posters by members of the Alliance Graphique Internationale, **Rizolli, New York, 1986**

Art direction bij GKf fotografen, **P/F, 1986**

Hayakawa, Fukuda, Nakahara, International biennial of Illustrations **Vol. 1, Rikuyosha, Tokyo, 1986**

Susanne Piët, 'Ben Bos, Het bedrijf is niet alleen het pakpapier', Elsevier's Weekblad, **special on 'De cultuur van de ondernemer', 1987, p. 161-165**

Erik Terlouw, **'De huisstijl, meer dan etiketjes plakken'**, Trouw, **21 February, 1987, p. 33**

André Toet en Ben Bos, **Rietveld Academie, Amsterdam, 1987**

Takenobu Igarashi, World Trademarks and Logotypes II, **Graphic Sha, Tokyo, 1987**

Gert Staal and Hester Wolters, Holland in Vorm, **Stichting Holland in Vorm, The Hague, 1987, p. 260,**

Susanne Piët, '"Kennen, vertrouwen, dienen": Nieuwe huisstijl na explosieve groei bij Randstad', Randstad Data **1, 1988, Randstad Uitzendbureau, Diemen, p. 16-19**

Cees van Staal, '25 jaar Total Design', Nieuwstribune **20, 1988**

'Cheops Ben Bos en Auke de Vries', Uit in Breda, **September, 1988, p. 5**

'Ben Bos verwacht veel werk voor designers', Adformatie, **1 december 1998, p. 21**

'Ben Bos en Total Design al 25 jaar samen', Randstad Revue, **November/December, 1988, p. 11**

Tracy Metz, 'Total Design', Graphis **263, Graphis Press, New York, 1989**

A.G. Fronzoni, Marchio progetti, proposte per il Credito industriale sardo, **CIS, Cagliari, 1989**

FHK Henrion, AGI annals, **Graphic Sha, Tokyo, 1989, p. 190, 236, 245, 274**

Ken Cato, First choice; leading international designers select the best of their own work, **Graphic Sha, Tokyo, 1989**

Hub. Hubben, Ontwerp: Total design - de jaren tachtig, **Inmerc, Wormer, 1989**

'Totaal ontworpen!', Compres **29, Leiden, 1989 p. 41-43**

Edward Gottschall, Typographic Communications Today, **MIT Press, Boston, 1989, p. 148-151**

HQ **14, Heidelberg, p. 5**

Herman Hoeneveld en Flip Bool, Fotografen aan het werk voor Randstad, **Randstad Uitzendbureau, Diemen, 1990**

David E.Carter, World corporate identity 1, **Art Direction Book Cy., New York, 1990, p. 34-37**

Typography Twelve, The annual of the Type Directors Club of New York, **Watsun Guptill Publications, New York, 1991 (work by Bos op p. 12, 22, 23)**

Roos Kuip, 'Ontwerper Ben Bos balanceert tussen goed en mooi', Quote **12, 1991, p. 106-109**

Hans Vonk, 'De Wet van Bos', VNU Blad voor bladen **2, 1991, p. 49-51**

Paul Ibou, Worldwide banking symbols collection 1, **Interecho Press, Antwerp, 1991, p. 19**

Paul Ibou, Famous animal symbols 1, **Interecho Press, Antwerp, 1991, p. 198**

Henriëtte Verburgh, 'Total Design, typical Dutch', Business Class **2, Maartensdijk, 1991, p. 14-19**

Hub. Hubben, 'Nestor van Total Design stapt op', De Volkskrant, **12 September, 1991**

'Bos stapt uit Total Design', Adformatie **38, Alphen aan de Rijn, 1991, p. 1-4**

Titus Yocarini, 'Vak in beweging', Lecturis, **Eindhoven, Documentaire, 1992, p. 33**

B. Martin Pedersen, Graphis Design, **Graphis Press, Zürich, 1992, p. 20-25**

Margo Rouard-Snowman, Museum graphics, **Thames and Hudson, London, 1992, p. 108, 109**

Henriëtte Verburgh, 'Design, creatieve vonk', Business Class, **Maartensdijk, 1992, p. 25-30**

'DSM-kalender, meer boek dan ooit', Graficus **7, 1992, p. 65-67**

'Ben Bos (2D3D) schrijft boek vol over verschijnsel design management', Graficus **15, 1992 p. 9**

Rob Beemster, 'Grafisch ontwerpers kampen met instroom en Macintosh terreur', Graficus **16, 1992, p. 26-29**

Daphne Duyvelshoff, 'Daar komen de meiden', Vormberichten **9, p. 22-23**

Tineke Stevens, 'Het is allemaal de schuld van Ben Bos', Vormberichten **11, p. 24-25**

Paul Ibou, Famous Animal Symbols **1, Sygma Union, 1992**

W.M.Lookman, 'Design managers verschillen van mening over vakopleiding', Het Financieele Dagblad, **10 April, 1992, p. 13**

70 affiches pour le droit des prisoniers ordinaires, **Observatoire international des prisons, Paris, 1993**

Peter Zec, Mythos aus des Flasche: Coca-Cola-Kultur im 20. Jahrhundert, **Design Zentrum Nordrhein Westfalen, Essen, 1994**

Kees Broos en Paul Hefting, Grafische Vormgeving in Nederland, een eeuw, **V+K Publishing, Laren, 1993, p. 174, 175**

Peter Sierksma, 'De schoonheid van het logo is niet meer', Kunstkatern van Trouw, **17 August, 1995, p. 1-2**

Armando Milano, A double life of 80 AGI designers, **Cartiere Burgo, Turin, 1996, p. 40-41**

Dirk de Wit, 60+40 is waarschijnlijk honderd: Ahrend - passers, pennen, potloden en projecten, **Waanders, Zwolle, 1996, p. 156**

'Designmanagers zijn nog steeds zeldzame vogels', Design in Business **vol. 1 no. 1, Amsterdam, p. 70-73**

Toon van Severen, 'Design management is een leerschool voor het leven', Adformatie **27/28, 1997**

Frederike Huygen en Hugues C. Boekraad, Wim Crouwel: Mode en module, **Uitgeverij 010, Rotterdam, 1997, p. 135 e.v.**

Reyer Kras, '"Nederlands Fabrikaat": industriële vormgeving' Hoofdstuk 4 van Huisstijl en identiteit, **Teleac/NOT, Utrecht, 1997, p. 80-92**

B. Martin Pedersen, Typography 2, **Graphis Press, New York, 1997, p. 58, 98, 99**

Hans Hoekstra, 'Stoel terug gevonden: collectie Ahrend tentoongesteld', Het Parool, **21 February, 1998**

Hub. Hubben, 'Affiche: Ontwerp Ben Bos', De Volkskrant, **30 April, 1998**

'Logodesign Award voor Ben Bos', Adformatie **27/28, 1998 p. 4**

'World Logo Design Award voor Ben Bos', Vormberichten **July, 1998, p. 37**

Gerard Mulder, 'Bevlogen ontwerpers versus rommelige journalisten', De Volkskrant, **21 November, 1998**

'Ben Bos', folding sheet, Bij-voorbeeld/Equipage/bNO, 1988

Dr Frieder Mellinghoff, Kindheit ist kein Kinderspiel, **Deutsches Plakat Museum, Essen, 1998**

Hub. Hubben, 'Het gaat om visibility', De Volkskrant, **1 juni 1999**

Rob Overwater, 'The Randstad collection of photographs', The Randstad International Review, **augustus 1999**

Video

Jaap Drupsteen, Een videomonument voor PTT Kunst en Vormgeving, **1985**

Educational television series Nederlands Fabrikaat, **Teleac, 1997**

Publications by Ben Bos

Film

Straminologie, **with Dick Schwarz, 16 mm film, Total Design, 1967**

Books and brochures

Vormgeving '61, **Gemeente Museum Arnhem (Introduction)**

De vormgeving van het personeelsblad, **Total Design, Amsterdam, 1976**

Indruk in druk, **Lecturis, Eindhoven (in the 'Documentaires' series), 1977**

Gemeenten, wapens, gemeentewapens, **GVN Amsterdam, 1981 (co-written with Henk 't Jong)**

'Bespiegelingen van een archiefadept', preface to Cas Oorthuys, fotograaf, **Geschiedenis van de Nederlandse fotografie 2, Uitgeverij Fragment, Amsterdam, 1982**

Huisstijl, een expressie van kwaliteitszin, **Van Loghum Slaterus, Deventer, 1987**

Ontwerpers m/v, visueel vertalers tussen producent en consument, **Van Loghum Slaterus, Houten, 1989**

Graphic Design in the service of industry and trade, **Biennale Brno 1990, Symposium, p. 70-73**

The Image of a Company, **Sdu, The Hague, 1991 (co-author)**

Design, de ontworpen meerwaarde, **BIS, Amsterdam, 1992**

Benno Wissing, **bNO, Amsterdam, 1993**

Meester/Leerling, **Tecno Forum 4, Amsterdam, 1994 (co-author)**

Je goeie gezicht, **Walburg Pers, Zutphen, 1995**

Huisstijl: spoor en bovenleiding, **Handboek Interne communicatie, 1996**

Ahrend Museum, **Koninklijke Ahrend NV, 1997**

Magazine articles and contributions to books

1973

'Tijdvorm: onvolledige studie over winstloze tijdschriften', Kontekst, vakblad voor kommunikatiedeskundigen

1976

'Horizontaal/vertikaal; lezen of ontcijferen', De Vorm **6**

'"Doeltreffend koppen": samenspel vorm/inhoud; onverborgen verleiders', de Bedrijfsjournalist **4**

1978

'"Ordening, toelichting of georganiseerde chaos": de rol van de vormgeving bij gedrukte massa-media', Mare **17, Leiden**

1988

'Dezelfde huisstijl, maar dan anders', Memorandstad, **Special (January issue), p. 6-9, Randstad Dienstengroep bv**

1989

'Vernieuwde knollen voor de geur van wilde limoenen', De Gids, **Vol. 152, no. 8/9, p. 702-706**

1990

'Lifestyle is zoiets als kwartarine uit een design-dispenser', Studium Generale Rijksuniversiteit Leiden, Leefstijl, **levensstijl of lifestyle, p. 29-32**

1991

'Of mice and men', Desktop Publishing Commentary **77**

'Typography Twelve' Judges' Choice, **NY Typedirectors Club, p. 22-23**

'Teksten op verpakkingen', Art View **6, p. 53-55**

'Schrijven, typografie en De Vooruitgang', Art View **8, p. 37**

1992

'Foreword', Graphis Design 92, **Graphis Inc., p. 20-25**

'Waar blijven de meiden?', Art View **9, p. 37-38**

'Ha, daar zijn de meiden!', Vormberichten **10, p. 24,25**

'Het tweede leven: de recycling van de huisstijl', Art View **10, p. 60-65**

'Het tweede leven of de volgende generatie?', Art View **11, p. 64-68**

'Het tweede leven: corporate identity in de slagschaduw van een cultuuromslag', Art View **12, p. 100-103**

1993

'Visuele programma's in revisie', Art View **13, p. 78-79**

'Over fabels, de eeuwigheid en nog wat', Art View **14, p. 46-48**

1994

'Penthouse with a view: Metaform', Art View **19, p. 58-61**

'AGI, een club in de houdgreep van kwaliteit', Art View **20, p. 67-70**

1995

'Een menselijk wezen uit de sector "diversen"', Art View **23, p. 68-70**

1996

'Ontdekkingsreiziger in Design-land', Art View **30, p. 42-48**

'Nog weinig last van muizen in Polen', Art View **31, p. 30-34**

'New York Times, krant der kranten', Art View **32, p. 32-39**

'Huisstijl, een expressie van kwaliteitszin' in U nu! **(Studium Generale, Hogeschool Constantijn Huygens), p. 16-21**

1997

'The singing bird', Graphis Typography 2, **Graphis Inc., p. 98, 99**

'The Uncrowned Authorities', High Quality, HQ **37, Heidelberg Press, p. 30-35**

'"Een eeuw precisie, vorm en publiciteit": Ahrend", Art View **34, p. 62-67**

'De muurbloempjes zijn uitgebloeid', Art View **36, p. 26-31**

'De volwassenwording van het grafisch ontwerpen', Art View **37, p. 22-27**

'From here to eternity', Design in Business, **jrg 2,6, p. 26-29**

1998

'"Blind date met de toekomst": ken uw klassieken', Art View **38, p. 42-47**

'Verpakking: een cultuurverschijnsel van de bovenste plank', Art View **40, p. 36-41**

'Het verslag, de verplichte striptease in ondernemersland', Art View **41, p. 28-33**

'"Wachten op het Bauhaus": de fotografie in de visuele communicatie', Art View **42, p. 56-59**

1999

'Flevopolder - fantasie', Identity Matters, **iM-02, p. 37-39**

'Over ijsvogels, pelikanen, ooievaars en leesbaarheid', Identity Matters, **iM-03, p. 34-38**

'Logos R Us', Identity Matters, **iM-04, p. 32-35**

'Noorder Dierenpark', Identity Matters, **iM-05, p. 44-48**

'Hoeveel identitteit behoeft de winkelier?', Identity Matters, **iM-06, p. 32-35**

2000

'Stuurlui aan wal', Identity Matters, **iM-07,p. 62-63**

'De beste logo's van de eeuw?', Identity Matters, **iM-08, p. 66-71**

'Omzien in verwondering: ontwerp 1969', Identity Matters, **iM-09**

'Lyon, identiteiten in en van een miskende stad', Identity Matters, **iM-10**

'Paris faut bien un logo', Identity Matters, **iM-11**

Colophon

Initiative
Jantien Bos†
Text
Dirk van Ginkel
Paul Hefting
Illustrations editor, image processing, graphic design and lay-out
Lex Reitsma, Haarlem
Translation
Jan Willem Reitsma
Lithography
Bij-voorbeeld, Amsterdam
Paper
Grafisch Papier, Andelst
Printing
Rosbeek, Nuth
Binding
Boekbinderij M. Geertsen, Nijmegen

Publisher
BIS Publishers
Nieuwe Spiegelstraat 36
1017 DG Amsterdam
The Netherlands
T +31(0)20-6205171
F +31(0)20-6279251
E bis@bispublishers.nl
www.bispublishers.nl

First edition, November 2000
ISBN 90-72007-81-6

This book could only be realized thanks to the support and dedication of
Elly Bonsen
Bij-voorbeeld Pre-press, Amsterdam
Dirk van Ginkel
Grafisch Papier, Andelst
Paul Hefting
Paul Mertz
Jan Willem Reitsma
Lex Reitsma
Drukkerij Rosbeek, Nuth
Antoinette van Schendelen

Thanks also to
Randstad Staffing Services, Atlanta
Koninklijke Ahrend, Amsterdam

Much of Ben Bos's work was produced in pleasant collaboration with photographers
Bert Berghuis
Tjeerd Frederikse
Sherry Kamp
Aart Klein
Dolf Kruger
Peter Marcuse
Cas Oorthuys (archive)
Yves Paternoster
Arjé Plas
Jan Versnel

Over the years Ben Bos received some remarkable support from studio staff, including
Guido van Breda
Daphne Duyvelshoff
Caspari de Geus
Renée van de Griend
Liz James
Karin Janssen
Joost Klinkenberg
Toshiko Oiyama-Habir
Zdena Sernets
Evert Snellenberg†
Ben Snijder (Bij-voorbeeld bv)
Georg Staehelin
Wim Verboven
Wim van der Weerd

Photo credits

Front cover photography by Koos Breukel
Back cover self-portrait by Ben Bos
p. 1 1984, Hotel New Otani, Tokyo
p. 2-3 Paris, 16 October, 1983
p. 4-5 1930, Birth announcement card/Pennant Dutch Alpine Association, Design by Ben Bos / 1933, Brother and sister, Ben and Clara ('Kees') Bos, Photo by Godfried de Groot / Book bound by Ben's father, Jacobus Bos / 1975, Daughter Ingeborg Bos travelling to Iceland / 1977, Son Ingmar Bos on the Piz Corvatsch, in the Bernina mountain range above Pontresina, Switzerland / 1986, European track and field championships for masters, Malmö, Sweden, Series 100 metres / 1983, The 20 km of Paris
p. 7 1997, St.-Tropez, Photograph by Jantien Bos
p. 8 1999, Bergen (N-H), Photography by Koos Breukel
p. 10 1993, Presentation of awards for annual reports, Amsterdam, Jantien Bos, Paul Hefting, Ben Bos/ 1978, After the climbing of the Kala Patar near Mount Everest, Nepal
p. 14 1980, AGI conference Alpbach, Designers Bruno Monguzzi, Suzanne Morin and Ben Bos